HISTORY

OF

AMERICAN LITERATURE

BY

REUBEN POST HALLECK, M.A. (YALE)

AUTHOR OF "HISTORY OF ENGLISH LITERATURE"

NEW YORK ∴ CINCINNATI ∴ CHICAGO
AMERICAN BOOK COMPANY

Copyright, 1911, by
AMERICAN BOOK COMPANY.

Entered at Stationers' Hall, London.

HALLECK'S HIST. AM. LIT.

W. P. 16

175

THE RETURN OF RIP VAN WINKLE

PREFACE

THE wide use of the author's *History of English Literature*, the favor with which it has been received in all parts of the United States, and the number of earnest requests for a *History of American Literature* on the same plan, have led to the writing of this book. It has not appeared sooner because the author has followed his rule of making a careful first-hand study, not only of all the matter discussed, but also of a far greater amount, which, although it must be omitted from a condensed textbook, is, nevertheless, necessary as a background for judgment and selection.

The following chapters describe the greatest achievements in American literature from the earliest times until the present. Many pupils fail to obtain a clear idea of great American authors and literary movements because textbook writers and teachers ignore the element of truth in the old adage, "The half is greater than the whole," and dwell too much on minor authors and details, which could reasonably be expected to interest only a specialist. In the following pages especial attention has been paid, not only to the individual work of great authors, but also to literary movements, ideals, and animating principles, and to the relation of all these to English literature.

The author has further aimed to make this work both interesting and suggestive. He has endeavored to present the subject in a way that necessitates the comparison of authors and movements, and leads to stimulating thinking. He has tried to communicate enough of the spirit of our literature to make students eager for a first-hand acquaintance with it, to cause them to investigate for themselves this remarkable American record of spirituality, initiative, and democratic accomplishment. As a guide to such study, there have been placed at the end of each chapter *Suggested Readings* and still further hints, called *Questions and Suggestions*. In *A Glance Backward* (p. 396), the author emphasizes in brief compass the most important truths that American literature teaches, truths that have resulted in raising the ideals of Americans and in arousing them to greater activity.

Any one who makes an original study of American literature will not be a mere apologist for it. He will marvel at the greatness of the moral lesson, at the fidelity of the presentation of the thought which has molded this nation, and at the peculiar aptness which its great authors have displayed in ministering to the special needs and aspirations of Americans. He will realize that the youth who stops with the indispensable study of English literature is not prepared for American citizenship, because our literature is needed to present the ideals of American life. There may be greater literatures, but none of them can possibly take the place of ours for citizens of this democracy.

The moral element, the most impressive quality in American literature, is continuous from the earliest colonial days until the present. Teachers should be careful not to obscure this quality. As the English scientist, John Tyndall, has shown in the case of Emerson (p. 192), this moral stimulus is capable of adding immeasurably to the achievement of the young.

The temptation to slight the colonial period should be resisted. It has too often been the fashion to ask, Why should the student not begin the study of American literature with Washington Irving, the first author read for pure pleasure? The answer is that the student would not then comprehend the stages of growth of the new world ideals, that he would not view our later literature through the proper atmosphere, and that he would lack certain elements necessary for a sympathetic comprehension of the subject.

The seven years employed in the preparation of this work would have been insufficient, had not the author been assisted by his wife, to whom he is indebted not only for invaluable criticism but also for the direct authorship of some of the best matter in this book.

R. P. H.

CONTENTS

CHAPTER I
COLONIAL LITERATURE 9

CHAPTER II
THE EMERGENCE OF A NATION 65

CHAPTER III
THE NEW YORK GROUP 107

CHAPTER IV
THE NEW ENGLAND GROUP 153

CHAPTER V
SOUTHERN LITERATURE 287

CHAPTER VI
WESTERN LITERATURE 341

CHAPTER VII
THE EASTERN REALISTS 367

A GLANCE BACKWARD 396

SUPPLEMENTARY LIST OF AUTHORS AND THEIR CHIEF WORKS 399

INDEX 423

HISTORY OF AMERICAN LITERATURE

CHAPTER I

COLONIAL LITERATURE

Relation to English Literature. — The literature produced in that part of America known as the United States did not begin as an independent literature. The early colonists were Englishmen who brought with them their own language, books, and modes of thought. England had a world-famous literature before her sons established a permanent settlement across the Atlantic. Shakespeare had died four years before the Pilgrims landed at Plymouth. When an American goes to Paris he can neither read the books, nor converse with the citizens, if he knows no language but his own. Let him cross to London, and he will find that, although more than three hundred years have elapsed since the first colonists came to America, he immediately feels at home, so far as the language and literature are concerned.

For nearly two hundred years after the first English settlements in America, the majority of the works read there were written by English authors. The hard struggle necessary to obtain a foothold in a wilderness is not favorable to the early development of a literature. Those who remained in England could not clear away the forest, till the soil, and conquer the Indians, but they could write the books and send them across the ocean. The early settlers were for the most part content to allow English authors to do this. For these reasons it would be surprising if early American literature could vie with that produced in England during the same period.

When Americans began to write in larger numbers, there was at first close adherence to English models. For a while it seemed as if American literature would be only a feeble imitation of these models, but a change finally came, as will be shown in later chapters. It is to be hoped, however, that American writers of the future will never cease to learn from Chaucer, Spenser, Shakespeare, Milton, Bunyan, and Wordsworth.

American Literature an Important Study. — We should not begin the study of American literature in an apologetic spirit. There should be no attempt to minimize the debt that America owes to English literature, nor to conceal the fact that American literature is young and has not had time to produce as many masterpieces as England gave to the world during a thousand years. However, it is now time also to record the fact that the literature of England gained something from America. Cultivated Englishmen to-day willingly admit that without a study of Cooper, Poe, and Hawthorne no one could give an adequate account of the landmarks of achievement in fiction, written in our common tongue. French critics have even gone so far as to canonize Poe. In a certain field he and Hawthorne occupy a unique place in the world's achievement. Again, men like Bret Harte and Mark Twain are not common in any literature. Foreigners have had American books translated into all the leading languages of the world. It is now more than one hundred years since

Franklin, the great American philosopher of the practical, died, and yet several European nations reprint nearly every year some of his sayings, which continue to influence the masses. English critics, like John Addington Symonds, Robert Louis Stevenson, and Edward Dowden, have testified to the power of the democratic element in our literature and have given the dictum that it cannot be neglected.

Some of the reasons why American literature developed along original lines and thus conveyed a message of its own to the world are to be found in the changed environment and the varying problems and ideals of American life. Even more important than the changed ways of earning a living and the difference in climate, animals, and scenery were the struggles leading to the Revolutionary War, the formation and guidance of the Republic, and the Civil War. All these combined to give individuality to American thought and literature.

Taken as a whole, American literature has accomplished more than might reasonably have been expected. Its study is especially important for us, since the deeds associated with our birthplace must mean more to us than more remarkable achievements of men born under other skies. Our literature, even in its humble beginnings, contains a lesson that no American can afford to miss. Unless we know its ideals and moral aims and are swayed by them, we cannot keep our heritage.

Why Virginia was Colonized. — In 1607 the first permanent English colony within the present limits of the United States was planted at Jamestown in Virginia. The colony was founded for commercial reasons by the London Company, an organization formed to secure profits from colonization. The colonists and the company that furnished their ship and outfit expected large profits from the gold mines and the precious stones which were believed to await discovery. Of course, the adventurers were also influenced by the honor and the romantic interest which they thought would result from a successful settlement.

When the expedition sailed from England in December, 1606, Michael Drayton, an Elizabethan poet, wrote verses dedicated "To the Virginian Voyage." These stanzas show the reason for sending the colonizers to Virginia: —

> "You brave heroic minds,
> Worthy your country's name,
> That honor still pursue,
> Whilst loit'ring hinds
> Lurk here at home with shame,
> Go and subdue.
>
> . . . . . .
>
> And cheerfully at sea,
> Success you still entice,
> To get the pearl and gold;
> And ours to hold
> Virginia,
> Earth's only paradise."

The majority of the early Virginian colonists were unfit for their task. Contemporary accounts tell of the "many unruly gallants, packed hither by their friends to escape ill destinies." Beggars, vagabonds, indentured servants, kidnapped girls, even convicts, were sent to Jamestown and became the ancestors of some of the "poor white trash" of the South. After the execution of Charles I. in 1649, and the setting up of the Puritan Commonwealth, many of the royalists, or Cavaliers, as they were called, came to Virginia to escape the obnoxious Puritan rule. They became the ancestors of Presidents and statesmen, and of many of the aristocratic families of the South.

WHY THE PURITANS COLONIZED NEW ENGLAND 13

The ideals expressed by Captain John Smith, the leader and preserver of the Jamestown colony, are worthy to rank beside those of the colonizers of New England. Looking back at his achievement in Virginia, he wrote, " Then seeing we are not born for ourselves but each to help other ... Seeing honor is our lives' ambition ... and seeing by no means would we be abated of the dignities and glories of our predecessors; let us imitate their virtues to be worthily their successors."

Why the Puritans colonized New England. — During the period from 1620 to 1640, large numbers of Englishmen migrated to that part of America now known as New England. These emigrants were not impelled by hope of wealth, or ease, or pleasure. They were called Puritans because they wished to purify the Church of England from what seemed to them great abuses; and the purpose of these men in emigrating to America was to lay the foundations of a state built upon their religious principles. These people came for an intangible something — liberty of conscience, a fuller life of the spirit — which has never commanded a price on any stock exchange in the world. They looked beyond

> " Things done that took the eye and had the price;
>   O'er which, from level stand,
>   The low world laid its hand,
> Found straightway to its mind, could value in a trice."

These Puritans had been more than one century in the making. We hear of them in the time of Wycliffe (1324-1384). Their religion was a constant command to put the unseen above the seen, the eternal above the temporal, to satisfy the aspiration of the spirit. James I. (reign, 1603-1625) told them that he would harry them out of the kingdom unless they conformed to the rites of the Established Church. His son and successor Charles I. (reign, 1625–1649) called to his aid Archbishop Laud (1573–1645), a bigoted official of that church. Laud hunted the dissenting clergy like wild beasts, threw them into prison, whipped them in the pillory, branded them, slit their nostrils, and mutilated their ears. **John Cotton**, pastor of the church of Boston, England, was told that if he had been guilty only of an infraction of certain of the Ten Commandments, he might have been pardoned, but since his crime was Puritanism, he must suffer. He had great trouble in escaping on a ship bound for the New England Boston.

JOHN COTTON

Professor Tyler says: "New England has perhaps never quite appreciated its great obligations to Archbishop Laud. It was his overmastering hate of nonconformity, it was the vigilance and vigor and consecrated cruelty with which he scoured his own diocese and afterward all England, and hunted down and hunted out the ministers who were committing the unpardonable sin of dissent, that conferred upon the principal colonies of New England their ablest and noblest men."

It should be noted that the Puritan colonization of New England took place in a comparatively brief space of time, during the twenty years from 1620 to 1640. Until 1640 persecution drove the Puritans to New England in multitudes, but in that year they suddenly stopped coming. "During the one hundred and twenty-five years following that date, more persons, it is supposed, went back from the New to the Old England than came from the Old England to the New," says Professor Tyler. The year 1640 marks the assembling of the Long Parliament, which finally brought to the block both Archbishop Laud (1645) and King Charles I. (1649), and chose the great Puritan, Oliver Cromwell, to lead the Commonwealth.

Elizabethan Traits. — The leading men in the colonization of Virginia and New England were born in the reign of Queen Elizabeth (1558-1603), and they and their descendants showed on this side of the Atlantic those characteristics which made the Elizabethan age preëminent.

In the first place, the Elizabethans possessed initiative. This power consists, first, in having ideas, and secondly, in passing from the ideas to the suggested action. Some people merely dream. The Elizabethans dreamed glorious dreams, which they translated into action. They defeated the Spanish Armada; they circumnavigated the globe; they made it possible for Shakespeare's pen to mold the thought and to influence the actions of the world.

If we except those indentured servants and apprentices who came to America merely because others brought them, we shall find not only that the first colonists were born in an age distinguished for its initiative, but also that they came because they possessed this characteristic in a greater degree than those who remained behind. It was easier for the majority to stay with their friends; hence England was not depopulated. The few came, those who had sufficient initiative to cross three thousand miles of unknown sea, who had the power to dream dreams of a new commonwealth, and the will to embody those dreams in action.

In the second place, the Elizabethans were ingenious, that is, they were imaginative and resourceful. Impelled by the mighty forces of the Reformation and the Revival of Learning which the England of Elizabeth alone felt at one and the same time, the Elizabethans craved and obtained variety of experience, which kept the fountain-head of ingenuity filled. It is instructive to follow the lives of Elizabethans as different as Sir Philip Sidney, William Shakespeare, Sir Walter Raleigh, Captain John Smith, and John Winthrop, and to note the varied experiences of each. Yankee ingenuity had an Elizabethan ancestry. The hard conditions of the New World merely gave an opportunity to exercise to the utmost an ingenuity which the colonists brought with them.

In the third place, the Elizabethans were unusually democratic; that is, the different classes mingled together in a marked degree, more than in modern England, more even than in the United States to-day. This intermingling was due in part to increased travel, to the desire born of the New Learning to live as varied and as complete a life as possible, and to the absence of overspecialization among individuals. This chance for varied experience with all sorts and conditions of men enabled Shakespeare to speak to all humanity. All England was represented in his plays. When the Rev. Thomas Hooker, born in the last half of Elizabeth's reign, was made pastor at Hartford, Connecticut, he suggested to his flock a democratic form of government much like that under which we now live.

Let us remember that American life and literature owe their most interesting traits to these three Elizabethan qualities — initiative, ingenuity, and democracy. Let us not forget that the Cambridge University graduate, the cooper, cloth-maker, printer, and blacksmith had the initiative to set out for the New World, the ingenuity to deal with its varied exigencies, and the democratic spirit that enabled them to work side by side, no matter how diverse their former trades, modes of life, and social condition.

CAPTAIN JOHN SMITH, 1579-1631

The hero of the Jamestown colony, and its savior during the first two years, was Captain John Smith, born in Willoughby, Lincolnshire, in 1579, twenty-four years before the death of Elizabeth and thirty-seven before the death of Shakespeare. Smith was a man of Elizabethan stamp, — active, ingenious, imaginative, craving new experiences. While a mere boy, he could not stand the tediousness of ordinary life, and so betook himself to the forest where he could hunt and play knight.

In the first part of his young manhood he crossed the Channel, voyaged in the Mediterranean, fought the Turks, killing three of them in single combat, was taken prisoner and enslaved by the Tartars, killed his inhuman master, escaped into Russia, went thence through Europe to Africa, was in desperate naval battles, returned to England, sailing thence for Virginia, which he reached at the age of twenty-eight.

He soon became president of the Jamestown colony and labored strenuously for its preservation. The first product of his pen in America was *A True Relation of Virginia*, written in 1608, the year in which John Milton was born. The last work written by Smith in America is entitled: *A Map of Virginia, with a Description of the Country, the Commodities, People, Government, and Religion.* His description of the Indians shows his capacity for quickly noting their traits : —

"They are inconstant in everything, but what fear constraineth them to keep. Crafty, timorous, quick of apprehension and very ingenious. Some are of disposition fearful, some bold, most cautious, all savage. Generally covetous of copper, beads, and such like trash. They are soon moved to anger, and so malicious that they seldom forget an injury: they seldom steal one from another, lest their conjurors should reveal it, and so they be pursued and punished. That they are thus feared is certain, but that any can reveal their offences by conjuration I am doubtful."

Smith has often been accused of boasting, and some have said that he was guilty of great exaggeration or something worse, but it is certain that he repeatedly braved hardships, extreme dangers, and captivity among the Indians to provide food for the colony and to survey Virginia. After carefully editing *Captain John Smith's Works* in a volume of 983 pages, Professor Edwin Arber says: "For our own part, beginning with doubtfulness and wariness we have gradually come to the unhesitating conviction, not only of Smith's truthfulness, but also that, in regard to all personal matters, he systematically understates rather than exaggerates anything he did."

Although by far the greater part of Smith's literary work was done after he returned to England, yet his two booklets written in America entitle him to a place in colonial literature. He had the Elizabethan love of achievement, and he records his admiration for those whose 'pens writ what their swords did.' He was not an artist with his pen, but our early colonial literature is the richer for his rough narrative and for the description of Virginia and the Indians.

In one sense he gave the Indian to literature, and that is his greatest achievement in literary history. Who has not heard the story of his capture by the Indians, of his rescue from torture and death, by the beautiful Indian maiden, Pocahontas, of her risking her life to save him a second time from Indian treachery, of her bringing corn and preserving the colony from famine, of her visit to England in 1616, a few weeks after the death of Shakespeare, of her royal reception as a princess, the daughter of an Indian king, of Smith's meeting her again in London, where their romantic story aroused the admiration of the court and the citizens for the brown-eyed princess? It would be difficult to say how many tales of Indian adventure this romantic story of Pocahontas has suggested. It has the honor of being the first of its kind written in the English tongue.

Did Pocahontas actually rescue Captain Smith? In his account of his adventures, written in Virginia in 1608, he does not mention this rescue, but in his later writings he relates it as an actual occurrence. When Pocahontas visited London, this story was current, and there is no evidence that she denied it. Professor Arber says, "To deny the truth of the Pocahontas incident is to create more difficulties than are involved in its acceptance." But literature does not need to ask whether the story of Hamlet or of Pocahontas is true. If this unique story of American adventure is a product of Captain Smith's creative imagination, the literary critic must admit the captain's superior ability in producing a tale of such vitality. If the story is true, then our literature does well to remember whose pen made this truth one of the most persistent of our early romantic heritages. He is as well known for the story of Pocahontas as for all of his other achievements. The man who saved the Virginia colony and who first suggested a new field to the writer of American romance is rightly considered one of the most striking figures in our early history, even if he did return to England in less than three years and end his days there in 1631.

LITERARY ACTIVITY IN VIRGINIA COLONY

A Possible Suggestion for Shakespeare's Tempest. — **William Strachey,** a contemporary of Shakespeare and secretary of the Virginian colony, wrote at Jamestown and sent to London in 1610 the manuscript of *A True Repertory of the Wrack and Redemption of Sir Thomas Gates, Kt., upon and from the Islands of the Bermudas.* This is a story of shipwreck on the Bermudas and of escape in small boats. The book is memorable for the description of a storm at sea, and it is possible that it may even have furnished suggestions to Shakespeare for *The Tempest.* If so, it is interesting to compare these with what they produced in Shakespeare's mind. Strachey tells how "the sea swelled above the clouds and gave battle unto heaven." He speaks of "an apparition of a little round light, like a faint star, trembling and streaming along with a sparkling blaze, half the height upon the main mast, and shooting sometimes from shroud to shroud." Ariel says to Prospero: —

> "I boarded the king's ship; now on the beak,
> Now in the waist, the deck, in every cabin,
> I flam'd amazement: Sometimes I'ld divide,
> And burn in many places; on the topmast,
> The yards, and bowsprit, would I flame distinctly,
> Then meet and join."

Strachey voices the current belief that the Bermudas were harassed by tempests, devils, wicked spirits, and other fearful objects. Shakespeare has Ferdinand with fewer words intensify Strachey's picture: —

> "Hell is empty,
> And all the devils are here."

The possibility that incidents arising out of Virginian colonization may have turned Shakespeare's attention to "the still vex'd Bermoothes" and given him suggestions for one of his great plays lends added interest to Strachey's *True Repertory*. But, aside from Shakespeare, this has an interest of its own. It has the Anglo-Saxon touch in depicting the wrath of the sea, and it shows the character of the early American colonists who braved a wrath like this.

Poetry in the Virginia Colony. — George Sandys (1577-1644), during

GEORGE SANDYS

his stay in the colony as its treasurer, translated ten books of Ovid's *Metamorphoses*, sometimes working by the light of a pine knot. This work is rescued from the class of mere translation by its literary art and imaginative interpretation, and it possesses for us an additional interest because of its nativity amid such surroundings. Two lines telling how Philemon

> "Took down a flitch of bacon with a prung,
> That long had in the smoky chimney hung,"

show that his environment aided him somewhat in the translation. He himself says of this version that it was "bred in the new world, whereof it cannot but participate, especially having wars and tumults to bring it to light, instead of the muses." He was read by both Dryden and Pope in their boyhood, and the form of their verse shows his influence.

The only original poem which merits our attention in the early Virginian colony was found soon after the Revolutionary War in a collection of manuscripts, known as the *Burwell Papers*. This poem is an elegy on the death of Nathaniel Bacon (1676), a young Virginian patriot and military hero, who resisted the despotic governor, Sir William Berkeley. It was popularly believed that Bacon's mysterious death was due to poison. An unknown friend wrote the elegy in defense of Bacon and his rebellion. These lines from that elegy show a strength unusual in colonial poetry: —

> "Virginia's foes,
> To whom, for secret crimes, just vengeance owes
> Deserved plagues, dreading their just desert,
> Corrupted death by Paracelsian art,
> Him to destroy . . .
> Our arms, though ne'er so strong,
> Will want the aid of his commanding tongue,
> Which conquered more than Cæsar."

Descriptions of Virginia. — **Robert Beverly,** clerk of the Council of Virginia, published in London in 1705 a *History and Present State of Virginia.* This is to-day a readable account of the colony and its people in the first part of the eighteenth century. This selection shows that in those early days Virginians were noted for what has come to be known as southern hospitality: —

> "The inhabitants are very courteous to travellers, who need no other recommendation, but the being human creatures. A stranger has no more to do, but to inquire upon the road where any gentleman or good housekeeper lives, and there he may depend upon being received with hospitality. This good nature is so general among their people, that the gentry, when they go abroad, order their principal servant to entertain all visitors with everything the plantation affords. And the poor planters who have but one bed, will very often sit up, or lie upon a form or couch all night, to make room for a weary traveller to repose himself after his journey."

Colonel William Byrd (1674–1744), a wealthy Virginian, wrote a *History of the Dividing Line run in the Year* 1728. He was commissioned by the Virginian colony to run a line between it and North Carolina. This book is a record of personal experiences, and is as interesting as its title is forbidding. This selection describes the Dismal Swamp, through which the line ran: —.

WILLIAM BYRD

> "Since the surveyors had entered the Dismal they had laid eyes on no living creature; neither bird nor beast, insect nor reptile came in view. Doubtless the eternal shade that broods over this mighty bog and hinders the sunbeams from blessing the ground, makes it an uncomfortable habitation for anything that has life. Not so much as a Zealand frog could endure

so aguish a situation. It had one beauty, however, that delighted the eye, though at the expense of all the other senses: the moisture of the soil preserves a continual verdure, and makes every plant an evergreen, but at the same time the foul damps ascend without ceasing, corrupt the air, and render it unfit for respiration. Not even a turkey buzzard will venture to fly ove. it, no more than the Italian vultures will fly over the filthy lake Avernus or the birds in the Holy Land over the salt sea where Sodom and Gomorrah formerly stood.

"In these sad circumstances the kindest thing we could do for our suffering friends was to give them a place in the Litany. Our chaplain for his part did his office and rubbed us up with a seasonable sermon. This was quite a new thing to our brethren of North Carolina, who live in a climate where no clergyman can breathe, any more than spiders in Ireland."

These two selections show that American literature, even before the Revolution, came to be something more than an imitation of English literature. They are the product of our soil, and no critic could say that they might as well have been written in London as in Virginia. They also show how much eighteenth-century prose had improved in form. Even in England, modern prose may almost be said to begin with John Dryden, who died at the beginning of the eighteenth century. In addition to improvement in form, we may note the appearance of a new quality — humor. Our earliest writers have few traces of humor because colonization was a serious life and death affair to them.

Different Lines of Development of Virginia and New England. — As we now go back more than a hundred years to the founding of the Plymouth colony in 1620, we may note that Virginia and New England developed along different lines. We shall find more dwellers in towns, more democracy and mingling of all classes, more popular education, and more literature in New England. The ruling classes of Virginia were mostly descendants of the Cavaliers who had sympathized with monarchy, while the Puritans had fought the Stuart kings and had approved a Commonwealth. In Virginia a wealthy class of landed gentry came to be an increasing power in the political history of the country. The ancestors of George Washington and many others who did inestimable service to the nation were among this class. It was long the fashion for this aristocracy to send their children to England to be educated, while the Puritans trained theirs at home.

New England started a printing press, and was printing books by 1640. In 1671 Sir William Berkeley, governor of Virginia, wrote, " I thank God there are no free schools, nor printing, and I hope we shall not have these hundred years; for learning has brought disobedience and heresy and sects into the world, and printing has developed them."

Producers of literature need the stimulus of town life. The South was chiefly agricultural. The plantations were large, and the people lived in far greater isolation than in New England, where not only the town, but more especially the church, developed a close social unit.

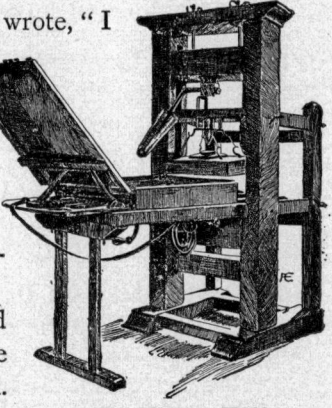

EARLY PRINTING PRESS

One other reason served to make it difficult for a poet of the plowman type, like Robert Burns, or for an author from the general working class, like Benjamin Franklin, to arise in the South. Labor was thought degrading, and the laborer did not find the same chance as at the North to learn from close association with the intelligent class.

The reason for this is given by Colonel William Byrd, from whom we have quoted in the preceding section. He wrote in 1736 of the leading men of the South:—

"They import so many negroes hither, that I fear this Colony will some time or other be confirmed by the name of New Guinea. I am sensible of many bad consequences of multiplying these Ethiopians amongst us. They blow up the pride and ruin the industry of our white people, who seeing a rank of poor creatures below them, detest work, for fear it should make them look like slaves."

WILLIAM BRADFORD, 1590–1657

William Bradford was born in 1590 in the Pilgrim district of England, in the Yorkshire village of Austerfield, two miles north of Scrooby. While a child, he attended the religious meetings of the Puritans. At the age of eighteen he gave up a good position in the post service of England, and crossed to Holland to escape religious persecution. His *History of Plymouth Plantation* is not a record of the Puritans as a whole, but only of that branch known as the Pilgrims, who left England for Holland in 1607 and 1608, and who, after remaining there for nearly twelve years, had the initiative to be the first of their band to come to the New World, and to settle at Plymouth in 1620.

For more than thirty years he was governor of the Plymouth colony, and he managed its affairs with the discretion of a Washington and the zeal of a Cromwell. His *History* tells the story of the Pilgrim Fathers from the time of the formation of their two congregations in England, until 1647.

In 1897 the United States for the first time came into possession of the manuscript of this famous *History of*

Plymouth Plantation, which had in some mysterious manner been taken from Boston in colonial times and had found its way into the library of the Lord Bishop of London. Few of the English seem to have read it. Even its custodian miscalled it *The Log of the Mayflower*, although after the ship finally cleared from England, only five incidents of the voyage are briefly mentioned: the death of a young seaman who cursed the Pilgrims on the

FACSIMILE OF FIRST PARAGRAPH OF BRADFORD'S "HISTORY OF PLYMOUTH PLANTATION"

voyage and made sport of their misery; the cracking of one of the main beams of the ship; the washing overboard in a storm of a good young man who was providentially saved; the death of a servant; and the sight of Cape Cod. On petition, the Lord Bishop of London generously gave this manuscript of 270 pages to the Commonwealth of Massachusetts. In a speech at the time of its formal reception, Senator Hoar eloquently summed up the subject matter of the volume as follows:—

"I do not think many Americans will gaze upon it without a little trembling of the lips and a little gathering of mist in the eyes, as they think of the story of suffering, of sorrow, of peril, of exile, of death, and of lofty triumph which that book tells, — which the hand of the great leader and founder of America has traced on those pages. There is nothing like it in human annals since the story of Bethlehem. These Englishmen and English women going out from their homes in beautiful Lincoln and York, wife separated from husband and mother from child in that hurried embarkation for Holland, pursued to the beach by English horsemen; the thirteen years of exile; the life at Amsterdam, 'in alley foul and lane obscure'; the dwelling at Leyden; the embarkation at Delfthaven; the farewell of Robinson; the terrible voyage across the Atlantic; the compact in the harbor; the landing on the rock; the dreadful first winter; the death roll of more than half the number; the days of suffering and of famine; the wakeful night, listening for the yell of wild beast and the war whoop of the savage; the building of the State on those sure foundations which no wave or tempest has ever shaken; the breaking of the new light; the dawning of the new day; the beginning of the new life; the enjoyment of peace with liberty, — of all these things this is the original record by the hand of our beloved father and founder."

In addition to giving matter of unique historical importance, Bradford entertains his readers with an account of Squanto, the Pilgrims' tame Indian, of Miles Standish capturing the "lord of misrule" at Merrymount, and of the failure of an experiment in tilling the soil in common. Bradford says that there was immediate improvement when each family received the full returns from working its own individual plot of ground. He thus philosophizes about this social experiment of the Pilgrims: —

"The experience that was had in this common course and condition, tried sundry years, and that amongst godly and sober men, may well evince the vanity of that conceit of Plato's and other ancients, applauded by some of later times; —— that the taking away of property and bringing in community into a common wealth would make them happy and flourishing. . . . Let none object this is men's corruption, and nothing to the course itself. I answer, seeing all men have this corruption in them, God in his wisdom saw another course fitter for them."

America need not be ashamed of either the form or the subject matter of her early colonial prose in comparison with that produced in England at the same time.

JOHN WINTHROP, 1588-1649

On March 29, 1630, John Winthrop made the first entry in his *Journal* on board the ship *Arbella*, before she left the Isle of Wight for Massachusetts Bay. This *Journal* was to continue until a few months before his death in 1649, and was in after times to receive the dignified name of *History of New England*, although it might more properly still be called his *Journal*, as its latest editor does indeed style it.

John Winthrop was born in the County of Suffolk, England, in 1588, the year of the defeat of the Spanish Armada. He was a wealthy, well-educated Puritan, the owner of broad estates. As he paced the deck of the *Arbella*, the night before he sailed for Massachusetts, he knew that he was leaving comfort, home, friends, position, all for liberty of conscience. Few men have ever voluntarily abandoned more than Winthrop, or clung more tenaciously to their ideals.

After a voyage lasting more than two months, he settled with a large number of Puritans on the site of modern Boston. For the principal part of the time from his arrival in 1630 until his death in 1649, he served as governor of the Massachusetts Bay Colony. Not many civil leaders of any age have shown more sagacity, patriotism, and tireless devotion to duty than John Winthrop.

His *Journal* is a record of contemporaneous events from 1630 to 1648. The early part of this work might with some justice have been called the *Log of the Arbella*.

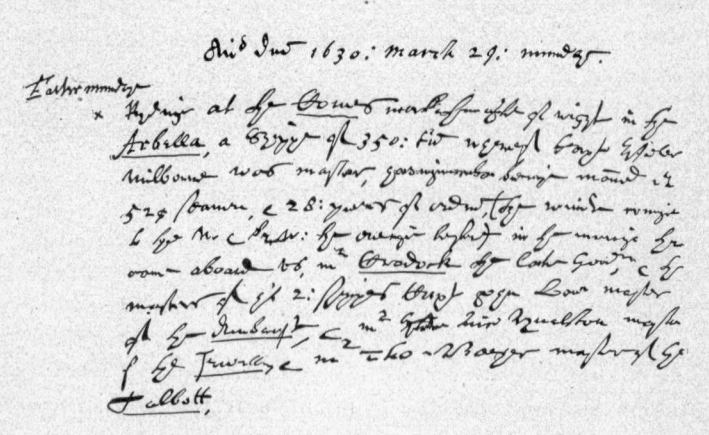

FACSIMILE OF BEGINNING OF MS. OF WINTHROP'S "JOURNAL"

TRANSLITERATION OF FACSIMILE OF WINTHROP'S "JOURNAL"

"ANNO DOMINI 1630, MARCH 29, MONDAY.
"EASTER MONDAY.

"Riding at the Cowes, near the Isle of Wight, in the *Arbella*, a ship of 350 tons, whereof Capt. Peter Milborne was master, being manned with 52 seamen. and 28 pieces of ordnance, (the wind coming to the N. by W. the evening before,) in the morning there came aboard us Mr. Cradock, the late governor, and the masters of his 2 ships, Capt. John Lowe, master of the *Ambrose*, and Mr. Nicholas Hurlston, master of the *Jewel*, and Mr. Thomas Beecher, master of the *Talbot*."

The entry for Monday, April 12, 1630, is:—

"The wind more large to the N. a stiff gale, with fair weather. In the afternoon less wind, and our people began to grow well again. Our children and others, that were sick and lay groaning in the cabins, we fetched out, and having stretched a rope from the steerage to the mainmast, we made them stand, some of one side and some of the other, and sway it up and down till they were warm, and by this means they soon grew well and merry."

The following entry for June 5, 1644, reflects an interesting side light on the government of Harvard, our first American college:—

"Two of our ministers' sons, being students in the college, robbed two dwelling houses in the night of some fifteen pounds. Being found out, they were ordered by the governors of the college to be there whipped, which was performed by the president himself — yet they were about twenty years of age; and after they were brought into the court and ordered to twofold satisfaction, or to serve so long for it. We had yet no particular punishment for burglary."

Another entry for 1644 tells of one William Franklin, condemned for causing the death of his apprentice:—

"The case was this. He had taken to apprentice one Nathaniel Sewell, one of those children sent over the last year for the country; the boy had the scurvy and was withal very noisome, and otherwise ill disposed. His master used him with continual rigour and unmerciful correction, and exposed him many times to much cold and wet in the winter season, and used divers acts of rigour towards him, as hanging him in the chimney, etc., and the boy being very poor and weak, he tied him upon an horse and so brought him (sometimes sitting and sometimes hanging down) to Boston, being five miles off, to the magistrates, and by the way the boy calling much for water, would give him none, though he came close by it, so as the boy was near dead when he came to Boston, and died within a few hours after."

Winthrop relates how Franklin appealed the case when he was found guilty, and how the Puritans inflicted the death penalty on him after searching the *Bible* for a rule on which to base their decision. The most noticeable qualities of this terrible story are its simplicity, its repression, its lack of striving after effect. Winthrop, Bradford, and Bunyan had learned from the 1611 version of the *Bible* to be content to present any situation as simply as possible and to rely on the facts themselves to secure the effect.

Winthrop's finest piece of prose, *Concerning Liberty*, appears in an entry for the year 1645. He defines liberty as the power "to do that which is good, just, and honest. This liberty you are to stand for, with the hazard, not only of your goods, but of your lives, if need be." Winthrop saw clearly what many since his day have failed to see, that a government conducted by the people could not endure, if liberty meant more than this.

Winthrop's *Journal* records almost anything which seemed important to the colonists. Thus, he tells about storms, fires, peculiar deaths of animals, crimes, trials, Indians, labor troubles, arrival of ships, trading expeditions, troubles with England about the charter, politics, church matters, events that would point a moral, like the selfish refusal of the authorities to loan a quantity of gunpowder to the Plymouth colony and the subsequent destruction of that same powder by an explosion, or the drowning of a child in the well while the parents were visiting on Sunday. In short, this *Journal* gives valuable information about the civil, religious, and domestic life of the early days of the Massachusetts Bay Colony. The art of modern prose writing was known neither in England nor in America in Winthrop's time. The wonder is that he told the story of this colony in such good form and that he still holds the interest of the reader so well.

THE RELIGIOUS IDEAL

William Bradford and John Winthrop were governors of two religious commonwealths. We must not forget that the Puritans came to America to secure a higher form of spiritual life. In the reign of Elizabeth, it was thought that the Revival of Learning would cure all ills and unlock the gates of happiness. This hope had met with disappointment. Then Puritanism came, and ushered in a new era of spiritual aspiration for something better, nobler, and more satisfying than mere intellectual attainments or wealth or earthly power had been able to secure.

The Puritans chose the *Bible* as the guidebook to their Promised Land. The long sermons to which they listened were chiefly biblical expositions. The Puritans considered the saving of the soul the most important matter, and they neglected whatever form of culture did not directly tend toward that result. They thought that entertaining reading and other forms of amusement were contrivances of the devil to turn the soul's attention away from the *Bible*. Even beauty and art were considered handmaids of the Evil One. The *Bible* was read, reread, and constantly studied, and it took the place of secular poetry and prose.

The New England Puritan believed in the theology of

John Calvin, who died in 1564. His creed, known as Calvinism, emphasized the importance of the individual, of life's continuous moral struggle, which would land each soul in heaven or hell for all eternity. In the *New England Primer*, the children were taught the first article of belief, as they learned the letter A: —

> "In Adam's fall,
> We sinnèd all."

Calvinism stressed the doctrine of foreordination, that certain ones, "the elect," had been foreordained to be saved. **Thomas Shepard** (1605–1649), one of the great Puritan clergy, fixed the mathematical ratio of the damned to the elect as "a thousand to one." On the physical side, scientists have pointed out a close correspondence between Calvin's creed and the theory of evolution, which emphasizes the desperate struggle resulting from the survival of the fittest. The "fittest" are the "elect"; those who perish in the contest, the "damned." In the evolutionary struggle, only the few survive, while untold numbers of the unfit, no matter whether seeds of plants, eggs of fish, human beings, or any other form of life, go to the wall.

In spite of the apparent contradiction between free will and foreordination, each individual felt himself fully responsible for the saving of his soul. A firm belief in this tremendous responsibility made each one rise the stronger to meet the other responsibilities of life. Civil responsibility seemed easier to one reared in this school. The initiative bequeathed by Elizabethan times was increased by the Puritans' religion.

Although there were probably as many university men in proportion to the population in early colonial Massachusetts as in England, the strength and direction of their religious ideals helped to turn their energy into activities outside the field of pure literature. In course of time, however, Nathaniel Hawthorne appeared to give lasting literary expression to this life.

The New England Clergy. — The clergy occupied a leading place in both the civil and religious life of New England. They were men of energy and ability, who could lead their congregations to Holland or to the wilds of New England. For the purpose in hand the world has never seen superior leaders. Many of them were graduates of Cambridge University, England. Their great authority was based on character, education, and natural ability. A contemporary historian said of John Cotton, who came as pastor from the old to the new Boston in 1633, that whatever he "delivered in the pulpit was soon put into an order of court . . . or set up as a practice in the church."

The sermons, from two to four hours long, took the place of magazines, newspapers, and modern musical and theatrical entertainments. The church members were accustomed to hard thinking and they enjoyed it as a mental exercise. Their minds had not been rendered flabby by such a diet of miscellaneous trash or sensational matter as confronts modern readers. Many of the congregation went with notebooks to record the different heads and the most striking thoughts in the sermon, such, for instance, as the following on the dangers of idleness: —

"Whilst the stream keeps running, it keeps clear; but let it stand still, it breeds frogs and toads and all manner of filth. So while you keep going, you keep clear."

The sermons were often doctrinal, metaphysical, and extremely dry, but it is a mistake to conclude that the clergy did not speak on topics of current interest. Winthrop in his *Journal* for 1639 relates how the Rev. John Cotton discussed whether a certain shopkeeper, who had been arraigned before the court for extortion, for having taken "in some small things, above two for one," was guilty of sin and should be excommunicated from the church, or only publicly admonished. Cotton prescribed admonition and he laid down a code of ethics for the guidance of sellers.

With the exception of Roger Williams (1604?-1683), who had the modern point of view in insisting on complete "soul liberty," on the right of every man to think as he pleased on matters of religion, the Puritan clergy were not tolerant of other forms of worship. They said that they came to New England in order to worship God as they pleased. They never made the slightest pretense of establishing a commonwealth where another could worship as he pleased, because they feared that such a privilege might lead to a return of the persecution from which they had fled. If those came who thought differently about religion, they were told that there was sufficient room elsewhere, in Rhode Island, for instance, whither Roger Williams went after he was banished from Salem. The history of the Puritan clergy would have been more pleasing had they been more tolerant, less narrow, more modern, like Roger Williams. Yet perhaps it is best not to complain overmuch of the strange and somewhat repellent architecture of the bridge which bore us over the stream dividing the desert of royal and ecclesiastical tyranny from the Promised Land of our Republic. Let us not forget that the clergy insisted on popular education; that wherever

POETRY

The trend of Puritan theology and the hard conditions of life did not encourage the production of poetry. The Puritans even wondered if singing in church was not an exercise which turned the mind from God. The Rev. John Cotton investigated the question carefully under four main heads and six subheads, and he cited scriptural authority to show that Paul and Silas (*Acts*, xvi., 25) had sung a *Psalm* in the prison. Cotton therefore concluded that the *Psalms* might be sung in church.

Bay Psalm Book.—"The divines in the country" joined to translate "into English metre." the whole book of *Psalms* from the original Hebrew, and they probably made the worst metrical

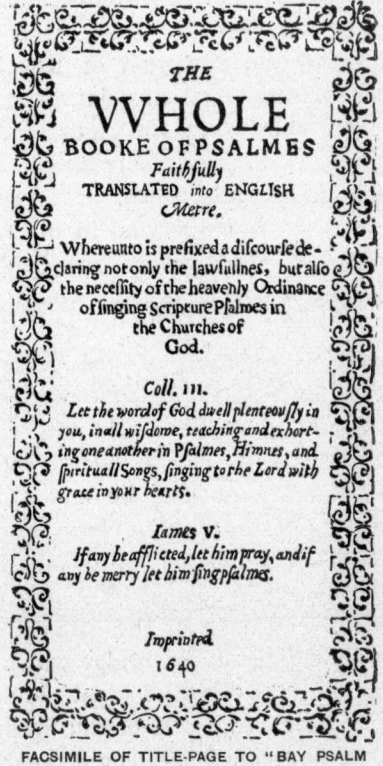

FACSIMILE OF TITLE-PAGE TO "BAY PSALM BOOK"

translation in existence. In their preface to this work, known as the *Bay Psalm Book* (1640), the first book of verse printed in the British American colonies, they explained that they did not strive for a more poetic translation because "God's altar needs not our polishings." The following verses from *Psalm* cxxxvii. are a sample of the so-called metrical translation which the Puritans sang : —

"1. The rivers on of Babilon
   there when wee did sit downe :
  yea even then wee mourned, when
   wee remembred Sion.

"2. Our Harps wee did it hang amid,
   upon the willow tree.

"3. Because there they that us away
   led in captivitee,
  Requir'd of us a song, & thus
   askt mirth : us waste who laid,
  sing us among a Sion's song,
   unto us then they said."

Michael Wigglesworth (1631-1705). — This Harvard graduate and Puritan preacher published in 1662 a poem setting forth some of the tenets of Calvinistic theology. This poem, entitled *The Day of Doom, or a Poetical Description of the Great and Last Judgment*, had the largest circulation of any colonial poem. The following lines represent a throng of infants at the left hand of the final Judge, pleading against the sentence of infant damnation : —

"'Not we, but he ate of the tree,
   whose fruit was interdicted;
 Yet on us all of his sad fall
   the punishment's inflicted.
 How could we sin that had not been,
   or how is his sin our,
 Without consent, which to prevent
   we never had the pow'r ? ' "

Wigglesworth represents the Almighty as replying:—

> " 'You sinners are, and such a share
> as sinners may expect;
> Such you shall have, for I do save
> none but mine own Elect.
> Yet to compare your sin with their
> who liv'd a longer time,
> I do confess yours is much less,
> though every sin's a crime.
>
> " 'A crime it is, therefore in bliss
> you may not hope to dwell;
> But unto you I shall allow
> the easiest room in Hell.' "

When we read verse like this, we realize how fortunate the Puritanism of Old England was to have one great poet schooled in the love of both morality and beauty. John Milton's poetry shows not only his sublimity and high ideals, but also his admiration for beauty, music, and art. Wigglesworth's verse is inferior to much of the ballad doggerel, but it has a swing and a directness fitted to catch the popular ear and to lodge in the memory. While some of his work seems humorous to us, it would not have made that impression on the early Puritans. At the same time, we must not rely on verse like this for our understanding of their outlook on life and death. Beside Wigglesworth's lines we should place the epitaph, "Reserved for a Glorious Resurrection," composed by the great orthodox Puritan clergyman, Cotton Mather (p. 46), for his own infant, which died unbaptized when four days old. It is well to remember that both the Puritans and their clergy had a quiet way of believing that God had reserved to himself the final interpretation of his own word.

Anne Bradstreet (1612-1672). — Colonial New England's best poet, or "The Tenth Muse," as she was called by her friends, was a daughter of the Puritan governor, Thomas Dudley, and became the wife of another Puritan governor, Simon Bradstreet, with whom she came to New England in 1630. Although she was born before the death of Shakespeare, she seems never to have studied the works of that great dramatist. Her models were what Milton called the "fantastics," a school of poets who mistook for manifestations of poetic power, far-fetched and strained metaphors, oddities of expression, remote comparisons, conceits, and strange groupings of thought. She had especially studied Sylvester's paraphrase of *The Divine Weeks and Works* of the French poet Du Bartas, and probably also the works of poets like George Herbert (1593–1633), of the English fantastic school. This paraphrase of Du Bartas was published in a folio of 1215 pages, a few years before Mrs. Bradstreet came to America. This book shows the taste which prevailed in England in the latter part of the first third of the seventeenth century, before Milton came into the ascendency. The fantastic comparison between the "Spirit Eternal," brooding upon chaos, and a hen, is shown in these lines from Du Bartas: —

> "Or as a Hen that fain would hatch a brood
> (Some of her own, some of adoptive blood)
> Sits close thereon, and with her lively heat,
> Of yellow-white balls, doth live birds beget:
> Even in such sort seemed the Spirit Eternal
> To brood upon this Gulf with care paternal."

A contemporary critic thought that he was giving her early work high praise when he called her "a right Du Bartas girl." One of her early poems is *The Four Elements*, where Fire, Air, Earth, and Water

" . . . did contest
Which was the strongest, noblest, and the best,
Who was of greatest use and mightiest force."

Such a debate could never be decided, but the subject was well suited to the fantastic school of poets because it afforded an opportunity for much ingenuity of argument and for far-fetched comparisons, which led nowhere.

Late in life, in her poem, *Contemplations*, she wrote some genuine poetry, little marred by imitation of the fantastic school. Spenser seems to have become her master in later years. No one without genuine poetic ability could have written such lines as: —

"I heard the merry grasshopper then sing,
The black-clad cricket bear a second part,
They kept one tune, and played on the same string,
Seeming to glory in their little art."

These lines show both poetic ease and power: —

"The mariner that on smooth waves doth glide
Sings merrily, and steers his bark with ease,
As if he had command of wind and tide,
And now become great master of the seas."

The comparative excellence of her work in such an atmosphere and amid the domestic cares incident to rearing eight children is remarkable.

NATHANIEL WARD, 1578?–1652

In 1647 Nathaniel Ward, who had been educated for the law, but who afterward became a clergyman, published a strange work known as *The Simple Cobbler of Agawam, in America* "willing," as the sub-title continues, "to help mend his native country, lamentably tattered, both in the upper leather and sole, with all the honest stitches he can take." He had been assistant pastor at Agawam (Ipswich) until ill health caused him to resign. He then busied himself in compiling a code of laws and in other writing before he returned to England in 1647. The following two sentences from his unique book show two points of the religious faith of the Puritans: (1) the belief in a personal devil always actively seeking the destruction of mankind, and (2) the assumption that the vitals of the "elect" are safe from the mortal sting of sin.

FACSIMILE OF TITLE-PAGE TO WARD'S "SIMPLE COBBLER OF AGAWAM"

"Satan is now in his passions, he feels his passion approaching, he loves to fish in roiled waters. Though that dragon cannot sting the vitals of the elect mortally, yet that Beelzebub can fly-blow their intellectuals miserably."

He is often a bitter satirist, a sort of colonial Carlyle, as this attack on woman shows: —

"I honor the woman that can honor herself with her attire; a good text always deserves a fair margent; I am not much offended if I see a trim far trimmer than she that wears it. In a word, whatever Christianity or civility will allow, I can afford with London measure: but when I hear a nugiperous gentledame inquire what dress the Queen is in this week:

what the nudiustertian fashion of the Court; I mean the very newest; with egg to be in it in all haste, whatever it be; I look at her as the very gizzard of a trifle, the product of a quarter of a cipher, the epitome of nothing, fitter to be kicked, if she were of a kickable substance, than either honored or humored."

He does not hesitate to coin a word. The preceding short selection introduces us to "nugiperous" and "nudiustertian." Next, he calls the women's tailor-made gowns "the very pettitoes of infirmity, the giblets of perquisquilian toys."

The spirit of a reformer always sees work to be done, and Ward emphasized three remedies for mid-seventeenth-century ills: (1) Stop toleration of departure from religious truth; (2) banish the frivolities of women and men; and (3) bring the civil war in England to a just end. In proportion to the population, his *Simple Cobbler*, designed to mend human ways, was probably as widely read as Carlyle's *Sartor Resartus* in later days.

In criticism, Ward deserves to be remembered for these two lines: —

> "Poetry's a gift wherein but few excel;
> He doth very ill that doth not passing well."

SAMUEL SEWALL, 1652-1730

There was born in 1652 at Bishopstoke, Hampshire, England, a boy who sailed for New England when he was nine years old, and who became our greatest colonial diarist. This was Samuel Sewall, who graduated from Harvard in 1671 and finally became chief justice of Massachusetts.

His *Diary* runs with some breaks from 1673 to 1729, the year before his death. Good diaries are scarce in any literature. Those who keep them seldom commit to writing many of the most interesting events and secrets of their lives. This failing makes the majority of diaries and memoirs very dry, but this fault cannot be found with Samuel Sewall. His *Diary* will more and more prove a mine of wealth to the future writers of our literature, to our dramatists, novelists, poets, as well as to our historians. The early chronicles and stories on which Shakespeare founded many of his plays were no more serviceable to him than this *Diary* may prove to a coming American writer with a genius like Hawthorne's.

SAMUEL SEWALL

In Sewall's *Diary* we at once feel that we are close to life. The following entry brings us face to face with the children in a Puritan household: —

"Nov. 6, 1692. Joseph threw a knop of brass and hit his sister Betty on the forehead so as to make it bleed and swell; upon which, and for his playing at Prayer-time, and eating when Return Thanks, I whipped him pretty smartly. When I first went in (called by his Grandmother) he sought to shadow and hide himself from me behind the head of the cradle: which gave me the sorrowful remembrance of Adam's carriage."

Sewall was one of the seven judges who sentenced nineteen persons to be put to death for witchcraft at Salem. After this terrible delusion had passed, he had the manliness to rise in church before all the members, and after acknowledging "the blame and shame of his decision," call for "prayers that God who has an unlimited authority would pardon that sin."

Sewall's *Diary* is best known for its faithful chronicle of his courtship of Mrs. Catharine Winthrop. Both had been married twice before, and both had grown children. He was sixty-nine and she fifty-six. No record of any other Puritan courtship so unique as this has been given to the world. He began his formal courtship of Mrs. Winthrop, October 1, 1720. His *Diary* contains records of each visit, of what they said to each other, of the Sermons, cake, and gingerbread that he gave her, of the healths that he drank to her, the lump of sugar that she gave him, of how they "went into the best room, and clos'd the shutters."

"Nov. 2. Gave her about ½ pound of sugar almonds, cost 3 shillings per £. Carried them on Monday. She seem'd pleas'd with them, ask'd what they cost. Spake of giving her a hundred pounds per annum if I died before her. Ask'd her what sum she would give me, if she should die first?"

"Monday, Nov. 7. I went to Mad. Winthrop; found her rocking her little Katy in the cradle. I excus'd my coming so late (near eight). She set me an arm'd chair and cushion; and so the cradle was between her arm'd chair and mine. Gave her the remnant of my almonds. She did not eat of them as before. . . . The fire was come to one short brand besides the block, which brand was set up in end; at last it fell to pieces and no recruit was made. . . . Took leave of her. . . . Her dress was not so clean as sometime it had been. Jehovah jireh!"

Acute men have written essays to account for the aristocratic Mrs. Winthrop's refusal of Chief-Justice Sewall. Some have said that it was due to his aversion to slavery and to his refusal to allow her to keep her slaves. This episode is only a small part of a rich storehouse. The greater part of the *Diary* contains only the raw materials of literature, yet some of it is real literature, and it ranks among the great diaries of the world.

Cotton Mather.

COTTON MATHER, 1663-1728

Life and Personality. — Cotton Mather, grandson of the Rev. John Cotton (p. 14), and the most distinguished of the old type of Puritan clergymen, was born in Boston and died in his native city, without ever having traveled a hundred miles from it. He entered Harvard at the age of eleven, and took the bachelor's degree at fifteen. His life shows such an overemphasis of certain Puritan traits as almost to presage the coming decline of clerical influence. He says that at the age of only seven or eight he not only composed forms of prayer for his schoolmates, but also obliged them to pray, although some of them cuffed him for his pains. At fourteen he began a series of fasts to crucify the flesh, increase his holiness, and bring him nearer to God.

He endeavored never to waste a minute. In his study, where he often worked sixteen hours a day, he had in large letters the sign, "BE SHORT," to greet the eyes of visitors. The amount of writing which he did almost baffles belief. His published works, numbering about four hundred, include sermons, essays, and books. During all of his adult life, he also preached in the North Church of Boston.

He was a religious "fantastic" (p. 40), that is, he made far-fetched applications of religious truth. A tall man suggested to him high attainments in Christianity; washing his hands, the desirability of a clean heart.

Although Cotton Mather became the most famous clergyman of colonial New England, he was disappointed in two of his life's ambitions. He failed to become president of Harvard and to bring New England back in religious matters to the first halcyon days of the colony. On the contrary, he lived to see Puritan theocracy suffer a great decline. His fantastic and strained application of religious truth, his overemphasis of many things, and especially his conduct in zealously aiding and abetting the Salem witchcraft murders, were no mean factors in causing that decline.

His intentions were certainly good. He was an apostle of altruism, and he tried to improve each opportunity for doing good in everyday life. He trained his children to do acts of kindness for other children. His *Essays to Do Good* were a powerful influence on the life of Benjamin Franklin. Cotton Mather would not have lived in vain if he had done nothing else except to help mold Franklin for the service of his country; but this is only one of

Mather's achievements. We must next pass to his great work in literature.

The Magnalia.— This "prose epic of New England Puritanism," the most famous of Mather's many works, is a large folio volume entitled *Magnalia Christi Americana: or the Ecclesiastical History of New England*. It was published in London in 1702, two years after Dryden's death.

The book is a remarkable compound of whatever seemed to the author most striking in early New England history. His point of view was of course religious. The work contains a rich store of biography of the early clergy, magistrates, and governors, of the lives of eleven of the clerical graduates of Harvard, of the faith, discipline, and government of the New England churches, of remarkable manifestations of the divine providence, and of the "Way of the Lord" among the churches and the Indians.

We may to-day turn to the *Magnalia* for vivid accounts of early New England life. Mather has a way of selecting and expressing facts in such a way as to cause them to lodge in the memory. These two facts about John Cotton give us a vivid impression of the influence of the early clergy:—

"The keeper of the inn where he did use to lodge, when he came to Derby, would profanely say to his companions, that he wished Mr. Cotton were gone out of his house, for he was not able to swear while that man was under his roof. . . .

"The Sabbath he began the evening before, for which keeping of the Sabbath from evening to evening he wrote arguments before his coming to New England; and I suppose 'twas from his reason and practice that the Christians of New England have generally done so too."

We read that the daily vocation of Thomas Shepard, the first pastor at Cambridge, Massachusetts, was, to quote Mather's noble phrase, "*A Trembling Walk with God.*" He speaks of the choleric disposition of Thomas Hooker, the great Hartford clergyman, and says it was "useful unto him," because "he had ordinarily as much government of his choler as a man has of a mastiff dog in a chain; he 'could let out his dog, and pull in his dog, as he pleased.'" Some of Mather's prose causes modern readers to wonder if he was not a humorist. He says that a fire in the college buildings in some mysterious way influenced the President of Harvard to shorten one of his long prayers, and gravely adds, "that if the devotions had held three minutes longer, the Colledge had been irrecoverably laid in ashes." One does not feel sure that Mather saw the humor in this demonstration of practical religion. It is also doubtful whether he is intentionally humorous in his most fantastic prose, such, for instance, as his likening the Rev. Mr. Partridge to the bird of that name, who, because he "had no defence neither of beak nor claw," took "a flight over the ocean" to escape his ecclesiastical hunters, and finally "took wing to become a bird of paradise, along with the winged seraphim of heaven."

Such fantastic conceits, which for a period blighted the literature of the leading European nations, had their last great exponent in Cotton Mather. Minor writers still indulge in these conceits, and find willing readers among the uneducated, the tired, and those who are bored when they are required to do more than skim the surface of things. John Seccomb, a Harvard graduate of 1728, the year in which Mather died, then gained fame from such lines as: —

"A furrowed brow,
Where corn might grow,"

but the best prose and poetry have for a long time won their readers for other qualities. Even the taste of the next generation showed a change, for Cotton Mather's son, Samuel, noted as a blemish his father's "straining for far-fetched and dear-bought hints." Cotton Mather's most repellent habit to modern readers is his overloading his pages with quotations in foreign languages, especially in Latin. He thus makes a pedantic display of his wide reading.

He is not always accurate in his presentation of historical or biographical matter, but in spite of all that can be said against the *Magnalia*, it is a vigorous presentation of much that we should not willingly let die. In fact, when we read the early history of New England, we are frequently getting from the *Magnalia* many things in changed form without ever suspecting the source.

JONATHAN EDWARDS, 1703-1758

Life and Writings. — Jonathan Edwards, who ranks among the world's greatest theologians and metaphysicians, was born in 1703 in East Windsor, Connecticut. Like Cotton Mather, Edwards was precocious, entering Yale before he was thirteen. The year previous to his going to college, he wrote a paper on spiders, showing careful scientific observation and argument. This paper has been called "one of the rarest specimens of precocious scientific genius on record." At fourteen, he read Locke's *Essay on the Human Understanding*, receiving from it, he says, higher pleasure "than the most greedy miser finds when gathering up handfuls of silver and gold from some newly discovered treasure." Before he was seventeen, he had graduated from Yale, and he had become a tutor there before he was twenty-one.

Like Dante, he had a Beatrice. Thinking of her, he wrote this prose hymn of a maiden's love for the Divine Power: —

"They say there is a young lady in New Haven who is beloved of that great Being who made and rules the world, and there are certain seasons in which this great Being, in some way or other invisible, comes to her and fills her mind with exceeding sweet delight, and that she hardly cares for anything except to meditate on Him; that she expects after a while to be received up where He is, to be raised up out of the world and caught up into heaven; being assured that He loves her too well to let her remain at a distance from Him always. . . . She will sometimes go about from place to place singing sweetly; and seems to be always full of joy and pleasure, and no one knows for what. She loves to be alone, walking in the fields and groves, and seems to have some one invisible always conversing with her."

Jonathan Edwards thus places before us Sarah Pierrepont, a New England Puritan maiden. To note the similarity of thought between the Old

MEMORIAL TABLET TO JONATHAN EDWARDS
(First Church, Northampton, Mass.)

Puritan England and the New, let us turn to the maiden in Milton's *Comus:*—

"A thousand liveried angels lackey her,
　Driving far off each thing of sin and guilt;
　And in clear dream and solemn vision,
　Tell her of things that no gross ear can hear,
　Till oft converse with heav'nly habitants

> Begin to cast a beam on th'outward shape,
> The unpolluted temple of the mind,
> And turns it by degrees to the soul's essence,
> Till all be made immortal."

Unlike Dante, Edwards married his Beatrice at the age of seventeen. In 1727, the year of his marriage, he became pastor of the church in Northampton, Massachusetts. With the aid of his wife, he inaugurated the greatest religious revival of the century, known as the "Great Awakening," which spread to other colonial churches, crossed the ocean, and stimulated Wesley to call sinners to repentance.

Early in life, Edwards formed a series of resolutions, three of which are:—

"To live with all my might, while I do live."

"Never to do anything, which, if I should see in another, I should count a just occasion to despise him for, or to think any way the more meanly of him."

"Never, henceforward, till I die, to act as if I were any way my own, but entirely and altogether God's."

He earnestly tried to keep these resolutions until the end. After a successful pastorate of twenty-three years at Northampton, the church dismissed him for no fault of his own.

Like Dante, he was driven into exile, and he went from Northampton to the frontier town of Stockbridge, where he remained for seven years as a missionary to the Indians. His wife and daughters did their utmost to add to the family income, and some contributions were sent him from Scotland, but he was so poor that he wrote his books on the backs of letters and on the blank margins cut from newspapers. His fame was not swallowed up in the wilderness. Princeton College called him to its presidency in 1757. He died in that office in 1758, after less than three months' service in his new position. His wife was still in Stockbridge when he passed away. "Tell her," he said to his daughter, "that the uncommon union which has so long subsisted between us has been of such a nature as I trust is spiritual, and therefore will continue forever." In September of the same year she came to lie beside him in the graveyard at Princeton.

In 1900, the church that had dismissed him one hundred and fifty years before placed on its walls a bronze tablet in his memory, with the noble inscription from *Malachi* ii., 6.

As a writer, Jonathan Edwards won fame in three fields. He is (1) America's greatest metaphysician, (2) her greatest theologian, and (3) a unique poetic interpreter of the universe as a manifestation of the divine love.

His best known metaphysical work is *The Freedom of the Will* (1754). The central point of this work is that the will is determined by the strongest motive, that it is "repugnant to reason that one act of the will should come into existence without a cause." He boldly says that God is free to do only what is right. Edwards emphasizes the higher freedom, gained through repeated acts of the right kind, until both the inclination and the power to do wrong disappear.

As a theologian, America has not yet produced his superior. His *Treatise concerning the Religious Affections*, his account of the Great Awakening, called *Faithful Narrative of the Surprising Work of God*, and *Thoughts on the Revival*, as well as his more distinctly technical theological works, show his ability in this field. Unfortunately, he did not rise superior to the Puritan custom of preaching about hell fire. He delivered on that subject a sermon which causes modern readers to shudder; but this, although the most often quoted, is the least typical of the man and his writings. Those in search of really typical statements of his theology will find them in such specimens as, "God and real existence is the same. God is and there is nothing else." He was a theological idealist, believing that all the varied phenomena of the universe are "constantly proceeding from God, as light from the sun." Such statements suggest Shelley's lines, which tell how

> ". . . the one Spirit's plastic stress
> Sweeps through the dull dense world compelling there
> All new successions to the forms they wear."

Dr. Allen, Edwards's biographer and critic, and a careful student of his unpublished, as well as of his published, writings, says, "He was at his best and greatest, most original and creative, when he described the divine love." Such passages as the following, and also the one quoted on page 51, show this quality: —

"When we behold the fragrant rose and lily, we see His love and purity. So the green trees and fields and singing of birds are the emanations of His infinite joy and benignity. The easiness and naturalness of trees and vines are shadows of His beauty and loveliness."

His favorite text was, "I am the Rose of Sharon and the Lily of the valleys," and his favorite words were "sweet and bright."

ENGLISH LITERATURE OF THE PERIOD

The great English writers between the colonization of Jamestown in 1607 and the outbreak of the French and Indian War in 1754 are: (1) **John Milton** (1608–1674), the great poetic spokesman of Puritan England, whose *Comus* is addressed to those, who: —

"... by due steps aspire
To lay their just hands on that golden key
That opes the palace of eternity,"

whose *Sonnets* breathe a purposeful prayer to live this life as ever in his great Taskmaster's eye, and whose *Paradise Lost* is the colossal epic of the loss of Eden through sin; (2) **John Bunyan** (1628-1688), whose *Pilgrim's Progress* addressed itself in simple, earnest English to each individual human being, telling him what he must do to escape the City of Destruction and to reach the City of All Delight; (3) **John Dryden** (1631-1700), a master in the field of satiric and didactic verse and one of the pioneers in the field of modern prose criticism; (4) **Alexander Pope** (1688-1744), another poet of the satiric and didactic school, who exalted form above matter, and wrote polished couplets which have been models for so many inferior poets; (5) the essayists, **Richard Steele** (1672-1729) and **Joseph Addison** (1672-1719), the latter being especially noted for the easy, flowing prose of his papers in the *Spectator;* (6) **Jonathan Swift** (1667-1745), a master of prose satire, whose *Gulliver's Travels* has not lost its fascination; (7) **Daniel Defoe** (1661 ?-1731) whose *Robinson Crusoe* continues to increase in popularity; (8) **Samuel Richardson** (1689-1761), and **Henry Fielding** (1707-1754), the two great mid-eighteenth-century novelists.

The colonial literature of this period was influenced only in a very minor degree by the work of these men, for a generation usually passed before the influence of contemporary English authors appeared in American literature. In the next chapter, we shall see evidences of the influence of Pope. Benjamin Franklin will tell us how Bunyan and Addison were his teachers, and the early fiction will show its indebtedness to the work of Samuel Richardson.

LEADING HISTORICAL FACTS

Virginia and Massachusetts produced the most of our colonial literature. There were, however, thirteen colonies stretched along the seaboard from Georgia (1733), the last to be founded, to Canada. Although these colonies were established under different grants or charters, and although some had more liberty and suffered less from the interference of England than others, it is nevertheless true that every colony was a school for a self-governing democracy. No colonies elsewhere in the world had the same amount of liberty. This period was a necessary preparation for the coming republic.

We must not suppose that there was complete liberty in those days. Such a state has not been reached even in the twentieth century. The early government of Virginia was largely aristocratic; that of Massachusetts, theocratic. Virginia persecuted the Puritans. The early settlers of Massachusetts drove out Roger Williams and hanged Quakers. New York persecuted those who did not join the Church of England. The central truth, however, is that these thirteen colonies were making the greatest of all world experiments in democracy and liberty.

The important colony of New Netherland (New York) was settled by the Dutch early in the seventeenth century. They established an aristocracy with great landed estates along the Hudson. The student of literature is specially interested in this colony because Washington Irving (p. 112) has invested it with a halo of romance. He shows us the sturdy Knickerbockers, the Van Cortlands, the Van Dycks, the Van Wycks, and other chivalrous Dutch burghers, sitting in perfect silence, puffing their pipes, and thinking of nothing for hours together in those "days of simplicity and sunshine." For literary reasons it is well that this was not made an English colony until the Duke of York took possession of it in 1664.

At the beginning of the eighteenth century, the colonists in the middle and northern part of the country divided their energies almost equally between trade and agriculture. At the South, agriculture was the chief occupation and tobacco and rice were the two leading staples. These were produced principally by the labor of negro slaves. There were also many indentured servants at the South, where the dividing lines between the different classes were most strongly marked.

Up to 1700 the history of each colony is practically that of a separate unit. Almost all the colonies had trouble with Indians and royal governors. Pirates, rapacious politicians, religious matters, or witchcraft were sometimes sources of disturbance. All knew the hard labor and the privations involved in subduing the wilderness and making permanent settlements in a new land. History tells of the abandonment of many other colonies and of the subjugation of many other races, but no difficulty and no foe daunted this Anglo-Saxon stock.

In 1700 the population of New England was estimated at about one hundred and ten thousand. In 1754, the beginning of the French and Indian War, Connecticut alone had that number, while all New England probably had at this time nearly four hundred thousand. The middle colonies began the eighteenth century with about fifty-nine thousand and grew by the middle of the century to about three hundred and fifty-five thousand. During the same period, the southern group increased from about ninety thousand to six hundred thousand. By 1750 the thirteen colonies probably had a total population of nearly fourteen hundred thousand. Since no census was taken until 1790, these figures are only approximately correct.

Such development serves to show the trend of coming events. This remarkable increase in population soon caused numbers to go farther west. This movement resulted in collision with the French, who were at this time holding the central part of the country, from the Gulf into Canada. One other result followed. The colonies began to seem valuable to England because they furnished a market for English manufactures and a carrying trade for English ships. The previous comparative insignificance of the colonies and the trouble in England had served to protect them, but their trade had now assumed a proportion that made the mother country realize what a valuable commercial asset she would have if she regulated the colonies in her own interest.

SUMMARY

In this chapter we have traced the history of American colonial literature from the foundation of the Jamestown Colony until 1754. Before 1607 Chaucer, Spenser, and Shakespeare had written, and before 1620 the King James version of the *Bible* had been produced. England had, therefore, a wonderful literature before her colonies came to America. They were the heirs of all that the English race had previously accomplished; and they brought to these shores an Elizabethan initiative, ingenuity, and democratic spirit.

The Virginia colony was founded, as colonies usually are, for a commercial reason. The Virginians and the other southern colonists lived more by agriculture, were more widely scattered, had fewer schools, more slaves, and less town life than the New Englanders. Under the in-

SUMMARY

fluence of a commanding clergy, common schools, and the stimulus of town life, the New England colony produced more literature.

The chief early writers of Virginia are: (1) Captain John Smith, who described the country and the Indians, and gave to literature the story of Pocahontas, thereby disclosing a new world to the imagination of writers; (2) William Strachey, who outranks contemporary colonial writers in describing the wrath of the sea, and who may even have furnished a suggestion to Shakespeare for *The Tempest;* (3) two poets, (*a*) George Sandys, who translated part of Ovid, and (*b*) the unknown author of the elegy on Nathaniel Bacon; and (4) Robert Beverly and William Byrd, who gave interesting descriptions of early Virginia.

The chief colonial writers of New England are: (1) William Bradford, whose *History of Plymouth Plantation* tells the story of the first Pilgrim colony; (2) John Winthrop, who wrote in his *Journal* the early history of the Massachusetts Bay Colony; (3) the poets, including (*a*) the translators of the *Bay Psalm Book*, the first volume of so-called verse printed in the British American colonies, (*b*) Wigglesworth, whose *Day of Doom*, was a poetic exposition of Calvinistic theology, (*c*) Anne Bradstreet, who wrote a small amount of genuine poetry, after she had passed from the influence of the "fantastic" school of poets; (4) Nathaniel Ward, the author of *The Simple Cobbler of Agawam*, an attempt to mend human ways; (5) Samuel Sewall, New England's greatest colonial diarist; (6) Cotton Mather, the most famous clerical writer, whose *Magnalia* is a compound of early colonial history and biography, sometimes written in a "fantastic" style; (7) Jonathan Edwards, America's greatest metaphysician and theologian, who maintained that the action of the human will is determined by the strongest motive, that the substance of this universe is nothing but "the divine Idea," communicated to human consciousness, and who could invest spiritual truth with the beauty of the Rose of Sharon and the Lily of the valleys.

The New England colonist came to America because of religious feeling. His religion was to him a matter of eternal life or eternal death. From the modern point of view, this religion may seem too inflexibly stern, too little illumined by the spirit of love, too much darkened by the shadow of eternal punishment, but unless that religion had communicated something of its own dominating inflexibility to the colonist, he would never have braved the ocean, the wilderness, the Indians; he would never have flung the gauntlet down to tyranny at Lexington and Concord.

The greatest lesson taught by colonial literature, by men like Bradford, Winthrop, Edwards, and the New England clergy in general, is moral heroism, the determination to follow the shining path of the Eternal over the wave and through the forest to a new temple of human liberty. Their aspiration, endeavor, suffering, accomplishment, should strengthen our faith in the worth of those spiritual realities which are not quoted in the markets of the world, but which alone possess imperishable value.

REFERENCES FOR FURTHER STUDY

HISTORICAL

English History. — In either Gardiner's *Students' History of England*, Walker's *Essentials in English History*, Andrews's *History of England*, or Cheney's *Short History of England*, read the chapters dealing with the time of Elizabeth, James I., Charles I., the Commonwealth, Charles II., James II., William and Mary, Anne, George I. and

II. A work like Halleck's *History of English Literature*, covering these periods, should be read.

American History. — Read the account from the earliest times to the outbreak of the French and Indian War in any of the following : —

Thwaites's *The Colonists*, 1492-1750.

Fisher's *Colonial Era*.

Lodge's *A Short History of the English Colonies in America*.

Doyle's *The English in America*.

Hart's *Essentials in American History*.

Channing's *A Students' History of the United States*.

Eggleston's *A Larger History of the United States of America*.

James and Sanford's *American History*.

For an account of special colonies, consult the volumes in *American Commonwealths* series, and also,

Fiske's *Beginnings of New England, The Dutch and Quaker Colonies in America, Old Virginia and Her Neighbors*.

LITERARY

Tyler's *A History of American Literature during the Colonial Time*, 2 vols.

Otis's *American Verse*, 1625-1807.

Richardson's *American Literature*, 2 vols.

Trent's *A History of American Literature*, 1607-1865.

Wendell's *History of Literature in America*.

Narratives of Early Virginia, edited by Tyler.

Bradford's *History of Plymouth Plantation*. New edition, edited by Davis. (Scribner, 1908.)

Winthrop's *Journal* ("History of New England"). New edition, edited by Hosmer, 2 vols., (Scribner, 1908.)

Chamberlain's *Samuel Sewall and the World He Lived in*.

Lodge's "A Puritan Pepys" (Sewall) in *Studies in History*.

Campbell's *Anne Bradstreet and her Time*.

Twichell's *John Winthrop*.

Walker's *Thomas Hooker*.

Wendell's *Life of Cotton Mather*.

Allen's *Life of Jonathan Edwards*.

Gardiner's *Jonathan Edwards, a Retrospect*.

SUGGESTED READINGS

The following volumes of selections from American Literature will be referred to either by the last name of the author, or, if there are more authors than one, by the initials of the last names: —

Cairns's *Selections from Early American Writers*, 1607-1800. (Macmillan.)

Trent and Wells's *Colonial Prose and Poetry*, 3 vols., 1607-1775. (Crowell.)

Stedman and Hutchinson's *A Library of American Literature*, 1608-1890, 11 vols. (Benjamin.)

Carpenter's *American Prose Selections*. (Macmillan.)

Trent's *Southern Writers: Selections in Prose and Verse*. (Macmillan.)

At least one of the selections indicated for each author should be read.

John Smith. — The Beginnings of Jamestown (from *A True Relation of Virginia*, 1608); The Religious Observances of the Indians (from *A Map of Virginia*, published in 1612), Cairns, pp. 2-4, 10-14; The Romance of Pocahontas (from *The General History of Virginia*, 1624), S. & H., Vol. I., pp. 10-17; T. & W., Vol. I., pp. 12-22.

William Strachey. — Read the selection from *A True Repertory of the Wrack and Redemption of Sir Thomas Gates*, in Cairns, 19-26.

Poetry in the Virginian Colony. — For George Sandys, see pp. 51-58 in Vol. I. of Tyler's *A History of American Literature during the Colonial Time*.

For the elegy on the death of Nathaniel Bacon, see Tyler, Vol. I., 78, 79; Cairns, 185-188; T. & W., II., 166-169; S. & H., I., 456-458; Trent, 12-14.

Descriptions of Virginia. — The best selection from Beverly's *History and Present State of Virginia* may be found in T. & W., II., 354-360. See also Trent, 16-18; S. & H., II., 270-272.

For selections from Byrd's *History of the Dividing Line*, see Cairns, *passim*, 259-272; Trent, 19-22; T. & W., III., 23-32; S. & H., II., 302-305.

William Bradford. — The Voyage of the Mayflower, Cairns, 31-35; Early Difficulties of the Pilgrim Fathers, T. & W., I., 42-45; The Communal System Abandoned, T. & W., I., 46-49; The Landing of the Pilgrims and their Settlement at Plymouth, S. & H., I., 124-130.

John Winthrop. — Twenty-five entries from his *Journal* or *History of New England* are given in Cairns, 44-48, and fourteen in T. & W., I., 99-105.

His famous speech on *Liberty* may be found in T. & W., I., 106-116; in S. & H., I., 302-303; and in Cairns, 50-53.

Early New England Verse. — The selection in the text (p. 38) from the *Bay Psalm Book* is sufficient.

For Wigglesworth's *Day of Doom*, see Cairns, 166-177; T. & W., II., 54-60; S. & H., *passim*, II., 3-16.

Anne Bradstreet's best poem, *Contemplations*, may be found in Cairns, 154-162; T. & W., I., 280-283; S. & H., I., 314, 315.

Ward's Simple Cobbler of Agawam. — His view of religious toleration is given in Cairns, 113-118, and T. & W., I., 253-259. For the satiric essay on women's fashions, see Cairns, 119-124; T. & W., I., 260-266; S. & H. I., 276-280.

Samuel Sewall. — Cairns, 240-243, gives from the *Diary* the events of a month. Notes on the Witchcraft Persecution and his prayer of repentance for "the blame and shame of it" may be found in T. & W., II., 294-296. The record of his courtship of Madam Winthrop is given in Cairns, 245-249; T. & W., II., 304-319; and S. & H., II., 192-200. For his early anti-slavery tract, see T. & W., II., 320-326; S. & H., II., 189-192.

Cotton Mather. — His fantastic life of Mr. Ralph Partridge from the *Magnalia* is given in Cairns, 228, 229. The interesting story of the New England argonaut, Sir William Phips, may be found in T. & W., II., 257-266, and in S. & H., II., 143-149. One of his best biographies is that of Thomas Hooker, S. & H., II., 149-156.

Jonathan Edwards. — For a specimen of an almost poetic exposition of the divine love, read the selection in Cairns, 280, 281; T. & W., III., 148, 149; S. & H., II., 374; and Carpenter, 16, 17, beginning, "I am the Rose of Sharon and the Lily of the valleys." Selections from his *Freedom of the Will* are given in Cairns, 291-294; T. & W., III., 185-187; and S. & H., II., 404-407 (the best).

QUESTIONS AND SUGGESTIONS

Is Captain John Smith more remarkable for chronicling what passed before his senses or for explaining what he saw? How does his account of the Indians (p. 18 of this text) compare with modern accounts? Is he apparently a novice, or somewhat skilled in writing prose ? Does he seem to you to be a romancer or a narrator of a plain unvarnished tale ?

Compare Strachey's storm at sea with *Act I.* of Shakespeare's *Tempest*. In what part of this *Act* and under what circumstances does he mention "the still-vex'd Bermoothes"?

Compare the ability of the three great early colonizers, Smith, Bradford, and Winthrop, in writing narrative prose. Smith's story of Pocahontas is easily accessible. Those who can find the complete works of Bradford and Winthrop may select from Bradford for comparison his story of Squanto, the Pilgrims' tame Indian. Winthrop's *Journal* contains many specimens of brief narrative, such as the story of the voyage across the Atlantic from March 29 to June 14, 1630; of Winthrop's losing himself in the wood, October 11, 1631; of shipwreck on the Isle of Shoals, August 16, 1635; of an indentured servant, March 8, 1636; of an adventure with Indians, July 20–30, August 24, and October 8, 1636. Those without opportunity to consult the works of Bradford and Winthrop will find in the books of selections sufficient material for comparison.

Is brevity or prolixity a quality of these early narrators ? What English prose written before 1640 is superior to the work of these three men ? Why is it especially important for Americans to know something of their writings ? What advance in prose narrative do you find in Beverly and Byrd ?

What characteristic of a famous English prose writer of the nineteenth century is noticeable in Ward's essay on fashions ?

Why could fine poetry not be reasonably expected in early Virginia and New England ? What are some of the Calvinistic tenets expounded in Wigglesworth's *Day of Doom?* Choose the best two short selections of colonial poetry.

What are some of the qualifications of a good diarist ? Which of these do you find in the *Diary* of Samuel Sewall ?

Point out some of the fantastic prose expressions of Cotton Mather. Compare his narrative of Captain Phips with the work of Smith, Bradford, and Winthrop, on the one hand, and of Beverly and Byrd, on the other.

Compare the theology in Edwards's "Rose of Sharon" selection (p. 54) with that in Wigglesworth's *Day of Doom*. Why may this selection from Edwards be called a "poetic exposition of the divine love" ? What is his view of the freedom of the will ?

CHAPTER II

THE EMERGENCE OF A NATION

Progress toward Nationality. — The French and Indian War, which began in 1754, served its purpose in making the colonists feel that they were one people. At this time most of them were living on the seacoast from Georgia to Maine, and had not yet even crossed the great Appalachian range of mountains. The chief men of one colony knew little of the leaders in the other colonies. This war made George Washington known outside of Virginia. There was not much interchange of literature between the two leading colonies, Virginia and Massachusetts. Prior to this time, the other colonies had not produced much that had literary value. No national literature could be written until the colonists were welded together.

The French and Indian War, which decided whether France or England was to be supreme in America, exposed the colonists to a common danger. They fought side by side against the French and Indians, and learned that the defeat of one was the defeat of all. After a desperate struggle France lost, and the Anglo-Saxon race was dominant on the new continent. By the treaty of Paris, signed in 1763, England became the possessor of Canada and the land east of the Mississippi River.

The Revolution. — All of the colonies had been under English rule, although they had in large part managed in one way or another to govern themselves. At the close of the French and Indian War, the colonists had not thought of breaking away from England, although they had learned the lesson of union against a common foe. George III. came to the throne in 1760. By temperament he was unusually adapted to play his part in changing the New World's history. He was determined to rule according to his own personal inclinations. He dominated his cabinet and controlled Parliament by bribery. He decided that the American colonies should feel the weight of his authority, and in 1763 his prime minister, George Grenville, undertook to execute measures in restraint of colonial trade. Numbers of commodities, like tobacco, for instance, could not be traded with France or Spain or Holland, but must be sent to England. If there was any profit to be made in selling goods to foreign nations, England would make that profit. He also planned to tax the colonists and to quarter British troops among them. These measures aroused the colonies to armed resistance and led to the Revolutionary War, which began in 1775.

Freneau (p. 96), a poet of the Revolution, thus expresses in verse some of these events: —

> "When a certain great king, whose initial is G,
> Shall force stamps upon paper and folks to drink tea;
> When these folks burn his tea and stampt paper like stubble,
> You may guess that this king is then coming to trouble."

THE ESSAYISTS

The pen helped to prepare the way for the sword and to arouse and prolong the enthusiasm of those who had taken arms. Before the battle of Lexington (1775), writers were busy on both sides of the dispute, for no great movement begins without opposition. Many colonists did not favor resistance to England. Even at the time of the first battle, comparatively few wished absolute separation from the mother country.

Thomas Paine (1737–1809) was an Englishman who came to America in 1774 and speedily made himself master of colonial thought and feeling. Early in 1776 he published a pamphlet entitled *Common Sense,* which advocated complete political independence of England. The sledge hammer blows which he struck hastened the *Declaration of Independence.* Note the energy, the directness, and the employment of the concrete method in the following:—

THOMAS PAINE

"But Britain is the parent country, say some. Then the more shame upon her conduct. Even brutes do not devour their young, nor savages make war upon their families; wherefore, the assertion, if true, turns to her reproach. . . . This new world hath been the asylum for the persecuted lovers of civil and religious liberty from *every part* of Europe. Hither have they fled, not from the tender embraces of the mother, but from the cruelty of the monster; and it is so far true of England, that the same tyranny which drove the first emigrants from home, pursues their descendants still."

In the latter part of 1776 Washington wrote, "If every nerve is not strained to recruit the new army with all possible expedition, I think the game is pretty nearly up." In those gloomy days, sharing the privations of the army, Thomas Paine wrote the first number of an irregularly issued periodical, known as the *Crisis*, beginning:—

"These are the times that try men's souls. The summer soldier and the sunshine patriot will, in this crisis, shrink from the service of his country; but he that stands it now, deserves the love and thanks of man and woman."

Some have said that the pen of Thomas Paine was worth more to the cause of liberty than twenty thousand men. In the darkest hours he inspired the colonists with hope and enthusiasm. Whenever the times seemed to demand another number of the *Crisis*, it was forthcoming. Sixteen of these appeared during the progress of the struggle for liberty. He had an almost Shakespearean intuition of what would appeal to the exigencies of each case. After the Americans had triumphed, he went abroad to aid the French, saying, "Where Liberty is not, there is my home." He died in America in 1809. He is unfortunately more remembered for his skeptical *Age of Reason* than for his splendid services to the cause of liberty.

Thomas Jefferson (1743–1826), the third President of the United States, wrote much political prose and many letters, which have been gathered into ten large volumes. Ignoring these, he left directions that the words, "Author of the Declaration of American Independence," should immediately follow his name on his monument. No other American prose writer has, in an equal number of words, yet surpassed this *Declaration of Independence*. Its influence has encircled the world and modified the opinions of nations as widely separated as the French and the Japanese.

THOMAS JEFFERSON

Jefferson may have borrowed some of his ideas from *Magna Charta* (1215) and the *Petition of Right* (1628); he may have incorporated in this *Declaration* the yearnings that thousands of human souls had already felt, but he voiced those yearnings so well that his utterances have become classic. It has been said that he "poured the soul of the continent" into that *Declaration*, but he did more than that. He poured into it the soul of all freedom-loving humanity, and he was accepted as the spokesman of the dweller on the Seine as enthusiastically as of the revolutionists in America. Those who have misconstrued the meaning of his famous expression, "All men are created equal" have been met with the adequate reply, "No intelligent man has ever misconstrued it except intentionally."

America has no *Beowulf* celebrating the slaying of land-devastating monsters, but she has in this *Declaration* a deathless battle song against the monsters that would throttle Liberty. Outside of Holy Writ, what words are more familiar to our ears than these?—

"We hold these truths to be self-evident: That all men are created equal; that they are endowed by their Creator with certain unalienable rights; that among these are life, liberty, and the pursuit of happiness. That, to secure these rights, governments are instituted among men, deriving their just powers from the consent of the governed."

Every student will find his comprehension of American literature aided by a careful study of this *Declaration*. This trumpet-tongued declaration of the fact that every man has an equal right with every other man to his own life, liberty, and the pursuit of happiness has served as an ideal to inspire some of the best things in our literature. This ideal has not yet been completely reached, but it is finding expression in every effort for the social and moral improvements of our population. Jefferson went a step beyond the old Puritans in maintaining that happiness is a worthy object of pursuit. Modern altruists are also working on this line, demanding a fuller moral and industrial liberty, and endeavoring to develop a more widespread capacity for happiness.

Alexander Hamilton (1757-1804), because of his wonderful youthful precocity, reminds us of Jonathan Edwards (p. 50). In 1774, at the age of seventeen, Hamilton wrote in answer to a Tory who maintained that England had given New York no charter of rights, and that she could not complain that her rights had been taken away: —

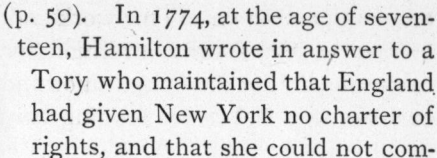

"The sacred rights of mankind are not to be rummaged for among old parchments or musty records. They are written as with a sunbeam, in the whole volume of human nature, by the hand of the Divinity itself, and can never be erased or obscured by mortal power."

ALEXANDER HAMILTON

A profound student of American constitutional history says of Hamilton's pamphlets: "They show great maturity, a more remarkable maturity than has ever been exhibited by any other person, at so early an age, in the same department of thought."

After the Americans were victorious in the war, Hamilton suggested that a constitutional convention be called. For seven years this suggestion was not followed, but in 1787 delegates met from various states and framed a federal constitution to be submitted to the states for ratification. Hamilton was one of the leading delegates. After the convention had completed its work, it seemed probable that the states would reject the proposed constitution. To win its acceptance, Hamilton, in collaboration with **James Madison** (1751-1836) and **John Jay** (1745-1829), wrote the famous *Federalist* papers. There were eighty-five of these, but Hamilton wrote more than both of his associates together. These papers have been collected into a volume, and to this day they form a standard commentary on our Constitution. This work and Hamilton's eloquence before the New York convention for ratification helped to carry the day for the Constitution and to terminate a period of dissension which was tending toward anarchy.

THE ORATORS

There are times in the history of a nation when there is unusual need for the orator to persuade, to arouse, and to encourage his countrymen. Many influential colonists disapproved of the Revolution; they wrote against it and talked against it. When the war progressed slowly, entailing not only severe pecuniary loss but also actual suffering to the revolutionists, many lost their former enthusiasm and were willing to have peace at any price. At this period in our history the orator was as necessary as the soldier. Orators helped to launch the Revolution, to continue the war, and, after it was finished, to give the country united constitutional government. It will be instructive to make the acquaintance of some of these orators and to learn the secret of their power.

James Otis (1725-1783) was born in Massachusetts and educated at Harvard. He studied literature for two years after he graduated and then became a lawyer. He was appointed to the position of king's advocate-general, a high-salaried office. There came an order from England, allowing the king's officers to search the houses of Americans at any time on mere suspicion of the concealment of smuggled goods. Otis resigned his office and took the side of the colonists, attacking the constitutionality of a law that allowed the right of unlimited search and that was really designed to curtail the trade of the colonies. He had the advantage of many modern orators in having something to say on his subject, in feeling deeply interested in it, and in talking to people who were also interested in the same thing. Without these three essentials, there cannot be oratory of the highest kind. We can imagine the voice of Otis trembling with feeling as he said in 1761: —

JAMES OTIS

"Now one of the most essential branches of English liberty is the freedom of one's house. A man's house is his castle; and whilst he is quiet, he is as well guarded as a prince in his castle. This writ, if it should be declared legal, would totally annihilate this privilege. Custom-house officers may enter our houses, when they please; we are commanded to permit their entry. Their menial servants may enter, may break locks, bars, and everything in their way; and whether they break through malice or revenge, no man, no court, can inquire."

We may to-day be more interested in other things than in the homes and unrestricted trade of our colonial ancestors, but Otis was willing to give up a lucrative office to speak for the rights of the humblest cottager. He, like the majority of the orators of the Revolution, also possessed another quality, often foreign to the modern orator. What this quality is will appear in this quotation from his speech: —

"Let the consequences be what they will, I am determined to proceed. The only principles of public conduct that are worthy of a gentleman or a man are to sacrifice estate, ease, health, and applause, and even life, to the sacred calls of his country. These manly sentiments, in private life, make the good citizen; in public life, the patriot and the hero."

John Adams, who became the second President of the United States, listened to this speech for five hours, and called Otis "a flame of fire." "Then and there," said Adams, with pardonable exaggeration, "the child Independence was born."

Patrick Henry (1736–1799), a young Virginia lawyer, stood before the First Continental Congress, in 1774, saying: —

"Where are your landmarks, your boundaries of Colonies? The distinctions between Virginians, New Yorkers, and New Englanders are no more. I am not a Virginian, but an American."

These words had electrical effect on the minds of his listeners, and helped to weld the colonies together. In 1775 we can hear him again speaking before a Virginian Convention of Delegates: —

PATRICK HENRY

"Mr. President, it is natural to man to indulge in the illusions of hope. We are apt to shut our eyes against a painful truth, and listen to the song of that siren, till she transforms us into beasts. . . .

"I have but one lamp by which my feet are guided; and that is the lamp of experience. I know of no way of judging of the future but by the past. And judging by the past, I wish to know what there has been in the conduct of the British ministry for the last ten years, to justify those hopes with which gentlemen have been pleased to solace themselves and the House? . . .

"Why stand we here idle? What is it that gentlemen wish? What would they have? Is life so dear, or peace so sweet, as to be purchased at the price of chains and slavery? Forbid it, Almighty God! I know not what course others may take; but as for me, give me liberty or give me death."

It is hardly too much to say that these words have communicated to the entire American nation an intenser desire for liberty, that their effect has not yet passed away, and that they may during the coming centuries serve to awaken Americans in many a crisis.

Samuel Adams (1722–1803), a Bostonian and graduate of Harvard, probably gave his time in fuller measure to the cause of independence than any other writer or speaker. For nine years he was a member of the Continental Congress. When there was talk of peace between the colonies and the mother country, he had the distinction of being one of two Americans for whom England proclaimed in advance that there would be no amnesty granted. We can seem to hear him in 1776 in the Philadelphia State House, replying to the argument that the colonists should obey England, since they were her children : —

SAMUEL ADAMS

"Who among you, my countrymen, that is a father, would claim authority to make your child a slave because you had nourished him in his infancy ?"

After he had signed the *Declaration of Independence*, he spoke to the Pennsylvanians like a Puritan of old : —

"We have explored the temple of royalty, and found that the idol we have bowed down to has eyes which see not, ears that hear not our prayer, and a heart like the nether millstone. We have this day restored the Sovereign, to whom alone men ought to be obedient. He reigns in heaven, and with a propitious eye beholds His subjects assuming that freedom of thought and dignity of self-direction which He bestowed on them."

These sentences plainly show the influence of biblical thought and diction. A century before, this compound of patriot, politician, orator, and statesman would also have been a clergyman.

An examination of these three typical orators of the Revolution will show that they gained their power (1) from intense interest in their subject matter, (2) from masterful knowledge of that matter, due either to first-hand acquaintance with it or to liberal culture or to both, (3) from the fact that the subject of their orations appealed forcibly to the interest of that special time, (4) from their character and personality. Most of what they said makes dry reading to-day, but we shall occasionally find passages, like Patrick Henry's apotheosis of liberty, which speak to the ear of all time and which have in them something of a Homeric or Miltonic ring.

Increasing Influence of the Legal Profession. — Not one of the great orators of the Revolution was a clergyman. The power of the clergy in political affairs was declining, while the legal profession was becoming more and more influential. James Otis, Patrick Henry, Alexander Hamilton, and John Jay (p. 71) were lawyers. Life was becoming more diversified, and there were avenues other than theology attractive to the educated man. At the same time, we must remember that the clergy have never ceased to be a mighty power in American life. They were not silent or uninfluential during the Revolution. Soon after the battle of Bunker Hill, John Adams wrote from Philadelphia to his wife in Boston, asking, " Does Mr. Wibird preach against oppression and other cardinal vices of the time? Tell him the clergy here of every denomination, not excepting the Episcopalian, thunder and lighten every Sabbath."

BENJAMIN FRANKLIN, 1706-1790

Autobiography and Life. — Franklin's *Autobiography* stands first among works of its kind in American literature. The young person who does not read it misses both profit and entertainment. Some critics have called it "the equal of Robinson Crusoe, one of the few everlasting books in the English language." In this small volume, begun in 1771, Franklin tells us that he was born in Boston in 1706, one of the seventeen children of a poor tallow chandler, that his branch of the Franklin family had lived for three hundred years or more in the village of Ecton,

Northamptonshire, where the head of the family, in Queen Mary's reign, read from an English *Bible* concealed under a stool, while a child watched for the coming of the officers. He relates how he attended school from the age of eight to ten, when he had to leave to help his father mold and wick candles. His meager schooling was in striking contrast to the Harvard education of Cotton Mather and the Yale training of Jonathan Edwards, who was only three years Franklin's senior. But no man reaches Franklin's fame without an education. His early efforts to secure this are worth giving in his own language: —

"From a child I was fond of reading, and all the little money that came into my hands was ever laid out in books. Pleased with the *Pilgrim's Progress*, my first collection was of John Bunyan's works in separate little volumes.... Plutarch's *Lives* there was in which I read abundantly, and I still think that time spent to great advantage. There was also a book of De Foe's, called an *Essay on Projects*, and another of Dr. Mather's, called *Essays to do Good*, which perhaps gave me a turn of thinking that had an influence on some of the principal future events of my life.... Often I sat up in my room reading the greatest part of the night."

He relates how he taught himself to write by reading and reproducing in his own language the papers from Addison's *Spectator*. Franklin says that the "little ability" in writing, developed through his self-imposed tasks, was a principal means of his advancement in after life.

He learned the printer's trade in Boston, and ran away at the age of seventeen to Philadelphia, where he worked at the same trade. Keith, the proprietary governor, took satanic pleasure in offering to purchase a printing outfit for the eighteen-year-old boy, to make him independent. Keith sent the boy to London to purchase this outfit, assuring him that the proper letters to defray the cost would be sent on the same ship. No such letters were ever written, and the boy found himself without money three thousand miles from home. By working at the printer's trade he supported himself for eighteen months in London. He relates how his companions at the press drank six pints of strong beer a day, while he proved that the "Water-American," as he was called, was stronger than any of them. The workmen insisted that he should contribute to the general fund for drink. He refused, but so many things happened to his type whenever he left the room that he came to the following conclusion: "Notwithstanding the master's protection, I found myself oblig'd to comply and pay the money, convinc'd of the folly of being on ill terms with those one is to live with continually." Such comments on the best ways of dealing with human nature are frequent in the *Autobiography*.

At the age of twenty, he returned to Philadelphia, much wiser for his experience. Here he soon had a printing establishment of his own. By remarkable industry he had at the age of forty-two made sufficient money to be able to retire from the active administration of this business. He defined leisure as "time for doing something useful." When he secured this leisure, he used it principally for the benefit of others. For this reason, he could write in his *Autobiography* at the age of seventy-six:—

" . . . were it offered to my choice, I should have no objection to a repetition of the same life from its beginning, only asking the advantages authors have in a second edition, to correct some faults of the first. So I might, besides correcting the faults, change some sinister accidents and events of it for others more favorable. But though this were denied, I should still accept the offer. Since such a repetition is not to be expected, the next thing like living one's life over again seems to be a recollection of that life."

The twentieth century shows an awakened sense of civic responsibility, and yet it would be difficult to name a man who has done more for his commonwealth than Franklin. He started the first subscription library, organized the first fire department, improved the postal service, helped to pave and clean the streets, invented the Franklin stove, for which he refused to take out a patent, took decided steps toward improving education and founding the University of Pennsylvania, and helped establish a needed public hospital. The *Autobiography* shows his pleasure at being told that there was no such thing as carrying through a public-spirited project unless he was concerned in it.

His electrical discoveries, especially his identification of lightning with electricity, gained him world-wide fame. Harvard and Yale gave him honorary degrees. England made him a Fellow of the Royal Society and awarded him the Copley Medal. The foremost scientists in France gave him enthusiastic praise.

The *Autobiography*, ending with 1757, does not tell how he won his fame as a statesman. In 1764 he went to England as colonial agent to protest against the passage of the Stamp Act. All but two and one half of the next twenty years he spent abroad, in England and France. The report of his examination in the English House of Commons, relative to the repeal of the Stamp Act, impressed both Europe and America with his wonderful capacity. Never before had an American given Europe such an exhibition of knowledge, powers of argument, and shrewdness, tempered with tact and good humor. In 1773 he increased his reputation as a writer and threw more light on English colonial affairs by publishing, in London, *Rules for Reducing a Great Empire to a Small One*, and *An Edict by the King of Prussia*.

In 1776, at the age of seventy, he became commissioner to the court of France, where he remained until 1785.

Every student of American history knows the part he played there in popularizing the American Revolution, until France aided us with her money and her navy. It is doubtful if any man has ever been more popular away from home than Franklin was in France. The French regarded him as "the personification of the rights of man." They followed him on the streets, gave him almost frantic applause when he appeared in public, put his portrait in nearly every house and on almost every snuff box, and bought a Franklin stove for their houses.

He returned to Philadelphia in 1785, revered by his country. He was the only man who had signed four of the most famous documents in American history: the Declaration of Independence, the treaty of alliance with France, the treaty of peace with England at the close of the Revolution, and the Constitution of the United States. He had also become, as he remains to-day, America's most widely read colonial writer. When he died in 1790, the American Congress and the National Assembly of France went into mourning.

General Characteristics.— As an author, Franklin is best known for his philosophy of the practical and the useful. Jonathan Edwards turned his attention to the next world; Franklin, to this world. The gulf is as vast between these two men as if they had lived on different planets. To the end of his life, Franklin's energies were bent toward improving the conditions of this mundanc existence. He advises honesty, not because an eternal spiritual law commands it, but because it is the best policy. He needs to be supplemented by the great spiritual teachers. He must not be despised for this reason, for the great spiritual forces fail when they neglect the material foundations imposed on mortals. Franklin was as necessary as Jonathan Edwards.

Franklin knew the importance of those foundation habits, without which higher morality is not possible. He impressed on men the necessity of being regular, temperate, industrious, saving, of curbing desire, and of avoiding vice. The very foundations of character rest on regularity, on good habits so inflexibly formed that it is painful to break them. Franklin's success in laying these foundations was phenomenal. His *Poor Richard's Almanac*, begun in 1733, was one of his chief agencies in reaching the common people. They read, reread, and acted on such proverbs as the following, which he published in this *Almanac* from year to year: —

"He has chang'd his one ey'd horse for a blind one" (1733).[1]

"Three may keep a secret, if two of them are dead" (1735).

"Wealth is not his that has it, but his that enjoys it" (1736).

FACSIMILE OF TITLE-PAGE, TO "POOR RICHARD'S ALMANAC" FOR 1733

"Fly pleasures and they'll follow you" (1738).

"Have you somewhat to do to-morrow; do it to-day" (1742).

"Tart words make no friends: a spoonful of honey will catch more flies than a gallon of vinegar" (1744).

---

[1] The figures in parenthesis indicate the year of publication.

In 1757 Franklin gathered together what seemed to him the most striking of these proverbs and published them as a preface to the *Almanac* for 1758. This preface, the most widely read of all his writings, has since been known as *The Way to Wealth*. It had been translated into nearly all European languages before the end of the nineteenth century. It is still reprinted in whole or part almost every year by savings banks and societies in France and England, as well as in the United States. "Dost thou love life?" asks Poor Richard in *The Way to Wealth*. "Then," he continues, "do not squander time, for that's the stuff life is made of." Franklin modestly disclaimed much originality in the selection of these proverbs, but it is true that he made many of them more definite, incisive, and apt to lodge in the memory. He has influenced, and he still continues to influence, the industry and thrift of untold numbers. In one of our large cities, a branch library, frequented by the humble and unlearned, reports that in one year his *Autobiography* was called for four hundred times, and a life of him, containing many of Poor Richard's sayings, was asked for more than one thousand times.

He is the first American writer to show a keen sense of humor. There may be traces of humor in *The Simple Cobbler of Agawam* (p. 41) and in Cotton Mather (p. 46), but Franklin has a rich vein. He used this with fine effect when he was colonial agent in England. He determined to make England see herself from the American point of view, and so he published anonymously in a newspaper *An Edict of the King of Prussia*. This *Edict* proclaimed that it was a matter of common knowledge that Britain had been settled by Hengist and Horsa and other German colonists, and that, in consequence of this fact, the King of

Prussia had the right to regulate the commerce, manufactures, taxes, and laws of the English. Franklin gave in this *Edict* the same reasons and embodied the same restrictions, which seemed so sensible to George III. and the Tories. Franklin was the guest of an English Lord, when a man burst into the room with the newspaper containing the *Edict*, saying, " Here's news for ye! Here's the King of Prussia claiming a right to this kingdom!"

In writing English prose, Franklin was fortunate in receiving instruction from Bunyan and Addison. The pleasure of reading Franklin's *Autobiography* is increased by his simple, easy, natural way of relating events. Simplicity, practicality, suggestiveness, common sense, were his leading attributes. His sense of humor kept him from being tiresome and made him realize that the half may be greater than the whole. The two people most useful to the age in which they lived were George Washington and Benjamin Franklin.

JOHN WOOLMAN, 1720-1772

A Great Altruist. — This Quaker supplements Franklin in teaching that the great aim in life should be to grow more capable of seeing those spiritual realities which were before invisible. Life's most beautiful realities can never be seen with the physical eye. The *Journal* of John Woolman will help one to increase his range of vision for what is best worth seeing. It will broaden the reader's sympathies and develop a keener sense of responsibility for lessening the misery of the world and for protecting even the sparrow from falling. It will cultivate precisely that side of human nature which stands most in need of development. To emphasize these points, Charles Lamb said,

"Get the writings of John Woolman by heart," and Whittier wrote of Woolman's *Journal*, which he edited and made easily accessible, "I have been awed and solemnized by the presence of a serene and beautiful spirit redeemed of the Lord from all selfishness, and I have been made thankful for the ability to recognize and the disposition to love him."

John Woolman was born of Quaker parentage in Northampton, New Jersey. He never received much education. Early in life he became a shopkeeper's clerk and then a tailor. This lack of early training and broad experience affects his writings, which are not remarkable for ease of expression or for imaginative reach; but their moral beauty and intensity more than counterbalance such deficiencies.

A part of his time he spent traveling as an itinerant preacher. He tried to get Quakers to give up their slaves, and he refused to write wills that bequeathed slaves. He pleaded for compassion for overworked oxen and horses. He journeyed among the Indians, and endeavored to improve their condition. It cut him to the quick to see traders try to intoxicate them so as to get their skins and furs for almost nothing. He took passage for England in the steerage, and learned the troubles of the sailors. From this voyage he never returned, but died in York in 1772.

In the year of his death, he made in his *Journal* the following entry, which is typical of his gentle, loving spirit:

"So great is the hurry in the spirit of this world, that in aiming to do business quickly and to gain wealth, the creation at this day doth loudly groan."

When a former president of Harvard issued a list of books for actual reading, he put Franklin's *Autobiography* first and John Woolman's *Journal* second. Franklin looked steadily at this world, Woolman at the next. Each record is supplementary to the other.

EARLY AMERICAN FICTION

The First Attempts. — **Mrs. Sarah Morton** published in Boston in 1789 a novel entitled *The Power of Sympathy*. This is probably the first American novel to appear in print. The reason for such a late appearance of native fiction may be ascribed to the religious character of the early colonists and to the ascendency of the clergy, who would not have tolerated novel reading by members of their flocks. Jonathan Edwards complained that some of his congregation were reading forbidden books, and he gave from the pulpit the names of the guilty parties. These books were probably English novels. Sir Leslie Stephen thinks that Richardson's *Pamela* (1740) may have been one of the books under the ban. There is little doubt that a Puritan church member would have been disciplined if he had been known to be a reader of some of Fielding's works, like *Joseph Andrews* (1742). The Puritan clergy, even at a later period, would not sanction the reading of novels unless they were of the dry, vapid type, like the earliest Sunday school books. Jonathan Edwards wrote the story of one of his youthful experiences, but it was "the story of a spiritual experience so little involved with the earth, that one might fancy it the story of a soul that had missed being born."

Timothy Dwight (p. 92), who became president of Yale in 1795, said that there is a great gulf fixed between novels and the *Bible*. Even later than 1800 there was a widespread feeling that the reading of novels imperiled the salvation of the soul. To-day we know that certain novels are as dangerous to the soul as leprosy to the body, but we have become more discriminating. We have learned that the right type of fiction, read in moderation, cultivates the imagination, broadens the sympathetic powers, and opens up a new, interesting, and easily accessible land of enjoyment.

A quarter of a century before the *Declaration of Independence*, the great eighteenth-century English writers of fiction had given a new creation to the literature of England. Samuel Richardson (1689-1761) had published *Pamela* in 1740 and *Clarissa Harlowe* in 1748. Henry Fielding (1707-1754) had given his immortal *Tom Jones* to the world in 1749.

Mrs. Morton's *Power of Sympathy*, a novel written with a moral purpose, is a poorly constructed story of characters whom we fortunately do not meet outside of books. One of these characters, looking at some flowers embroidered by the absent object of his affections, says, "It shall yield more fragrance to my soul than all the bouquets in the universe."

The majority of the early novels, in aiming to teach some lesson, show the influence of Samuel Richardson, the father of English fiction. This didactic spirit appears in sober statement of the most self-evident truths. "Death, my dear Maria, is a serious event," says the heroine of one of these novels. Another characteristic is tepid or exaggerated sentimentality. The heroine of *The Power of Sympathy* dies of a broken heart "in a lingering graceful manner."

At least twenty-two American novels had been published between 1789 and the appearance of Charles Brockden Brown's *Wieland* in 1798. Only an antiquary need linger over these. We must next study the causes that led to a pronounced change in fiction.

Difference between the Classic and the Romantic School. — The next step in fiction will show a breaking away from the classic or didactic school of Samuel Richardson and a turning toward the new Gothic or romantic school. To understand these terms, we must know something of the English influences that led to this change.

For the first two thirds of the eighteenth century, English literature shows the dominating influence of the classic school. Alexander Pope (1688-1744) in poetry and Samuel Johnson (1709-1784) in prose were the most influential of this school. They are called *classicists* because they looked to the old classic authors for their guiding rules. Horace, more than any other classic writer, set the standard for poetry. Pope and his followers cared more for the excellence of form than for the worth of the thought. Their keynote was: —

> " True Wit is Nature to advantage dress'd,
> What oft was thought, but ne'er so well express'd." [1]

In poetry the favorite form was a couplet, that is, two lines which rhymed and usually made complete sense. This was not inaptly termed "rocking horse meter." The prose writers loved the balanced antithetical sentences used by Dr. Johnson in his comparison of Pope and Dryden: —

" If the flights of Dryden, therefore, are higher, Pope continues longer on the wing. . . . Dryden is read with frequent astonishment and Pope with perpetual delight."

Such overemphasis placed on mere form tended to draw the attention of the writer away from the matter. The American poetry of this period suffered more than the prose from this formal influence.

Since the motto of the classicists was polished regularity, they avoided the romantic, irregular, and improbable, and condemned the *Arabian Nights*, *A Midsummer Night's Dream*, *The Tempest*, and other "monstrous irregularities of Shakespeare." This school loved to teach and to point

[1] Pope's *Essay on Criticism*, lines 297-8.

out shortcomings, hence the terms "didactic" and "satiric" are often applied to it.

The last part of the eighteenth century showed a revolt against the classicists. Victory came to the new romantic school, which included authors like Wordsworth (1770–1850), Coleridge (1772–1834), Shelley (1792–1822), and Keats (1795–1821). The terms "romantic" and "imaginative" were at first in great measure synonymous. The romanticists maintained that a reality of the imagination might be as satisfying and as important as a reality of the prosaic reason, since the human mind had the power of imagining as well as of thinking.

The term "Gothic" was first applied to fiction by Horace Walpole (1717–1797), who gave to his famous romance the title of *The Castle of Otranto: A Gothic Romance*" (1764). "Gothic" is here used in the same sense as "romantic." Gothic architecture seemed highly imaginative and overwrought in comparison with the severe classic order. In attempting to avoid the old classic monotony, the Gothic school of fiction was soon noted for its lavish use of the unusual, the mysterious, and the terrible. Improbability, or the necessity for calling in the supernatural to untie some knot, did not seriously disturb this school. The standard definition of "Gothic" in fiction soon came to include an element of strangeness added to terror. When the taste for the extreme Gothic declined, there ensued a period of modified romanticism, which demanded the unusual and occasionally the impossible. This influence persisted in the fiction of the greatest writers, until the coming of the realistic school (p. 367). We are now better prepared to understand the work of Charles Brockden Brown, the first great American writer of romance, and to pass from him to Cooper, Hawthorne, and Poe.

CHARLES BROCKDEN BROWN, 1771-1810

Philadelphia has the honor of being the birthplace of Brown, who was the first professional man of letters in America. Franklin is a more famous writer than Brown, but, unlike Brown, he did not make literature the business of his life. Descended from ancestors who came over on the ship with William Penn, Brown at the age of ten had read, with Quaker seriousness, every book that he could find. He did not go to college, but studied law, which he soon gave up for literature as a profession.

Depression from ill health and the consciousness that

he would probably die young colored all his romances. He has the hero of one of his tales say, "We are exposed, in common with the rest of mankind, to innumerable casualties; but, if these be shunned, we are unalterably fated to die of consumption." In 1810, before he had reached forty, he fell a victim to that disease. Near the end of his days, he told his wife that he had not known what health was longer than a half hour at a time.

Brown deserves a place in the history of American literature for his four romances: *Wieland, Ormond, Arthur Mervyn,* and *Edgar Huntly*. These were all published within the space of three years from 1798, the date of the publication of *Wieland*. These romances show a striking change from the American fiction which had preceded them. They are no longer didactic and sentimental, but Gothic or romantic. Working under English influence, Brown gave to America her first great Gothic romances. The English romance which influenced him the most was *Caleb Williams* (1794), the work of William Godwin (1756–1836), the father-in-law of the poet Shelley.

Wieland is considered the strongest of Brown's Gothic romances, but it does not use as distinctively American materials as his three other stories of this type, *Ormond, Arthur Mervyn, or Memoirs of the Year 1793,* and *Edgar Huntly*. The results of his own experience with the yellow fever plague in Philadelphia give an American touch to *Ormond* and *Arthur Mervyn,* and at the same time add the Gothic element of weirdness and horror. *Arthur Mervyn* is far the better of the two.

Edgar Huntly, or Memoirs of a Sleep Walker, shows a Gothic characteristic in its very title. This book is noteworthy in the evolution of American fiction, not because of the strange actions of the sleep walker, but for the reason that Brown here deliberately determines, as he states in his prefatory note *To the Public*, to give the romance an American flavor, by using "the incidents of Indian hostility and the perils of the Western wilderness." If we assume that John Smith's story of Pocahontas is not fiction, then to Brown belongs the honor of first recognizing in the Indian a valuable literary asset from the Gothic romancer's point of view. In Chapter XVI., he reverses Captain Smith's story and has Edgar Huntly rescue a young girl from torture and kill an Indian. In the next two chapters, the hero kills four Indians. The English recognized this introduction of a new element of strangeness added to terror and gave Brown the credit of developing an "Americanized" Gothic. He disclosed to future writers of fiction, like James Fenimore Cooper (p. 125), a new mine of American materials. This romance has a second distinguishing characteristic, for Brown surpassed contemporary British novelists in taking his readers into the open air, which forms the stage setting for the adventures of *Edgar Huntly*. The hero of that story loves to observe the birds, the squirrels, and the old Indian woman "plucking the weeds from among her corn, bruising the grain between two stones, and setting her snares for rabbits and opossums." He takes us where we can feel the exhilaration from "a wild heath, whistled over by October blasts meagerly adorned with the dry stalks of scented shrubs and the bald heads of the sapless mullein."

Brown's place in the history of fiction is due to the fact that he introduced the Gothic romance to American literature. He loved to subject the weird, the morbid, the terrible, to a psychological analysis. In this respect he suggests Hawthorne, although there are more points of difference than of likeness between him and the great New

England romancer. In weird subject matter, but not in artistic ability, he reminds us of Poe. Brown could devise striking incidents, but he lacked the power to weave them together in a well-constructed plot. He sometimes forgot that important incidents needed further elaboration or reference, and he occasionally left them suspended in mid-air. His lack of humor was too often responsible for his imposing too much analysis and explanation on his readers. Although he did not hesitate to use the marvelous in his plots, his realistic mind frequently impelled him to try to explain the wonderful occurrences. He thus attempted to bring in ventriloquism to account for the mysterious voices which drove Wieland to kill his wife and children.

It is, however, not difficult for a modern reader to become so much interested in the first volume of *Arthur Mervyn* as to be unwilling to leave it unfinished. Brown will probably be longest remembered for his strong pictures of the yellow fever epidemic in Philadelphia, his use of the Indian in romance, and his introduction of the outdoor world of the wilderness and the forest.

POETRY—THE HARTFORD WITS

The Americans were slow to learn that political independence could be far more quickly gained than literary independence. A group of poets, sometimes known as the Hartford Wits, determined to take the kingdom of poetry by violence. The chief of these were three Yale graduates, Timothy Dwight, Joel Barlow, and John Trumbull.

Timothy Dwight (1752–1817).— Before he became president of Yale, Dwight determined to immortalize himself by an epic poem. He accordingly wrote the *Conquest of Canaan* in 9671 lines, beginning:—

"The Chief, whose arms to Israel's chosen band
  Gave the fair empire of the promis'd land,
  Ordain'd by Heaven to hold the sacred sway,
  Demands my voice, and animates the lay."

This poem is written in the rocking horse couplets of Pope, and it is well-nigh unreadable to-day. It is doubtful if twenty-five people in our times have ever read it through. Even where the author essays fine writing, as in the lines: —

"On spicy shores, where beauteous morning reigns,
  Or Evening lingers o'er her favorite plains,"

there is nothing to awaken a single definite image, nothing but glittering generalities. Dwight's best known poetry is found in his song, *Columbia*, composed while he was a chaplain in the Revolutionary War: —

TIMOTHY DWIGHT

"Columbia, Columbia, to glory arise,
  The queen of the world, and the child of the skies."

Joel Barlow (1755–1812) was, like Dwight, a chaplain in the war, but he became later a financier and diplomat, as well as a poet. He determined in *The Vision of Columbus* (1787), afterwards expanded into the ponderous *Columbiad*, to surpass Homer and all preceding epics. Barlow's classical couplets thus present a general in the Revolution, ordering a cannonade: —

> "When at his word the carbon cloud shall rise,
> And well-aim'd thunders rock the shores and skies."

Hawthorne ironically suggested that the *Columbiad* should be dramatized and set to the accompaniment of cannon and thunder and lightning. Barlow, like many others, certainly did not understand that bigness is not necessarily greatness. He is best known by some lines from his less ambitious *Hasty Pudding:* —

> "E'en in thy native regions, how I blush
> To hear the Pennsylvanians call thee *Mush!*"

JOEL BARLOW

John Trumbull (1750–1831). — The greatest of the Hartford wits was John Trumbull. His father, a Congregational clergyman living at Waterbury, Connecticut, prepared boys for college. In 1757 he sent two candidates to Yale to be examined, one pupil of nineteen, the other of seven. Commenting on this, the *Connecticut Gazette* of September 24, 1757, says, "the Son of Rev'd. Mr. Trumble of Waterbury . . . passed a good Examination, altho but little more than seven years of age; but on account of his Youth his father does not intend he shall at present continue at College." This boy waited until he was thirteen to enter Yale, where he graduated in due course. After teaching for two years in that college, he became a lawyer by profession. Although he did not die until 1831, the literary work by which he is known was finished early.

Trumbull occupied the front rank of the satiric writers of that age. Early in his twenties he satirized in classical couplets the education of the day, telling how the students: —

> "Read ancient authors o'er in vain,
> Nor taste one beauty they contain,
> And plodding on in one dull tone,
> Gain ancient tongues and lose their own."

His masterpiece was a satire on British sympathizers. He called this poem *M'Fingal*, after a Scotch Tory. The first part was published in 1775 and it gave a powerful impetus to the Continental cause. It has been said that the poem "is to be considered as one of the forces of the Revolution, because as a satire on the Tories it penetrated into every farmhouse, and sent the rustic volunteers laughing into the ranks of Washington and Greene."

One cannot help thinking of Butler's *Hudibras* (1663), when reading *M'Fingal*. Of course

JOHN TRUMBULL

the satiric aim is different in the two poems. Butler ridiculed the Puritans and upheld the Royalists, while Trumbull discharged his venomed shafts at the adherents of the king. In *M'Fingal*, a Tory bent on destroying a liberty pole drew his sword on a Whig, who had no arms except a spade. The Whig, however, employed his weapon with such good effect on the Tory that: —

> "His bent knee fail'd, and void of strength,
> Stretch'd on the ground his manly length.
> Like ancient oak, o'erturn'd, he lay,
> Or tower to tempests fall'n a prey,
> Or mountain sunk with all his pines,
> Or flow'r the plough to dust consigns,
> And more things else — but all men know 'em,
> If slightly versed in epic poem."

Some of the incisive lines from *M'Fingal* have been wrongly ascribed to Butler's *Hudibras*. The following are instances: —

> "No man e'er felt the halter draw
> With good opinion of the law."

> "For any man with half an eye
> What stands before him may espy;
> But optics sharp it needs, I ween,
> To see what is not to be seen."

Trumbull's *M'Fingal* is a worthy predecessor of Lowell's *Biglow Papers*. Trumbull wrote his poem as a "weapon of warfare." The first part of *M'Fingal* passed through some forty editions, many of them printed without the author's consent. This fact is said to have led Connecticut to pass a copyright law in 1783, and to have thus constituted a landmark in American literary history.

PHILIP FRENEAU, 1752–1832

New York City was the birthplace of Freneau, the greatest poet born in America before the Revolutionary War. He graduated at Princeton in 1771, and became a school teacher, sea captain, poet, and editor.

The Revolution broke out when he was a young man, and he was moved to write satiric poetry against the British. Tyler says that "a running commentary on his Revolutionary satires would be an almost complete commentary on the whole Revolutionary struggle; nearly every important emergency and phase of which are photographed in his keen, merciless, and often brilliant lines." In one of these satires Freneau represents Jove investigating the records of Fate:—

"And first on the top of a column he read—
 Of a king with a mighty soft place in his head,
 Who should join in his temper the ass and the mule,
 The Third of his name and by far the worst fool."

PHILIP FRENEAU

We can imagine the patriotic colonists singing as a refrain:—

". . . said Jove with a smile,
 Columbia shall never be ruled by an isle,"

or this:—

"The face of the Lion shall then become pale,
 He shall yield fifteen teeth and be sheared of his tail,"

but Freneau's satiric verse is not his best, however important it may be to historians.

His best poems are a few short lyrics, remarkable for their simplicity, sincerity, and love of nature. His lines:—

"A hermit's house beside a stream
 With forests planted round,"

are suggestive of the romantic school of Wordsworth and Coleridge, as is also *The Wild Honeysuckle*, which begins as follows:—

"Fair flower, that dost so comely grow,
　Hid in this silent, dull retreat,
Untouched thy honied blossoms blow,
　Unseen thy little branches greet.

"By Nature's self in white arrayed,
　She bade thee shun the vulgar eye,
And planted here the guardian shade,
　And sent soft waters murmuring by."

Although Freneau's best poems are few and short, no preceding American poet had equaled them. The following will repay careful reading: *The Wild Honeysuckle*, *The Indian Burying Ground*, and *To a Honey Bee*.

He died in 1832, and was buried near his home at Mount Pleasant, Monmouth County, New Jersey.

ENGLISH LITERATURE OF THE PERIOD

The great prose representatives of the first half of the eighteenth century, Swift, Addison, Steele, and Defoe, had passed away before the middle of the century. The creators of the novel, Samuel Richardson and Henry Fielding, had done their best work by 1750.

The prose writers of the last half of the century were **Oliver Goldsmith** (1728–1774), who published the *Vicar of Wakefield* in 1766; **Edward Gibbon** (1737–1794), who wrote *The History of the Decline and Fall of the Roman Empire;* **Edmund Burke** (1729–1797), best known to-day for his *Speech on Conciliation with America;* and **Samuel Johnson** (1709–1784), whose *Lives of the Poets* is the best specimen of eighteenth-century classical criticism.

The most noteworthy achievement of the century was the victory of romanticism (p. 88) over classicism. Pope's polished satiric and didactic verse, neglecting the primrose by the river's brim, lacking deep feeling, high ideals, and heaven-climbing imagination, had long been the model that inspired cold intellectual poetry. In the latter part of the century, romantic feeling and imagination won their battle and came into their own heritage in literature. **Robert Burns** (1759–1796) wrote poetry that touched the heart. A classicist like Dr. Johnson preferred the town to the most beautiful country scenes, but **William Cowper** (1731–1800) says: —

> "God made the country, and man made the town."

Romantic poetry culminated in the work of **William Wordsworth** and **Samuel Taylor Coleridge**, whose *Lyrical Ballads* (1798) included the wonderful romantic poem of *The Ancient Mariner*, and poems by Wordsworth, which brought to thousands of human souls a new sense of companionship with nature, a new feeling

> ". . . that every flower
> Enjoys the air it breathes,"

and that all nature is anxious to share its joy with man and to introduce him to a new world. The American poets of this age, save Freneau in a few short lyrics, felt but little of this great impulse; but in the next period we shall see that William Cullen Bryant heard the call and sang: —

> "Scarce less the cleft-born wild-flower seems to enjoy
> Existence than the wingèd plunderer
> That sucks its sweets."

The romantic prose was not of as high an order as the poetry. Writers of romances like **Walpole's** *Castle of Otranto* and **Godwin's** *Caleb Williams* did not allow their imaginations to be fettered by either the probable or the possible. In America the romances of Charles Brockden Brown show the direct influence of this school.

LEADING HISTORICAL FACTS

The French and Indian War accomplished two great results. In the first place, it made the Anglo-Saxon race dominant in North America. Had the French won, this book would have been chiefly a history of French literature. In the second place, the isolated colonies learned to know one another and their combined strength.

Soon after the conclusion of this war, the English began active interference with colonial imports and exports, laid taxes on certain commodities, passed the Stamp Act, and endeavored to make the colonists feel that they were henceforth to be governed in fact as well as in name by England. The most independent men that the world has ever produced came to America to escape tyranny at home. The descendants of these men started the American Revolution, signed the Declaration of Independence in 1776, and, led by George Washington (1732–1799), one of the greatest heroes of the ages, won their independence. They had the assistance of the French, and it was natural that the treaty of peace with England should be signed at Paris in 1783.

Then followed a period nearly as trying as that of the Revolution, an era called by John Fiske "The Critical Period of American History, 1783–1789." Because of the jealousy of the separate states and the fear that tyranny at home might threaten liberty, there was no central government vested with adequate power. Sometimes there was a condition closely bordering on anarchy. The wisest men feared that the independence so dearly bought would be lost. Finally, the separate states adopted a Constitution which united them, and in 1789 they chose Washington as the president of this Union. His *Farewell Address*, issued to the American people toward the end of his administration, breathes the prayer "that your union and brotherly affection may be perpetual; that the free constitution which is the work of your hands, may be sacredly maintained; that its administration in every part may be stamped with wisdom and virtue." A leading thought from this great *Address* shows that the Virginian agreed with the New Englander in regard to the chief cornerstone of this Republic:—

"Of all the dispositions and habits which lead to political prosperity, Religion and Morality are indispensable supports."

The student of political rather than of literary history is interested in the administrations of John Adams (1797–1801), Thomas Jefferson (1801–1809), and James Madison (1809–1817). The acquisition in 1803 of the vast central territory, known as the Louisiana Purchase, affected the entire subsequent development of the country and its literature. Thomas Jefferson still exerts an influence on our literature and institutions; for he championed the democratic, as opposed to the aristocratic, principle of government. His belief in the capacity of the common people for progress and self-government still helps to mold public opinion.

Next in importance to the victorious struggle of the Revolution and the adoption of the Constitution, is the wonderful pioneer movement toward the West. Francis A. Walker, in his *Making of the Nation, 1783–1817*, says:—

"During the period of thirty-four years covered by this narrative, a movement had been in continuous progress for the westward extension of population, which far transcended the limits of any of the great migrations of mankind upon the older continents. . . . From 1790 to 1800, the mean population of the period being about four and a half millions, sixty-five thousand square miles were brought within the limits of settlement; crossed with rude roads and bridges; built up with rude houses and barns; much of it, also, cleared of primeval forests.

"In the next ten years, the mean population of the decade being about six and a half millions, the people of the United States extended settlement over one hundred and two thousand square miles of absolutely new territory. . . . No other people could have done this. No: nor the half of it. Any other of the great migratory races — Tartar, Slav, or German — would have broken hopelessly down in an effort to compass such a field in such a term of years."

SUMMARY

The early essays of the period, Paine's *Common Sense* and the *Crisis*, Jefferson's *Declaration of Independence*, Hamilton's pamphlets and papers, all champion human liberty and show the influence of the Revolution. The orators, James Otis, Patrick Henry, and Samuel Adams, were inspired by the same cause. The words of Patrick Henry, "Give me liberty or give me death," have in them the essence of immortality because they voice the supreme feeling of one of the critical ages in the world's history.

Benjamin Franklin was the greatest writer of the period. His *Autobiography* has a value possessed by no other work of the kind. This and his *Poor Richard's Almanac* have taught generations of Americans the duty of self-culture, self-reliance, thrift, and the value of practical common sense. He was the first of our writers to show a balanced sense of humor and to use it as an agent in impressing truth on unwilling listeners. He is an equally great apostle of the practical and the altruistic, although he lacked the higher spirituality of the old Puritans and of the Quaker, John Woolman. This age is marked by a comparative decline in the influence of the clergy. Not a single clerical name appears on the list of the most prominent writers.

This period shows the beginning of American fiction, dominated by English writers, like Samuel Richardson.

The early novels, like Mrs. Morton's *The Power of Sympathy*, were usually prosy, didactic, and as dull as the Sunday school books of three quarters of a century ago. The victory of the English school of romanticists influenced Charles Brockden Brown, the first professional American author, to throw off the yoke of classical didacticism and regularity and to write a group of Gothic romances, in which the imagination was given a freer rein than the intellect. While he freely employed the imported Gothic elements of "strangeness added to terror," he nevertheless managed to give a distinctively American coloring to his work by showing the romantic use to which the Indian and the forest could be put.

Authors struggled intensely to write poetry. "The Hartford Wits," Dwight, Barlow, and Trumbull, wrote a vast quantity of verse. The most of this is artificial, and reveals the influence of the classical school of Alexander Pope. Freneau wrote a few short lyrics which suggest the romantic school of Wordsworth.

The American literature of this period shows in the main the influence of the older English classical school. America produced no authors who can rank with the contemporary school of English writers, such as Burns, Wordsworth, and Coleridge. Of all the writers of this age, Franklin alone shows an undiminished popularity with readers of the twentieth century.

Three events in the history of the period are epoch-making in the world's history; (*a*) the securing of independence through the Revolutionary War, (*b*) the adoption of a constitution and the formation of a republic, and (*c*) the magnitude of the work of the pioneer settlers, who advanced steadily west from the coast, and founded commonwealths beyond the Alleghanies.

REFERENCES FOR FURTHER STUDY

HISTORICAL

The course of English events (reign of George III.) may be traced in any of the English histories mentioned on p. 60. For the English literature of the period, see the author's *History of English Literature*.

Valuable works dealing with special periods of the American history of the time are: —

Hart's *Formation of the Union*.

Parkman's *Half Century of Conflict* and *Montcalm and Wolfe*, 2 vols. (French and Indian War.)

Fiske's *American Revolution*, 2 vols.

Fiske's *Critical Period of American History*.

Walker's *The Making of the Nation*.

Johnston's *History of American Politics*.

Schouler's *History of the United States of America under the Constitution*, 6 vols.

The works by Hart, Channing, and James and Sanford, referred to on p. 61, will give the leading events in brief compass. An account of much of the history of the period is given in the biographies of Washington by Lodge, of Franklin by Morse, of Hamilton by Lodge, and of Jefferson by Morse. (*American Statesmen Series*.)

LITERARY

Tyler's *The Literary History of the American Revolution*, 2 vols.

Richardson's *American Literature*, 2 vols.

Wendell's *Literary History of America*.

Trent's *A History of American Literature*.

McMaster's *Benjamin Franklin*.

Ford's *The Many-Sided Franklin*.

Erskine's *Leading American Novelists*, pp. 3-49, on Charles Brockden Brown.

Loshe's *The Early American Novel*.

SUGGESTED READINGS

The Essayists. — Selections from Thomas Paine's *Common Sense*, — Cairns,[1] 344-347; Carpenter, 66-70; S. & H., III., 219-221. From the *Crisis*, — Cairns, 347-352; Carpenter, 70, 71; S. & H., III., 222-225.

---

[1] For full titles see p. 62.

Jefferson's *Declaration of Independence* — which may be found in Carpenter, 79–83; S. & H., III., 286–289; and in almost all the histories of the United States — should be read several times until the very atmosphere or spirit of those days comes to the reader.

Selections from Alexander Hamilton, including a paper from the *Federalist*, may be found in Cairns, 363–369; S. & H., IV., 113–116.

The Orators. — A short selection from Otis is given in this work, p. 72. A longer selection may be found in Vol. I. of Johnston's *American Orations*, 11–17. For Patrick Henry's most famous speech, see Cairns, 335–338; S. & H., III., 214–218; Johnston, I., 18–23. The speech of Samuel Adams on American Independence is given in Johnston, I., 24–38, and in Moore's *American Eloquence*, Vol. I.

Benjamin Franklin. — Every one should read his *Autobiography*. Selections may be found in Carpenter, 31–36; Cairns, 322–332; T. & W., III., 192–201; S. & H., III., 3–13.

Read his *Way to Wealth* either in the various editions of *Poor Richard's Almanac* or in Cairns, 315–319; Carpenter, 36–43; T. & W., III., 202–213; S. & H., III., 17–21.

John Woolman. — Cairns, 307–313; S. & H., III., 78–80, 82–85.

Charles Brockden Brown. — The first volume of *Arthur Mervyn* with its account of the yellow fever epidemic in Philadelphia is not uninteresting reading. Chaps. XVI., XVII., and XVIII. of *Edgar Huntly* show the hero of that romance rescuing a girl from torture and killing Indians. These and the following chapters, especially XIX., XX., and XXI., give some vigorous out-of-door life.

Selections giving incidents of the yellow fever plague may be found in Cairns, 482–488; Carpenter, 97–100. For Indian adventures or out-of-door life in *Edgar Huntly*, see Cairns, 488–493; Carpenter, 89–97; S. & H., IV., 273–292.

Poetry. — Selections from Dwight, Barlow, and Trumbull may be found in Cairns, 395–430; S. & H., III., 403–413, 426–429, IV., 47–55. For Freneau's best lyrics, see Cairns, 440, 441, 447; S. & H., III., 452, 453, 456; Stedman, *An American Anthology*, 4, 7, 8.

QUESTIONS AND SUGGESTIONS

Prose. — After reading some of the papers of Thomas Paine, state why they were unusually well suited to the occasion. Why is the *Declaration of Independence* likened to the old battle songs of the

Anglo-Saxon race? What is remarkable about Jefferson's power of expression? In the orations of Otis, Patrick Henry, and Samuel Adams, what do you find to account for their influence? To what must an orator owe his power?

Contrast the writings of Benjamin Franklin with those of Jonathan Edwards and John Woolman. What are some of the most useful suggestions and records of experience to be found in Franklin's *Autobiography?* In what ways are his writings still useful to humanity? Select the best four maxims from *The Way to Wealth*. What are some of the qualities of Franklin's style? Compare it with Woolman's style.

Why are Brown's romances called "Gothic"? What was the general type of American fiction preceding him? Specify three strong or unusual incidents in the selections read from Brown. What does he introduce to give an American color to his work?

Poetry. — In the selections read from Dwight, Barlow, and Trumbull, what general characteristics impress you? Do these poets belong to the classic or the romantic school? What English influences are manifest? What qualities in Freneau's lyrics show a distinct advance in American poetry?

CHAPTER III

THE NEW YORK GROUP

A New Literary Center. — We have seen that Massachusetts supplied the majority of the colonial writers before the French and Indian War. During the next period, Philadelphia came to the front with Benjamin Franklin and Charles Brockden Brown. In this third period, New York forged ahead, both in population and in the number of her literary men. Although in 1810 she was smaller than Philadelphia, by 1820 she had a population of 123,706, which was 15,590 more than Philadelphia, and 80,408 more than Boston.

This increase in urban population rapidly multiplied the number of readers of varied tastes and developed a desire for literary entertainment, as well as for instruction. Works like those of Irving and Cooper gained wide circulation only because of the new demands, due to the increasing population, to the decline in colonial provincialism, and to the growth of the new national spirit. Probably no one would have been inspired, twenty-five years earlier, to write a work like Irving's *Knickerbocker's History of New York*. Even if it had been produced earlier, the country would not have been ready to receive it. This remarkable book was published in New York in 1809, and more than a quarter of a century had passed before Massachusetts could produce anything to equal that work.

In the New York group there were three great writers whom we shall discuss separately: Washington Irving,

James Fenimore Cooper, and William Cullen Bryant. Before we begin to study them, however, we may glance at two of the minor writers, who show some of the characteristics of the age.

DRAKE AND HALLECK

Two friends, who in their early youth styled themselves "The Croakers," were Joseph Rodman Drake (1795–1820) and Fitz-Greene Halleck (1790–1867), "the Damon and Pythias of American poets." Drake was born in New York City in the same year as the English poet, John Keats, in London. Both Drake and Keats studied medicine, and both died of consumption at the age of twenty-five. Halleck was born in Guilford, Connecticut, but moved to New York in early youth, where he became a special accountant for John Jacob Astor. Although Halleck outlived Drake forty-seven years, trade seems to have sterilized Halleck's poetic power in his later life.

JOSEPH RODMAN DRAKE

The early joint productions of Drake and Halleck were poems known as *The Croakers*, published in 1819, in the New York *Evening Post*. This stanza from *The Croakers* will show the character of the verse and its avowed object: —

"There's fun in everything we meet,
    The greatest, worst, and best;
Existence is a merry treat,
    And every speech a jest:

> Be't ours to watch the crowds that pass
> Where Mirth's gay banner waves;
> To show fools through a quizzing-glass
> And bastinade the knaves."

This was written by Drake, but he and Halleck together "croaked" the following lines, which show that New York life at the beginning of the nineteenth century had something of the variety of London in the time of Queen Anne, at the beginning of the eighteenth century:—

> "The horse that twice a week I ride
> At Mother Dawson's eats his fill;
> My books at Goodrich's abide,
> My country seat is Weehawk hill;
> My morning lounge is Eastburn's shop,
> At Poppleton's I take my lunch,
> Niblo prepares my mutton chop,
> And Jennings makes my whiskey punch."

FITZ-GREENE HALLECK

Such work indicates not only a diversified circle of readers, who were not subject to the religious and political stress of earlier days, but it also shows a desire to be entertained, which would have been promptly discouraged in Puritan New England. We should not be surprised to find that the literature of this period was swayed by the new demands, that it was planned to entertain as well as to instruct, and that all the writers of this group, with the exception of Bryant, frequently placed the chief emphasis on the power to entertain.

Fortunately instruction often accompanies entertainment, as the following lines from *The Croakers* show:—

> "The man who frets at worldly strife
>   Grows sallow, sour, and thin;
> Give us the lad whose happy life
>   Is one perpetual grin,
> He, Midas-like, turns all to gold."

Drake's best poem, which is entirely his own work, is *The Culprit Fay*, written in 1816 when he was twenty-one years of age. This shows the influence of the English romantic school, and peoples the Hudson River with fairies. Before the appearance of this poem, nothing like these lines could have been found in American verse:—

> "The winds are whist, and the owl is still,
>   The bat in the shelvy rock is hid;
> And naught is heard on the lonely hill
> But the cricket's chirp and the answer shrill
>   Of the gauze-winged katydid;
> And the plaint of the wailing whip-poor-will,
>   Who moans unseen, and ceaseless sings,
> Ever a note of wail and woe,
>   Till morning spreads her rosy wings
> And earth and sky in her glances glow."

Although *The Culprit Fay* shows the influence of Coleridge's *Christabel*, yet this American poem could not have been written by an English poet. Drake did not sing the praises of the English lark and the nightingale; but chose instead an American bird, the whippoorwill, and a native insect, the katydid, and in writing of them showed the enjoyment of a true poet.

Drake's best known poem, *The American Flag*, which was signed "Croaker & Co.," because Halleck wrote the last four lines, is a good specimen of rhetorical verse, but lacks the poetic feeling of *The Culprit Fay*.

Fitz-Greene Halleck's best known poem is *Marco Bozzaris* (1827), an elegy on the death of a Grecian leader, killed in 1823. America's sympathies went out to Greece in her struggles for independence against the Turks. In celebrating the heroic death of Bozzaris, Halleck chose a subject that was naturally fitted to appeal to all whose liberties were threatened. This poem has been honored with a place in almost all American anthologies. Middle-aged people can still remember the frequency with which the poem was declaimed. At one time these lines were perhaps as often heard as any in American verse: —

> "Strike — till the last armed foe expires;
> Strike — for your altars and your fires;
> Strike — for the green graves of your sires;
> God — and your native land!"

Fifty years ago the readers of this poem would have been surprised to be told that interest in it would ever wane, but it was fitted to arouse the enthusiasm, not of all time, but of an age, — an age that knew from first-hand experience the meaning of a struggle for hearth fires and freedom. Most critics to-day prefer Halleck's lines *On the Death of Joseph Rodman Drake:* —

> "Green be the turf above thee,
> Friend of my better days!
> None knew thee but to love thee,
> Nor named thee but to praise."

This poem is simpler, less rhetorical, and the vehicle of more genuine feeling than *Marco Bozzaris*.

The work of Drake and Halleck shows an advance in technique and imaginative power. Their verse, unlike the satires of Freneau and Trumbull, does not use the maiming cudgel, nor is it ponderous like Barlow's *Columbiad* or Dwight's *Conquest of Canaan*.

WASHINGTON IRVING, 1783-1859

Life. — Irving was born in New York City in 1783, the year in which Benjamin Franklin signed at Paris the treaty of peace with England after the Revolutionary War. Irving's father, a Scotchman from the Orkney Islands, was descended from De Irwyn, armor bearer to Robert Bruce. Irving's mother was born in England, and the English have thought sufficiently well of her son to claim that he belonged to England as much as to America. In fact, he sometimes seemed to them to be more English than

American, especially after he had written something unusually good.

When Irving was a boy, the greater part of what is now New York City was picturesque country. He mingled with the descendants of the Dutch, passed daily by their old-style houses, and had excellent opportunities for hearing the traditions and learning the peculiarities of Manhattan's early settlers, whom he was afterwards to immortalize in American literature. On his way to school he looked at the stocks and the whipping post, which had a salaried official to attend to the duties connected with it. He could have noticed two prisons, one for criminals and the other for debtors. He could scarcely have failed to see the gallows, in frequent use for offenses for which the law to-day prescribes only a short term of imprisonment. Notwithstanding the twenty-two churches, the pious complained that the town was so godless as to allow the theaters to be open on Saturday night.

Instead of going to bed after the family prayers, Irving sometimes climbed through a window, gained the alley, and went to the theater. In school he devoured as many travels and tales as possible, and he acquired much early skill in writing compositions for boys in return for their assistance in solving his arithmetical problems — a task that he detested.

At the age of fifteen he was allowed to take his gun and explore the Sleepy Hollow region, which became the scene of one of his world-famous stories. When he was seventeen, he sailed slowly up the Hudson River on his own voyage of discovery. Hendrick Hudson's exploration of this river gave it temporarily to the Dutch; but Irving annexed it for all time to the realm of the romantic imagination. The singers and weavers of legends were more than a thousand years in giving to the Rhine its high position in that realm; but Irving in a little more than a decade made the Hudson almost its peer.

In such unique environment, Irving passed his boyhood. Unlike his brothers, he did not go to Columbia College, but like Charles Brockden Brown studied law, and like him never seriously practiced the profession. Under the pen name of "Jonathan Oldstyle," he was writing, at the age of nineteen, newspaper letters, modeled closely after Addison's *Spectator*. Ill health drove Irving at twenty-one to take a European trip, which lasted two years. His next appearance in literature after his return was in connection with his brother, William Irving, and James K. Paulding. The three started a semi-monthly periodical called *Salmagundi*, fashioned after Addison's *Spectator* and Goldsmith's *Citizen of the World*. The first number was published January 24, 1807, and the twentieth and last, January 25, 1808. "In Irving's contributions to it," says his biographer, "may be traced the germs of nearly everything he did afterwards."

The year 1809 was the most important in Irving's young life. In that year Matilda Hoffman, to whom he was engaged, died in her eighteenth year. Although he out-

IRVING AT THE AGE OF TWENTY-TWO

lived her fifty years, he remained a bachelor, and he carried her *Bible* with him wherever he traveled in Europe or America. In the same year he finished one of his masterpieces, Diedrich Knickerbocker's *History of New York*. Even at this time he had not decided to follow literature as a profession.

In 1815 he went to England to visit his brother, who was in business there. It was not, however, until the failure of his brother's firm in 1818 that Irving determined to make literature his life work. While in London he wrote the *Sketch Book* (1819), which added to his fame on both sides of the Atlantic. This visit abroad lasted seventeen years. Before he returned, in 1832, he had finished the greater part of the literary work of his life. Besides the *Sketch Book*, he had written *Bracebridge Hall, Tales of a Traveller, Life and Voyages of Christopher Columbus, The Conquest of Granada, The Companions of Columbus,* and *The Alhambra*. He had been secretary of the American legation at Madrid and at London. He had actually lived in the Alhambra.

Soon after his return, he purchased a home at Tarrytown (now Irvington) in the Sleepy Hollow district on the Hudson. He named his new home "Sunnyside." With the exception of four years (1842–1846), when he served as minister to Spain, Irving lived here, engaged in literary work, for the remainder of his life. When he died in 1859, he was buried in the Sleepy Hollow cemetery, near his home.

Long before his death he was known on both sides of the Atlantic as America's greatest author. Englishmen who visited this country expressed a desire to see its two wonders, Niagara Falls and Irving. His English publishers alone paid him over $60,000 for copyright sales of his books in England. Before he died, he had earned more than $200,000 with his pen.

Irving's personality won him friends wherever he went. He was genial and kindly, and his biographer adds that it was never Irving's habit to stroke the world the wrong way. One of his maxims was, "When I cannot get a dinner to suit my taste, I endeavor to get a taste to suit my dinner."

SUNNYSIDE, IRVING'S HOME AT TARRYTOWN

Knickerbocker's History of New York. — The New York *Evening Post* for December 28, 1809, said: "This work was found in the chamber of Mr. Diedrich Knickerbocker, the old gentleman whose sudden and mysterious disappearance has been noticed. It is published in order to discharge certain debts he has left behind." This disguise, however, was too thin to deceive the public, and the work was soon popularly called Irving's *Knickerbocker's History of New York.*

Two hundred years before its publication, Hendrick Hudson, an explorer in the service of Holland, had sailed into New York Bay and discovered Manhattan Island and the Hudson River for the Dutch. They founded the city of New Amsterdam and held it until the English captured it in 1664. Irving wrote the history of this settlement during the Dutch occupation. He was led to choose this subject, because, as he tells us, few of his fellow citizens were aware that New York had ever been called New Amsterdam, and because the subject, "poetic from its very obscurity," was especially available for an American author, since it gave him a chance to adorn it with legend and fable. He states that his object was "to embody the traditions of our city in an amusing form" and to invest it "with those imaginative and whimsical associations so seldom met with in our country, but which live like charms and spells about the cities of the old world."

Irving achieved his object and produced an entertaining compound of historical fact, romantic sentiment, exaggeration, and humor. He shows us the contemplative Dutchmen on their first voyage in the *Half Moon*, sailing into New York Bay, prohibited by Hudson "from wearing more than five jackets and six pair of breeches." We see the scrupulously "honest" Dutch traders buying furs from the Indians, using an invariable scale of avoirdupois weights, a Dutchman's hand in the scale opposite the furs weighing one pound, his foot

THE OFFICIAL WEIGHT

two pounds. We watch the puzzled Indians trying to account for the fact that the largest bundle of furs never weighed more than two pounds. We attend a council of burghers at Communipaw, called to devise means to protect their town from an English expedition. While they are thoughtfully smoking, the English sail by without seeing the smoke-enveloped town. Irving shows us the Dutchmen estimating their distances and time by the period consumed in smoking a pipe, — Hartford, Connecticut, being two hundred pipes distant. He allows us to watch a housewife emptying her pocket in her search for a wooden ladle and filling two corn baskets with the contents.

A ONE-PIPE JOURNEY

He takes us to a tea party attended by "the higher classes or noblesse, that is to say such as kept their own cows and drove their own wagons," where we can see the damsels knitting their own woolen stockings and the vrouws serving big apple pies, bushels of doughnuts, and pouring tea out of a fat Delft teapot. He draws this picture of Wouter Van Twiller, Governor of New Amsterdam: —

"The person of this illustrious old gentleman was formed and proportioned as though it had been moulded by the hands of some cunning Dutch statuary, as a model of majesty and lordly grandeur. He was exactly five feet six inches in height, and six feet five inches in circumference. His head was a perfect sphere. . . .

WOUTER VAN TWILLER

"His habits were as regular as his person. He daily took his four stated meals, appropriating exactly an hour to each; he smoked and doubted eight hours, and he slept the remaining twelve of the four-and-twenty."

The Sketch Book Group. — The only one of his productions to which Irving gave the name of *The Sketch Book* was finished in 1820, the year in which Scott's *Ivanhoe*, Keats's *Eve of St. Agnes*, and Shelley's *Prometheus Unbound* appeared. Of the same general order as *The Sketch Book* are Irving's *Bracebridge Hall* (1822) and *Tales of a Traveller* (1824). These volumes all contain short stories, essays, or sketches, many of which are suggestive of Addison's *Spectator*. *The Sketch Book* is the most famous of Irving's works of this class. While it contains some excellent essays or descriptions, such as those entitled *Westminster Abbey* and *Stratford-on-Avon*, the book lives to-day because of two short stories, *Rip Van Winkle* and *The Legend of Sleepy Hollow*. These were not equaled by Addison, and they have not been surpassed by any English writers of the nineteenth century. Both stories take their rise from the "Knickerbocker Legend," and they are thoroughly American in coloring and flavor, even if they did happen to be written in England. No story in our literature is better known than that of Rip Van Winkle watching Hendrick Hudson and his ghostly crew playing ninepins in the Catskill Mountains and quaffing the magic liquor which caused him to sleep for twenty years.

For nearly one hundred years Ichabod Crane's courtship of Katrina Van Tassel, in *The Legend of Sleepy Hollow*, has continued to amuse its readers. The Indian summer haze is still resting on Sleepy Hollow, our American

ICHABOD CRANE

Utopia, where we can hear the quail whistling, see the brook bubbling along among alders and dwarf willows, over which amber clouds float forever in the sky; where the fragrant buckwheat fields breathe the odor of the beehive; where the slapjacks are "well buttered and garnished with honey or treacle, by the delicate little dimpled hand of Katrina Van Tassel," where a greeting awaits us from the sucking pigs already roasted and stuffed with pudding; where the very tea tables of the Dutch housewives welcome us with loads of crisp crumbling crullers, honey cakes, and "the whole family of cakes," surrounded by pies, preserves, roast chicken, bowls of cream, all invested with a halo from the spout of the motherly Dutch teapot.

The Alhambra, a book of tales of the old Moorish palace in Granada, Spain, has been aptly termed "The Spanish Sketch Book." This has preserved the romance of departed Moorish glory almost as effectively as the Knickerbocker sketches and stories have invested the early Dutch settlers of New York with something like Homeric immortality. A traveler in Spain writes of *The Alhambra:* "Not Ford, nor Murray, nor Hare has been able to replace it. The tourist reads it within the walls it commemorates as conscientiously as the devout read Ruskin in Florence."[1]

In his three works, *The Sketch Book*, *The Tales of a Traveller*, and *The Alhambra*, Irving proved himself the first American master of the short tale or sketch, yet he is not the father of the modern short story, which aims to avoid every sentence unless it directly advances the narrative or heightens the desired impression. His description and presentation of incident do not usually tend to one definite goal, after the fashion theoretically prescribed by the art of the modern short story. The author of a modern

[1] Introduction to Pennell's illustrated edition of *The Alhambra*.

short tale would need to feel the dire necessity of recording the sage observation of a Dutch housewife, that "ducks and geese are foolish things, and must be looked after, but girls can take care of themselves." Irving, however, in *The Legend of Sleepy Hollow*, has sufficient leisure to make this observation and to stop to listen to "the pensive whistle of the quail," or to admire "great fields of Indian corn, with its golden ears peeping from their leafy coverts, and holding out the promise of cakes and hasty puddings."

Some have even proposed that his stories be called "narrative-essays," but they show a step beyond Addison in the evolution of the short story because they contain less essay and more story. It is true that Irving writes three pages of essay before beginning the real story in *The Legend of Sleepy Hollow*, but the most of this preliminary matter is very interesting description. The quiet valley with its small brook, the tapping woodpecker, the drowsy shade of the trees, the spots haunted by the headless Hessian, — all fascinate us and provide an atmosphere which the modern short-story teller too seldom secures. The novice in modern short-story writing should know at the outset that it takes more genius to succeed with a story like *The Legend of Sleepy Hollow* than with a tale where the writer relies on the more strait-laced narration of events to arouse interest.

History and Biography. — Of *The Life and Voyages of Christopher Columbus* (1828), Irving said "it cost me more toil and trouble than all my other productions." While the method of scientific historical study has completely changed since his time, no dry-as-dust historian has yet equaled Irving in presenting the human side of Columbus, his ideals, his dreams, and his mastery of wind and wave and human nature in the greatest voyage of the ages. Others have written of him as a man who once lived but who died so very long ago that he now has no more life than the portraits of those old masters who made all their figures look like paralytics. Irving did not write this work as if he were imagining a romance. He searched for his facts in all the musty records which he could find in Spain, but he then remembered that they dealt with a living, enthusiastic human being, sometimes weak, and sometimes invested with more than the strength of all the generations that had died without discovering the New World. It was this work which, more than any other, brought Irving the degree of D.C.L. from Oxford University. And yet, when he appeared to take his degree, the undergraduates of Oxford voiced the judgment of posterity by welcoming him with shouts of "Diedrich Knickerbocker!" "Ichabod Crane!" "Rip Van Winkle!"

The Conquest of Granada (1829) is a thrilling narrative of the subjugation by Ferdinand and Isabella of the last kingdom of the Moors in Spain. In this account, royal leaders, chivalrous knights, single-handed conflicts, and romantic assaults make warfare seem like a carnival instead of a tragedy.

The life of *Oliver Goldsmith* (1849) ranks among the best biographies yet written by an American, not because of its originality, but for its exquisitely sympathetic portraiture of an English author with whom Irving felt close kinship.

His longest work, the *Life of George Washington* (1855-1859), lacks the imaginative enthusiasm of youth, but it does justice to "the magnificent patience, the courage to bear misconstruction, the unfailing patriotism, the practical sagacity, the level balance of judgment combined with the wisest toleration, the dignity of mind, and the lofty moral nature," which made George Washington the one man capable of leading a forlorn army in the Revolution, of presiding over the destinies of the young Republic, and of taking a sure place among the few great heroes of all time. This work is also an almost complete history of the Revolutionary War. It is unfortunate that the great length of this *Life* (eight volumes) has resulted in such a narrowing of its circle of readers.

General Characteristics.—Washington Irving is the earliest American whose most popular works are read for pure pleasure and not for some historical or educational significance. His most striking qualities are humor and restrained sentiment. The work by which he will be longest known is his creation of the "Knickerbocker Legend" in the *History of New York* and his two most famous short stories, *Rip Van Winkle* and *The Legend of Sleepy Hollow*. Although he is not the father of the modern short story, which travels like an airship by the shortest line to its destination, he is yet one of the great nineteenth-century story tellers. Some of his essays or papers, like *Westminster Abbey*, *Stratford-on-Avon*, and *Christmas* do not suffer by comparison with Addison's writings.

Much of Irving's historical work and many of his essays do not show great depth or striking originality. He did some hack writing, dealing with our great West, but the work by which he is best known is so original that no other American writers can for a moment compare with him in his special field. He gave us our own Homeric age and peopled it with Knickerbockers, who are as entertaining as Achilles, Priam, or Circe.

His best work is a product of the romantic imagination, but his romanticism is of a finer type than that of Charles Brockden Brown and the English Gothic school (p. 88), for

Irving's fondness for Addison and Goldsmith, in conjunction with his own keen sense of humor, taught him restraint, balance, and the adaptation of means to ends.

Irving has an unusual power of investing his subjects with the proper atmosphere. In this he resembles the greatest landscape painters. If he writes of the early settlers of New York, we are in a Dutch atmosphere. If he tells the legends of the Alhambra, the atmosphere is Moorish. If he takes us to the Hudson or the Catskills or Sleepy Hollow or Granada, he adds to our artistic enjoyment by enveloping everything in its own peculiar atmosphere.

IRVING'S GRAVE IN THE SLEEPY HOLLOW CEMETERY

His clear, simple, smooth prose conceals its artistic finish so well and serves as the vehicle for so much humor, that readers often pass a long time in his company without experiencing fatigue. His style has been criticized for lack of vigor and for resemblance to Goldsmith's. Irving's style, however, is his own, and it is the style natural to a man of his placid, artistic temperament.

America takes special pride in Washington Irving, because he was the first author to invest her brief history with the enduring fascination of romance. We shall the better appreciate our debt to him, if we imagine that some wizard has the power to subtract from our literature the inimitable Knickerbocker, Rip Van Winkle, Sleepy Hollow, and our national romantic river, the storied Hudson.

JAMES FENIMORE COOPER, 1789-1851

Youth.— Cooper's place in American literature is chiefly based on his romantic stories of the pioneer and the Indian. We have seen how Captain John Smith won the ear of the world by his early story of Indian adventure, how Charles Brockden Brown in *Edgar Huntly* deliberately selected the Indian and the life of the wilderness as good material for an American writer of romance. Cooper chose these very materials and used them with a success attained by no other writer. Let us see how his early life fitted him to write of the Indian, the pioneer, the forest, and the sea.

He was born in Burlington, New Jersey, in 1789, the year made memorable by the French Revolution. While he was still an infant, the Cooper family moved to the southeastern shore of Otsego Lake and founded the village of Cooperstown, at the point where the Susquehanna River furnishes an outlet for the lake. In this romantic place he passed the most impressionable part of his boyhood.

At the close of the eighteenth century, Cooperstown was one of the outposts of civilization. Few clearings had been made in the vast mysterious forests, which appealed so deeply to the boy's imagination, and which still sheltered deer, bear, and Indians. The most vivid local story which his young ears heard was the account of the Cherry Valley massacre, which had taken place a few miles from Cooperstown only eleven years before he was born. Cooper himself felt the fascination of the trackless forests before he communicated it to his readers.

He entered Yale in 1802, but he did not succeed in eradicating his love of outdoor life and of the unfettered habits of the pioneer, and did not remain to graduate. The faculty dismissed him in his junior year. It was unfortunate that he did not study more and submit to the restraints and discipline of regular college life; for his prose often shows in its carelessness of construction and lack of restraint his need for that formal discipline which was for the moment so grievous to him.

After Cooper had left college, his father decided to have him prepare for the navy. As there was no naval academy, he adopted the usual course of having the boy serve a year on a merchant vessel. After this apprenticeship, Cooper entered the navy as a midshipman. From such experiences he gained sufficient knowledge of the ocean and ships to enable him to become the author of some of our best tales of the sea. He resigned from the navy, however, in 1811, when he married.

Becomes an Author. — Cooper had reached the age of thirty without even attempting to write a book. In 1820 he remarked one day to his wife that he thought he could write a better novel than the one which he was then reading to her. She immediately challenged him to try, and he promply wrote the novel called *Precaution*. He chose to have this deal with English life because the critics of his time considered American subjects commonplace and uninteresting. As he knew nothing of English life at first hand, he naturally could not make the pages of *Precaution* vivid with touches of local color.

This book was soon forgotten, and Cooper might never have written another, had not some sensible friends insisted that it was his patriotic duty to make American subjects fashionable. A friend related to him the story of a spy of Westchester County, New York, who during the Revolution served the American cause with rare fidelity and sagacity. Cooper was then living in this very county, and, being attracted by the subject, he soon completed the first volume of *The Spy*, which was at once printed. As he still doubted, however, whether his countrymen would read "a book that treated of their own familiar interests," he delayed writing the second volume for several months. When he did start to write it, his publisher feared that it might be too long to pay, so before Cooper had thought out the intervening chapters, he wrote the last chapter and had it printed and paged to satisfy the publisher. When *The Spy* was published in 1821, it immediately sold well in America, although such was the bondage to English standards of criticism that many who read the book hesitated to express an opinion until they had heard the verdict from

England. When the English received the book, however, they fairly devoured it, and it became one of the most widely read tales of the early nineteenth century. Harvey Birch, the hero of the story, is one of the great characters of our early fiction.

Cooper now adopted writing as a profession. In less than thirty years, he wrote more than thirty romances, in

OTSEGO HALL, COOPERSTOWN

most cases of two volumes each. When he went to Europe in 1826, the year of the publication of *The Last of the Mohicans*, he found that his work was as well known abroad as at home. Sir Walter Scott, who met Cooper in Paris, mentions in his diary for November 6, 1826, a reception by a French princess, and adds the note, "Cooper was there, so the American and Scotch lions took the field together."

Later Years. — After Cooper's return from Europe in 1833, he spent the most of the remaining seventeen years of his life in writing books at his early home, known as Otsego Hall, in Cooperstown. Here in the summer of 1837 there occurred an unfortunate incident which embittered the rest of his life and for a while made him the most unpopular of American authors. Some of his townspeople cut down one of his valuable trees and otherwise misused the picnic grounds on a part of his estate fronting the lake. When he remonstrated, the public denounced him and ordered his books removed from the local library. He then forbade the further use of his grounds by the public. Many of the newspapers throughout the state misrepresented his action, and he foolishly sued them for libel. From that time the press persecuted him. He sued the Albany *Evening Journal*, edited by Thurlow Weed, and received four hundred dollars damage. Weed thereupon wrote in the New York *Tribune:* —

"The value of Mr. Cooper's character has been judicially determined. It is worth exactly four hundred dollars."

Cooper promptly sued *The Tribune*, and was awarded two hundred dollars. In the heat of this controversy Thurlow Weed incautiously opened Cooper's *The Pathfinder*, which had just appeared, and sat up all night to finish the book. During the progress of these suits, Cooper unfortunately wrote a novel, *Home as Found*, satirizing, from a somewhat European point of view, the faults of his countrymen. A friend, trying to dissuade him from publishing such matter, wrote, "You lose hold on the American public by rubbing down their shins with brickbats, as you do." Cooper, however, published the book in 1838, and then there was a general rush to attack him. A critic of his *History of the Navy of the United States of America* (1839), a work which is still an authority for the time of which it treats, abused the book and made reflections on Cooper's veracity. The author brought suit for libel, and won his case in a famous trial in which he was his own lawyer. These unfortunate incidents, which would have been avoided by a man like Benjamin Franklin, diminished the circulation of Cooper's books in America during the rest of his life.

Even on his deathbed he thought of the unjust criticism from which he had suffered, and asked his family not to aid in the preparation of any account of his life. He died in 1851 at the age of sixty-two, and was buried at Cooperstown. Lounsbury thus concludes an excellent biography of this great writer of romance: —

"America has had among her representatives of the irritable race of writers many who have shown far more ability to get on pleasantly with their fellows than Cooper. . . . But she counts on the scanty roll of her men of letters the name of no one who acted from purer patriotism or loftier principle. She finds among them all no manlier nature and no more heroic soul."

STATUE OF LEATHERSTOCKING OVERLOOKING OTSEGO LAKE

Greatest Romances. — Cooper's greatest achievement is the series known as *The Leatherstocking Tales*. These all have as their hero Leatherstocking, a pioneer variously known as Hawkeye, *La Longue Carabine* (The Long Rifle), and Natty Bumppo. A statue of this great original creation of American fiction now overlooks Otsego Lake. Leatherstocking embodies the fearlessness, the energy, the rugged honesty, of the worthiest of our pioneers, of those men who opened up our vast inland country and gave it to us to enjoy. Ulysses is no more typically Grecian than Leatherstocking is American.

The Leatherstocking Tales are five in number. The order in which they should be read to follow the hero from youth to old age is as follows: —

The Deerslayer; or The First War Path (1841).[1]
The Last of the Mohicans; a Narrative of 1757 (1826).
The Pathfinder; or the Inland Sea (1840).
The Pioneers; or the Sources of the Susquehanna (1823).
The Prairie; a Tale (1827).

This sequence may be easily remembered from the fact that the first chief words in the titles, "Deerslayer," "Mohicans," "Pathfinder," "Pioneers," and "Prairie," are arranged in alphabetical order. These books are the prose *Iliad* and *Odyssey* of the eighteenth-century American pioneer. Instead of relating the fall of Ilium, Cooper tells of the conquest of the wilderness. The wanderings of Leatherstocking in the forest and the wilderness are substituted for those of Ulysses on the sea. This story could not have been related with much of the vividness of an eye-witness of the events, if it had been postponed beyond Cooper's day. Before that time had forever passed, he fixed in

LEATHERSTOCKING

[1] The figures in parenthesis refer to the date of publication.

living romance one remarkable phase of our country's development. The persons of this romantic drama were the Pioneer and the Indian; the stage was the trackless forest and the unbroken wilderness.

The Last of the Mohicans has been the favorite of the greatest number of readers. In this story Chingachgook, the Indian, and Uncas, his son, share with Hawkeye our warmest admiration. The American boy longs to enter the fray to aid Uncas. Cooper knew that the Indian had good traits, and he embodied them in these two red men. Scott took the same liberty of presenting the finer aspects of chivalry and neglecting its darker side. Cooper, however, does show an Indian fiend in Magua.

Cooper's work in this series brings us face to face with the activities of nature and man in God's great out of doors.

COOPER AT THE AGE OF FORTY-FIVE

Cooper makes us realize that the life of the pioneer was not without its elemental spirit of poetry. We may feel something of this spirit in the reply of Leatherstocking to the trembling Cora, when she asked him at midnight what caused a certain fearful sound: —

"'Lady,' returned the scout, solemnly, 'I have listened to all the sounds of the woods for thirty years, as a man will listen, whose life and death depend so often on the quickness of his ears. There is no whine of the panther, no whistle of the catbird, nor any invention of the devilish Mingos, that can cheat me. I have heard the forest moan like mortal men in their affliction; often and again have I listened to the wind playing its music in the branches of the girdled trees; and I have heard the lightning cracking in the air, like the snapping of blazing brush, as it spitted forth sparks and forked flames; but never have I thought that I heard more than the pleasure of him, who sported with the things of his hand. But neither the Mohicans, nor I, who am a white man without a cross, can explain the cry just heard.'"

In addition to the five *Leatherstocking Tales*, three other romances show special power. They are:—

The Spy; a Tale of the Neutral Ground (1821).
The Pilot; a Tale of the Sea (1824).
The Red Rover; a Tale (1828).

The last two show Cooper's mastery in telling stories of the sea. Tom Coffin, in *The Pilot*, is a fine creation.

Some of the more than thirty works of fiction that Cooper wrote are almost unreadable, and some appeal more to special students than to general readers. *Satanstoe* (1845), for instance, gives vivid pictures of mid-eighteenth century colonial life in New York.

The English critic's query, "Who reads an American book?" could have received the answer in 1820, "The English public is reading Irving." In 1833, Morse, the inventor of the electric telegraph, had another answer ready — "Europe is reading Cooper." He said that as soon as Cooper's works were finished they were published in thirty-four different places in Europe. American literature was commanding attention for its original work.

General Characteristics. — Cooper's best romances are masterpieces of action and adventure in the forest and on the sea. No other writer has so well told the story of the pioneer. He is not a successful novelist of the drawing-room. His women are mediocre and conventional, of the type described in the old Sunday school books. But when he leaves the haunts of men and enters the forest, power comes naturally to his pen. His greatest stage of action is the forest. He loved wild nature and the sea.

He often availed himself of the Gothic license of improbability, his characters being frequently rescued from well-nigh impossible situations. His plots were not carefully planned in advance; they often seem to have been suggested by an inspiration of the moment. He wrote so rapidly that he was careless about the construction of his sentences, which are sometimes not even grammatical.

It is easy, however, to exaggerate Cooper's faults, which do not, after all, seriously interfere with the enjoyment of his works. A teacher, who was asked to edit critically *The Last of the Mohicans*, said that the first time he read it, the narrative carried him forward with such a rush, and bound him with such a spell, that he did not notice a single blemish in plot or style. A boy reading the same book obeyed the order to retire at eleven, but having reached the point where Uncas was taken prisoner by the Hurons, found the suspense too great, and quietly got the book and read the next four chapters in bed. Cooper has in a preëminent degree the first absolutely necessary qualification of the writer of fiction — the power to hold the interest. In some respects he resembles Scott, but although the "Wizard of the North" has a far wider range of excellence, Leatherstocking surpasses any single one of Scott's creations and remains a great original character added to the literature of the world. These romances have strong ethical influence over the young. They are as pure as mountain air, and they teach a love for manly, noble, and brave deeds. "He fought for a principle," says Cooper's biographer, "as desperately as other men fight for life."

WILLIAM CULLEN BRYANT, 1794-1878

Life. — The early environment of each of the three great members of the New York group determined to an unusual degree the special literary work for which each became famous. Had Irving not been steeped in the legends of the early Dutch settlers of Manhattan, hunted squirrels in Sleepy Hollow, and voyaged up the Hudson past the Catskills, he would have had small chance of becoming famous as the author of the "Knickerbocker Legend." Had Cooper not spent his boyhood on the frontier, living in close touch with the forest and the pioneer, we should probably not have had *The Leatherstocking Tales.* Had it not been for Bryant's early Puritan training and his association with a peculiar type of nature, he might have ended his days as a lawyer.

Bryant was born in Cummington, among the hills of western Massachusetts. In her diary, his mother thus records his birth: —

"Nov. 3, 1794. Stormy, wind N. E. Churned. Seven in the evening a son born."

His poetry will be better understood, if we emphasize two main facts in his early development. In the first place, he was descended from John and Priscilla Alden of Mayflower stock and reared in strict Puritan fashion. Bryant's religious training determined the general attitude of all his poetry toward nature. His parents expected their children to know the *Bible* in a way that can scarcely be comprehended in the twentieth century. Before completing his fourth year, his older brother "had read the *Scriptures* through from beginning to end." At the age of nine, the future poet turned the first chapter of *Job* into classical couplets, beginning: —

> "Job, good and just, in Uz had sojourned long,
> He feared his God and shunned the way of wrong.
> Three were his daughters and his sons were seven,
> And large the wealth bestowed on him by heaven."

Another striking fact is that the prayers which he heard from the Puritan clergy and from his father and grandfather in family worship gave him a turn toward noble poetic expression. He said that these prayers were often "poems from beginning to end," and he cited such expressions from them as, "Let not our feet stumble on the dark mountains of eternal death." From the Puritan point of view, the boy made in his own prayers one daring variation from the petitions based on scriptural sanction. He prayed that he "might receive the gift of poetic genius, and write verses that might endure." His early religious training was responsible for investing his poetry with the dignity, gravity, and simplicity of the Hebraic *Scriptures*.

In the second place, he passed his youth in the fine scenery of western Massachusetts, which is in considerable measure the counterpart of the Lake Country which bred Wordsworth. The glory of this region reappears in his verse; the rock-ribbed hills, the vales stretching in pensive quietness between them, the venerable woods of ash, beech, birch, hemlock, and maple, the complaining brooks that make the valleys green, the rare May days: —

"When beechen buds begin to swell,
And woods the blue bird's warble know."[1]

BRYANT AS A YOUNG MAN

His association with such scenes determined the subject matter of his poetry, and his Puritan training prescribed the form of treatment.

He had few educational advantages, — a little district schooling, some private tutoring by a clergyman, seven months' stay in Williams College, which at the time of his

[1] Bryant: *The Yellow Violet.*

entrance in 1810 had a teaching staff of one professor and two tutors, besides the president. Bryant left Williams, intending to enter Yale; but his father, a poor country physician who had to ride vast distances for small fees, was unable to give him any further college training.

Bryant, at about the age of eighteen, soon after leaving Williams, wrote *Thanatopsis*, — with the exception of the opening and the closing parts. He had already written at the age of thirteen a satiric poem, *The Embargo*, which had secured wide circulation in New England. Keenly disappointed at not being able to continue his college education, he regretfully began the study of law in order to earn his living as soon as possible. He celebrated his admission to the bar by writing one of his greatest short poems, *To a Waterfowl* (1815). When he was a lawyer practicing in Great Barrington, Massachusetts, he met Miss Fanny Fairchild, to whom he addressed the poem; —

"O fairest of the rural maids!"

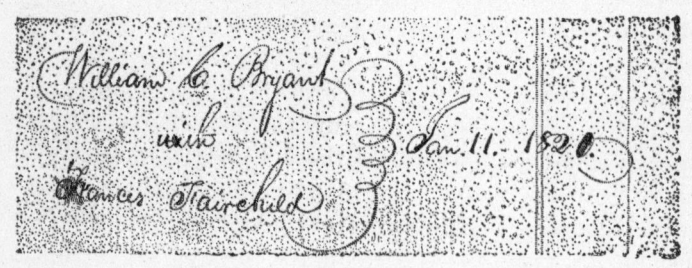

FACSIMILE OF RECORD OF BRYANT'S MARRIAGE

Religious in all things, he prepared this betrothal prayer, which they repeated together before they were married in the following year: —

"May Almighty God mercifully take care of our happiness here and hereafter. May we ever continue constant to each other, and mindful of our mutual promises of attachment and truth. In due time, if it be the will of Providence, may we become more nearly connected with each other, and together may we lead a long, happy, and innocent life, without any diminution of affection till we die."

In 1821, the year in which Cooper published *The Spy* and Shelley wrote his *Adonais* lamenting the death of Keats, Bryant issued the first volume of his verse, which contained eight poems, *Thanatopsis, The Inscription for Entrance to a Wood, To a Waterfowl, The Ages, The Fragment from Simonides, The Yellow Violet, The Song,* and *Green River*. This was an epoch-making volume for American poetry. Freneau's best lyrics were so few that they had attracted little attention, but Bryant's 1821 volume of verse furnished a new standard of excellence, below which poets who aspired to the first rank could not fall. During the five years after its publication, the sales of this volume netted him a profit of only $14.92, but a Boston editor soon offered him two hundred dollars a year for an average of one hundred lines of verse a month. Bryant accepted the offer, and wrote poetry in connection with the practice of law.

Unlike Irving and Charles Brockden Brown, Bryant attended to his legal work doggedly and conscientiously for nine years, but he never liked the law, and he longed to be a professional author. In 1825 he abandoned the law and went to New York City. Here he managed to secure a livelihood for awhile on the editorial force of short-lived periodicals. In 1827, however, he became assistant editor, and in 1829 editor-in-chief, of *The New York Evening Post* —a position which he held for nearly fifty years, until his death.

The rest of his life is more political and journalistic than literary. He made *The Evening Post* a power in the development of the nation, but his work as editor interfered with his poetry, although he occasionally wrote verse to the end of his life.

In middle life he began a series of trips abroad, and wrote many letters describing his travels. To occupy his attention after his wife died in 1866, he translated Homer's *Iliad* and *Odyssey*, at the nearly uniform rate of forty lines a day. This work still remains one of the standard poetic translations of Homer.

As the years passed, he became New York's representative citizen, noted for high ideals in journalism and for incorruptible integrity, as well as for the excellence of his poetry. He died in 1878, at the age of eighty-four, and was buried at Roslyn, Long Island, beside his wife.

BRYANT'S HOME, ROSLYN, L. I.

Poetry. — *Thanatopsis*, probably written in 1811, was first published in 1817 in *The North American Review*, a Boston periodical. One of the editors said to an associate, "You have been imposed upon. No one on this side of the Atlantic is capable of writing such verses." The associate insisted that Dr. Bryant, the author, had left them at the office, and that the Doctor was at that moment sitting in the State Senate, representing his county. The editor at once dashed away to the State House, took a long look at the Doctor, and reported, "It is a good head, but I do not see *Thanatopsis* in it." When the father was aware of the misunderstanding, he corrected it, but there were for a long time doubts whether a boy could have written a poem of this rank. In middle age the poet wrote the following to answer a question in regard to the time of the composition of *Thanatopsis:*—

"It was written when I was seventeen or eighteen years old — I have not now at hand the memorandums which would enable me to be precise — and I believe it was composed in my solitary rambles in the woods. As it was first committed to paper, it began with the half line — 'Yet a few days, and thee' — and ended with the beginning of another line with the words — 'And make their bed with thee.' The rest of the poem — the introduction and the close — was added some years afterward, in 1821."

Thanatopsis remains to-day Bryant's most famous production. It is a stately poem upon death, and seems to come directly from the lips of Nature : —

". . . from all around —
Earth and her waters and the depth of air —
Comes a still voice. —
Yet a few days, and thee
The all-beholding sun shall see no more. . ."

No other poem presents "all-including death" on a scale of such vastness. The majestic solemnity of the poem and the fine quality of its blank verse may be felt in this selection : —

". . . The hills
Rock-ribbed and ancient as the sun, — the vales
Stretching in pensive quietness between;
The venerable woods — rivers that move
In majesty, and the complaining brooks
That make the meadows green; and, poured round all,
Old Ocean's gray and melancholy waste, —
Are but the solemn decorations all
Of the great tomb of man."

Thanatopsis shows the old Puritan tendency to brood on death, but the *Inscription for Entrance to a Wood*, written in 1815 and published in the same number of *The North American Review* as his first great poem, takes us where

> ". . . the thick roof
> Of green and stirring branches is alive
> And musical with birds."

The gladness of the soft winds, the blue sky, the rivulet, the mossy rocks, the cleft-born wild-flower, the squirrels, and the insects, — all focus our attention on the "deep content" to be found in "the haunts of Nature," and suggest Wordsworth's philosophy of the conscious enjoyment of the flower, the grass, the mountains, the bird, and the stream, voicing their "thousand blended notes."

We may say of Bryant what was true of Cooper, that when he enters a forest, power seems to come unbidden to his pen. Bryant's *Forest Hymn* (1825) finds God in those green temples: —

> "Thou art in the soft winds
> That run along the summit of these trees
> In music."

He points out the divinity that shapes our ends in: —

> "That delicate forest flower,
> With scented breath and look so like a smile."

No Puritan up to this time had represented God in a guise more pleasing than the smile of a forest flower. This entire *Hymn* seems like a great prayer rooted deep in those earlier prayers to which the boy used to listen.

Although Bryant lived to be eighty-four, he wrote less poetry than Keats, who died at the age of twenty-five, and about one third as much as Shelley, who was scarcely thirty when he was drowned. It is not length of days that makes a poet. Had Bryant died in his thirtieth year, his excellence and limitations would be fairly well shown in his work finished at that time. At this age, in addition to the five poems in his 1821 volume (p. 139), he had written *The Winter Piece*, *A Forest Hymn*, and *The Death of the Flowers*. These and a number of other poems, written before he had finished his thirtieth year, would have entitled him to approximately the same rank that he now holds in the history of American poetry. It is true that if he had then passed away, we should have missed his exquisite call to *The Evening Wind* (1829), and some of his other fine productions, such as *To the Fringed Gentian* (1829), *The Prairies* (1832), *The Battle-Field* (1837), with its lines which are a keynote to Bryant's thought and action: —

> "Truth, crushed to earth, shall rise again,
> Th' eternal years of God are hers."

We are thankful for the ideals voiced in *The Poet* (1863), and we listen respectfully to *The Flood of Years* (1876), as the final utterance of a poet who has had the experience of fourscore years.

General Characteristics. — Bryant is the first great American poet. His poetry is chiefly reflective and descriptive, and it is remarkable for its elevation, simplicity, and moral earnestness. He lacks dramatic power and skill in narration. Calmness and restraint, the lack of emotional intensity, are also evident in his greatest work. His depths of space are vast, but windless. In *The Poet* he says that verse should embody: —

> "... feelings of calm power and mighty sweep,
> Like currents journeying through the windless deep."

His chosen field is describing and interpreting nature. He has been called an American Wordsworth. In the following lines Bryant gives poetic expression to his feeling that a certain maiden's heart and face reflected the beauty of the natural scenes amid which she was reared:—

> ". . . all the beauty of the place
> Is in thy heart and on thy face.
> The twilight of the trees and rocks
> Is in the light shade of thy locks." [1]

With these lines compare Wordsworth's *Three Years She Grew in Sun and Shower* (1799):—

> ". . . she shall lean her ear
> In many a secret place
> Where rivulets dance their wayward round,
> And beauty born of murmuring sound
> Shall pass into her face."

Bryant himself says that under the influence of Wordsworth, nature suddenly changed "into a strange freshness and life." It is no discredit to him to have been Wordsworth's pupil or to have failed to equal the magic of England's greatest poet of nature.

Bryant's range was narrow for a great poet, and his later verse usually repeated his earlier successes. As a rule, he presented the sky, forest, flower, stream, animal, and the composite landscape, only as they served to illumine the eternal verities, and the one verity toward which nature most frequently pointed was death. His heart, unlike Wordsworth's, did not dance with the daffodils waving in the breeze, for the mere pleasure of the dancing.

The blank verse of his *Thanatopsis* has not been surpassed since Milton. In everything that he did, Bryant was a careful workman. Painters have noticed his skill in the use of his poetic canvas and his power to suggest subjects to them, such as:—

[1] "O Fairest of the Rural Maids." (1820.)

"... croft and garden and orchard,
  That bask in the mellow light."

Three vistas from *To a Waterfowl*, — "the plashy brink of weedy lake," "marge of river wide," and "the chafed ocean side," — long ago furnished the suggestion for three paintings.

Bryant's Puritan ancestry and training laid a heavy hand upon him. Thoughts of "the last bitter hour" are constantly recurring in his verse. The third line of even his poem *June* brings us to the grave. His great poems are often like a prayer accompanied by the subdued tones of a mighty organ. Nothing foul or ignoble can be found in his verse. He has the lofty ideals of the Puritans.

ENGLISH LITERATURE OF THE PERIOD

As we saw in the preceding chapter, **Wordsworth** and **Coleridge** at the close of the last century began to exert a new influence on literature. Wordsworth's new philosophy of nature (p. 99) can be traced in the work of Bryant. The other poets of this age belong to the romantic school. **Byron** (1788–1824), the poet of revolt against the former world, shows the same influences that manifest themselves in the American and the French Revolution. He voices the complaints, and, to some extent, the aspirations of Europe. He shows his influence in Fitz-Greene Halleck's *Marco Bozzaris*. **Shelley**, who also belongs to the school of revolt, has a peculiar position as a poet of ethereal, evanescent, and spirit-like beauty. He is heard in the voice of the West Wind, the Cloud, the unseen Skylark, the "Spirit of Night," and "the white radiance of Eternity." Bryant's call in *The Evening Wind* (1829) to

> ". . . rouse
> The wide old wood from his majestic rest,
> Summoning from the innumerable boughs
> The strange, deep harmonies that haunt his breast,"

may even have been suggested by Shelley's *Ode to the West Wind* (1819): —

> "Make me thy lyre, even as the forest is:
> What if my leaves are falling like its own?
> The tumult of thy mighty harmonies
> Will take from both a deep autumnal tone."

In the early part of this period, Wordsworth and Shelley were both making these harmonies of nature audible to ears which had hitherto not heard them. **Keats** (1795–1821) is the poet of beauty, and he makes more of an appeal to the senses than Shelley. The favorite creed of Keats was: —

> "A thing of beauty is a joy forever."

His influence will gradually extend to later American verse.

Sir Walter Scott was the great prose writer of the age preceding the Victorian. The first of his series of *Waverley* novels was published in 1814, and he continued until his death in 1832 to delight the world with his genius as a writer of romances. His influence may be traced in Cooper's work, although the American author occupies an original field. Readers are still charmed with the exquisite flavor and humor in the essays of **Charles Lamb** (1775–1834). The essays of **De Quincey** (1785–1859) are remarkable for precision, stateliness, and harmony.

LEADING HISTORICAL FACTS, 1809–1849.

During these forty years, the facts most important for the student of literature are connected with the expansion and social ideals of the country. Progress was specially manifest in two ways: in "the manufacture of farms" and in the introduction and use of steam. At the time of the inauguration of Washington in 1789, the center of population of the entire country was thirty miles east of Baltimore. The progress of settlements westward, which had already begun in the last period, became in an increasing degree one of the remarkable events in the history of the world.

We may observe that the second war with England (1812) resulted in welding the Union more closely together and in giving it more prestige abroad. We should next note the unparalleled material development of the country; the opening of the Erie Canal in 1825, the rapid extension of steamboats on rivers, the trial of the first steam locomotive in 1828, the increased westward movement of population, which reached California in 1849, several hundred years ahead of schedule time, as those thought who prophesied before the introduction of steam. The story of the material progress of the country sounds like a new *Arabian Nights' Tale.*

The administration of Andrew Jackson (1829-1837) is really the beginning of the modern history of the United States. The change during these years was due more to steam than to any other single cause. At the beginning of his administration, there were no steam railroads, but fifteen hundred miles were in operation before the end of his second term. His predecessor in the presidential chair was John Quincy Adams, a Harvard graduate and an aristocrat. Jackson was illiterate, a man of the people. There was an extension of the social democratic feeling.

All classes, the poor as well as the rich, spoke their

minds more freely on every subject. Even Jackson's messages relating to foreign nations were sometimes not couched in very diplomatic terms. Every one felt that he was as good as anybody else, and in the new settlements all mingled on terms of equality. When Cooper came back to the United States in 1833, after an absence of six years in Europe, he found that he had returned to a new country, where "everybody was everywhere," and nobody was anywhere, and where the chase for the dollar seemed to have grown more absorbing than ever before.

Slavery had become one of the leading questions of the day. To keep the balance between the North and the South, states were often admitted in pairs, one free and one slave state. In 1845 there were in the Union thirteen free and fourteen slave states. The decade between 1840 and 1850 witnessed the war with Mexico and the acquisition from her of our vast southwestern territory, — Texas, California, Utah, Nevada, Arizona, New Mexico, and some interior lands to the north of these. The South was chiefly instrumental in bringing about this extension of our boundaries, hoping that this additional territory would be open for the employment of slaves and would tend to make more nearly even the influence of each section in the national government.

SUMMARY

With the publication of Irving's *Knickerbocker's History of New York* in 1809, the literary center of the United States shifted to New York, then the second city in the country. Drake and Halleck, two minor poets, calling themselves "The Croakers," issued a series of poems with the principal object of entertaining readers. Drake wrote a fine romantic poem called *The Culprit Fay*. Halleck's best works are the poems on the death of Drake and *Marco Bozzaris*.

Washington Irving's chief fame is based on his original creation of the "Knickerbocker Legend" in his *History of New York*, *Rip Van Winkle*, and *The Legend of Sleepy Hollow*. He is an unusually successful writer of short stories, of essays like those in Addison's *Spectator*, and of popular history and biography. He is the first American writer whose works are still read for pure pleasure. Humor and restrained sentiment are two of his pronounced qualities. While the subject matter of his best work is romantic, in his treatment of that matter he shows the restraint of the classical school. His style is simple and easy-flowing but not remarkable for vigor.

James Fenimore Cooper's *Leatherstocking Tales* recreate in a romantic way the life of the pioneer in the forest and the wilderness. The Indian figures more largely in these *Tales* than in those of any preceding writer. Leatherstocking deserves a place in the world's temple of fame as a great original character in fiction. Cooper is also our greatest writer of stories of the sea. *The Pilot* and *The Red Rover* still fascinate readers with the magic of the ocean. The scenes of all of his best stories are laid out of doors. His style is often careless, and he sometimes does not take the trouble to correct positive errors, but his power of arousing interest is so great that these are seldom noticed. His romances are pure, and they inspire a love for what is noble and manly. Irving was almost as popular in England as in the United States, but Cooper was the first American author to be read widely throughout Europe.

William Cullen Bryant is the first great American poet. He belongs to Wordsworth's school of nature poets. Bryant's verse, chiefly reflective and descriptive, is characterized by elevation, simplicity, and moral earnestness. His range is narrow. His communion with nature often leads him to the grave, but no other American poet invests it with as much majesty as is found in *Thanatopsis*. His strict Puritan training causes him to present the eternal verities in his poetry. Unlike Irving, Cooper, and the minor writers, his object is not entertainment.

The influence of steam, the more rapid emigration westward, the increase of the democratic spirit, and the beginning of the modern era with its strenuous materialistic trend in the administration of Andrew Jackson marked a great change in the development of the nation. The taking of our vast southwest territory from Mexico was an event second only in importance to the Louisiana Purchase.

REFERENCES FOR FURTHER STUDY

HISTORICAL

In addition to the American and English histories suggested on pp. 60, 61, the following may be consulted : Burgess's *The Middle Period, 1817–1858*; Coman's *The Industrial History of the United States*, Chaps. VI. and VII.; Bogart's *Economic History of the United States*, Chap. XIV; Sparks's *The Expansion of the American People*.

LITERARY

Richardson's *American Literature*.
Trent's *A History of American Literature*.
Wendell's *History of Literature in America*.
Stanton's *A Manual of American Literature*.
Herford's *The Age of Wordsworth*.
Stedman's *Poets of America*. (Drake, Halleck, Bryant.)
The Croakers, pp. 255–385, in *The Poetical Writings of Fitz-Greene Halleck*, edited by James Grant Wilson.
Wilson's *Fitz-Greene Halleck's Life and Letters*.
Irving's, Pierre M.: *Life and Letters of Washington Irving*, 4 vols.

Warner's *The Work of Washington Irving* (60 pages, excellent).
Warner's *Washington Irving* (304 pages, *American Men of Letters*).
Payne's *Leading American Essayists*, pp. 43-134. (Irving.)
Canby's *The Short Story in English*, pp. 218-226. (Irving.)
Lounsbury's *James Fenimore Cooper*. (*American Men of Letters*; excellent.)
Clymer's *James Fenimore Cooper*. (*Beacon Biographies*.)
Brownell's *American Prose Masters*. (Cooper.)
Erskine's *Leading American Novelists*, pp. 51-129. (Cooper.)
Cooper's *Last of the Mohicans*, edited with *Introduction* by Halleck.
Godwin's *A Biography of William Cullen Bryant, with Extracts from his Private Correspondence*, 2 vols. (The standard authority.)
Godwin's *The Poetical Works of William Cullen Bryant*, 2 vols.
Bigelow's *William Cullen Bryant*. (*American Men of Letters*.)
Bradley's *William Cullen Bryant*. (*English Men of Letters, American Series*.)
Chadwick's *The Origin of a Great Poem* (*Thanatopsis*), *Harper's Magazine*, September, 1894.

SUGGESTED READINGS

Minor Writers. — *The Croakers*, in Wilson's edition of Halleck's *Poetical Writings*.

Selections from the poetry of Drake and Halleck may be found in Stedman's *American Anthology*, pp. 36-47, and in S. & H., Vol. V.

Irving. — His *Knickerbocker's History of New York* begins with somewhat tiresome matter, condensed from chapters which he and his brother had jointly written on a different plan. The first part may well be omitted, but *Books III., V., VI., VII.* should at least be read.

Read his best two short stories, *Rip Van Winkle* and *The Legend of Sleepy Hollow*. Lovers of Irving will also wish to read some tales from *The Alhambra*, and some of his essays: *e.g. Westminster Abbey* and *Stratford-on-Avon*. For selections from his various works, see Carpenter, 124-134; S. & H., V., 41-62.

Cooper. — One of his *Leatherstocking Tales* (p. 131), *e.g. The Last of the Mohicans*, which is deservedly the most popular, should be read. If a tale of the sea is desired, read either *The Pilot* or *The Red Rover*. Selections may be found in Carpenter, 124-134; S. & H., V., 138-183.

Bryant. — Read *Thanatopsis*, *To a Waterfowl*, *O Fairest of the Rural Maids*, *A Forest Hymn*, *The Death of the Flowers*, *The Evening Wind*, *To the Fringed Gentian*, and *The Poet*. All of these are accessible in Bryant's poetical works, and almost all may be found in Page's *The Chief American Poets*. Selections are given in Stedman's *American Anthology*; S. & H., Vol. V.; and Long's *American Poems, 1776–1900*.

QUESTIONS AND SUGGESTIONS

What are some of the chief qualities in the poetry of "The Croakers"? What do these qualities indicate in the readers of contemporary New York? Do you find a genuine romantic element in Drake's *Culprit Fay*? Compare Halleck's *Marco Bozzaris* with his lines on the death of Drake, and give reasons for your preference.

Select what you consider the best three specimens of humor in Irving's *Knickerbocker's History of New York*. How is the humorous effect secured? Why does it not make us dislike the Dutch? Why is this *History* an original work? Why have *Rip Van Winkle* and *The Legend of Sleepy Hollow* been such general favorites? Compare these with any of Addison's *Sir Roger de Coverley Papers* and with any modern short story. Is Irving a romantic writer? Compare his style with Addison's and with Goldsmith's in *The Vicar of Wakefield*.

Why does Cooper deserve to rank as an original American author? What is his chosen field? In what does his special power consist? Who before him made use of the Indian in literature? Can you find any point of similarity between his work and *The Legend of Sleepy Hollow*? What are the most striking points of dissimilarity? How does his use of the romantic element differ from Irving's? What blemishes have you actually noticed in Cooper?

What lines in Bryant's *Thanatopsis* are the keynote of the entire poem? What are its general qualities? What are the finest thoughts in *A Forest Hymn*? What do these suggest in regard to Bryant's early training and the cast of his mind? Of all Bryant's poems indicated for reading, which do you prefer? Which of his references to nature do you like best? Compare his poem: *O fairest of the rural maids!* with Wordsworth's: *Three years she grew in sun and shower*. In Bryant's *The Poet*, what noteworthy poetical ideals do you find?

CHAPTER IV

THE NEW ENGLAND GROUP

Change in Religious Thought. — Since the death of Jonathan Edwards in the middle of the seventeenth century, New England had done little to sustain her former literary reputation. As the middle of the nineteenth century approaches, however, we shall find a remarkable group of writers in Boston and its vicinity. The causes of this wonderful literary awakening are in some respects similar to those which produced the Elizabethan age. In the sixteenth century the Reformation and the Revival of Learning exerted their joint force on England. In the nineteenth century, New England also had its religious reformation and intellectual awakening. We must remember that "re-formation" strictly means "forming again" or "forming in a different way." It is not the province of a history of literature to state whether a change in religious belief is for the better or the worse, but it is necessary to ascertain how such a change affects literature.

The old Puritan religion taught the total depravity of man, the eternal damnation of the overwhelming majority, of all but the "elect." A man's election to salvation depended on God's foreordination. If the man was not elected, he was justly treated, for he merely received his deserts. Even Jonathan Edwards, in spite of his sweet nature, felt bound to preach hell fire in terms of the old Puritan theology. In one of his sermons, he says: —

> "The God that holds you over the pit of hell, much as one holds a spider, or some loathsome insect, over the fire, abhors you, and is dreadfully provoked; his wrath toward you burns like fire; he looks upon you as worthy of nothing else but to be cast into the fire."

This quotation was not given when we discussed the works of Edwards, because it misrepresents his most often recurring idea of God. But the fact that even he felt impelled to preach such a sermon shows most emphatically that hell fire was supposed to be a necessary part of scriptural diet.

A tremendous reaction from such beliefs came in the first quarter of the nineteenth century. William Ellery Channing (1780-1842), pastor of the Federal Street Church in Boston and one of the greatest leaders of this religious reform, wrote in 1809 of the old Puritan creed: —

> "A man of plain sense, whose spirit has not been broken to this creed by education or terror, will think that it is not necessary for us to travel to heathen countries, to learn how mournfully the human mind may misrepresent the Deity."

He maintained that human nature, made in the image of God, is not totally depraved, that the current doctrine of original sin, election, and eternal punishment "misrepresents the Deity" and makes him a monster. This view was speedily adopted by the majority of cultivated people in and around Boston. The Unitarian movement rapidly developed and soon became dominant at Harvard College. Unitarianism was embraced by the majority of Congregational churches in Boston, including the First Church, and the Second Church, where the great John Cotton (see p. 14.) and Cotton Mather (p. 46.) had preached the sternest Puritan theology. Nearly all of the prominent writers mentioned in this chapter adopted liberal religious views. The recoil had been violent, and in the long run recoil will usually be found proportional to the strength of the repression. Dr. Oliver Wendell Holmes even called the old theology largely "diabology." The name of one of his poems is *Homesick in Heaven*. Had he in the early days chosen such a title, he would either, like Roger Williams, have been exiled, or, like the Quakers, have suffered a worse fate.

Many adopted more liberal religious beliefs without embracing Unitarianism. Perhaps these three lines voice most briefly the central thought in man's new creed and his changed attitude toward God: —

> "For Thou and I are next of kin;
> The pulses that are strong within,
> From the deep Infinite heart begin."

The New England Renaissance. — The stern theology of the Puritans may have been absolutely necessary to make them work with a singleness and an inflexibility of purpose to lay the foundations of a mighty republic; but this very singleness of aim had led to a narrowness of culture which had starved the emotional and æsthetic nature. Art, music, literature, and the love of beauty in general had seemed reprehensible because it was thought that they took away the attention from a matter of far graver import, the salvation of the immortal soul. Now there gradually developed the conviction that these agencies not only helped to save the soul, but made it worth saving. People began to search for the beautiful and to enjoy it in both nature and art. Emerson says: —

> ". . . if eyes were made for seeing,
> Then Beauty is its own excuse for being."

The first half of the nineteenth century saw the New Englanders engaged in a systematic attempt at self-culture, to an extent never before witnessed in America and rarely elsewhere. Many with an income barely sufficient for comfortable living set aside a fund for purchasing books before anything else. Emerson could even write to Carlyle that all the bright girls in New England wanted something better than morning calls and evening parties, and that a life of mere trade did not promise satisfaction to the boys.

In 1800 there were few foreign books in Boston, but the interest in them developed to such an extent that Hawthorne's father-in-law and sister-in-law, Dr. and Miss Peabody, started a foreign bookstore and reading room. Longfellow made many beautiful translations from foreign poetry. In 1840 Emerson said that he had read in the original fifty-five volumes of Goethe. Emerson superintended the publication in America of Carlyle's early writings, which together with some of Coleridge's works introduced many to German philosophy and idealism.

In this era, New England's recovery from emotional and æsthetic starvation was rapid. Her poets and prose writers produced a literature in which beauty, power, and knowledge were often combined, and they found a cultivated audience to furnish a welcome.

The Transcendental Philosophy. — The literature and thought of New England were profoundly modified by the transcendental philosophy. Ralph Waldo Emerson (p. 178) was the most celebrated expounder of this school of thought. The English philosopher, Locke, had maintained that intellectual action is limited to the world of the senses. The German metaphysician, Kant, claimed that the soul has ideas which are not due to the activity of any of the senses: that every one has an idea of time and space although no one has ever felt, tasted, seen, eaten, or smelled time or space. He called such an idea an intuition or transcendental form.

The student of literature need not worry himself greatly about the metaphysical significance of transcendentalism, but he must understand its influence on literary thought. It is enough for him to realize that there are two great classes of fact confronting every human being. There are the ordinary phenomena of life, which are apparent to the senses and which are the only things perceived by the majority of human beings. But behind all these appearances are forces and realities which the senses do not perceive. One with the bodily eye can see the living forms moving around him, but not the meaning of life. It is something more than the bodily hand that gropes in the darkness and touches God's hand. To commune with a Divine Power, we must transcend the experience of the senses. We are now prepared to understand what a transcendentalist like Thoreau means when he says:—

> "I hear beyond the range of sound,
> I see beyond the range of sight."

The transcendentalists, therefore, endeavored to transcend, that is, to pass beyond, the range of human sense and experience. We are all in a measure transcendentalists when we try to pierce the unseen, to explain existence, to build a foundation of meaning under the passing phenomena of life. To the old Puritan, the unseen was always fraught with deeper meaning than the seen. Sarah Pierrepont and Jonathan Edwards (p. 51) were in large measure transcendentalists. The trouble was that the former Puritan philosophy of the unseen was too rigid and limited to satisfy the widening aspirations of the soul.

It should be noted that in this period the term "transcendentalist" is extended beyond its usual meaning and loosely applied to those thinkers who (1) preferred to rely on their own intuitions rather than on the authority of any one, (2) exalted individuality, (3) frowned on imitation and repetition, (4) broke with the past, (5) believed that a new social and spiritual renaissance was necessary and forthcoming, (6) insisted on the importance of culture, on "plain living and high thinking," and (7) loved isolation and solitude. An excellent original exposition of much of this philosophy may be found in Emerson's *Nature* (1836) and in his lecture on *The Transcendentalist* (1842).

The Ecstasy of the Transcendentalists. — Any age that accomplishes great things is necessarily enthusiastic. According to Emerson, one of the articles of the transcendental creed was a belief "in inspiration and ecstasy." With this went an overmastering consciousness of newly discovered power. "Do you think me the child of circumstances?" asked the transcendentalist, and he answered in almost the same breath, "I make my circumstance."

The feeling of ecstasy, due to the belief that he was really a part of an infinite Divine Power, made Emerson say: —

"I see the spectacle of morning from the hill-top over against my house, from daybreak to sunrise, with emotions which an angel might share. The long slender bars of cloud float like fishes in the sea of crimson light. From the earth, as a shore, I look out into that silent sea. I seem to partake its rapid transformations; the active enchantment reaches my dust, and I dilate and conspire with the morning wind."

The greatest of the women transcendentalists, **Margaret Fuller** (1810–1850), a distinguished early pleader for equal rights for her sex, believed that when it was fashionable for women to bring to the home " food and fire for the mind as well as for the body," an ecstatic " harmony of the spheres would ensue."

To her, as to Emerson, Nature brought an inspiring message. On an early May day she wrote: —

" The trees were still bare, but the little birds care not for that; they revel and carol and wildly tell their hopes, while the gentle voluble south wind plays with the dry leaves, and the pine trees sigh with their soul-like sounds for June. It was beauteous; and care and routine fled away, and I was as if they had never been."

The transcendentalist, while voicing his ecstasy over life, has put himself on record as not wishing to do anything more than once. For him God has enough new experiences, so that repetition is unnecessary. He dislikes routine. "Everything," Emerson says, "admonishes us how needlessly long life is," that is, if we walk with heroes and do not repeat. Let a machine add figures while the soul moves on. He dislikes seeing any part of a universe that he does not use. Shakespeare seemed to him to have lived a thousand years as the guest of a great universe in which most of us never pass beyond the antechamber.

MARGARET FULLER

Critics were not wanting to point out the absurdity of many transcendental ecstasies. **Amos Bronson Alcott** (1799–1888), one of the leading transcendentalists, wrote a peculiar poem called *The Seer's Rations*, in which he speaks of

"Bowls of sunrise for breakfast,
Brimful of the East."

His neighbors said that this was the diet which he provided for his hungry family. His daughter, Louisa May, the author of that fine juvenile work, *Little Women* (1868), had a sad struggle with poverty while her father was living in the clouds. The extreme philosophy of the intangible was soon called "transcendental moonshine." The tenets of Bronson Alcott's transcendental philosophy required him to believe that human nature is saturated with divinity. He therefore felt that a misbehaving child in school would be most powerfully affected by seeing the suffering which his wrongdoing brought to others. He accordingly used to shake a good child for the bad deeds of others. Sometimes when the class had offended, he would inflict corporal punishment on himself. His extreme applications of the new principle show that lack of balance which many of this school displayed, and yet his reliance on sympathy instead of on the omnipresent rod marks a step forward in educational practice. Emerson was far-seeing enough to say of those who carried the new philosophy to an extreme, "What if they eat clouds and drink wind, they have not been without service to the race of man."

The New View of Nature. — To the old Puritan, nature seemed to groan under the weight of sin and to bear the primal curse. To the transcendentalist, nature was a part of divinity. The question was sometimes asked whether nature had any real existence outside of God, whether it was not God's thoughts. Emerson, being an idealist, doubted whether nature had any more material existence than a thought.

ORCHARD HOUSE, HOME OF THE ALCOTTS

The majority of the writers did not press this idealistic conception of nature, but much of the nature literature of this group shows a belief in the soul's mystic companionship with the bird, the flower, the cloud, the ocean, and the stars. Emerson says: —

"The greatest delight which the fields and woods minister is the suggestion of an occult relation between man and the vegetable. I am not alone and unacknowledged. They nod to me, and I to them."

Hawthorne exclaims: —

"O, that I could run wild! — that is, that I could put myself into a true relation with Nature, and be on friendly terms with all congenial elements."

Thoreau (p. 194) often enters Nature's mystic shrine and dilates with a sense of her companionship. Of the song of the wood thrush, he says: —

"Whenever a man hears it, he is young, and Nature is in her spring. Whenever he hears it, it is a new world and a free country, and the gates of heaven are not shut against him. . . . It changes all hours to an eternal morning. It banishes all trivialness. It reinstates me in my dominion, makes me the lord of creation, is chief musician of my court. This minstrel sings in a time, a heroic age, with which no event in the village can be contemporary."

Thoreau could converse with the Concord River and hear the sound of the rain in its "summer voice." Hiawatha talked with the reindeer, the beaver, and the rabbit, as with his brothers. In dealing with nature, Whittier caught something of Wordsworth's spirituality, and Lowell was impressed with the yearnings of a clod of earth as it

"Climbs to a soul in grass and flowers."

One of the chief glories of this age was the fuller recognition of the companionship that man bears to every child of nature. This phase of the literature has reacted on the ideals of the entire republic. Flowers, trees, birds, domestic animals, and helpless human beings have received more sympathetic treatment as a result. In what previous time have we heard an American poet ask, as Emerson did in his poem *Forbearance* (1842): —

"Hast thou named all the birds without a gun?
Loved the wood-rose, and left it on its stalk?"

The Dial. — Transcendentalism had for its organ a magazine called *The Dial*, which was published quarterly for four years, from 1840 to 1844. Margaret Fuller, its first editor, was a woman of wide reading and varied culture, and she had all the enthusiasm of the Elizabethans. Carlyle said of her, "Such a predetermination to eat this

big Universe as her oyster or her egg, and to be absolute empress of all height and glory in it that her heart could conceive, I have not before seen in any human soul."
She was determined to do her part in ushering in a new social and spiritual world, and it seemed to her that *The Dial* would be a mighty lever in accomplishing this result. She struggled for two years to make the magazine a success. Then ill health and poverty compelled her to turn the editorship over to Emerson, who continued the struggle for two years longer.

MARGARET FULLER'S COTTAGE, BROOK FARM

Some of Emerson's best poems were first published in *The Dial*, as were his lecture on *The Transcendentalist* and many other articles by him. Thoreau wrote for almost every number. Some of the articles were dull, not a few were vague, but many were an inspiration to the age, and their resultant effect is still felt in our life and literature. Much of the minor poetry was good and stimulating. William Channing (1818–1901) published in *The Dial* his *Thoughts*, in which we find lines that might serve as an epitaph for a life approved by a transcendentalist: —

>"It flourished in pure willingness;
> Discovered strongest earnestness;
> Was fragrant for each lightest wind;
> Was of its own particular kind; —
> Nor knew a tone of discord sharp;
> Breathed alway like a silver harp;
> And went to immortality."

While turning the pages of *The Dial*, we shall often meet with sentiments as full of meaning to us as to the people of that time. Among such we may instance: —

> "Rest is not quitting
> The busy career;
> Rest is the fitting
> Of self to its sphere."

Occasionally we shall find an expression fit to become a fireside motto: —

> "I slept, and dreamed that life was beauty;
> I woke, and found that life was duty."

The prose in *The Dial* reflects the new spirit. In the first volume we may note such expressions of imaginative enthusiasm as: —

"The reason why Homer is to me like dewy morning is because I too lived while Troy was and sailed in the hollow ships of the Grecians. . . . And Shakespeare in *King John* does but recall me to myself in the dress of another age, the sport of new accidents. I, who am Charles, was sometime Romeo. In *Hamlet* I pondered and doubted. We forget that we have been drugged with the sleepy bowl of the Present."

In the same volume we find some of Alcott's famous *Orphic Sayings*, of which the following is a sample: —

"Engage in nothing that cripples or degrades you. Your first duty is self-culture, self-exaltation: you may not violate this high trust. Yourself is sacred, profane it not. Forge no chains wherewith to shackle your own members. Either subordinate your vocation to your life or quit it forever."

A writer on *Ideals of Every Day Life* in *The Dial* for January, 1841, suggested a thought that is finding an echo in the twentieth century: —

"No one has a right to live merely to get a living. And this is what is meant by drudgery."

Two lines in the last volume voice the new spirit of growth and action: —

> "I am never at anchor, I never shall be;
> I am sailing the glass of infinity's sea."

The Dial afforded an outlet for the enthusiasms, the aspirations, the ideals of life, during a critical period in New England's renaissance. No other periodical during an equal time has exerted more influence on the trend of American literature.

Brook Farm. — In 1841 a number of people, headed by **George Ripley** (1802–1880), a Unitarian clergyman, purchased a tract of land of about two

POOL AT BROOK FARM

hundred acres at West Roxbury, nine miles from Boston. This was known as Brook Farm, and it became the home of a group who wished to exemplify in real life some of the principles that *The Dial* and other agencies of reform were advocating.

In *The Dial* for January, 1842, we may find a statement of the aims of the Brook Farm community. The members especially wanted "*leisure to live in all the faculties of the soul*," and they determined to combine manual and mental labor in such a way as to achieve this result. Probably the majority of Americans are in sympathy with such an aim. Many have striven to find sufficient release from their hard, unimproving routine work to enable them to escape its dwarfing effects and to live a fuller life on a higher plane.

The Brook Farm settlement included such people as Nathaniel Hawthorne, Charles A. Dana (1819–1897), afterward editor of the New York *Sun*, George Ripley, in later times distinguished as the literary critic of the New York *Tribune*, and **George William Curtis** (1824–1892), who became a well-known essayist, magazine editor, and civil service reformer. The original pioneers numbered about twenty; but the membership increased to nearly one hundred and fifty. Brook Farm had an influence, however, that could not be measured by the number of its inmates. In one year more than four thousand visitors came to see this new social settlement.

Hawthorne, the most famous literary member of the Brook Farm group, has recorded many of his experiences during his residence there in 1841: —

"April 13. I have not yet taken my first lesson in agriculture, except that I went to see our cows foddered, yesterday afternoon. We have eight of our own; and the number is now increased by a transcendental heifer belonging to Miss Margaret Fuller. She is very fractious, I believe, and apt to kick over the milk pail. . . . April 16. I have milked a cow!!! . . . May 3. The whole fraternity eat together, and such a delectable way of life has never been seen on earth since the days of the early Christians. . . . May 4. . . . there is nothing so unseemly and disagreeable in this sort of toil as you could think. It defiles the hands, indeed, but not the soul."

Unfortunately, in order to earn a living, it was found necessary to work ten hours a day in the summer time, and this toil was so fatiguing that the mind could not work clearly at the end of the day. We find Hawthorne writing on June 1 of the same year: —

"It is my opinion that a man's soul may be buried and perish. . . in a furrow of the field, just as well as under a pile of money."

On August 12, he asks: —

"Is it a praiseworthy matter that I have spent five golden months in providing food for cows and horses? It is not so."

On Octber 9, he says: —

"Our household, being composed in great measure of children and young people, is generally a cheerful one enough, even in gloomy weather. . . . It would be difficult to conceive beforehand how much can be added to the enjoyment of a household by mere sunniness of temper and liveliness of disposition. . . ."

Hawthorne remained at Brook Farm for only one of the six years of its existence. An important building, on which there was no insurance, burned in 1846, and the next year the association was forced for financial reasons to disband. This was probably the most ideal of a series of social settlements, every one of which failed. The problem of securing sufficient leisure to live in all the faculties of the soul has not yet been solved, but attempts toward a satisfactory solution have not yet been abandoned.

The influence of Brook Farm on our literature survives in Hawthorne's *Blithedale Romance* (p. 219), in his *American Note Books*, in Emerson's miscellaneous writings, and in many books and hundreds of articles by less well-known people. Almost all of those who participated in this social experiment spoke of it in after years with strong affection.

Ideals of the New England Authors. — When we examine with closest scrutiny the lives of the chief New England authors, of Emerson and Thoreau, Longfellow and Whittier,

Holmes and Lowell, we find that all were men of the highest ideals and character. Not one could be accused of double dealing and intentional misrepresentation, like Alexander Pope; not one was intemperate, like Robert Burns or Edgar Allan Poe; not one was dissolute, like Byron; not one uttered anything base, like many a modern novelist and dramatist.

The mission of all the great New England writers of this age was to make individuals freer, more cultivated, more self-reliant, more kindly, more spiritual. Puritan energy and spirituality spoke through them all. Nearly all could trace their descent from the early Puritans. It is not an infusion of new blood that has given America her greatest writers, but an infusion of new ideals. Some of these ideals were illusions, but a noble illusion has frequently led humanity upward. The transcendentalists could not fathom the unknowable, but their attempts in this direction enabled them to penetrate deeper into spiritual realities.

The New Englander demanded a cultivated intellect as the servant of the spirit. He still looked at the world from the moral point of view. For the most part he did not aim to produce a literature of pleasure, but of spiritual power, which he knew would incidentally bring pleasure of the highest type. Even Holmes, the genial humorist, wished to be known to posterity by his trumpet call to the soul to build itself more stately mansions.

The Influence of Slavery. — The question of human slavery profoundly modified the thought and literature of the nation. In these days we often make the mistake of thinking that all of the people of New England disapproved of slavery at the end of the first half of the nineteenth century. The truth is that many of the most influential people in that section agreed with the South on the question of slavery. Not a few of the most cultivated people at the North thought that an antislavery movement would lead to an attack on other forms of property and that anarchy would be the inevitable result.

Opposition to slavery developed naturally as a result of the new spirit in religion and human philosophy. This distinctly affirmed the right of the individual to develop free from any trammels. *The Dial* and Brook Farm were both steps toward fuller individuality and more varied life, and both were really protests against all kinds of slavery. This new feeling in the air speedily passed beyond the color line, and extended to the animals.

One of the earliest to advocate the abolition of slavery was **William Lloyd Garrison** (1805–1879), a printer at Newburyport, Massachusetts. In 1831 he founded *The Liberator*, which became the official organ of the New England abolitionists. He influenced the Quaker poet Whittier to devote the best years of his life to furthering the cause of abolition. Emerson and Thoreau spoke forcibly against slavery. Lowell attacked it with his keenest poetic shafts.

Harriet Beecher Stowe (1811–1896). — It was, however, left for the daughter of an orthodox Congregational clergyman of New England to surpass every other antislavery champion in fanning into a flame the sentiment against enslaving human beings. Harriet Beecher, the sister of Henry Ward Beecher, the greatest pulpit orator of antislavery days, was born in Litchfield, Connecticut. When she was twenty-one, she went with her father, Lyman Beecher, to Cincinnati. Her new home was on the borderland of slavery, and she often saw fugitive slaves and heard their stories at first hand. In 1833 she made a visit to a slave plantation in Kentucky and obtained additional material for her most noted work.

In 1836 she married Calvin E. Stowe, a colleague of her father in the Lane Theological Seminary in Cincinnati. During the next twelve years she had six children to rear. In 1850 Professor Stowe and his family moved to Bowdoin College, in Brunswick, Maine. This year saw the passage of the Fugitive Slave Act, which required the citizens of free states to aid in catching and returning escaped slaves. This Act roused Mrs. Stowe, and she began *Uncle Tom's Cabin*, which was published in book form in 1852.

HARRIET BEECHER STOWE

Perhaps no other American book of note has been written under so great a handicap. When Mrs. Stowe began this work, one of her large family of children was not a year old, and the others were a constant care. Nevertheless, she persevered with her epoch-making story. One of her friends has given us a picture of the difficulties in her way, the baby on her knee, the new hired girl asking whether the pork should be put on top of the beans, and whether the gingerbread should stay longer in the oven.

In *Uncle Tom's Cabin* Mrs. Stowe endeavored to translate into concrete form certain phases of the institution of slavery, which had been merely an abstraction to the North. Of Senator John Bird, who believed in stringent laws for the apprehension of fugitive slaves, she wrote:—

". . . his idea of a fugitive was only an idea of the letters that spell the word, — or, at the most, the image of a little newspaper picture of a man with a stick and bundle, with 'Ran away from the subscriber' under it. The magic of the real presence of distress, — the imploring human eye, the frail, trembling human hand, the despairing appeal of helpless agony, — these he had never tried. He had never thought that a fugitive might be a hapless mother, a defenceless child. . . ."

In chapters of intense dramatic power, Mrs. Stowe shows a slave mother and her child escaping on the floating ice across the Ohio. They come for refuge to the home of Senator Bird.

"'Were you a slave?' said Mr. Bird.
"'Yes, sir; I belonged to a man in Kentucky.'
"'Was he unkind to you?'
"'No, sir; he was a good master.'
"'And was your mistress unkind to you?'
"'No, sir,— no! my mistress was always good to me.'"

Senator Bird learned that the master and mistress were in debt, and that a creditor had a claim which could be discharged only by the sale of the child. "Then it was," said the slave mother, "I took him and left my home and came away."

Mrs. Stowe's knowledge of psychological values is shown in the means taken to make it appear to Senator John Bird that it would be the natural thing for him to defeat his own law, by driving the woman and her child seven miles in the dead of night to a place of greater safety.

All sections of the country do not agree in regard to whether *Uncle Tom's Cabin* gives a fairly representative picture of slavery. This is a question for the historian, not for the literary critic. We study *Macbeth* for its psychology, its revelation of human nature, its ethics, more than for its accurate exposition of the Scottish history of the time. We read *Uncle Tom's Cabin* to find out how the pen of one woman proved stronger than the fugitive slave laws of the United States, how it helped to render of no avail the decrees of the courts, and to usher in a four years' war. We decide that she achieved this result because the pictures, whether representative or not, which she chose to throw on her screen, were such as appealed to the most elemental principles of human nature, such as the mother could not forget when she heard her own children say their evening prayer, such as led her to consent to send her firstborn to the war, such as to make *Uncle Tom's Cabin* outsell every other book written by an American, to cause it to be translated into more than thirty foreign languages, to lead a lady of the Siamese court to free all her slaves in 1867, and to say that Mrs. Stowe "had taught her as even Buddha had taught kings to respect the rights of her fellow creatures."

It may be noted in this connection that Mark Twain, who was of southern descent and whose parents and relatives owned slaves, introduces in his greatest work, *Huckleberry Finn* (1884), a fugitive slave to arouse our sympathies. The plot of *Pudd'nhead Wilson* (1894) turns on one of Mrs. Stowe's points of emphasis, the fear of the mother that her child would be sold and taken away from her, down the river.

The story of *Uncle Tom's Cabin* is intensely dramatic, and it accomplished its author's purpose far beyond her expectations. When we study it merely as a literary performance, we shall notice the effect of the handicap under which Mrs. Stowe labored at the time of composition, as well as her imperfect conception of the art technique of the modern novel. There are faults of plot, style, and characterization. Modern fiction would call for more differentiation in the dialogue of the different characters and for more unity of structure, and yet there are stories with all these technical excellencies which do not live a year. We may say with W. P. Trent, a Virginian by birth, and a critic who has the southern point of view: "*Uncle Tom's Cabin* is alive with emotion, and the book that is alive with emotion after the lapse of fifty years is a great book. The critic of to-day cannot do better than to imitate George Sand when she reviewed the story on its first appearance — waive its faults and affirm its almost unrivaled emotional sincerity and strength."

Oratory.—The orators of this period made their strongest speeches on questions connected with human liberty and the preservation of the Union. Most public speeches die with the success or the failure of the reforms that they champion or the causes that they plead. A little more than half a century ago, schoolboys declaimed the speeches of **Edward Everett** (1794-1865), **Charles Sumner** (1811-1874), and **Wendell Phillips** (1811-1884), all born in Massachusetts, and all graduates of Harvard. But even the best speeches of these men are gradually being forgotten, although a stray sentence or paragraph may still occasionally be heard, such as Wendell Phillips's reply to those who hissed his antislavery sentiments, "Truth dropped into the pit of hell would make a noise just like that," or Edward Everett's apostrophe to "that one solitary adventurous vessel, the *Mayflower* of a forlorn hope, freighted with the prospects of a future state and bound across the unknown sea."

Daniel Webster (1782-1852). — New England furnished in Daniel Webster one of the world's great orators. He was born in Salisbury, New Hampshire, and educated at Dartmouth College. It was said half humorously that no one could really be as great as he looked. Whittier called him

> "New England's stateliest type of man,
> In port and speech Olympian;
> Whom no one met, at first, but took
> A second awed and wondering look."

Before his death he was known as the best lawyer, the most noted statesman, and the greatest orator in the country. He is still considered America's greatest orator.

A study of the way in which Webster schooled himself to become a speaker will repay every one who wishes to use our spoken language effectively. In Webster's youth, a stilted, unnatural style was popular for set speeches. He was himself influenced by the prevailing fashion, and we find him writing to a friend: —

DANIEL WEBSTER

"In my melancholy moments I presage the most dire calamities. I already see in my imagination the time when the banner of civil war shall be unfurled; when Discord's hydra form shall set up her hideous yell, and from her hundred mouths shall howl destruction through our empire."

Such unnatural prose impresses us to-day as merely an insincere play with words, but in those days many thought a stilted, ornate style as necessary for an impressive occasion as Sunday clothes for church. An *Oratorical Dictionary*, for the use of public speakers, was actually published in the first part of the nineteenth century. This contained a liberal amount of sonorous words derived from the Latin, such as "campestral," "lapidescent," "obnubilate," and "adventitious." Such words were supposed to give dignity to spoken utterance.

Edward Everett, the most finished classical speaker of the time, loved to introduce the "Muses of Hellas," and to make allusions to the fleets "of Tyre, of Carthage, of Rome," and to Hannibal's slaughtering the Romans "till the Aufidus ran blood." He painted Warren "moving resplendent over the field of honor, with the rose of Heaven upon his cheek, and the fire of liberty in his eye."

Webster was cured of such tendencies by an older lawyer, Jeremiah Mason, who graduated at Yale about the time Webster was born. Mason, who was frequently Webster's opponent, took pleasure in ridiculing all ornate efforts and in pricking rhetorical bubbles. Webster says that Mason talked to the jury "in a plain conversational way, in short sentences, and using no word that was not level to the comprehension of the least educated man on the panel. This led me to examine my own style, and I set about reforming it altogether." Note the simplicity in the following sentences from Webster's speech on *The Murder of Captain Joseph White:* —

"Deep sleep had fallen on the destined victim, and on all beneath his roof. A healthful old man, to whom sleep was sweet, and the first sound slumbers of the night held him in their soft but strong embrace. . . . The face of the innocent sleeper is turned from the murderer, and the beams of the moon, resting on the gray locks of his aged temple, show him where to strike."

In his speech on *The Completion of the Bunker Hill Monument*, we find the following paragraph, containing two sentences which present in simple language one of the great facts in human history: —

"America has furnished to the world the character of Washington! And if our American institutions had done nothing else, that alone would have entitled them to the respect of mankind."

He knew when illustrations and figures of rhetoric could be used to advantage to impress his hearers. In discussing the claim made by Senator Calhoun of South Carolina that a state could nullify a national law, Webster said: —

"To begin with nullification, with the avowed intent, nevertheless, not to proceed to secession, dismemberment, and general revolution, is as if one were to take the plunge of Niagara, and cry out that he would stop half way down."

To show the moral bravery of our forefathers and the comparative greatness of England, at that time, he said: —

"On this question of principle, while actual suffering was yet afar off, they raised their flag against a power, to which, for purposes of foreign conquest and subjugation, Rome, in the height of her glory, is not to be compared; a power which has dotted over the surface of the whole globe with her possessions and military posts, whose morning drumbeat, following the sun, and keeping company with the hours, circles the earth with one continuous and unbroken strain of the martial airs of England."

For nearly a generation prior to the Civil War, schoolboys had been declaiming the peroration of his greatest speech, his *Reply to Hayne* (1830): —

"When my eyes shall be turned to behold for the last time the sun in heaven, may I not see him shining on the broken and dishonored fragments of a once glorious Union ; on States dissevered, discordant, belligerent ; on a land rent with civil feuds, or drenched, it may be, in fraternal blood!"

This peroration brought Webster as an invisible presence into thousands of homes in the North. The hearts of the listeners would beat faster as the declaimer continued : —

"Let their last feeble and lingering glance rather behold the gorgeous ensign of the republic, now known and honored throughout the earth, still full high advanced, its arms and trophies streaming in their original luster, not a stripe erased or polluted, nor a single star obscured. . . . "

When the irrepressible conflict came, it would be difficult to estimate how many this great oration influenced to join the army to save the Union. The closing words of that speech, " Liberty and Union, now and forever, one and inseparable ! " kept sounding like the voice of many thunders in the ear of the young men, until they shouldered their muskets. His *Seventh of March Speech* (1850), which seemed to the North to make compromises with slavery, put him under a cloud for awhile, but nothing could stop youth from declaiming his *Reply to Hayne*.

Although the majority of orators famous in their day are usually forgotten by the next generation, it is not improbable that three American orations will be quoted hundreds of years hence. So long as the American retains his present characteristics, we cannot imagine a time when he will forget Patrick Henry's speech in 1775, or Daniel Webster's peroration in his *Reply to Hayne*, or Abraham Lincoln's *Gettysburg Address* (p. 344), entrusting the American people with the task of seeing " that government of the people, by the people, and for the people shall not perish from the earth."

RALPH WALDO EMERSON, 1803-1882

Life. — Ralph Waldo Emerson, the most distinguished of New England transcendentalists, came from a family of clergy. Peter Bulkeley, his ancestor, was the first pastor of Concord in 1635. William Emerson, his grandfather, was pastor in Concord at the opening of the Revolutionary War and witnessed the fight of Concord Bridge from the window of the Old Manse, that famous house which he had built and which Hawthorne afterwards occupied. By that

Bridge there stands a monument, commemorating the heroic services of the men who there made the world-famous stand for freedom. On the base of this monument are Ralph Waldo Emerson's lines: —

> "By the rude bridge that arched the flood,
>   Their flag to April's breeze unfurled,
> Here once the embattled farmers stood,
>   And fired the shot heard round the world."

Ralph Waldo Emerson was born in Boston in 1803. His father, who was pastor of the First Church in Boston, died when Ralph Waldo was eight years old, leaving in poverty a widow with six children under ten years of age. His church promptly voted to pay his widow five hundred dollars a year, for seven years, but even with this help the family was so poor that in cold weather it was noticed that Ralph and his brother went to school on alternate days. The boys divined the reason, and were cruel enough to call out, "Whose turn is it to wear the coat to-day?" But the mother struggled heroically with poverty, and gave her sons a good education. Ralph Waldo entered Harvard in 1817. He saved the cost of his lodging by being appointed "President's Freshman," as the official message bearer was called, and earned most of his board by waiting on the table at the college Commons.

Emerson was descended from such a long line of clergymen that it was natural for him to decide to be a minister. After graduating at Harvard and taking a course in theology, he received a call from Cotton Mather's (p. 46) church and preached there for a short time; but he soon resigned because he could not conscientiously conform to some of the customs of the church. Although he occasionally occupied pulpits for a few years after this, the greater part of his time for the rest of his life was spent in writing and lecturing.

When he was temporarily preaching in Concord, New Hampshire, in 1827, he met Miss Ellen Tucker, then sixteen years old. This meeting was for two reasons a noteworthy event in his life. In the first place, her inspiration aided in the development of his poetical powers. He seemed to hear the children of Nature say to her: —

> "Thou shalt command us all, —
>   April's cowslip, summer's clover,
> To the gentian in the fall,
>   Blue-eyed pet of blue-eyed lover."

His verses tell how the flower and leaf and berry and rosebud ripening into rose had seemed to copy her. He married her in 1829 and wrote the magnificent prophecy of their future happiness in the poem beginning: —

"And Ellen, when the graybeard years,"

a poem which he could not bear to have published in his lifetime, for Mrs. Emerson lived but a few years after their marriage.

In the second place, in addition to stimulating his poetical activity, his wife's help did not end with her death; for she left him a yearly income of twelve hundred dollars, without which he might never have secured the leisure necessary to enable him "to live in all the faculties of his soul" and to become famous in American literature.

ELLEN TUCKER

In the fall of 1833 he sailed for Europe, going by way of the Mediterranean. Returning by way of England, he met Coleridge, Wordsworth, and Carlyle, whose influence he had already felt. His visit to Carlyle led to a lifelong friendship. Emerson helped to bring out an American edition of the *Sartor Resartus* (1836) before it was published in England.

After returning from Europe, Emerson permanently settled at Concord, Massachusetts, the most famous literary

EMERSON'S STUDY

town of its size in the United States. The appreciation of the Concord people for their home is shown by the naïve story, told by a member of Emerson's family, of a fellow townsman who read of the rapidly rising price of building lots in Chicago, and remarked, "Can't hardly believe that any lands can be worth so much money, so far off." After

Henry D. Thoreau (p. 194) had received a medal at school for proficiency in geography, he went home and asked his mother if Boston was located in Concord. It was to Concord that Emerson brought his second wife, Lidian Jackson Emerson, whom he married in 1835. In Concord he wrote his most famous *Essays*, and from there he set out on his various lecturing tours. There he could talk daily to celebrities like Nathaniel Hawthorne, Henry Thoreau, and Bronson Alcott. Louisa May Alcott relates that when eight years old she was sent to the Emerson home to inquire about the health of his oldest son, a boy of five. Emerson answered her knock, and replied, "Child, he is dead!" Years later she wrote, "I never have forgotten the anguish that made a familiar face so tragical, and gave those few words more pathos than the sweet lamentation of the *Threnody*." Like Milton and Tennyson, Emerson voiced his grief in an elegy, to which he gave the title *Threnody*. In this poem the great teacher of optimism wrote: —

> "For this losing is true dying;
> This is lordly man's down-lying,
> This his slow but sure reclining,
> Star by star his world resigning."

Aside from domestic incidents, his life at Concord was uneventful. As he was by nature averse to contests, he never took an extreme part in the antislavery movement, although he voiced his feelings against slavery, even giving antislavery lectures, when he thought the occasion required such action. His gentleness and tenderness were inborn qualities. Oliver Wendell Holmes said that Emerson removed men's "idols from their pedestals so tenderly that it seemed like an act of worship."

He widened his influence by substituting the platform

for the pulpit, and year after year he enlarged his circle of hearers. He lectured in New England, the South, and the West. Sometimes these lecture tours kept him away from home the entire winter. In 1847 he lectured in England and Scotland. He visited Carlyle again, and for four days listened to "the great and constant stream" of his talk. On this second trip abroad, Emerson met men like De Quincey, Macaulay, Thackeray, and Tennyson. Emerson gained such fame in the mother country that, long after he had returned, he was nominated for the Lord Rectorship of Glasgow University and received five hundred votes against seven hundred for Disraeli, one of England's best known statesmen.

Something of his character and personality may be learned from the accounts of contemporary writers. James Russell Lowell, who used to go again and again to hear him, even when the subject was familiar, said, "We do not go to hear what Emerson says so much as to hear Emerson." Hawthorne wrote, "It was good to meet him in the wood paths or sometimes in our avenue with that pure intellectual gleam diffusing about his presence like the garment of a shining one." Carlyle speaks of seeing him "vanish like an angel" from his lonely Scotch home.

Emerson died in 1882 and was buried near Hawthorne, in Sleepy Hollow cemetery at Concord, on the "hilltop hearsed with pines." Years before he had said, "I have scarce a daydream on which the breath of the pines has not blown and their shadow waved." The pines divide with an unhewn granite boulder the honor of being his monument.

Early Prose. — Before he was thirty-five, Emerson had produced some prose which, so far as America is concerned, might be considered epoch-making in two respects: (1) in a new philosophy of nature, not new to the world, but new in the works of our authors and fraught with new inspiration to Americans; and (2) in a new doctrine of self-reliance and intellectual independence for the New World.

In 1836 he published a small volume entitled *Nature*, containing fewer than a hundred printed pages, but giving

EMERSON'S GRAVE, CONCORD

in embryo almost all the peculiar, idealistic philosophy that he afterwards elaborated. By "Nature" he sometimes means everything that is not his own soul, but he also uses the word in its common significance, and talks of the beauty in cloud, river, forest, and flower. Although *Nature* is written in prose, it is evident that the author is a poet. He says: —

"How does Nature deify us with a few and cheap elements! Give me health and a day, and I will make the pomp of emperors ridiculous. The dawn is my Assyria; the sunset and moonrise my Paphos, and unimaginable realms of faerie; broad noon shall be my England of the senses and the understanding; the night shall be my Germany of mystic philosophy and dreams."

Emerson tried to make men feel that the beauty of the universe is the property of every individual, but that the many divest themselves of their heritage. When he undertook to tell Americans how to secure a warranty deed to the beauties of nature, he specially emphasized the moral element in the process. The student who fails to perceive that Emerson is one of the great moral teachers has studied him to little purpose. To him all the processes of nature "hint or thunder to man the laws of right and wrong, and echo the Ten Commandments." In *Nature*, he says: —

"All things with which we deal, preach to us. What is a farm but a mute gospel? The chaff and the wheat, weeds and plants, blight, rain, insects, sun, — it is a sacred emblem from the first furrow of spring to the last stack which the snow of winter overtakes in the fields."

In *Nature*, Emerson sets forth his idealistic philosophy. "Idealism sees the world in God" is with him an axiom. This philosophy seems to him to free human beings from the tyranny of materialism, to enable them to use matter as a mere symbol in the solution of the soul's problems, and to make the world conformable to thought. His famous sentence in this connection is, "The sensual man conforms thoughts to things; the poet conforms things to his thoughts."

In *The American Scholar*, an address delivered at Cambridge in 1837, Emerson announced what Oliver Wendell Holmes calls "our intellectual Declaration of Independence." Tocqueville, a gifted Frenchman who visited America in 1831, wrote: "I know no country in which there is so little independence of opinion and freedom of discussion as in America. . . . If great writers have not existed in America, the reason is very simply given in the fact that there can be no literary genius without freedom of opinion, and freedom of opinion does not exist in America." Harriet Martineau, an English woman, who came to America in 1830, thought that the subservience to opinion in and around Boston amounted to a sort of mania. We have already seen how Cooper in his early days deferred to English taste (p. 127), and how Andrew Jackson in his rough way proved something of a corrective (p. 148).

Emerson proceeded to deal such subserviency a staggering blow. He denounced this "timid, imitative, tame spirit," emphasized the new importance given to the single person, and asked, "Is it not the chief disgrace in the world not to be a unit; — not to be reckoned one character; — not to yield that peculiar fruit which each man was created to bear; but to be reckoned in the gross, in the hundred, or the thousand, of the party, the section, to which we belong, and our opinion predicted geographically, as the North, or the South?" Then followed his famous declaration to Americans, "We will walk on our own feet; we will work with our own hands; we will speak our own minds."

No American author has done more to exalt the individual, to inspire him to act according to his own intuitions and to mold the world by his own will. Young Americans especially listened to his call, "O friend, never strike sail to a fear! Come into port greatly, or sail with God the seas."

Essays. — The bulk of Emerson's work consists of essays, made up in large part from lectures. In 1841 he published a volume, known as *Essays, First Series*, and in 1844, another volume, called *Essays, Second Series*. Other volumes followed from time to time, such as *Miscel-*

lanies (1849), *Representative Men* (1850), *English Traits* (1856), *The Conduct of Life* (1860), *Society and Solitude* (1870). While the *First Series* of these *Essays* is the most popular, one may find profitable reading and even inspiring passages scattered through almost all of his works, which continued to appear for more than forty years.

When we examine his *Essays, First Series*, we find that the volume is composed of short essays on such subjects as *History, Self-Reliance, Friendship, Heroism,* and the *Over-Soul*. If we choose to read *Self-Reliance*, one of his most typical essays, we shall find that the sentences, or the clauses which take the place of sentences, are short, vigorous, and intended to reach the attention through the ear. For instance, he says in this essay:—

"There is a time in every man's education when he arrives at the conviction that envy is ignorance; that imitation is suicide; that he must take himself for better, for worse, as his portion."

Before we have finished *Self-Reliance*, he has made us feel that, with the exercise of self-trust, new powers will appear; that a man should not postpone his life, but live *now;* that a man is weak if he expects aid from others; that discontent is want of self-reliance.

We pick up another volume of essays, *Society and Solitude*, and wonder whether we shall read *Success*, or *Books*, or *Civilization*, or any one of nine others. While we are turning the pages, we see this sentence:—

"Hitch your wagon to a star,"

and we decide to read *Civilization*.

"Now that is the wisdom of a man, in every instance of his labor, to hitch his wagon to a star, and see his chore done by the gods themselves. . . . We cannot bring the heavenly powers to us, but, if we will only choose our jobs in directions in which they travel, they will undertake them with the greatest pleasure. . . . Let us not lie and steal. No god will help. We shall find all their teams going the other way."

The youth is to be pitied if this does not quicken his determination to choose his work in the direction in which the aiding forces of the universe are traveling.

Some of Emerson's best social philosophy may be found in the essay, *Considerations by the Way*, published in the volume called *The Conduct of Life*. His *English Traits* records in a vigorous, interesting, common-sense way his impressions from his travels in the mother country. The English find in this volume some famous sentences, which they love to quote, such as, —

"That which lures a solitary American in the woods with the wish to see England, is the moral peculiarity of the Saxon race, — its commanding sense of right and wrong, — the love and devotion to that, — this is the imperial trait which arms them with the sceptre of the globe."

Poetry. — Emerson's verse is noteworthy for its exposition (1) of nature and (2) of his transcendental philosophy. He produced a comparatively small amount of poetry, but much more than he is popularly supposed to have written. Some of his verse is of a high degree of excellence; in fact, his nature poetry deserves to be ranked with the best that America has produced. Like Bryant, Emerson loves the forest. He says: —

> "I go to the god of the wood
> To fetch his word to men."

In *The Poet*, we see how great he thought the poet's debt to communion with nature: —

> "The gods talk in the breath of the woods,
>   They talk in the shaken pine,
> And fill the long reach of the old seashore
>   With dialogue divine;
> And the poet who overhears
>   Some random word they say

> Is the fated man of men
> Whom the ages must obey."

Hawthorne saw Emerson one August day, wandering in Sleepy Hollow near Concord, and wrote, "He appeared to have had a pleasant time; for he said there were Muses in the woods to-day and whispers to be heard in the breezes." When Emerson was twenty-four years old, he wrote the following lines, which show the new feeling of mystic companionship with nature:—

> "These trees and stones are audible to me,
> These idle flowers, that tremble in the wind,
> I understand their faery syllables."

His verses make us feel how nature enriches human life, increases its joys, and lessens its sorrows. What modern lover of nature has voiced a more heartfelt, unaffected appreciation of her ministrations than may be found in these lines from Emerson's *Musketaquid?*—

> "All my hurts
> My garden spade can heal. A woodland walk,
> A quest of river grapes, a mocking thrush,
> A wild rose or rock-loving columbine,
> Salve my worst wounds."

From reading his best nature poem, *Woodnotes*, first published in *The Dial*, an appreciative person may find it easy to become

> "Lover of all things alive,
> Wonderer at all he meets,"

to feel that in the presence of nature, every day is the best day of the year, and possibly even to sing with Emerson of any spring or summer day:—

> "'Twas one of the charmed days
> When the genius of God doth flow;
> The wind may alter twenty ways,
> A tempest cannot blow;

It may blow north, it still is warm;
  Or south, it still is clear;
Or east, it smells like a clover farm;
  Or west, no thunder fear."

All who love nature or who wish to become interested in her should read at least his *Woodnotes*, *The Humble Bee*, *The Rhodora*, *Each and All*, *The Snow Storm*, and *To Ellen at the South*.

Some of his philosophy may be found in poems like *The Problem* (1839), *The Sphinx* (1841), and *Brahma* (1857). The immanence of God in everything, in the sculptor's hand, for instance, is well expressed in *The Problem:* —

"The hand that rounded Peter's dome
And groined the aisles of Christian Rome
  Wrought in a sad sincerity;
Himself from God he could not free;
He builded better than he knew; —
  The conscious stone to beauty grew."

The Sphinx thus expresses one of Emerson's favorite thoughts: —

"To vision profounder,
  Man's spirit must dive,"

and concludes with the Sphinx's thought-provoking statement: —

"Who telleth one of my meanings,
  Is master of all I am."

This line in *Brahma:* —

"I am the doubter and the doubt,"

shows his belief in the unity of all things, his conviction that all existence and action result from one underlying force. His own personal philosophy, that which actuated him in dealing with his fellow-men, is expressed in the following lines, which are worthy a place in the active memory of every American: —

> "Life is too short to waste
>   In critic peep or cynic bark,
> Quarrel or reprimand:
>   'Twill soon be dark."

While we are enjoying his poetry, we feel its limitations. Having slight ear for music, he often wrote halting lines. Sometimes his poetic flight is marked by too sudden a descent, but we shall often find in his verse rare jewels, such as:—

> "When Duty whispers low, '*Thou must*,'
>   The youth replies, '*I can*.'"

These lines seemed to Oliver Wendell Holmes, the moment he saw them, as if they had been "carved on marble for a thousand years." Emerson's poetry does not pulsate with warm human feeling, but it "follows the shining trail of the ethereal," the ideal, and the eternal. His prose overshadows his poetry, but no one without natural poetical ability of a high order could have written the lines:—

> "O tenderly the haughty day
>   Fills his blue urn with fire,"

or even have seen

> "The frolic architecture of the snow."

General Characteristics. — The central aim of Emerson's writing is moral development. He is America's greatest ethical teacher. He thus voices his fixed belief:—

"A breath of will blows eternally through the universe of souls in the direction of the Right and Necessary."

This belief gives rise to his remarkable optimism for the future, to his conviction that evil is but a stepping stone to good.

In a material age he is the great apostle of the spiritual. "Will you not tolerate," he asks, "one or two solitary voices in the land, speaking for thoughts not marketable or perishable?" To him "mind is the only reality," and his great man is never the one who can merely alter matter, but who can change our state of mind. He believed in reaching truth, guided by intuition. He would not argue to maintain his positions. He said that he did not know what argument signified with reference to a thought. To him a thought was just as natural a product as a rose and did not need argument to prove or justify its existence. Much of his work is tinged with Plato's philosophy.

Of all American writers, he is the most inspiring teacher of the young. One of his chief objects is, in his own phrase, "to help the young soul, add energy, inspire hope, and blow the coals into a useful flame; to redeem defeat by new thought, by firm action." John Tyndall, the eminent English scientist, declared that the reading of two men, Carlyle and Emerson, had made him what he was. He said to his students: "I never should have gone through Analytical Geometry and Calculus, had it not been for these men. I never should have become a physical investigator, and hence without them I should not have been here to-day. They told me what I ought to do in a way that caused me to do it, and all my consequent intellectual action is to be traced to this purely moral force." After hearing one of Emerson's lectures, James Russell Lowell wrote, "Were we enthusiasts? I hope and believe we were, and am thankful to the man who made us worth something for once in our lives."

Few authors, excepting Shakespeare, have more of the quality of universality in their writings. Many things in Emerson will fit certain stages of individual development as well a thousand years hence as to-day and be as applicable to the moral improvement of the Chinese as of Americans. If he is not as much read in the future, it will be largely due to the fact that his most inspiring subject matter has been widely diffused through modern thought.

Emerson's style is condensed. He spoke of his own paragraphs as incompressible, "each sentence an infinitely repellent particle." Because of this condensation, it is best not to read more than one essay at a time. Years ago some joker said that Emerson's *Essays* could be read as well backward as forward, because there was no connection between the sentences. The same observation could have been made with almost equal truth about *Proverbs*, some of Bacon's *Essays*, Polonius's *Advice to Laertes*, parts of Hamlet's *Soliloquy*, and, in general, about any condensed sentences that endeavor to convey a complete, striking truth. Lowell remarks acutely: "Did they say he was disconnected? So were the stars. . . . And were *they* not knit together by a higher logic than our mere sense could master?" We should look for unity and connection in Emerson's chosen subject matter and trend of thought.

We must not forget that Emerson has in his prose as well as in his verse many of the general characteristics of a poet. In his *Essays*, he sometimes avails himself of the poetic license to be obscure and contradictory and to present philosophy that will not walk on all fours. When we examine some of the best passages on nature in his early prose (*e.g.* p. 158), we shall find that they are highly poetical.

Much of his verse is filled with the charm of nature and shows here and there remarkable power of putting great riches in a little room, although there may be intervening waste spaces. Critics may say that his poetry lacks deep feeling, that it is mostly intellectual; if so, it is nobly intellectual. Both his poetry and prose, to use an Emersonian expression, "sail the seas with God."

HENRY DAVID THOREAU, 1817-1862

Life. — Henry David Thoreau, America's poet-naturalist, was born in 1817 at Concord, Massachusetts. He was one of the youngest of the famous Concord group of writers and the only one who could claim Concord as his birthplace. He was a lifelong student of nature, and he loved the district around Concord. As a boy he knew its woods and streams because he had hunted and fished in them. After his graduation from Harvard in 1837, he substituted for the fishing rod and gun, the spyglass, microscope, measuring tape, and surveying instruments, and continued his out-of-door investigations.

He taught school with his brother and lectured, but in order to add to his slender income also did work unusual for a Harvard graduate, such as odd jobs of carpentering, planting trees, and surveying. He also assisted his father in his business of pencil making, and together they made the best pencils in New England. Whatever he undertook, he did thoroughly. He had no tolerance for the shoddy or for compromises. Exact workmanship was part of his religion. "Drive a nail home," he writes in *Walden*, "and clinch it so faithfully that you can wake up in the night and think of your work with satisfaction."

THOREAU'S SPY-GLASS, FLUTE, ETC.

Like so many of the transcendentalists, Thoreau desired to surround his life with a "wide margin of leisure" in order that he might live in his higher faculties and not be continuously dwarfed with the mere drudgery of earning his sustenance. He determined to divest himself of as many of the burdens of civilization as possible, to lead the simple life, and to waste the least possible time in the making of mere money. The leisure thus secured, he spent in studying birds, plants, trees, fish, and other objects of nature, in jotting down a record of his experiences, and in writing books.

Since he did not marry and incur responsibilities for others, he was free to choose his own manner of life. His regular habit was to reserve half of every day for walking in the woods; but for two years and two months he lived alone in the forest, in a small house that he himself built upon a piece of Emerson's property beside Walden Pond, about a mile south of Concord. Thoreau found that he could earn enough in six weeks to support himself in this simple way for the rest of the year. He thus acquired the leisure to write books that are each year read with increasing interest. The record of his life at Walden forms the basis for his best known work. A few people practice the return to nature for a short time, but Thoreau spent his available life with nature.

SITE OF THOREAU'S HUT, WALDEN POND

He was a pronounced individualist, carrying out Emerson's doctrine by becoming independent of others' opinions. What he thought right, he said or did. He disapproved, for example, of slavery, and consequently refused to pay his poll tax to a government that upheld slavery. When he was imprisoned because of non-payment, Emerson visited him and asked, "Why are you here, Henry?" Thoreau merely replied, "Why are you *not* here?"

His intense individualism made him angular, and his transcendental love of isolation caused him to declare that he had never found "the companion that was so companionable as solitude"; but he was, nevertheless, spicy, original, loyal to friends, a man of deep family affection, stoical in his ability to stand privations, and Puritanic in his conviction about the moral aim of life. His last illness, induced by exposure to cold, confined him for months away from the out of doors that he loved. In 1862, at the age of forty-five, he said, as he lay on his deathbed, "When I was a very little boy, I learned that I must die, and I set that down, so, of course, I am not disappointed now." He was buried not far from Emerson's lot in the famous Sleepy Hollow cemetery at Concord.

Works. — Only two of his books were published during his lifetime. These were *A Week on the Concord and Merrimac Rivers* (1849) and *Walden* (1854). The first of these, usually referred to as *The Week*, is the record of a week spent in a rowboat on the rivers mentioned in the title. The clearness and exactness of the descriptions are remarkable. Whenever he investigated nature, he took faithful notes so that when he came to write a more extended description or a book, he might have something more definite than vague memory impressions on which to rely. When he describes in *The Week* a mere patch of the river bank, this definiteness of observation is manifest: —

"The dead limbs of the willow were rounded and adorned by the climbing milkania, *Milkania scandens*, which filled every crevice in the leafy bank, contrasting agreeably with the gray bark of its supporter and the balls of the button-bush."

This book did not prove popular, and almost three fourths of the edition were left on his hands. This unfortunate venture caused him to say, "I have now a library of nearly nine hundred volumes, over seven hundred of which were written by myself."

Walden is the book by which Thoreau is best known. It is crisper, livelier, more concise and humorous, and less given to introspective philosophizing than *The Week*. *Walden*, New England's *Utopia*, is the record of Thoreau's experiment in endeavoring to live an ideal life in the forest. This book differs from most of its kind in presenting actual life, in not being mainly evolved from the inner consciousness on the basis of a very little experience. He thus states the reason why he withdrew to the forest: —

"I went to the woods because I wished to live deliberately, to front only the essential facts of life, and see if I could not learn what it had to teach, and not, when I came to die, discover that I had not lived. I did not wish to live what was not life, living is so dear."

His food during his twenty-six months of residence there cost him twenty-seven cents a week. "I learned," he says, "from my two years' experience that it would cost incredibly little trouble to obtain one's necessary food, even in this latitude; that a man may use as simple a diet as the animals, and yet retain health and strength.... I am convinced both by faith and experience that to maintain one's self on this earth is not a hardship, but a pastime." This book has, directly or indirectly, caused more to desire the simple life and a return to nature than any other work in American literature.

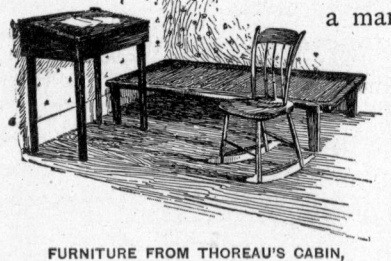

FURNITURE FROM THOREAU'S CABIN, WALDEN POND

In *Walden* he speaks of himself as a "self-appointed inspector of snowstorms and rainstorms." His companionship with nature became so intimate as to cause him to say, "Every little pine needle expanded and swelled with sympathy and befriended me." When a sparrow alighted upon his shoulder, he exclaimed, "I felt that I was more distinguished by that circumstance than I should have been by any epaulet I could have worn." When nature had some special celebration with the trees, such as decking them with snow or ice or the first buds of spring, he frequently tramped eight or ten miles "to keep an appointment with a beech-tree or a yellow-birch, or an old acquaintance among the pines." It is amusing to read how on such a walk he disturbed the daytime slumbers of a large owl, how the bird opened its eyes wide, "but their lids soon fell again, and he began to nod," and how a sympathetic hypnotization began to take effect on Thoreau. "I too," he says, "felt a slumberous influence after watching him half an hour, as he sat thus with his eyes half open, like a cat, winged brother of the cat."

In spite of some Utopian philosophy and too much insistence on the self-sufficiency of the individual, *Walden* has proved a regenerative force in the lives of many readers who have not passed the plastic stage. The book develops a love for even commonplace natural objects, and, like poetry, discloses a new world of enjoyment. *Walden* is Thoreau's most vital combination of his poetic apprehension of wild nature with his philosophy and aggressive individualism.

Almost all of his work is autobiographical, a record of actual experience. *The Maine Woods* (1864), *Cape Cod* (1865), and *A Yankee in Canada* (1866) are records of his tramps in the places named in the titles, but these works do not possess the interest of *Walden*.

His voluminous manuscript *Journal* is an almost daily

record of his observations of nature, mingled with his thoughts, from the time when he left college until his last sickness. At periods for nearly fifty years after his death, various works have been compiled from this *Journal.* The volumes published under the titles, *Early Spring in Massachusetts* (1881), *Summer* (1884), *Winter* (1887), *Autumn* (1892), and *Notes on New England Birds* (1910) were not arranged by him in their present form. Editors searched his *Journal* for entries dealing with the same season or type of life, and put these in the same volume. Sometimes, as, for instance, in *Winter*, paragraphs separated by an interval of nineteen years in composition become neighbors. In spite of the somewhat fragmentary nature of these works, lovers of Thoreau become intensely interested in them. His *Journal* in the form in which he left it was finally published in 1906, in fourteen volumes containing 6811 printed pages. He differs from the majority of writers because the interest in his work increases with the passing of the years.

General Characteristics. — Thoreau's object was to discover how to live a rich, full life with a broad margin of leisure. Intimate companionship with nature brought this secret to him, and he has taught others to increase the joys of life from sympathetic observation of everyday occurrences.

A mere unimaginative naturalist may be a bore; but Thoreau regarded nature with the eyes of a poet. His ear was thrilled with the vesper song of the whippoorwill, the lisping of the chickadee among the evergreens, and the slumber call of the toads. For him the bluebird "carries the sky on its back." The linnets come to him "bearing summer in their natures." When he asks, "Who shall stand godfather at the christening of the wild apples?" his reply shows rare poetic appreciation of nature's work: —

"We should have to call in the sunrise and the sunset, the rainbow and the autumn woods and the wild flowers, and the woodpecker and the purple finch and the squirrel and the jay and the butterfly, the November traveler and the truant boy, to our aid."

He is not only a poet-naturalist, but also a philosopher, who shows the influence of the transcendental school, particularly of Emerson. Some of Thoreau's philosophy is impractical and too unsocial, but it aims to discover the underlying basis of enchantment. He thus sums up the philosophy which his life at Walden taught him: —

"I learned this at least by my experiment — that if one advances confidently in the direction of his dreams, and endeavors to live the life which he has imagined, he will meet with a success unexpected in common hours. . . . If you have built castles in the air, your work need not be lost; that is where they should be. Now put the foundations under them."

The reason why he left Walden shows one of his pronounced transcendental characteristics, a dread of repetition. He gives an account of only his first year of life there, and adds, "the second year was similar to it." He says: —

"I left the woods for as good a reason as I went there. Perhaps it seemed to me that I had several more lives to live, and could not spare any more time for that one. It is remarkable how easily and insensibly we fall into a particular route, and make a beaten track for ourselves. I had not lived there a week before my feet wore a path from my door to the pond side."

He does not demand that other human beings shall imitate him in devoting their lives to a study of nature. He says, "Follow your genius closely enough, and it will not fail to show you a fresh prospect every hour." He thus expresses his conception of the fundamental basis of happiness in any of the chosen avenues of life: —

"Our whole life is startlingly moral. There is never an instant's truce between virtue and vice. Goodness is the only investment that never fails."

His insistence on the necessity of a moral basis for a happy life is a characteristic that he shared in common with the great authors of the New England group, but he had his own individual way of impressing this truth. He thought life too earnest a quest to tolerate the frivolous or the dilettante, and he issued his famous warning that no one can "kill time without injuring eternity." His aim in studying nature was not so much scientific discovery as the revelation of nature's joyous moral message to the spiritual life of man. He may have been unable to distinguish between the song of the wood thrush and the hermit thrush. To him the most important fact was that the thrush is a rare poet, singing of "the immortal wealth and vigor that is in the forest." "The thrush sings," says Thoreau, in his *Journal*, "to make men take higher and truer views of things."

The sterling honesty and directness of Thoreau's character are reflected in his style. He says, "The one great rule of composition — and if I were a professor of rhetoric I should insist on this — is to *speak the truth*." This was his aim in presenting the results of the experience of his soul, as well as of his senses. If he exaggerated the importance of a certain way of regarding things, he did so only because he thought the exaggeration was necessary to secure attention for that particular truth, which would even then not be apprehended at its full value. His style has a peculiar flavor, difficult to describe. Lowell's characterization of Thoreau's style has hardly been surpassed. "His range was narrow, but to be a master is to be a master. There are sentences of his as perfect as anything in the language, and thoughts as clearly crystallized; his metaphors and images are always fresh from the soil."

Thoreau's style shows remarkable power of description. No American has surpassed him in unique description of the most varied incidents in the procession of all the seasons. We shall find frequent illustrations of this power scattered through his *Journal:* —

"*June* 1, 1857. I hear the note of a bobolink concealed in the top of an apple tree behind me. . . . He is just touching the strings of his theorbo, his glassichord, his water organ, and one or two notes globe themselves and fall in liquid bubbles from his teeming throat. It is as if he touched his harp within a vase of liquid melody, and when he lifted it out, the notes fell like bubbles from the trembling string . . . the meadow is all bespattered with melody. His notes fall with the apple blossoms, in the orchard."

Even more characteristic is an entry in his *Journal* for June 11, 1840, where he tries to fathom the consciousness of the solitary bittern: —

"With its patient study by rocks and sandy capes, has it wrested the whole of her secret from Nature yet? It has looked out from its dull eye for so long, standing on one leg, on moon and stars sparkling through silence and dark, and now what a rich experience is its! What says it of stagnant pools, and reeds, and damp night fogs? It would be worth while to look in the eye which has been open and seeing in such hours and in such solitudes. When I behold that dull yellowish green, I wonder if my own soul is not a bright invisible green. I would fain lay my eye side by side with its and learn of it."

In this entry, which was probably never revised for publication, we note three of his characteristics: his images "fresh from the soil," adding vigor to his style; his mystic and poetic communion with nature; and the peculiar transcendental desire to pass beyond human experience and to supplement it with new revelations of the gospel of nature.

NATHANIEL HAWTHORNE, 1804-1864

Ancestry and Early Years. — William Hathorne, the ancestor of America's greatest prose writer, sailed at the age of twenty-three from England on the ship *Arbella* with John Winthrop (p. 30), and finally settled at Salem, Massachusetts. He brought with him a copy of Sir Philip Sidney's *Arcadia*, a very unusual book for the library of a New England Puritan.

John Hathorne, a son of the first settler, was a judge of the poor creatures who were put to death as witches at

Salem in 1692. The great romance writer says that this ancestor "made himself so conspicuous in the martyrdom of the witches, that their blood may fairly be said to have left a stain upon him. . . . I, the present writer, as their representative, hereby take shame upon myself for their sakes, and pray that any curse incurred by them — as I have heard, and as the dreary and unprosperous condition of the race, for many a long year back, would argue to exist — may be now and henceforth removed." Tradition says that the husband of one of the tortured victims appealed to God to avenge her sufferings and murder. Probably the ancestral curse hanging over *The House of the Seven Gables* would not have been so vividly conceived, if such a curse had not been traditional in the Hawthorne family.

HAWTHORNE'S BIRTHPLACE, SALEM, MASSACHUSETTS

Nathaniel Hawthorne, the sixth in descent from the first New England ancestor, and the first of his family to add a "w" to his name, was born in Salem in 1804. His father, a sea captain, died of a fever at a foreign port in 1808. Hawthorne's mother was twenty-seven years old at this time, and for forty years after this sad event, she usually took her meals in her own room away from her three children. Everybody in that household became accustomed to loneliness. At the age of fourteen, the boy went to live for a while on the shore of Sebago Lake, Maine. "I lived in Maine," he said, "like a bird of the air, so perfect was the freedom I enjoyed. But it was there I got my cursed habits of solitude." Shyness and aversion to meeting people became marked characteristics.

His solitariness predisposed him to reading, and we are told that Bunyan's *Pilgrim's Progress* and Shakespeare's plays were special favorites. Spenser's *Faerie Queene* was the first book that he bought with his own money. Bunyan and Spenser probably fostered his love of the allegorical method of presenting truth, a method that is in evidence in the bulk of Hawthorne's work. He even called his daughter Una, after one of Spenser's allegorical heroines, and, following the suggestion in the *Faerie Queene*, gave the name of "Lion" to the large cat that came to her as a playmate.

At the age of seventeen, Hawthorne went to Bowdoin College, Maine, where he met such students as Longfellow, Franklin Pierce, and Horatio Bridge, in after years a naval officer, who published in 1893 a delightful volume called *Personal Reminiscences of Nathaniel Hawthorne*. These friends changed the course of Hawthorne's life. In his dedication of *The Snow Image* to Bridge in 1850, Hawthorne says, "If anybody is responsible for my being at this day an author, it is yourself."

Literary Apprenticeship. — After leaving college, Milton spent nearly six years in studious retirement; but Hawthorne after graduating at Bowdoin, in 1825, passed in seclusion at Salem a period twice as long. Here he lived the life of a recluse, frequently postponing his walks until after dark. He was busy serving his apprenticeship as an author. In 1828 he paid one hundred dollars for the publication of *Fanshawe*, an unsuccessful short romance. In mortification he burned the unsold copies, and his rejected short stories often shared the same fate. He was so depressed that in 1836 his friend Bridge went quietly to a publisher and by guaranteeing him against loss induced him to bring out Hawthorne's volume entitled *Twice-Told Tales*.

The Peabodys of Salem then invited the author to their home, where he met the artistic Miss Sophia Peabody, who made an illustration for his fine historical story, *The Gentle Boy*. Of her he wrote, "She is a flower to be worn in no man's bosom, but was lent from Heaven to show the possibilities of the human soul." We find that not long after he wrote in his *American Note-Books:* —

MISS PEABODY'S DRAWING FOR "THE GENTLE BOY"

"All that seems most real about us is but the thinnest substance of a dream, — till the heart be touched. That touch creates us, — then we begin to be, — thereby we are beings of reality and inheritors of eternity."

He was thinking of Sophia Peabody's creative touch, for he had become engaged to her.

Fired with the ambition of making enough money to enable him to marry, he secured a subordinate position in the Boston customhouse, from which the spoils system was soon responsible for his discharge. He then invested in Brook Farm a thousand dollars which he had saved, thinking that this would prove a home to which he could bring his future wife and combine work and writing in an ideal way. A year's trial of this life convinced him of his mistake. He was then thirty-eight, and much poorer for his last experiment; but he withdrew and in a few months married Miss Peabody and took her to live in the famous Old Manse

"THE OLD MANSE," HAWTHORNE'S FIRST CONCORD HOME

at Concord. The first entry in his *American Note-Books* after this transforming event is: —

"And what is there to write about? Happiness has no succession of events, because it is a part of eternity; and we have been living in eternity ever since we came to this old manse. Like Enoch we seem to have been translated to the other state of being, without having passed through death."

The history of American literature can record no happier marriage and no more idyllic life than this couple lived for nearly four years in the Old Manse. While residing here, Hawthorne wrote another volume, known as *Mosses from an Old Manse* (1846). The only serpent to enter that Eden was poverty. Hawthorne's pen could not support his family. He found himself in debt before he had finished his fourth year in Concord. Moncure D. Conway, writing Hawthorne's *Life* in 1890, the year before American authors were protected by international copyright, says, "In no case has literature, pure and simple, ever supported an American author, unless, possibly, if he were a bachelor." Hawthorne's college friends, Bridge and Pierce, came to his assistance, and used their influence with President Polk to secure for Hawthorne the position of surveyor of customs at Salem, with a yearly salary of twelve hundred dollars.

His Prime and Later Years. — He kept his position as head customs officer at Salem for three years. Soon after President Taylor was inaugurated in 1849, the spoils system again secured Hawthorne's removal. When he came home dejected with this news, his wife smiled and said, "Oh, then you can write your book!" *The Scarlet Letter*, published in 1850, was the result. The publisher printed five thousand copies, all that he had ever expected to sell, and then ordered the type to be distributed at once. Finding in ten days, however, that every copy had been sold, he gave the order to have the type reset and permanent plates made. Hawthorne had at last, at the age of forty-six, become one of the greatest writers of English prose romance. From this time he wrote but few short tales.

He left Salem in the year of the publication of *The Scarlet Letter*, never again to return to it as a place of residence, although his pen continued to help immortalize his birthplace.

In 1852 he bought of Bronson Alcott in Concord a house since known as the "Wayside." This was to be Hawthorne's American home during his remaining years. Here he had a tower room so constructed as to be well-nigh inaccessible to visitors, and he also had a romantic study bower built in the pine trees on a hill back of his house.

His college friend, Pierce, was inaugurated President of the United States in 1853, and he appointed Hawthorne consul at Liverpool. This consulship then netted the holder between $5000 and $7000 a year. After nearly four years' service in this position, he resigned and traveled in Europe with his family. They lived in Rome sufficiently long for him to absorb the local color for his romance of *The Marble Faun*. He remained abroad for seven years. The record of his travels and impressions may be found in his *English Note-Books* and in his *French and Italian Note-Books*. *Our Old Home*, a volume based on his *English Note-Books*, is a more finished account of his thoughts and experiences in England.

HAWTHORNE'S PINE STUDY, CONCORD

In 1860 he returned quietly to his Concord home. His health was failing, but he promised to write for the *Atlantic Monthly* another romance, called *The Dolliver Romance*. This, however, was never finished, and *The Marble Faun* remains the last of his great romances. His health continued to fail, and in May, 1864, Pierce, thinking that a trip might prove beneficial, started with him on a journey to the

White Mountains. Hawthorne retired for the night at the hotel in Plymouth, New Hampshire, and the next morning Pierce found that Hawthorne's wish of dying unawares in his sleep had been gratified. He had passed away before the completion of his fifty-ninth year. He was buried underneath the pines in the Sleepy Hollow cemetery at Concord. His classmate, Longfellow, wrote: —

> "There in seclusion and remote from men,
> The wizard hand lies cold."

"Twice Told Tales" and "Mosses from an Old Manse." — Many do not realize that these two volumes contain eighty-two tales or sketches and that they represent the most of Hawthorne's surviving literary work for the first forty-five years of his life. The title for *Twice-Told Tales* (1837) was probably suggested by the line from Shakespeare's *King John:* "Life is as tedious as a twice-told tale." The second volume, *Mosses from an Old Manse* (1846), took its name from Hawthorne's first Concord home. His last collection is called *The Snow Image and Other Twice-Told Tales* (1851). Each one of these volumes contains some of his short-story masterpieces, although, taken as a whole, the collection in *Mosses from an Old Manse* shows the greatest power and artistic finish.

The so-called tales in these volumes are of several different types. (1) There is the story which presents chiefly allegorical or symbolic truth, such as *Rappacini's Daughter, The Great Stone Face, The Birthmark, The Artist of the Beautiful,* and *The Snow Image.* The last story, one of the greatest of this class, relates how two children make a companion out of a snow image, how Jack Frost and the pure west wind endow this image with life and give them a little "snow sister." She grows more vigorous with every life-giving breath inhaled from the west wind. She extends her hands to the snow-birds, and they joyously flock to her. The father of these children is a deadly literal man. No tale of fairy, no story of dryad, of Aladdin's lamp, or of winged sandal had ever carried magical meaning to his unimaginative literal mind, and he proceeds to disenchant the children. Like Nathan the prophet, Hawthorne wished to say, "Thou art the man," to some tens of thousands of stupid destroyers of those ideals which bring something of Eden back to our everyday lives. This story, like so many of the others, was written with a moral purpose. There are to-day people who measure their acquaintances by their estimates of this allegorical story.

(2) Another type of Hawthorne's stories illustrates the history of New England. Such are *The Gentle Boy*, *The Maypole of Merry Mount*, *Endicott's Red Cross*, and *Lady Eleanore's Mantle*. We may even include in this list *Young Goodman Brown*, in one sense an unreal and fantastic tale, but in another, historically true to the Puritanic idea of the orgies of witches in a forest. If we wish, for instance, to supplement the cold page of history with a tale that breathes the very atmosphere of the Quaker persecution of New England, let us open *The Twice-Told Tales* and read the story of *The Gentle Boy*, a Quaker child of six, found sobbing on his father's newly-made grave beside the scaffold under the fir tree. Let us enter the solemn meeting house, hear the clergyman inveigh against the Quakers, and sit petrified when, at the end of the sermon, that boy's mother, like a Daniel entering the lion's den, ascends the pulpit, and invokes woe upon the Puritans.

(3) We shall occasionally find in these volumes what eighteenth-century readers of the *Spectator* would have

called a "paper," that is, a delightful bit of mixed description and narration, "a narrative essay" or "a sketch," as some prefer to call it. In this class we may include *The Old Manse*, *The Old Apple-Dealer*, *Sights from a Steeple*, *A Rill from the Town Pump*, and the masterly *Introduction* to *The Scarlet Letter*.

The Old Manse, the first paper in *Mosses from an Old Manse*, is excellent. Hawthorne succeeds in taking his readers with him up the Assabeth River, in a boat made by Thoreau. We agree with Hawthorne that a lovelier river "never flowed on earth, — nowhere indeed except to lave the interior regions of a poet's imagination." When we return with him at the end of that day's excursion, we are almost tempted to say that we can never again be enslaved as before. We feel that we can say with him: —

"We were so free to-day that it was impossible to be slaves again to-morrow. When we crossed the threshold of the house or trod the thronged pavements of a city, still the leaves of the trees that overhang the Assabeth were whispering to us, 'Be free! Be free.'"

These volumes entitle Hawthorne to be ranked among the greatest of short-story writers. Like Irving, Hawthorne did not take the air line directness of narration demanded by the modern short story; but the moral truth and beauty of his tales will long prove their elixir of life, after the passing of many a modern short story which has divested itself of everything except the mere interest in narration.

Children's Stories. — Hawthorne's *Grandfather's Chair* (1841) is a series of simple stories of New England history, from the coming of the Mayflower to the death of Samuel Adams in 1803. Hawthorne's greatest success in writing for children is to be found in his *A Wonder Book* (1851) and *Tanglewood Tales* (1853). In these volumes he has adapted the old classical myths to the tastes of American children. His unusual version of these myths meets two supreme tests. Children like it, and are benefited by it. Many would rejoice to be young enough again to hear for the first time the story of *The Golden Touch*, — how Midas prized gold above all things, how he secured the golden touch, and how the flies that alighted on his nose fell off little nuggets of gold. What a fine thing we thought the golden touch until he touched his beautiful little daughter, Marygold! No sermon could better have taught us that gold is not the thing above all to be desired.

Hawthorne stands in the front rank of a very small number whose writings continue to appeal to the children of succeeding generations. He loved and understood children and shared their experiences. He was one of those whose sixteenth amendment to the Constitution reads, "The rights and caprices of children in the United States shall not be denied or abridged on account of age, sex, or formal condition of tutelage."

THE HOUSE OF THE SEVEN GABLES
(Copyright, 1898, by Houghton Mifflin Co.)

Great Romances. — Hawthorne wrote four long romances: *The Scarlet Letter* (1850), the scene of which is laid in Boston in Governor Winthrop's time, *The House of the Seven Gables* (1851), with the scene laid in Salem, *The Marble Faun* (1860), in Rome, and *The Blithedale Romance*

(1852), in an ideal community similar to Brook Farm. The first three of these works have a great moral truth to present. Accordingly, the details of scene, plot, description, and conversation are handled so as to emphasize this central truth.

The Scarlet Letter was written to show that the consequences of a sin cannot be escaped and that many different lives are influenced by one wrong deed. The lives of Hester Prynne, Reverend Arthur Dimmesdale, and Roger Chillingworth are wrecked by the crime in *The Scarlet Letter*. Roger Chillingworth is transformed into a demon of revenge. So malevolent does he become that Hester wonders "whether the tender grass of early spring would not be blighted beneath him." She would not be surprised to see him "spread bat's wings and flee away." The penalty paid by Arthur Dimmesdale is to appear to be what he is not, and this is a terrible punishment to his sensitive nature. The slow steps by which his soul is tortured and darkened are followed with wonderful clearness, and the agony of his soul alone with God is presented with an almost Shakespearean pen. The third sufferer is the beautiful Hester Prynne. Her fate is the most terrible because she not only writhes under a severe punishment inflicted by the authorities, but also suffers from daily, even hourly, remorse. To help assuage her grief and to purify her soul, Hester becomes the self-effacing good Samaritan of the village. Her uncomplaining courage, noble beauty, and self-sacrifice make her the center of this tragic story.

Shakespeare proposed no harder problem than the one in *The Scarlet Letter*, — the problem of the expiation of sin. The completeness with which everything is subordinated to the moral question involved, and the intensity with which this question is treated, show the Puritanic temperament and the imaginative genius of the author. Hawthorne is Puritan in the earnestness of his purpose, but he is wholly the artist in carrying out his design. Such a combination of Puritan and artist has given to American literature in *The Scarlet Letter* a masterpiece, somber yet beautiful, ethical yet poetic, incorporating both the spirit of a past time and the lessons of an eternal present. This incomparable romance is unified in conception, symmetrical in form, and nobly simple in expression.

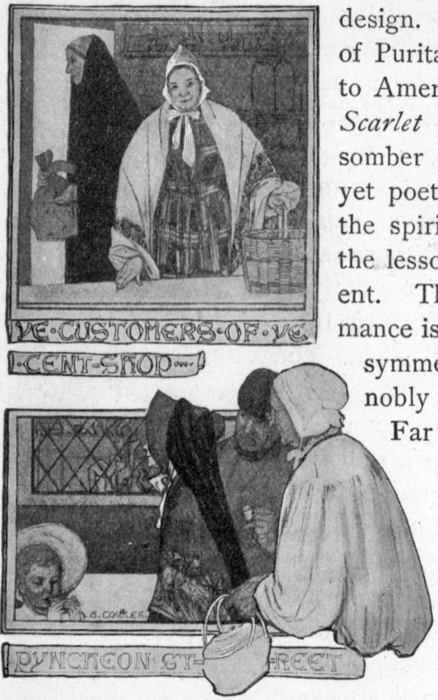

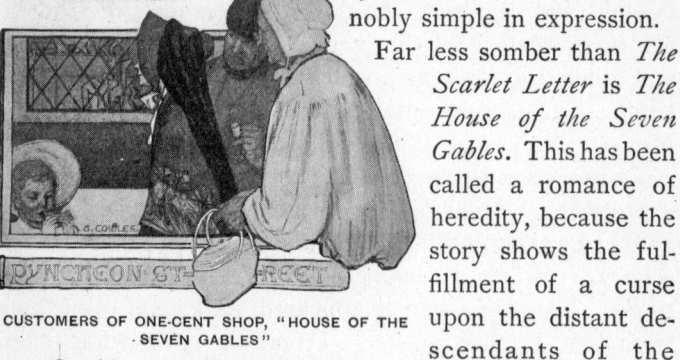

Far less somber than *The Scarlet Letter* is *The House of the Seven Gables*. This has been called a romance of heredity, because the story shows the fulfillment of a curse upon the distant descendants of the wrongdoer, old Judge Pyncheon. The present inhabitants of the Pyncheon mansion, who are among the worst sufferers, are Hepzibah Pyncheon and her brother Clifford. Hawthorne's pages contain nothing more pathetic than the picture of helplessness presented by these two innocent souls, bearing a burden

CUSTOMERS OF ONE-CENT SHOP, "HOUSE OF THE SEVEN GABLES"

(Copyright, 1898, by Houghton Mifflin Co.)

of crime not their own. The brightness of the story comes through the simple, joyous, home-making nature of Phœbe Pyncheon. She it is who can bring a smile to Clifford's face and can attract custom to Hepzibah's cent shop. Hawthorne never loses sight of his purpose. The curse finds its last victim, and the whole story is a slow preparation for this event. The scenes, however, in which Phœbe, that "fair maker of sunshine," reigns as queen, are so peaceful and attractive, the cent shop, which Hepzibah is forced to open for support, offers so many opportunities for comic as well as pathetic incidents, and the outcome of the story is so satisfactory that it is the brightest of all Hawthorne's long romances.

In *The Marble Faun*, Hawthorne's last complete romance, the Puritan problem of sin is transplanted to Italian soil. The scene is laid in Rome, where the art of Michael Angelo and Raphael, the secret orders of the Church, the tragic history of the eternal city, with its catacombs and ruins, furnish a rich and varied background for the story. So faithfully indeed are the galleries, churches, and historic corners of Rome described, that *The Marble Faun* has served as a guide for the cultured visitor. This expression of opinion by the late A. P. Stanley (1815–1881), a well-known author and dean of Westminster Abbey, is worth remembering: "I have read it seven times. I read it when it appeared, as I read everything from that English master. I read it again when I expected to visit Rome, then when on the way to Rome, again while in Rome, afterwards to revive my impressions of Rome. Recently I read it again because I wanted to." In this historic setting, Hawthorne places four characters: Donatello, the faun, Miriam, the beautiful and talented young artist, Kenyon, the American sculptor, and

Hilda, the Puritan maid who tends the lamp of the Virgin in her tower among the doves and makes true copies of the old masters. From the beginning of the story some mysterious evil power is felt, and this power gains fuller and fuller ascendency over the characters. What that is the author does not say. It seems the very spirit of evil itself that twines its shadow about human beings and crushes them if they are not strong enough to resist.

In *The Scarlet Letter* it was shown that the moral law forces evildoers to pay the last farthing of the debt of sinning. In *The Marble Faun* the effect of sin in developing character is emphasized, and Donatello, the thoughtless creature of the woods, is portrayed in his stages of growth after his moral nature has first been roused by a great crime. The question is raised, Can the soul be developed and strengthened by sin? The problem is handled with Hawthorne's usual moral earnestness of purpose, and is expressed in his easiest and most flexible style. Nevertheless this work has not the suppressed intensity, completeness of outline, and artistic symmetry possessed by *The Scarlet Letter*. The chief defects of *The Marble Faun* are a vagueness of form, a distracting variety of scene, and a lack of the convincing power of reality. The continued popularity of this romance, however, is justly

HILDA'S TOWER, VIA PORTOGHESE, ROME

due to its poetic conception, its atmosphere of ancient mystery, and its historic Roman background.

The Blithedale Romance and the coöperative settlement described in it were suggested to Hawthorne by his Brook Farm experience, although he disclaims any attempt to present an actual picture of that community. The idea of the division of labor, the transcendental conversations, and many of the incidents owe their origin to his sojourn at Brook Farm (p. 166). Although *The Blithedale Romance* does not equal the three romances already described, it contains one character, Zenobia, who is the most original and dramatic of Hawthorne's men and women, and some scenes which are as powerful as any drawn by him.

General Characteristics. — Hawthorne gave the Puritan to literature. This achievement suggests Irving's canonization of the Knickerbockers and Cooper's of the pioneer and the Indian. Himself a Unitarian and out of sympathy with the Puritans' creed, Hawthorne nevertheless says, "And yet, let them scorn me as they will, strong traits of their nature have intertwined themselves with mine." He and they had the same favorite subject, — the human soul in its relation to the judgment day. He could no more think of sin unrelated to the penalty, than of a serpent without shape or color. Unlike many modern novelists, his work never wanders beyond a world where the Ten Commandments rule. Critics have well said that he never painted a so-called man of the world, because such a man, by Hawthorne's definition, would really be a man out of the great moral world, which to Hawthorne seemed the only real world.

He is preëminently a writer of romance. He was always powerfully influenced by such romantic materials as may be found in the world of witchcraft and the supernatural, or such as are suggested by dim foreshadowings of evil and by the many mysteries for which human philosophy does not account. For this reason, his works are removed from the commonplace and enveloped in an imaginative atmosphere. He subjects his use of these romantic materials — the unusual, the improbable, and the supernatural — to only one touchstone. He is willing to avail himself of these, so long as he does not, in his own phrase, " swerve aside from the truth of the human heart."

His stories are frequently symbolic. He selects some object, token, or utterance, in harmony with his purpose, and uses it as a symbol to prefigure some moral action or result. The symbol may be an embroidered mantle, indicative of pride; a butterfly, typical of emergence from a dead chrysalis to a state of ideal beauty; or the words of a curse, which prophesy a ghastly death. His choice of scene, plot, and character is in harmony with the moral purpose indicated by the symbol. Sometimes this purpose is dimly veiled in allegory, but even when his stories are sermons in allegory, like *The Snow Image*, he so invests them with poetic fancy or spiritual beauty as to make them works of art. His extensive use of symbolism and allegory has been severely criticized. It is unfortunate that he did not learn earlier in life what *The Scarlet Letter* should have taught him, that he did not need to rely on these supports. He becomes one of the great masters when he paints character from the inside with a touch so vivid and compelling that the symbolism and the allegory vanish like a dissolving picture and reveal human forms. When he has breathed into them the creator's breath of life, he walks with them hand in hand in this lost Eden. He ascends the pillory with Hester Prynne, and writhes with Arthur Dimmesdale's agony. He plays on the seashore with little Pearl. He shares Hepzibah Pyncheon's solitude and waits on the customers in the cent shop with Phœbe. He eats two dromedaries and a gingerbread locomotive with little Ned Higgins.

Hawthorne did not care much for philosophical systems, and never concerned himself with the intricacies of transcendentalism. Yet he was affected by that philosophy, as is shown by his personal isolation and that of his characters. His intense belief in individuality is also a transcendental doctrine. He holds that the individual is his own jailer, his own liberator, the preserver or loser of his own Eden. Moral regeneration seems to him an individual, not a social, affair.

His style is easy, exact, flowing, and it shows the skill of a literary artist. He never strains after effect, never uses excessive ornament, never appears hurried. There was not another nineteenth-century prose master on either side of the Atlantic who could in fewer words or simpler language have secured the effect produced by *The Scarlet Letter*. He wished to be impressive in describing Phœbe, that sunbeam in *The House of the Seven Gables*, but he says simply : —

"She was like a prayer, offered up in the homeliest beauty of one's mother tongue."

Sincerity is the marked characteristic of this simplicity in style, and it makes an impression denied to the mere striver after effect, however cunning his art.

A writer of imperishable romances, a sympathetic revealer of the soul, a great moralist, a master of style, Hawthorne is to be classed with the greatest masters of English fiction. His artist's hand

"Wrought in a sad sincerity;
Himself from God he could not free."

HENRY WADSWORTH LONGFELLOW, 1807-1882

Life. — Longfellow, the most widely read of American poets, was born in Portland, Maine, in 1807. His father was a Harvard graduate, and his mother, like Bryant's, was descended from John and Priscilla Alden of Plymouth. Longfellow, when three years old, began to go to school, and, like Bryant, he published at the ripe age of thirteen his first poem, *Battle of Lovell's Pond*, which appeared in the *Portland Gazette*.

Portland made a great impression on the boy. To his early life there is due the love of the sea, which colors so much of his poetry. In his poem, *My Lost Youth*, he says: —

> "I remember the black wharves and the slips,
>   And the sea tides tossing free;
> And Spanish sailors with bearded lips,
> And the beauty and mystery of the ships,
>   And the magic of the sea."

He went to Bowdoin College, Maine, where he had Nathaniel Hawthorne for a classmate. In his senior year Longfellow wrote to his father, "I most eagerly aspire after future eminence in literature; my whole soul burns most ardently for it, and every earthly thought centers in it." His father replied, "There is not enough wealth in this country to afford encouragement and patronage to merely literary men. And as you have not had the fortune . . . to be born rich, you must adopt a profession which will afford you subsistence as well as reputation." The son then chose the law, saying, "This will support my real existence; literature, my ideal one." Bowdoin College, however, came to the rescue, and offered him the professorship of modern languages on condition that he would go abroad for study. He accepted the offer, and remained abroad three years. His travel sketches on this trip were published in book form in 1835, under the title of *Outre-Mer: A Pilgrimage beyond the Sea*. This is suggestive of the *Sketch Book* (p. 119), the earliest book which he remembered reading. After five years' service at Bowdoin, he accepted Harvard's offer of the professorship of modern languages and again went abroad. This journey was saddened by the death of his first wife. His prose romance, *Hyperion*, was one of the fruits of this sojourn abroad. The second Mrs. Longfellow, whose real name was Frances Appleton, appears in this book under the name of Mary

Ashburton. Her father bought the Craigie House, which had been Washington's headquarters in Cambridge, and gave it to Longfellow as a residence. In 1854, after eighteen years' teaching at Harvard, he resigned, for his means were then ample to enable him to devote his full time to literature.

From 1854 until 1861 he lived in reality the ideal existence of his youthful dreams. In 1861 his wife's summer

LONGFELLOW'S HOME, CRAIGIE HOUSE, CAMBRIDGE

dress caught fire, and although he struggled heroically to save her, she died the next day, and he himself was so severely burned that he could not attend her funeral. Years afterwards he wrote: —

> "Here in this room she died; and soul more white
> Never through martyrdom of fire was led
> To its repose."

Like Bryant, he sought refuge in translating. Longfellow chose Dante, and gave the world the fine rendering of his *Divine Comedy* (1867).

Outside of these domestic sorrows, Longfellow's life was

happy and prosperous. His home was blessed with attractive children. Loved by friends, honored by foreigners, possessed of rare sweetness and lovableness of disposition, he became the most popular literary man in America. He desired freedom from turmoil and from constant struggling for daily bread, and this freedom came to him in fuller measure than to most men.

The children of the country felt that he was their own special poet. The public schools of the United States celebrated his seventy-fifth birthday, February 27, 1882. Less than a month later he died, and was laid to rest in Mount Auburn cemetery, Cambridge.

"Laureate of the Common Human Heart." — "God must love the common people," said President Lincoln, "because he has made so many of them." Longfellow wrote for "the common human heart." In him the common people found a poet who could gild the commonplace things of life and make them seem more attractive, more easily borne, more important, more full of meaning.

In his first published volume of poems, *Voices of the Night* (1839), he shows his aim distinctly in such poems as *A Psalm of Life.*• Its lines are the essence of simplicity.

LONGFELLOW AS A YOUNG MAN

but they have instilled patience and noble purpose into many a humble human soul. The two stanzas beginning

"Life is real! Life is earnest,"

and

"Lives of great men all remind us,"

can be repeated by many who know but little poetry, and these very stanzas, as well as many others like them, have affected the lives of large numbers of people. Those born a generation ago not infrequently say that the following stanza from *The Ladder of St. Augustine* (1850) has been the stepping-stone to their success in life: —

"The heights by great men reached and kept
Were not attained by sudden flight,
But they, while their companions slept,
Were toiling upward in the night."

His poem, *The Rainy Day* (1841), has developed in many a person the qualities of patience, resignation, and hopefulness. Repetition makes the majority of things seem commonplace, but even repetition has not robbed lines like these of their power: —

"Be still, sad heart! and cease repining,
Behind the clouds is the sun still shining;
Thy fate is the common fate of all;
Into each life some rain must fall,
Some days must be dark and dreary."

Nine days before he died, he wrote his last lines with the same simplicity and hopefulness of former days: —

"Out of the shadows of night
The world rolls into light.
It is daybreak everywhere."

As we examine these typical poems, we shall find that all of them appeal to our common experiences or aspirations, and that all are expressed in that simple language which no one need read twice to understand.

Ballads. — Longfellow knew how to tell a story which preserved the simplicity and the vigor of the old ballad makers. His *The Wreck of the Hesperus* (1839) starts in the true fashion to make us wish to finish the tale: —

> "It was the schooner Hesperus,
>   That sailed the wintry sea;
> And the skipper had taken his little daughtèr
>   To bear him company."

Longfellow says that he wrote this ballad between twelve and three in the morning and that the composition did not come to him by lines, but by stanzas.

Even more vigorous is his ballad of *The Skeleton in Armor* (1840). The Viking hero of the tale, like young Lochinvar, won the heart of the heroine, the blue-eyed daughter of a Norwegian prince.

> "When of old Hildebrand
>   I asked his daughter's hand,
> Mute did the minstrels stand
>   To hear my story."

The Viking's suit was denied. He put the maiden on his vessel before he was detected and pursued by her father. Those who think that the gentle Longfellow could not write poetry as energetic as Scott's *Lochinvar* should read the following stanza: —

> "As with his wings aslant,
>   Sails the fierce cormorant,
>   Seeking some rocky haunt,
>   With his prey laden, —
> So toward the open main,
>   Beating to sea again,
>   Through the wild hurricane,
>   Bore I the maiden."

Those who are fond of this kind of poetry should turn to Longfellow's *Tales of a Wayside Inn* (1863), where they will find such favorites as *Paul Revere's Ride* and *The Birds of Killingworth*.

Longer Poems. — No other American poet has equaled Longfellow's longer narrative poems. Bryant and Poe would not attempt long poems. The flights of Whittier and Emerson were comparatively short. It is unusually difficult to write long poems that will be read. In the case of *Evangeline* (1847), *Hiawatha* (1855), and *The Courtship of Miles Standish* (1858), Longfellow proved an exception to the rule.

Evangeline is based upon an incident that occurred during the French and Indian War. In 1755 a force of British and colonial troops sailed from Boston to Acadia (Nova Scotia) and deported the French inhabitants. Hawthorne heard the story, how the English put Evangeline and her lover on different ships and how she began her long, sad search for him. When Hawthorne and Longfellow were discussing this one day at dinner at the Craigie House, the poet said, "If you really do not want this incident for a tale, let me have it for a poem." Hawthorne consented to give his classmate all poetical rights to the story.

Evangeline is the tale of a love "that hopes and endures and is patient." The metrical form, dactylic hexameter, is one that few of our poets have successfully used, and many have thought it wholly unfitted to English verse. Longfellow has certainly disproved their theory, for his success with this meter is pronounced. The long, flowing lines seem to be exactly adapted to give the scenes the proper atmosphere and to narrate the heroine's weary search. The poem became immediately popular. It was the first successful long narrative poem to appear in the United States. Whittier had studied the same subject, but had delayed making verses on it until he found that it had been suggested to Longfellow. In a complimentary review of the poem, Whittier said, " Longfellow was just the one to write it. If I had attempted it, I should have spoiled the artistic effect of the poem by my indignation at the treatment of the exiles by the colonial government."

From the moment that Evangeline appears, our interest does not lag.

" Fair was she to behold, that maiden of seventeen summers.

. . . .

When she had passed, it seemed like the ceasing of exquisite music."

The imagery of the poem is pleasing, no matter whether we are listening to "the murmuring pines and the hemlocks," the softly sounding Angelus, the gossiping looms, the whir of wings in the drowsy air, or seeing the barns bursting with hay, the air filled with a dreamy and mystical light, the forest arrayed in its robes of russet and scarlet and yellow, and the stars, those "forget-me-nots of the angels," blossoming "in the infinite meadows of heaven."

LONGFELLOW'S STUDY

The Song of Hiawatha was begun by Longfellow in 1854, after resigning the professorship of modern languages at Harvard. He seemed to revel in his new freedom, and in less than a year he had produced the poem by which he will probably be longest known to posterity. He studied Schoolcraft's *Algic Researches* and the same author's

History, Condition, and Prospects of the Indian Tribes of the United States, and familiarized himself with Indian legends. The simplicity of Longfellow's nature and his ability as a poetic artist seemed rarely suited to deal with these traditions of a race that never wholly emerged from childhood.

HIAWATHA

Longfellow's invitation to hear this *Song* does not include all, but only

"Ye whose hearts are fresh and simple,
Who have faith in God and nature."

Those who accept this invitation will rejoice to accompany Shawondasee, the South-Wind, when he sends northward the robin, bluebird, and swallow. They will also wish to go with Kabibonokka, the North-Wind, as he paints the autumn woods with scarlet and sends the snowflakes through the forests. They will be glad to be a child with Hiawatha, to hear again the magical voices of the forest, the whisper of the pines, the lapping of the waters, the hooting of the owl, to learn of every bird and beast its language, and especially to know the joy of calling them all brothers. They will gladly accompany Hiawatha to the land of the Dacotahs, when he woos Minnehaha, Laughing Water, and hears Owaissa, the bluebird, singing: —

"Happy are you, Hiawatha,
Having such a wife to love you!"

But the guests will be made of stern stuff if their eyes do not moisten when they hear Hiawatha calling in the midst of the famine of the cold and cruel winter: —

> "Give your children food, O father!
> Give us food or we must perish!
> Give me food for Minnehaha,
> For my dying Minnehaha."

Hiawatha overflows with the elemental spirit of childhood. The sense of companionship with all earth's creatures, the mystery of life and of Minnehaha's departure to the Kingdom of Ponemah, make a strong appeal to all who remember childhood's Eden.

The Courtship of Miles Standish (1858), in the same meter as *Evangeline*, is a romantic tale, the scene of which is laid

> "In the Old Colony days, in Plymouth, the land of the Pilgrims."

We see Miles Standish, the incarnation of the Puritan church militant, as he

> ". . . wistfully gazed on the landscape,
> Washed with a cold gray mist, the vapory breath of the east-wind,
> Forest and meadow and hill, and the steel-blue rim of the ocean,
> Lying silent and sad in the afternoon shadows and sunshine."

Priscilla Mullins, the heroine of the poem, is a general favorite. Longfellow and Bryant were both proud to trace their descent from her. This poem introduces her

> "Seated beside her wheel, and the carded wool like a snow-drift
> Piled at her knee, her white hands feeding the ravenous spindle,
> While with her foot on the treadle she guided the wheel in its motion.
>   .   .   .   .   .   .
> She, the Puritan girl, in the solitude of the forest,
> Making the humble house and the modest apparel of homespun
> Beautiful with her beauty, and rich with the wealth of her being!"

This story has more touches of humor than either *Evangeline* or *Hiawatha*. Longfellow uses with fine effect the contradiction between the preaching of the bluff old captain, that you must do a thing yourself if you want it well done, and his practice in sending by John Alden an offer of marriage to Priscilla. Her reply has become classic:

"Why don't you speak for yourself, John?"

Longfellow's *Christus, a Mystery*, was the title finally given by him to three apparently separate poems, published under the titles, *The Golden Legend* (1851), *The Divine Tragedy* (1871), and *The New England Tragedies* (1868). His idea was to represent the origin, the medieval aspect, and the Puritan conception of Christianity — a task not well suited to Longfellow's genius. *The Golden Legend* is the most poetic, but *The New England Tragedies* is the most likely to be read in future years, not for its poetic charms, but because it presents two phases of New England's colonial history, the persecution of the Quakers and the Salem witchcraft delusion.

General Characteristics. — An eminent Scotch educator says that Longfellow has probably taught more people to love poetry than any other nineteenth-century poet, English or American. He is America's best and most widely read story-teller in verse. Success in long narrative poems is rare in any literature. Probably the majority of critics would find it difficult to agree on any English poet since Chaucer who has surpassed Longfellow in this field.

He has achieved the unusual distinction of making the commonplace attractive and beautiful. He is the poet of the home, of the common people, and of those common objects in nature which in his verses convey a lesson to all. He has proved a moral stimulus to his age and he has further helped to make the world kindlier and its troubles more easily borne. This was his message: —

> "Bear through sorrow, wrong and ruth
> In thy heart the dew of youth,
> On thy lips the smile of truth."

His poetry is usually more tinctured with feeling than with thought. Diffuseness is his greatest fault. The *Sonnets* of his later years and an occasional poem, like *Morituri Salutamus* (1875), show more condensation, but parts of even *Hiawatha* would be much improved if told in fewer words.

Some complain that Longfellow finds in books too much of the source of his inspiration; that, although he did not live far from Evangeline's country, he never visited it, and that others had to tell him to substitute pines or hemlocks for chestnut trees. Many critics have found fault with his poetry because it does not offer "sufficient obstruction to the stream of thought," — because it does not make the mind use its full powers in wrestling with the meaning. It is a mistake, however, to underestimate the virtues of clearness and simplicity. Many great men who have been unsuccessful in their struggle to secure these qualities have consequently failed to reach the ear of the world with a message. While other poets should be read for mental development, the large heart of the world still finds a place for Longfellow, who has voiced its hopes that

> ". . . the night shall be filled with music,
> And the cares that infest the day,
> Shall fold their tents like the Arabs,
> And as silently steal away."

Like most Puritans, Longfellow is usually over-anxious to teach a lesson; but the world must learn, and no one has surpassed him as a poetic teacher of the masses.

THE NEW ENGLAND GROUP

JOHN GREENLEAF WHITTIER, 1807-1892

Life. — Whittier says that the only unusual circumstance about the migration of his Puritan ancestor to New England in 1638 was the fact that he brought over with him a hive of bees. The descendants of this very hive probably suggested the poem, *Telling the Bees*, for it was an old English custom to go straightway to the hive and tell the bees whenever a member of the family died. It was believed that they would swarm and seek another home if this information was withheld. The poet has made both the bees and the snows of his northern home famous. He was born in 1807 in the same house that his first American ancestor built in East Haverhill, about thirty-two miles northwest of Boston. The Whittiers were farmers who for generations had wrung little more than a bare subsistence from the soil. The boy's frail health was early broken by the severe labor. He had to milk seven cows, plow with a yoke of oxen, and keep busy from dawn until dark.

Unlike the other members of the New England group of authors, Whittier never went to college. He received only the scantiest education in the schools near his home. The family was so poor that he had to work as a cobbler, making slippers at eight cents a pair, in order to attend the Haverhill academy for six months. He calculated his expenses so exactly that he had just twenty-five cents left at the end of the term.

Two events in his youth had strong influence on his future vocation. When he was fourteen, his school-teacher read aloud to the family from the poems of Robert Burns. The boy was entranced, and, learning that Burns had been merely a plowman, felt that there was hope for himself. He borrowed the volume of poems and read them again and again. Of this experience, he says: "This was about the first poetry I had ever read (with the exception of the *Bible*, of which I had been a close student) and it had a lasting influence upon me. I began to make rhymes myself and to imagine stories and adventures." The second event was the appearance in print of some of his verses, which his sister had, unknown to him, sent to a Newburyport paper edited by William Lloyd Garrison. The great abolitionist thought enough of the poetry to ride out to

Whittier's home and urge him to get an education. This event made an indelible impression on the lad's memory.

Realizing that his health would not allow him to make his living on a farm, he tried teaching school, but, like Thoreau, found that occupation distasteful. Through Garrison's influence, Whittier at the age of twenty-one procured an editorial position in Boston. At various times he served as editor on more than half a dozen different papers, until his own health or his father's brought him back to the farm. Such occupation taught him how to write prose, of which he had produced enough at the time of his death to fill three good-sized volumes, but his prose did not secure the attention given to his verse. While in Hartford, editing *The New England Review*, he fell in love with Miss Cornelia Russ, and a few days before he finally left the city, he wrote a proposal to her in three hundred words of wandering prose. Had he expressed his feelings in one of his inimitable ballads, it is possible that he might have been accepted, for neither she nor he ever married. In the year of her death, he wrote his poem, *Memories*, which recounts some recollections earlier than his Hartford experiences: —

> "A beautiful and happy girl,
>   With step as light as summer air,
> Eyes glad with smiles, and brow of pearl
> Shadowed by many a careless curl
>   Of unconfined and flowing hair;
> A seeming child in everything,
>   Save thoughtful brow and ripening charms,
> As nature wears the smile of Spring
>   When sinking into Summer's arms."

He was a Quaker and he came to Hartford in the homespun clothes of the cut of his sect. He may have been thinking of Miss Russ and wondering whether theology had anything to do with her refusal, when in after years he wrote : —

"Thine the Genevan's sternest creed,
While answers to my spirit's need
The Derby dalesman's simple truth."

As Whittier was a skillful politician, he had hopes of making a name for himself in politics as well as in literature. He was chosen to represent his district in the state legislature and there is little doubt that he would have been sent to the national congress later, had he not taken

WHITTIER AT THE AGE OF TWENTY-NINE

a step which for a long time shut off all avenues of preferment. In 1833 he joined the abolitionists. This step had very nearly the same effect on his fortunes as the public declaration of an adherence to the doctrines of anarchy would to-day have on a man similarly situated. The best magazines at the North would not open their pages to him. He was even mobbed, and the office of an anti-slavery paper, which he was editing in Philadelphia, was sacked. He wrote many poems to aid the abolition cause. These were really editorials expressed in verse, which caught the attention in a way denied to prose. For more than thirty years such verse constituted the most of his poetical production. Lowell noticed that the Quaker doctrine of peace did not deter Whittier from his vigorous attack on slavery. In *A Fable for Critics* (1848), Lowell asks:—

> ". . . O leather-clad Fox?
> Can that be thy son, in the battle's mid din,
> Preaching brotherly love and then driving it in
> To the brain of the tough old Goliath of sin,
> With the smoothest of pebbles from Castaly's spring
> Impressed on his hard moral sense with a sling?"

Whittier did, however, try to keep the spirit of brotherly love warm throughout his life. He always preferred to win his cause from an enemy peacefully. When he was charged with hating the people of the South, he wrote:—

"I was never an enemy to the South or the holders of slaves. I inherited from my Quaker ancestry hatred of slavery, but not of slaveholders. To every call of suffering or distress in the South, I have promptly responded to the extent of my ability. I was one of the very first to recognize the rare gift of the Carolinian poet Timrod, and I was the intimate friend of the lamented Paul H. Hayne, though both wrote fiery lyrics against the North."

With a few striking exceptions, his most popular poems were written after the close of the Civil War. His greatest poem, *Snow-Bound*, was published in the year after the cessation of hostilities (1866). His last thirty years were a time of comparative calm. He wrote poetry as the spirit moved him. He had grown to be loved everywhere at the North, and his birthday, like Longfellow's, was the occasion for frequent celebrations. For years before the close of the war, in fact until *Snow-Bound* appeared, he was very poor, but the first edition of that poem brought him in ten thousand dollars, and after that he was never again troubled by poverty. In a letter written in 1866, he says:—

"If my health allowed me to write I could make money easily now, as my anti-slavery reputation does not injure me in the least, at the present time. For twenty years I was shut out from the favor of booksellers and magazine editors, but I was enabled by rigid economy to live in spite of them."

His fixed home for almost all of his life was in the valley of the Merrimac River, at East Haverhill, until 1836, and

KITCHEN FIREPLACE IN WHITTIER'S HOME, EAST HAVERHILL, MASS.

then at Amesbury, only a few miles east of his birthplace. He died in 1892 and was buried in the Amesbury cemetery.

Poetry. — Although Whittier wrote much forcible anti-slavery verse, most of this has already been forgotten, because it was directly fashioned to appeal to the interests of the time. One of the strongest of these poems is *Ichabod* (1850), a bitter arraignment of Daniel Webster, because Whittier thought that the great orator's *Seventh* *of March Speech* of that year advised a compromise with slavery. Webster writhed under Whittier's criticism more than under that of any other man.

> ". . . from those great eyes
> The soul has fled:
> When faith is lost, when honor dies
> The man is dead!"

Thirty years later, Whittier, feeling that perhaps Webster merely intended to try to save the Union and do away with slavery without a conflict, wrote *The Lost Occasion*, in which he lamented the too early death of the great orator:—

> " Some die too late and some too soon,
> At early morning, heat of noon,
> Or the chill evening twilight. Thou,
> Whom the rich heavens did so endow
> With eyes of power and Jove's own brow,
>
> . . . . . .
>
> Too soon for us, too soon for thee,
> Beside thy lonely Northern sea,
> Where long and low the marsh-lands spread,
> Laid wearily down thy august head."

Whittier is emphatically the poet of New England. His verses which will live the longest are those which spring directly from its soil. His poem entitled *The Barefoot Boy* tells how the typical New England farmer's lad acquired:—

> " Knowledge never learned of schools,
> Of the wild bee's morning chase,
> Of the wild flower's time and place,
> Flight of fowl and habitude
> Of the tenants of the wood."

His greatest poem, the one by which he will probably be chiefly known to posterity, is *Snow-Bound*, which describes the life of a rural New England household. At the beginning of this poem of 735 lines, the coming of the all-enveloping snowstorm, with its "ghostly finger tips of sleet" on the window-panes, is the central event, but we soon realize that this storm merely serves to focus intensely the New England life with which he was familiar. The household is shut in from the outside world by the snow, and there is nothing else to distract the attention from the picture of isolated Puritan life. There is not another poet

WHITTIER'S BIRTHPLACE IN WINTER (SCENE OF "SNOW-BOUND")

in America who has produced such a masterpiece under such limitations. One prose writer, Hawthorne, in *The Scarlet Letter*, had indeed taken even more unpromising materials and achieved one of the greatest successes in English romance, but in this special narrow field Whittier has not yet been surpassed by poets.

The sense of isolation and what painters would call "the atmosphere" are conveyed in lines like these: —

> "Shut in from all the world without,
> We sat the clean-winged hearth about,

> Content to let the north wind roar
> In baffled rage at pane and door,
> While the red logs before us beat
> The frost line back with tropic heat;
> And ever when a louder blast
> Shook beam and rafter as it passed,
> The merrier up its roaring draught
> The great throat of the chimney laughed."

In such a focus he shows the life of the household; the mother, who often left her home to attend sick neighbors, now: —

> "... seeking to express
> Her grateful sense of happiness
> For food and shelter, warmth and health,
> And love's contentment, more than wealth,"

the uncle: —

> "... innocent of books,
> Was rich in lore of fields and brooks,
>
> . . . . .
>
> A simple, guileless, childlike man,
> Strong only on his native grounds,
> The little world of sights and sounds
> Whose girdle was the parish bounds,"

the aunt, who: —

> "Found peace in love's unselfishness,"

the sister: —

> "A full rich nature, free to trust,
> Truthful and even sternly just,
> Impulsive, earnest, prompt to act,
> And make her generous thought a fact,
> Keeping with many a light disguise
> The secret of self-sacrifice."

Some read *Snow-Bound* for its pictures of nature and some for its still more remarkable portraits of the members of that household. This poem has achieved for the New England fireside what Burns accomplished for the hearths of Scotland in *The Cotter's Saturday Night*.

Whittier wrote many fine short lyrical poems, such as *Ichabod*, *The Lost Occasion*, *My Playmate* (which was Tennyson's favorite), *In School Days*, *Memories*, *My Triumph*, *Telling the Bees*, *The Eternal Goodness*, and the second part of *A Sea Dream*. His narrative poems and ballads are second only to Longfellow's. *Maud Muller*, *Skipper Ireson's Ride*, *Cassandra Southwick*, *Barbara Frietchie*, and *Mabel Martin* are among the best of these.

General Characteristics. — Whittier and Longfellow resemble each other in simplicity. Both are the poets of the masses, of those whose lives most need the consolation of poetry. Both suffer from diffuseness, Whittier in his greatest poems less than Longfellow. Whittier was self-educated, and he never traveled far from home. His range is narrower than Longfellow's, who was college bred and broadened by European travel. But if Whittier's poetic range is narrower, if he is the poet of only the common things of life, he shows more intensity of feeling. Often his simplest verse comes from the depths of his heart. He wrote *In School Days* forty years after the grass had been growing on the grave of the little girl who spelled correctly the word which the boy had missed: —

> "'I'm sorry that I spelt the word:
>   I hate to go above you,
> Because,' — the brown eyes lower fell, —
>   'Because you see, I love you!'
>
> . . . . .
>
> "He lives to learn, in life's hard school,
>   How few who pass above him
> Lament their triumph and his loss,
>   Like her, — because they love him."

Whittier's simplicity, genuineness, and sympathetic heart stand revealed in those lines.

His youthful work shows traces of the influence of many poets, but he learned most from Robert Burns. Whittier himself says that it was Burns who taught him to see

> ". . . through all familiar things
> The romance underlying,"

and especially to note that

> "Through all his tuneful art, how strong
> The human feeling gushes!"

The critics have found three indictments against Whittier; first, for the unequal value of his poetry; second, for its loose rhymes; and third, for too much moralizing. He would probably plead guilty to all of these indictments. His tendency to moralize is certainly excessive, but critics have too frequently forgotten that this very moralizing draws him closer to the heart of suffering humanity. There are times when the majority of human beings feel the need of the consolation which he brings in his religious verse and in such lines as these from *Snow-Bound:* —

> "Alas for him who never sees
> The stars shine through his cypress trees
> Who, hopeless, lays his dead away,
> Nor looks to see the breaking day
> Across the mournful marbles play!
> Who hath not learned, in hours of faith,
> The truth to flesh and sense unknown,
> That Life is ever lord of Death
> And Love can never lose its own!"

He strives to impress on all the duty of keeping the windows of the heart open to the day and of "finding peace in love's unselfishness."

JAMES RUSSELL LOWELL, 1819-1891

Early Years. — James Russell Lowell, the son of the Rev. Charles Lowell, was a descendant of one of the best of the old New England families. The city of Lowell and the Lowell Institute of Boston received their names from uncles of the author. His mother's name was Spence, and she used to tell her son that the Spence family, which was of Scotch origin, was decended from Sir Patrick Spens of ballad fame. She loved to sing to her boy in the gloaming : —

> "O forty miles off Aberdeen,
>   'Tis fifty fathoms deep,
> And there lies gude Sir Patrick Spens,
>   Wi' the Scots lords at his feet."

From her Celtic blood her son inherited a tendency toward poetry. When a child, he was read to sleep with Spenser's *Faerie Queene* and he found amusement in retelling its stories to his playmates.

James Russell Lowell was born in 1819, in the suburbs of Cambridge, Massachusetts, in the fine old historic home called "Elmwood," which was one of the few homes to witness the birth and death of a great American author and to remain his native residence for seventy-two years.

LOWELL'S MOTHER

His early opportunities were in striking contrast to those of Whittier; for Lowell, like his ancestors for three generations, went to Harvard. Because of what the Lowell side of his family called "the Spence negligence," he was suspended from college for inattention to his studies and sent to Concord to be coached by a tutor. We know, however, that a part of Lowell's negligence was due to his reading and imitating such poetry as suited his fancy. It was fortunate that he was sent to Concord, for there he had the opportunity of meeting Emerson and Thoreau and of drinking in patriotism as he walked "the rude bridge that arch'd the flood" (p. 179). He was elected class poet, but he was not allowed to return in time to deliver his poem before his classmates, although he received his degree with them in 1838.

Marriage and New Impulses. — Like Irving and Bryant, Lowell studied law, and then gave up that profession for literature. In 1839 he met Miss Maria White, a transcendentalist of noble impulses. Before this he had made fun of the abolitionists, but under her influence he followed men like Whittier into the anti-slavery ranks. She was herself a poet and she wrote to Lowell after they became engaged: —

> "I love thee for thyself — thyself alone;
>   For that great soul whose breath most full and rare
>   Shall to humanity a message bear,
> Flooding their dreary waste with organ tone."

Under such inspiration, "the Spence negligence" left him, and with rapid steps he entered the temple of fame. In December, 1844, the month in which he married her, he wrote the finest lines ever penned by him: —

> "Truth forever on the scaffold, Wrong forever on the throne,—
>   Yet that scaffold sways the future, and, behind the dim unknown,
>   Standeth God within the shadow, keeping watch above his own."

Lowell's twenty-ninth year, 1848, is called his *annus mirabilis*, the wonderful year of his life. He had published small volumes of poems in 1840, 1843, and 1847, but in 1848 there appeared three of his most famous works, — *The Biglow Papers, First Series, A Fable for Critics*, and *The Vision of Sir Launfal*.

As Mrs. Lowell's health was delicate, Lowell took her abroad, in 1851, for a year's stay. Thackeray came over on the same ship with them, on their return in 1852, and proved a genial companion. The next year Mrs. Lowell died. When he thought of the inspiration which she had given him and of the thirteen years of her companionship, he said, "It is a million times better to have had her and lost her, than to have had and kept any other woman I ever saw."

Later Work. — After his great bereavement in 1853, Lowell became one of America's greatest prose writers. In 1855 he was appointed Longfellow's successor in the Harvard professorship of modern languages and polite literature, a position which he held, with the exception of two years spent in European travel, until 1877. The duties of his chair called for wide reading and frequent lecturing, and he turned much of his attention toward writing critical essays. The routine work of his professorship often grew irksome and the "Spence negligence" was sometimes in evidence in his failure to meet his classes. As a teacher, he was, however, frequently very stimulating.

MRS. MARIA WHITE LOWELL

He was the editor of the *Atlantic Monthly*, from its beginning in 1857 until 1861. All of the second series of the *Biglow Papers* appeared in this magazine. From 1864 to 1872 he was one of the editors of the *North American Review*.

In 1877 he became the minister of the United States to Spain. The Spanish welcomed him to the post that Washington Irving had once filled. In 1880 Lowell was transferred to England, where he represented his country until 1885. No other American minister has ever proved a greater success in England. He was respected for his literary attainments and for his ability as a speaker. He had the reputation of being one of the very best speakers in the Kingdom, and he was in much demand to speak at banquets and on special occasions. Many of his articles and speeches were on political subjects, the greatest of these being his address on *Democracy*, at Birmingham, in 1884.

Although his later years showed his great achievements in prose, he did not cease to produce poetry. The second series of the *Biglow Papers* was written during the Civil War. His *Ode Recited at the Harvard Commemoration* in 1865, in honor of those who fell in freeing the slave,

"Who in warm life-blood wrote their nobler verse,"

his three memorial poems: (1) *Ode Read at the One Hundredth Anniversary of the Fight at Concord Bridge* (1875), (2) *Under the Old Elm* (1875), written in commemoration of Washington's taking command of the Continental forces under that tree, a century before, and (3) *Ode for the Fourth of July*, 1876, are well-known patriotic American poems.

After returning from England and passing from the excitement of diplomatic and social life to a quiet New England home, he wrote:—

"I take my reed again and blow it free
  Of dusty silence, murmuring, 'Sing to me.'
And, as its stops my curious touch retries,
The stir of earlier instincts I surprise,—
Instincts, if less imperious, yet more strong,
And happy in the toil that ends with song."

In 1888 he published a volume of poems called *Heartsease and Rue*. He died in 1891 and was buried in Mount Auburn Cemetery, near his "Elmwood" home, not far from the last resting place of Longfellow.

LOWELL'S STUDY, ELMWOOD

Poetry. — Lowell wrote many short lyrical poems, which rank high. Some of them, like *Our Love is not a Fading Earthly Flower*, *O Moonlight Deep and Tender*, *To the Dandelion*, and *The First Snow-Fall* are exquisite lyrics of nature and sentiment. Others, like *The Present Crisis*, have for their text, "Humanity sweeps onward," and teach high moral ideals. Still others, like his poems written in commemoration of some event, are instinct with patriotism.

He is best known for three long poems, *The Biglow Papers*, *A Fable for Critics*, and *The Vision of Sir Launfal*. All of these, with the exception of the second series of *The Biglow Papers*, appeared in his wonderful poetic year, 1848.

He will, perhaps, be longest known to posterity for that remarkable series of papers written in what he called the Yankee dialect and designed at first to stop the extension of slavery and afterwards to suppress it. These are called "Biglow Papers" because the chief author is represented to be Hosea Biglow, a typical New England farmer. The immediate occasion of the first series of these *Papers* was the outbreak of the Mexican War in 1846. Lowell said in after years, "I believed our war with Mexico to be essentially a war of false pretences, and that it would result in widening the boundaries and so prolonging the life of slavery." The second series of these *Papers*, dealing with our Civil War, began to be published in the *Atlantic Monthly* in 1862. The poem lives to-day, however, not for its censure of the war or for its attack on slavery, but for its expression of the mid-nineteenth century New England ideals, hard common sense, and dry humor. Where shall we turn for a more incisive statement of the Puritan's attitude toward pleasure?

> "Pleasure doos make us Yankees kind o' winch,
> Ez though 't wuz sunthin' paid for by the inch;
> But yit we du contrive to worry thru,
> Ef Dooty tells us thet the thing's to du,
> An' kerry a hollerday, ef we set out,
> Ez stiddily ez though 't wuz a redoubt."

The homely New England common-sense philosophy is in evidence throughout the *Papers*. We frequently meet such expressions as: —

> "I like the plain all wool o' common-sense
> Thet warms ye now, an' will a twelve-month hence."

> "Now's the only bird lays eggs o' gold."

"Democ'acy gives every man
The right to be his own oppressor."

"But Chance is like an amberill, — it don't take twice to lose it."

"An' you've gut to git up airly,
Ef you want to take in God."

In the second series of the *Papers*, there is one of Lowell's best lyrics, *The Courtin'*. It would be difficult to find another poem which gives within the compass of four lines a better characterization of many a New England maiden: —

". . . she was jes' the quiet kind
Whose natur's never vary,
Like streams that keep a summer mind,
Snowhid in Jenooary."

This series contains some of Lowell's best nature poetry. We catch rare glimpses of

"Moonshine an' snow on field an' hill
All silence an' all glisten,"

and we actually see a belated spring

"Toss the fields full o' blossoms, leaves, an' birds."

The Vision of Sir Launfal has been the most widely read of Lowell's poems. This is the *vision* of a search for the Holy Grail. Lowell in a letter to a friend called the poem "a sort of story and more likely to be popular than what I write about generally." But the best part of the poem is to be found in the apotheosis of the New England June, in the *Prelude* to *Part I.*: —

"And what is so rare as a day in June?
Then, if ever, come perfect days;
Then Heaven tries the earth if it be in tune,
And over it softly her warm ear lays."

The poem teaches a noble lesson of sympathy with suffering:—

> "Not what we give, but what we share,—
> For the gift without the giver is bare;
> Who gives himself with his alms feeds three,—
> Himself, his hungering neighbor, and Me."

Lowell said that he "scrawled at full gallop" *A Fable for Critics*, which is a humorous poem of about two thousand long lines, presenting an unusually excellent criticism of his contemporary authors. In this most difficult type of criticism, Lowell was not infallible; but a comparison of his criticisms with the verdicts generally accepted to-day will show his unusual ability in this field. Not a few of these criticisms remain the best of their kind, and they serve to focus many of the characteristics of the authors of the first half of the nineteenth century. It will benefit all writers, present and prospective, to read this criticism on Bryant:—

> "He is almost the one of your poets that knows
> How much grace, strength, and dignity lie in Repose;
> If he sometimes fall short, he is too wise to mar
> His thought's modest fulness by going too far;
> 'Twould be well if your authors should all make a trial
> Of what virtue there is in severe self-denial,
> And measure their writings by Hesiod's staff,
> Who teaches that all has less value than half."

Especially humorous are those lines which give a recipe for the making of a Washington Irving and those which describe the idealistic philosophy of Emerson:—

> "In whose mind all creation is duly respected
> As parts of himself — just a little projected."

Prose. — Lowell's literary essays entitle him to rank as a great American critic. The chief of these are to be found gathered in three volumes: *Among My Books* (1870), *My Study Windows* (1871), *Among My Books, Second Series* (1876). These volumes as originally issued contain 1140 pages. If we should wish to persuade a group of moderately intelligent persons to read less fiction and more solid literature, it is doubtful if we could accomplish our purpose more easily than by inducing them to dip into some of these essays. Lowell had tested many of them on his college students, and he had noted what served to kindle interest and to produce results. We may recommend five of his greater literary essays, which would give a vivid idea of the development of English poetry from Chaucer to the death of Pope. These five are: *Chaucer*, in *My Study Windows; Spenser*, in *Among My Books, Second Series; Shakespeare Once More*, and *Dryden*, in *Among My Books, First Series;* and *Pope*, in *My Study Windows*. If we add to these the short addresses on *Wordsworth* and *Coleridge*, delivered in England, and printed in the volume *Democracy and Other Addresses* (1886), we shall have the incentive to continue the study of poetry into the nineteenth century.

Lowell's criticism provokes thought. It will not submit to a passive reading. It expresses truth in unique and striking ways. Speaking of the French and Italian sources on which Chaucer drew, Lowell says : —

"Should a man discover the art of transmuting metals, and present us with a lump of gold as large as an ostrich egg, would it be in human nature to inquire too nicely whether he had stolen the lead ? . . .

"Chaucer, like Shakespeare, invented almost nothing. Wherever he found anything directed to Geoffrey Chaucer, he took it and made the most of it. . . .

"Sometimes he describes amply by the merest hint, as where the Friar, before setting himself softly down, drives away the cat. We know without need of more words that he has chosen the snuggest corner."

Lowell usually makes the laziest readers do a little pleasant thinking. It is common for even inert students to investigate his meaning; for instance, in his statements that in the age of Pope "everybody ceremoniously took a bushel basket to bring a wren's egg to market in," and that everybody "called everything something else."

The high ideals and sterling common sense of Lowell's political prose deserve special mention. In *Democracy* (1886), which should be read by every citizen, Lowell shows that old age had not shattered his faith in ideals. "I believe," he said, "that the real will never find an irremovable basis until it rests on the ideal." Voters and lawmakers are to-day beginning to realize that they will go far to find in the same compass a greater amount of common sense than is contained in these words: —

"It is only when the reasonable and the practicable are denied that men demand the unreasonable and impracticable; only when the possible is made difficult that they fancy the impossible to be easy. Fairy tales are made out of the dreams of the poor."[1]

General Characteristics. — Lowell has written verse which shows sympathetic treatment of nature. His lines *To the Dandelion:* —

"Dear common flower, that grow'st beside the way,
Fringing the dusty road with harmless gold,
    First pledge of blithesome May
Which children pluck, and full of pride uphold

. . . . .

. . . thou art more dear to me
Than all the prouder summer-blooms may be,"

[1] *Democracy and Other Addresses*, p. 15.

show rare genuineness of feeling.   No one not enthusiastic about nature would ever have heard her calling to him : —

> " To mix his blood with sunshine, and to take
> The winds into his pulses."

He invites us in March to watch : —

> " The bluebird, shifting his light load of song
> From post to post along the cheerless fence,"

and in June to lie under the willows and rejoice with

> " The thin-winged swallow, skating on the air."

Another pronounced characteristic which he has in common with the New England group is nobility of ideals. His poem entitled *For an Autograph*, voices in one line the settled conviction of his life : —

> "Not failure, but low aim, is crime."

He is America's greatest humorist in verse. *The Biglow Papers* and *A Fable for Critics* are ample justification for such an estimate.

As Lowell grew older, his poetry, dominated too much by his acute intellect, became more and more abstract. In *Under the Old Elm*, for example, he speaks of Washington as : —

> " The equestrian shape with unimpassioned brow
> That paces silent on through vistas of acclaim."

It is possible to read fifty consecutive lines of his *Commemoration Ode* without finding any but abstract or general terms, which are rarely the warp and woof out of which the best poetry is spun. This criticism explains why repeated readings of some of his poems leave so little impression on the mind. Some of the poetry of his later life is, however, concrete and sensuous, as the following lines from his poem *Agassiz* (1874) show : —

> "To lie in buttercups and clover-bloom,
>   Tenants in common with the bees,
>   And watch the white clouds drift through gulfs of trees,
> Is better than long waiting in the tomb."

In prose literary criticism, he keeps his place with Poe at the head of American writers. Lowell's sentences are usually simple in form and easily understood; they are frequently enlivened by illuminating figures of rhetoric and by humor, or rendered impressive by the striking way in which they express thought, *e.g.* "The foolish and the dead alone never change their opinion." A pun, digression, or out-of-the-way allusion may occasionally provoke readers, but onlookers have frequently noticed that few wrinkle their brows while reading his critical essays, and that a pleased expression, such as photographers like, is almost certain to appear. He has the rare faculty of making his readers think hard enough for agreeable exercise, and yet he spares them undue fatigue and rarely takes them among miry bogs or through sandy deserts.

Lowell's versatility is a striking characteristic. He was a poet, reformer, college professor, editor, literary critic, diplomatist, speaker, and writer on political subjects. We feel that he sometimes narrowly escaped being a genius, and that he might have crossed the boundary line into genius-land, if he had confined his attention to one department of literature and had been willing to write at less breakneck speed, taking time and thought to prune, revise, and suppress more of his productions. Not a few, however, think that Lowell, in spite of his defects, has left the impress of genius on some of his work. When his sonnet, *Our Love is not a Fading Earthly Flower*, was read to a cultured group, some who did not recognize the authorship of the verses thought that they were Shakespeare's.

OLIVER WENDELL HOLMES, 1809-1894

Life. — The year 1809 was prolific in the birth of great men, producing Holmes, Poe, Lincoln, Tennyson, and Darwin. Holmes was descended from Anne Bradstreet, New England's "Tenth Muse" (p. 39). His father was a Congregational clergyman, preaching at Cambridge when Oliver was born. The family was in comfortable circumstances, and the boy was reared in a cultured atmosphere. In middle age Holmes wrote, "I like books, — I was born and bred among them, and have the easy feeling, when I get into their presence, that a stable boy has among horses."

He graduated from Harvard in the famous class of 1829, for which he afterward wrote many anniversary poems. He went to Paris to study medicine, a science that held his interest through life. For thirty-five years he was professor of anatomy in the Harvard Medical School, where he was the only member of the faculty who could at the end of the day take the class, fagged and wearied, and by his wit, stories, and lively illustrations both instruct and interest the students.

His announcement, "small fevers gratefully received," his humor in general, and his poetry especially, did not aid him in securing patients. His biographer says that Holmes learned at his cost as a doctor that the world had made up its mind "that he who writes rhymes must not write prescriptions, and he who makes jests should not escort people to their graves." He later warned his students that if they would succeed in any one calling they must not let the world find out that they were interested in anything else. From his own point of view, he wrote:—

"It's a vastly pleasing prospect, when you're screwing out a laugh,
That your very next year's income is diminished by a half,
And a little boy trips barefoot that your Pegasus may go,
And the baby's milk is watered that your Helicon may flow."

He was driven, like Emerson and Lowell, to supplement his modest income by what he called "lecture peddling." Although Holmes did not have the platform presence of these two contemporaries, he had the power of reaching his audiences and of quickly gaining their sympathy, so that he was very popular and could always get engagements.

His scientific training made him intolerant of any philosophical or religious creed which seemed to him to be based merely upon superstition or tradition. He was thoroughly alert, open-minded, and liberal upon all such questions. On subjects of politics, war, or the abolition of slavery, he was, on the other hand, strongly conservative. He had the aristocratic dread of change. He was distinctly the courtly gentleman, the gifted talker, and the social, genial, refined companion.

Holmes was a conscientious worker, but he characteristically treated his mental processes in a joking way, and wrote to a friend: "I like nine tenths of any matter I study, but I do not like to *lick the plate*. If I did, I suppose I should be more of a man of science and find my brain tired oftener than I do." Again he wrote, "my nature is to snatch at all the fruits of knowledge and take a good bite out of the sunny side — after that let in the pigs." Despite these statements, Holmes worked steadily every year at his medical lectures. He was very particular about the exactness and finish of all that he wrote, and he was neither careless nor slipshod in anything. His life, while filled with steady, hard work, was a placid one, full of love and friendships, and he passed into his eightieth year with a young heart. He died in 1894, at the age of eighty-five, and was buried in Mt. Auburn cemetery not far from Longfellow and Lowell.

Poetry. — In 1836 he published his first volume of verse. This contained his first widely known poem, *Old Ironsides*, a successful plea for saving the old battleship, *Constitution*, which had been ordered destroyed. With the exception of this poem and *The Last Leaf*, the volume is remarkable for little except the rollicking fun which we find in such favorites as *The Ballad of the Oysterman* and *My Aunt*. This type of humor is shown in this simile from *The Ballad*: —

"Her hair drooped round her pallid cheeks, like seaweed on a clam,"

and in his description of his aunt: —

"Her waist is ampler than her life,
    For life is but a span."

He continued to write verses until his death. Among the last poems which he wrote were memorials on the death of Lowell (1891) and Whittier (1892). As we search the three volumes of his verse, we find few serious poems of a high order. The best, and the one by which he himself wished to be remembered, is *The Chambered Nautilus*. No member of the New England group voiced higher ideals than we find in the noble closing stanza of this poem: —

"Build thee more stately mansions, O my soul,
    As the swift seasons roll!
    Leave thy low-vaulted past!
Let each new temple, nobler than the last,
Shut thee from heaven with a dome more vast,
    Till thou at length art free,
Leaving thine outgrown shell by life's unresting sea!"

Probably *The Last Leaf*, which was such a favorite with Lincoln, would rank second. This poem is remarkable for preserving the reader's equilibrium between laughter and tears. Some lines from *The Voiceless* are not likely to be soon forgotten: —

"A few can touch the magic string,
    And noisy Fame is proud to win them: —
Alas for those that never sing,
    But die with all their music in them!"

He wrote no more serious poem than *Homesick in Heaven*, certain stanzas of which appeal strongly to bereaved hearts. It is not easy to forget the song of the spirits who have recently come from earth, of the mother who was torn from her clinging babe, of the bride called away with the kiss of love still burning on her cheek, of the daughter taken from her blind and helpless father : —

> " Children of earth, our half-weaned nature clings
> To earth's fond memories, and her whispered name
> Untunes our quivering lips, our saddened strings;
> For there we loved, and where we love is home."

When Holmes went to Oxford in 1886, to receive an honorary degree, it is probable that, as in the case of Irving (p. 122), the Oxford boys in the gallery voiced the popular verdict. As Holmes stepped on the platform, they called, " Did he come in the One-Hoss Shay?" This humorous poem, first known as *The Deacon's Masterpiece*, has been a universal favorite. *How the Old Hoss Won the Bet* tells with rollicking humor what the parson's nag did at a race. *The Boys*, with its mingled humor and pathos, written for the thirtieth reunion of his class, is one of the best of the many poems which he was so frequently asked to compose for special celebrations. No other poet of his time could equal him in furnishing to order clever, apt, humorous verses for ever recurring occasions.

Prose. — He was nearly fifty when he published his first famous prose work. He had named the *Atlantic Monthly*, and Lowell had agreed to edit it only on condition that Holmes would promise to be a contributor. In the first number appeared *The Autocrat of the Breakfast Table*. Holmes had hit upon a style that exactly suited his temperament, and had invented a new prose form. His great conversational gift was now crystallized in these breakfast table talks, which the Autocrat all but monopolizes. However, the other characters at the table of this remarkable boarding house in Boston join in often enough to keep up the interest in their opinions, feelings, and relations to each other. The reader always wants to know the impression that the Autocrat's fine talk makes upon "the young man whom they call 'John.'" John sometimes puts his feelings into action, as when the Autocrat gives a typical illustration of his mixture of reasoning and humor, in explaining that there are always six persons present when two people are talking:—

THE AUTOCRAT OF THE BREAKFAST TABLE

"Three Johns.
1. The real John; known only to his Maker.
2. John's ideal John; never the real one, and often very unlike him.
3. Thomas's ideal John; never the real John, nor John's John, but often very unlike either.

"Three Thomases.
1. The real Thomas.
2. Thomas's ideal Thomas.
3. John's ideal Thomas."

"A certain basket of peaches, a rare vegetable, little known to boarding-houses, was on its way to me," says the Autocrat, "*via* this unlettered Johannes. He appropriated the three that remained in the basket, remarking that there was just one apiece for him. I convinced him that his practical inference was hasty and illogical, but in the meantime he had eaten the peaches." When John enters the debates with his crushing logic of facts, he never fails to make a ten strike.

A few years after the *Autocrat* series had been closed, Holmes wrote *The Professor at the Breakfast Table;* many years later *The Poet at the Breakfast Table* appeared; and in the evening of life, he brought out *Over the Teacups*, in which he discoursed at the tea table in a similar vein, but not in quite the same fresh, buoyant, humorous way in which the Autocrat talked over his morning coffee. The decline in these books is gradual, although it is barely perceptible in the *Professor*. The *Autocrat* is, however, the brightest, crispest, and most vigorous of the series, while *Over the Teacups* is the calmest, as well as the soberest and most leisurely.

Holmes wrote three novels, *Elsie Venner*, *The Guardian Angel*, and *The Mortal Antipathy*, which have been called "medicated novels" because his medical knowledge is so apparent in them. These books also have a moral purpose, each in turn considering the question whether an individual is responsible for his acts. The first two of these novels are the strongest, and hold the attention to the end because of the interest aroused by the characters and by the descriptive scenes.

General Characteristics. — Humor is the most characteristic quality of Holmes's writings. He indeed is the only member of the New England group who often wrote with the sole object of entertaining readers. Lowell also was a humorist, but he employed humor either in the cause of reform, as in *The Biglow Papers*, or in the field of knowledge, in endeavoring to make his literary criticisms more expressive and more certain to impress the mind of his readers.

Whenever Holmes wrote to entertain, he did not aim to be deep or to exercise the thinking powers of his readers. Much of his work skims the surface of things in an amusing and delightful way. Yet he was too much of a New Englander not to write some things in both poetry and prose with a deeper purpose than mere entertainment. *The Chambered Nautilus*, for instance, was so written, as were all of his novels. His genial humor is thus frequently blended with unlooked-for wisdom or pathos.

Whittier has been called provincial because he takes only the point of view of New England. The province of Holmes is still narrower, being mainly confined to Boston. He expresses in a humorous way his own feelings, as well as those of his fellow townsmen, when he says in *The Autocrat of the Breakfast Table:* —

"Boston State House is the hub of the solar system. You couldn't pry that out of a Boston man if you had the tire of all creation straightened out for a crowbar."

Like Irving, Holmes was fond of eighteenth-century English writers, and much of his verse is modeled after the couplets of Pope. Holmes writes fluid and rippling prose, without a trace of effort. His meaning is never left to conjecture, but is stated in pure, exact English. He not only expresses his ideas perfectly, but he seems to achieve this result without premeditation. This apparent artlessness is a great charm. He has left America a new form of prose, which bears the stamp of pure literature, and which is distinguished not so much for philosophy and depth as for grace, versatility, refined humor, bright intellectual flashes, and artistic finish.

THE HISTORIANS

Three natives of Massachusetts and graduates of Harvard, William H. Prescott, John Lothrop Motley, and Francis Parkman, wrote history in such a way as to entitle it to be mentioned in our literature. We cannot class as literature those historical writings which are not enlivened with imagination, invested with at least an occasional poetic touch, and expressed in rare style. Unfortunately the very qualities that render history attractive as literature often tend to raise doubts about the scientific method and accuracy of the historian. For this reason few histories keep for a great length of time a place in literature, unless, like Irving's *Knickerbocker's History of New York*, they aim to give merely an imaginative interpretation of a past epoch. They may then, like Homer's *Iliad*, Shakespeare's *Macbeth*, and some of Irving's and Cooper's work, be, in Celtic phrase, "more historical than history itself." History of this latter type lives, and is a treasure in the literature of any nation.

William H. Prescott (1796–1859). — Like Washington Irving, Prescott was attracted by the romantic achievements of Spain during the years of her brilliant successes, and he wrote four histories upon Spanish subjects: a *History of the Reign of Ferdinand and Isabella* (1837), a *History of the Conquest of Mexico* (1843), a *History of the Conquest of Peru* (1847), and a *History of the Reign of*

WILLIAM H. PRESCOTT

Philip II. (1855–1858), the last of which he did not live to complete.

He was a careful, painstaking student. He learned the Spanish language, had copies made of all available manuscripts and records in Europe, and closely compared contemporary accounts so as to be certain of the accuracy of his facts. Then he presented them in an attractive form. His *Ferdinand and Isabella* and the part he finished of *Philip II.* are accurate and authoritative to-day because the materials which he found for them are true. The two histories on the Spanish conquests in the New World are not absolutely correct in all their descriptions of the Aztecs and Incas before the arrival of the Spaniards. This is due to no carelessness on Prescott's part, but to the highly colored accounts upon which he had to depend for his facts, and to the lack of the archæological surveys which have since been carried on in Mexico and Peru. These two histories of the daring exploits of a handful of adventurers in hostile lands are as thrilling and interesting as novels. We seem to be reading a tale from the *Arabian Nights*, as we follow Pizarro and see his capture of the Peruvian monarch in the very sight of his own army, and view the rich spoils in gold and silver and precious stones which were carried back to Spain. In relating the conquest of Mexico by Cortez, Prescott writes the history of still more daring adventures. His narrative is full of color, and he presents facts picturesquely.

John Lothrop Motley (1814–1877). — As naturally as the love of adventure sent Prescott to the daring exploits of the Spanish feats of arms, so the inborn zeal for civil and religious liberty and hatred of oppression led Motley to turn to the sturdy, patriotic Dutch in their successful struggle against the enslaving power of Spain. His histories are *The Rise of the Dutch Republic* (1856), *The History of the United Netherlands* (1860–1868), *The Life and Death of John of Barneveld, Advocate of Holland* (1874).

The difference in temperament between Prescott and Motley is seen in the manner of presenting the character of Philip II. In so far as Prescott drew the picture of Philip II., it is traced with a mild, cool hand. Philip is shown as a tyrant, but he is impelled to his tyranny by motives of conscience. In Motley's *The Rise of the Dutch Republic*, this oppressor is an accursed scourge of a loyal people, the enemy of progress, of liberty, and of justice. Motley's feelings make his pages burn and flash with fiery denunciation, as well as with exalted praise.

JOHN LOTHROP MOTLEY

The Rise of the Dutch Republic is the recital of as heroic a struggle as a small but determined nation ever made against tremendous odds. Amid the swarm of men that crowd the pages of this work, William the Silent, of Orange, the central figure, stands every inch a hero, a leader worthy of his cause and of his people. Motley with an artist's skill shows how this great leader launched Holland on her victorious career. This history is a living story, faithful to facts, but it is written to convince the reader that "freedom of thought, of speech, and of life" are "blessings without which everything that this earth can afford is worthless."

In choosing to write of the struggle of Holland for her

freedom, Motley was actuated by the same reason that prompted his forefathers to fight on Bunker Hill. He wanted to play at least a historian's part in presenting "the great spectacle which was to prove to Europe that principles and peoples still existed, and that a phlegmatic nation of merchants and manufacturers could defy the powers of the universe, and risk all their blood and treasure, generation after generation, in a sacred cause."

The History of the United Netherlands continues this story after Holland, free and united, proved herself a power that could no longer remain unheeded in Europe. *The Life and Death of John of Barneveld*, which brings the history of Holland down to about 1623, was planned as an introduction to a final history of that great religious and political conflict, called the Thirty Years' War, — a history which Motley did not live to finish.

Although no historian has spent more time than Motley in searching the musty records and state archives of foreign lands for matter relating to Holland, it was impossible for a man of his temperament, convictions, and purpose to write a calm, dispassionate history. He is not the cool judge, but the earnest advocate, and yet he does not distort facts. He is just and can be coldly critical, even of his heroes, but he is always on one side, the side of liberty and justice, pleading their cause. His temperament gives warmth, eloquence, and dramatic passion to his style. Individual incidents and characters stand forth sharply defined. His subject seems remarkably well suited to him because his love of liberty was a sacred passion. With this feeling to fire his blood, the unflinching Hollander to furnish the story, and his eloquent style to present it worthily, Motley's *Rise of the Dutch Republic* is a prose epic of Dutch liberty.

Francis Parkman (1823-1893).—The youngest and greatest of this group of historians was born of Puritan blood in Boston in 1823. Parkman's life from early childhood was a preparation for his future work, and when a mere lad at college, he had decided to write a history of the French and Indian War. He was a delicate child, and at the age of eight was sent to live with his grandfather, who owned at Medway, near Boston, a vast tract of woodland. The boy roamed at will through these forests, and began to amass that wood lore of which his histories hold such rich stores. At Harvard he overworked in the gymnasium with the mistaken purpose of strengthening himself for a life on the frontier.

In 1846, two years after graduation, he took his famous trip out west over the Oregon Trail, where he hunted buffalo on the plains, dragged his horse through the canyons to escape hostile Indians, lived in the camp of the warlike Dacota tribe, and learned by bitter experience the privations of primitive life.

His health was permanently impaired by the trip. He was threatened with absolute blindness, and was compelled to have all his notes read to him and to dictate his histories. For years he was forbidden literary work on account of insomnia and intense cerebral pain which threatened insanity, and on account of lameness he was long confined to a wheel chair. He rose above every obstacle, however, and with silent fortitude bore his sufferings, working whenever he could, if for only a bare half hour at a time.

His amazing activity during his trips, both in America and abroad, is shown in the Massachusetts Historical Society Library, which contains almost two hundred folio volumes, which he had experts copy from original sources. With few exceptions, he visited every spot which he described, and saw the life of nearly every tribe of Indians. His battle with ill health, his strength of character, and his energetic first-hand study of Indian and pioneer life are remarkable in the history of American men of letters. He died near Boston in 1893.

Because of their subject matter, Parkman's works are of unusual interest to Americans. When he returned from his pioneer western trip, he wrote a simple, straightforward account, which was in 1849 published in book form, under the title of *The California and Oregon Trail*. This book remains the most trustworthy, as well as the most entertaining, account of travel in the unsettled Northwest of that time. Indians, big game, and adventures enough to satisfy any reasonable boy may be found in this book.

FRANCIS PARKMAN

His histories cover the period from the early French settlements in the New World to the victory of the English over the French and Indian allies. The titles of his separate works, given in their chronological order, are as follows: —

The Pioneers of France in the New World (1865) describes the experiences of the early French sailors and explorers off the Newfoundland coast and along the St. Lawrence River.

The Jesuits in North America in the Seventeenth Century (1867) tells of the work of the self-forgetting Jesuit Fathers in their mission of mercy and conversion among the Indians. Fifty pages of the *Introduction* give an account of the religion, festivities, superstitions, burials, sacrifices, and military organization of the Indians.

La Salle, or the Discovery of the Great West (1869), is the story of La Salle's heroic endeavors and sufferings while exploring the West and the Mississippi River.

The Old Régime in Canada (1874) presents the internal conflicts and the social development of Canada in the seventeenth century.

Count Frontenac and New France under Louis XIV. (1877) continues the history of Canada as a French dependency, and paints in a lively manner Count Frontenac's character, his popularity with the Indians, and his methods of winning laurels for France.

A Half Century of Conflict (1892) depicts the sharp encounter between the French and English for the possession of the country, and the terrible deeds of the Indians against their hated foes, the English.

Montcalm and Wolfe (1884) paints the final scenes of the struggle between France and England, closing practically with the fall of Quebec.

The History of the Conspiracy of Pontiac (1851) shows one more desperate attempt of a great Indian chief to combine the tribes of his people and drive out the English. The volume closes with the general smoking of the pipe of peace and the swearing of allegiance to England. The first forty-five pages describe the manners and customs of the Indian tribes east of the Mississippi.

The general title, *France and England in North America*, indicates the subject matter of all this historical work. The central theme of the whole series is the struggle between the French and English for this great American continent. The trackless forests, the Great Lakes, the untenanted shores of the St. Lawrence and the Mississippi form an impressive background for the actors in this drama, — the Indians, traders, self-sacrificing priests, and the French and English contending for one of the greatest prizes of the world.

In his manner of presenting the different ideals and civilizations of England and France in this struggle, he shows keen analytical power and strong philosophical grasp. He is accurate in his details, and he summarizes the results of economic and religious forces in the strictly modern spirit. At the same time, these histories read like novels of adventure, so vivid and lively is the action. While scholars commend his reliability in dealing with facts, boys enjoy his vivid stories of heroism, sacrifice, religious enthusiasm, Indian craft, and military maneuvering. The one who begins with *The Conspiracy of Pontiac*, for instance, will be inclined to read more of Parkman.

In the first volumes the style is clear, nervous, and a trifle ornate. His facility in expression increased with his years, so that in *Montcalm and Wolfe* he has a mellowness and dignity that place him beside the best American prose writers. Although Prescott's work is more full of color, he does not surpass Parkman in the presentation of graphic pictures. Parkman has neither the solemn grandeur of Prescott nor the rapid eloquence of Motley, but Parkman has unique merits of his own, — the freshness of the pine woods, the reality and vividness of an eyewitness, an elemental strength inherent in the primitive nature of his novel subject. He secured his material at first hand in a way that cannot be repeated. Parkman's prose presents in a simple, lucid, but vigorous manner the story of the overthrow of the French by the English in the struggle for a mighty continent. As a result of this contest, Puritan England left its lasting impress upon this new land.

ENGLISH LITERATURE OF THE PERIOD

Most of the work of the great New England group of writers was done during the Victorian age — a time prolific of famous English authors. The greatest of the English writers were **Thomas Carlyle** (1795–1881), whose *Sartor Resartus* and *Heroes and Hero Worship* proved a stimulus to Emerson and to many other Americans; **Lord Macaulay** (1800–1859), whose *Essays* and *History of England*, remarkable for their clearness and interest, affected either directly or indirectly the prose style of numberless writers in the second half of the nineteenth century; **John Ruskin** (1819–1900), the apostle of the beautiful and of more ideal social relations; **Matthew Arnold** (1822–1888), the great analytical critic; **Charles Dickens** (1812–1870), whose novels of the lower class of English life are remarkable for vigor, optimism, humor, the power to caricature, and to charm the masses; **William Makepeace Thackeray** (1811–1863), whose novels, like *Vanity Fair*, remain unsurpassed for keen satiric analysis of the upper classes; and **George Eliot** (1819–1880), whose realistic stories of middle class life show a new art in tracing the growth and development of character instead of merely presenting it with the fixity of a portrait. To this list should be added **Charles Darwin** (1809–1882), whose *Origin of Species* (1859) affected so much of the thought of the second half of the nineteenth century.

The two greatest poets of this time were **Alfred Tennyson** (1809–1892) and **Robert Browning** (1812–1889). Browning's greatest poetry aims to show the complex development of human souls, to make us understand that: —

> "He fixed thee 'mid this dance
> Of plastic circumstance."[1]

[1] *Rabbi Ben Ezra.*

His influence on the American poets of this group was very slight. Whittier's comment on Browning's *Men and Women* is amusing : —

> "I have only dipped into it, here and there, but it is not exactly comfortable reading. It seemed to me like a galvanic battery in full play — its spasmodic utterances and intense passion make me feel as if I had been taking a bath among electric eels."

Tennyson through his artistic workmanship and poetry of nature exerted more influence. His Arthurian legends, especially *Sir Galahad* (1842), seem to have suggested Lowell's *Vision of Sir Launfal* (1848). The New England poets in general looked back to Burns, Wordsworth, Keats, and other members of the romantic school of poets. Lowell was a great admirer of Keats, and in early life, like Whittier, was an imitator of Burns.

LEADING HISTORICAL FACTS

As might be inferred from the literature of this period — from Whittier's early poems, Mrs. Stowe's *Uncle Tom's Cabin*, Lowell's *The Biglow Papers*, and from emphatic statements in Emerson and Thoreau — the question of slavery was the most vital one of the time. From 1849, when California, recently settled by gold seekers, applied for admission as a state, with a constitution forbidding slavery, until the end of the Civil War in 1865, slavery was the irrepressible issue of the republic. The Fugitive Slave Law, which was passed in 1850 to secure the return of slaves from any part of the United States, was very unpopular at the North and did much to hasten the war, as did also the decision of the United States Supreme Court in the Dred Scott case (1857), affirming that slaves were property, not persons, and could be moved the same as cattle from one state to another. Various compromise measures between the North and the South were vainly tried. When Abraham Lincoln was elected President in 1860, South Carolina led the South in seceding from the Union. In 1861 began the Civil War, which lasted four years and resulted in the restoration of the Union and the freeing of the slaves.

Before Holmes, the last member of this New England group, died in 1894, both North and South had more than regained the material prosperity which they had enjoyed before the war. The natural resources of the country were so great and the energy of her sons so remarkable that not only was the waste of property soon repaired, but a degree of prosperity was reached which would probably never have been possible without the war. More than one million human beings perished in the strife. Many of these were from the more cultured and intellectual classes on both sides. Centuries will not repair that waste of creative ability in either section. France, after the lapse of more than two hundred years, is still suffering from the loss of her Huguenots. It is impossible to compute what American literature has lost as a result of this war, not only from the double waste involved in turning the energies of men to destruction and subsequently to the necessary repairs, but also from the sacrifice of life of those who might have displayed genius with the pen or furnished an encouraging audience to the gifted ones who did not speak because there were none to hear.

The development of inventions during this period revolutionized the world's progress. Cities in various parts of the country had begun to communicate with each other by electricity, when Thoreau was living at Walden; when

Emerson was writing the second series of his *Essays;* Longfellow, his lines about cares "folding their tents like the Arabs and as silently stealing away"; Lowell, his verses *To the Dandelion;* and Holmes, his complaint that his humor was diminishing his practice. By the time that Longfellow had finished *The Courtship of Miles Standish*, and Holmes *The Autocrat of the Breakfast Table*, messages had been cabled across the Atlantic. A comparison with an event of the preceding period will show the importance of this method of communication. The treaty of peace to end the last war with England was signed in Belgium, December 24, 1814. On January 8, 1815, the bloody battle of New Orleans was fought. News of this fight did not reach Washington until February 4. A week later information of the treaty of peace was received at New York. A new process of welding the world together had begun, and this welding was further strengthened by the invention of that modern miracle, the telephone, in 1876.

The result of the battle between the ironclads, the *Monitor* and the *Merrimac* (1862), led to a change in the navies of the entire world. Alaska was bought in 1867, and added an area more than two thirds as large as the United States comprised in 1783. The improvement and extension of education, the interest in social reform, the beginning of the decline of the "let alone doctrine," the shortening of the hours of labor, and the consequent increase in time for self-improvement, — are all especially important steps of progress in this period.

Authors could no longer complain of small audiences. At the outbreak of the Civil War the United States had a population of thirty-one millions, while the combined population of Great Britain and Ireland was then only twenty-nine millions. Before Holmes passed away in 1894 the population of 1860 had doubled. The passage of an international copyright law in 1891 at last freed American authors from the necessity of competing with pirated editions of foreign works.

SUMMARY

The great mid-nineteenth century group of New England writers included Emerson, Thoreau, Hawthorne, who were often called the Concord group, and Harriet Beecher Stowe, Daniel Webster, Longfellow, Whittier, Lowell, Holmes, and the historians, Prescott, Motley, and Parkman.

The causes of this great literary awakening were in some measure akin to those which produced the Elizabethan age, — a " re-formation" of religious opinion and a renaissance, seen in a broader culture which did not neglect poetry, music, art, and the observation of beautiful things.

The philosophy known as transcendentalism left its impress on much of the work of this age. The transcendentalists believed that human mind could " transcend " or pass beyond experience and form a conclusion which was not based on the world of sense. They were intense idealists and individualists, who despised imitation and repetition, who were full of the ecstasy of discoveries in a glorious new world, who entered into a new companionship with nature, and who voiced in ways as different as *The Dial* and Brook Farm their desire for an opportunity to live in all the faculties of the soul.

The fact that the thought of the age was specially modified by the question of slavery is shown in Webster's orations, Harriet Beecher Stowe's *Uncle Tom's Cabin*, the poetry of Whittier and Lowell, and to a less degree in the work of Emerson, Thoreau, and Longfellow.

SUMMARY

We have found that Emerson's aim, shown in his *Essays* and all his prose work, is the moral development of the individual, the acquisition of self-reliance, character, spirituality. Some of his nature poetry ranks with the best produced in America. Thoreau, the poet-naturalist, shows how to find enchantment in the world of nature. Nathaniel Hawthorne, one of the great romance writers of the world, has given the Puritan almost as great a place in literature as in history. In his short stories and romances, this great artist paints little except the trial and moral development of human souls in a world where the Ten Commandments are supreme.

Longfellow taught the English-speaking world to love simple poetry. He mastered the difficult art of making the commonplace seem attractive and of speaking to the great common heart. His ability to tell in verse stories like *Evangeline* and *Hiawatha* remains unsurpassed among our singers. Whittier was the great antislavery poet of the North. Like Longfellow, he spoke simply but more intensely to that overwhelming majority whose lives stand most in need of poetry. His *Snow-Bound* makes us feel the moral greatness of simple New England life. The versatile Lowell has written exquisite nature poetry in his lyrics and *Vision of Sir Launfal* and *The Biglow Papers*. He has produced America's best humorous verse in *The Biglow Papers* and *A Fable for Critics*. He is a great critic, and his prose criticism in *Among My Books* and the related volumes is stimulating and interesting. His political prose, of which the best specimen is *Democracy*, is remarkable for its high ideals. Holmes is especially distinguished for his humor in such poems as *The Deacon's Masterpiece, or the Wonderful One-Hoss Shay* and for the pleasant philosophy and humor in such artistic prose as

The Autocrat of the Breakfast Table. He is the only member of this group who often wrote merely to entertain, but his *Chambered Nautilus* shows that he also had a more serious aim.

When we come to the historians, we find that Prescott wrote of the romantic achievements of Spain in the days of her glory; Motley, of the struggles of the Dutch Republic to keep religious and civil liberty from disappearing from this earth; Parkman, of the contest of the English against the French and Indians to decide whether the institutions and literature of North America should be French or English.

This New England literature is most remarkable for its moral quality, its gospel of self-reliance, its high ideals, its call to the soul to build itself more stately mansions.

REFERENCES FOR FURTHER STUDY

HISTORICAL

For contemporary English history consult the histories mentioned on p. 60. The chapter on Victorian literature in the author's *History of English Literature* gives the trend of literary movements on the other side of the Atlantic during this period.

Contemporary American history may be traced in the general works listed on p. 61, or in Woodrow Wilson's *Division and Reunion*.

LITERARY

General Works

In addition to the works of Richardson, Wendell, and Trent (p. 61), the following may be consulted: —

Nichol's *American Literature.*
Churton Collins's *The Poets and Poetry of America.*
Vincent's *American Literary Masters.*
Stedman's *Poets of America.*
Onderdonk's *History of American Verse.*

REFERENCES FOR FURTHER STUDY

Lawton's *The New England Poets*.
Erskine's *Leading American Novelists*. (Mrs. Stowe, Hawthorne.)
Brownell's *American Prose Masters*. (Especially Emerson and Lowell.)
Howells's *Literary Friends and Acquaintance*. (Longfellow, Lowell, Holmes.)

Special Works

Frothingham's *Transcendentalism in New England*.
Dowden's *Studies in Literature*. (Transcendentalism.)
Swift's *Brook Farm*.
Fields's *The Life and Letters of Harriet Beecher Stowe*.
Lodge's *Daniel Webster*.
Woodberry's *Ralph Waldo Emerson*.
Holmes's *Ralph Waldo Emerson*.
Garnett's *Life of Ralph Waldo Emerson*.
Sanborn's *Ralph Waldo Emerson*.
Cabot's *A Memoir of Ralph Waldo Emerson*, 2 vols.
E. W. Emerson's *Emerson in Concord*.
Lowell's *Emerson the Lecturer*, in *Works*, Vol. I.
Woodbury's *Talks with Ralph Waldo Emerson*.
Sanborn's *Henry David Thoreau*.
Salt's *Life of Henry David Thoreau*.
Channing's *Thoreau, The Poet Naturalist*.
Marble's *Thoreau, His Home, Friends, and Books*.
James Russell Lowell's *Thoreau*, in *Works*, Vol. I.
Burroughs's *Indoor Studies*, Chap. I., *Henry D. Thoreau*.
Woodberry's *Nathaniel Hawthorne*.
Henry James's *Hawthorne*.
Conway's *Life of Nathaniel Hawthorne*.
Fields's *Nathaniel Hawthorne*.
Julian Hawthorne's *Nathaniel Hawthorne and his Wife*.
George Parsons Lathrop's *A Study of Hawthorne*.
Bridge's *Personal Recollections of Nathaniel Hawthorne*.
Rose Hawthorne Lathrop's *Memories of Hawthorne*.
Julian Hawthorne's *Hawthorne and his Circle*.
Gates's *Studies and Appreciations*. (Hawthorne.)
Canby's *The Short Story in English*, Chap. XII. (Hawthorne.)
Samuel Longfellow's *Life of Henry Wadsworth Longfellow with Extracts from his Journals and Correspondence*, 3 vols.

Higginson's *Henry Wadsworth Longfellow*.
Carpenter's *Henry Wadsworth Longfellow*.
Robertson's *Life of Henry Wadsworth Longfellow*.
Carpenter's *John Greenleaf Whittier*.
Higginson's *John Greenleaf Whittier*.
Perry's *John Greenleaf Whittier*.
Pickard's *Life and Letters of John Greenleaf Whittier*, 2 vols.
Pickard's *Whittier-Land*.
Greenslet's *James Russell Lowell, his Life and Work*.
Hale's *James Russell Lowell*. (*Beacon Biographies*.)
Scudder's *James Russell Lowell, A Biography*, 2 vols.
Hale's *James Russell Lowell and his Friends*.
James Russell Lowell's *Letters*, edited by Charles Eliot Norton.
Morse's *Life and Letters of Oliver Wendell Holmes*, 2 vols.
Haweis's *American Humorists*.
Ticknor's *Life of William Hickling Prescott*.
Ogden's *William Hickling Prescott*.
Peck's *William Hickling Prescott*.
Holmes's *John Lothrop Motley, A Memoir*.
Curtis's *The Correspondence of John Lothrop Motley*.
Sedgwick's *Francis Parkman*.
Farnham's *A Life of Francis Parkman*.

SUGGESTED READINGS

Since the works of the authors of the New England group are nearly always accessible, it is not usually necessary to specify editions or the exact place where the readings may be found. Those who prefer to use books of selections will find that Page's *The Chief American Poets*, 713 pp., contains nearly all of the poems recommended for reading. Prose selections may be found in Carpenter's *American Prose*, and still more extended selections in Stedman and Hutchinson's *Library of American Literature*.

Transcendentalism and The Dial. — Read Emerson's lecture on *The Transcendentalist*, published in the volume called *Nature, Addresses, and Lectures*. *The Dial* is very rare and difficult to obtain outside of a large library. George Willis Cooke has collected in one volume under the title, *The Poets of Transcendentalism, An Anthology* (1903), 341 pp., some of the best of the poems published in *The Dial*, as well as much transcendental verse that appeared elsewhere.

Slavery and Oratory. — Selections from *Uncle Tom's Cabin* may be found in Carpenter, 312–322; S. & H., VII., 132–144. Webster's *Reply to Hayne* is given in Johnston's *American Orations*, Vol. I., 248–302. There are excellent selections from Webster in Carpenter, 105–118, and S. & H., IV., 462–469. Selections from the other orators mentioned may be found in Johnston and S. & H.

Emerson. — Read from the volume, *Nature, Addresses, and Lectures*, the chapters called *Nature, Beauty, Idealism*, and the "literary declaration of independence" in his lecture, *The American Scholar*. From the various other volumes of his *Essays*, read *Self-Reliance, Friendship, Character, Civilization*.

From his nature poetry, read *To Ellen at the South, The Rhodora, Each and All, The Humble-Bee, Woodnotes, The Snow-Storm*. For a poetical exposition of his philosophy, read *The Problem, The Sphinx*, and *Brahma*.

Thoreau. — If possible, read all of *Walden*; if not, Chaps. I., *Economy*, IV., *Sounds*, and XV., *Winter Animals* (Riverside Literature Series). From the volume called *Excursions*, read the essay *Wild Apples*. Many will be interested to read here and there from his *Notes on New England Birds* and from the four volumes, compiled from his *Journal*, describing the seasons.

Hawthorne. — At least one of each of the different types of his short stories should be read. His power in impressing allegorical or symbolic truth may be seen in *The Snow Image* or *The Great Stone Face*. As a specimen of his New England historical tales, read one or more of the following: *The Gentle Boy, The Maypole of Merry Mount, Lady Eleanore's Mantle*, or even the fantastic *Young Goodman Brown*, which presents the Puritan idea of witchcraft. For an example of his sketches or narrative essays, read *The Old Manse* (the first paper in *Mosses from an Old Manse*) or the *Introduction* to *The Scarlet Letter*.

The Scarlet Letter may be left for mature age, but *The House of the Seven Gables* should be read by all.

From his books for children, *The Golden Touch* (*Wonder Book*) at least should be read, no matter how old the reader.

Longfellow. — His best narrative poem is *Hiawatha*, and its strongest part is *The Famine*, beginning: —

"Oh, the long and dreary Winter!"

The opening lines of *Evangeline* should be read for both the beauty of the poetry and the novelty of the meter. The first four sections of *The Courtship of Miles Standish* should be read for its pictures of the early days of the first Pilgrim settlement. His best ballads are *The Wreck of the Hesperus, The Skeleton in Armor, Paul Revere's Ride,* and *The Birds of Killingworth.* For specimens of his simple lyrics, which have had such a wide appeal, read *A Psalm of Life, The Ladder of St. Augustine, The Rainy Day, The Day is Done, Daybreak, Resignation, Maidenhood, My Lost Youth.*

Whittier. — Read the whole of *Snow-Bound,* and for specimens of his shorter lyrics, *Ichabod, The Lost Occasion, My Playmate, Telling the Bees, The Barefoot Boy, In School Days, My Triumph, An Autograph,* and *The Eternal Goodness.* His best ballads are *Maud Muller, Skipper Ireson's Ride,* and *Cassandra Southwick.*

Lowell. — From among his shorter lyrical poems, read *Our Love is not a Fading Earthly Flower, To the Dandelion, The Present Crisis, The First Snow-Fall, After the Burial, For an Autograph, Prelude to Part I.* of *The Vision of Sir Launfal.* From *The Biglow Papers,* read *What Mr. Robinson Thinks* (No. III., *First Series*), *The Courtin'* (*Introduction* to *Second Series*), *Sunthin' in the Pastoral Line* (No. VI., *Second Series*). From *A Fable for Critics,* read the lines on Cooper, Poe, and Irving.

The five of Lowell's greater literary essays mentioned on page 254 show his critical powers at their best. The student who wishes shorter selections may choose those paragraphs which please him and any thoughts from the political essay *Democracy* which he thinks his neighbor should know.

Holmes. — Read *The Deacon's Masterpiece, or the Wonderful One-Hoss Shay, The Ballad of the Oysterman, The Boys, The Last Leaf,* and *The Chambered Nautilus.* From *The Autocrat of the Breakfast Table,* the student may select any pages that he thinks his friends would enjoy hearing.

The Historians. — Selections from Prescott, Motley, and Parkman may be found in Carpenter's *American Prose.*

QUESTIONS AND SUGGESTIONS

Poetry. — Compare Emerson's *Woodnotes* with Bryant's *Thanatopsis* and *A Forest Hymn.* Make a comparison of these three poems of

QUESTIONS AND SUGGESTIONS

motion: *The Evening Wind* (Bryant), *The Humble-Bee* (Emerson), and *Daybreak* (Longfellow), and give reasons for your preference. Compare in like manner *The Snow-Storm* (Emerson), the first sixty-five lines of *Snow-Bound* (Whittier), and *The First Snow-Fall* (Lowell). To which of these three simple lyrics of nature would you award the palm: *To the Fringed Gentian* (Bryant), *The Rhodora* (Emerson) *To the Dandelion* (Lowell)? After making your choice of these three poems, compare it with these two English lyrics of the same class: *To a Mountain Daisy* (Burns), *Daffodils* (Wordsworth, the poem beginning "I wandered lonely as a cloud"), and again decide which poem pleases you most.

Compare the humor of these two short poems describing a wooing: *The Courtin'* (Lowell), *The Ballad of the Oysterman* (Holmes). Discuss the ideals of these four poems: *A Psalm of Life* (Longfellow), *For an Autograph* (Lowell), *An Autograph* (Whittier), *The Chambered Nautilus* (Holmes).

What difference in the mental characteristics of the authors do these two retrospective poems show: *My Lost Youth* (Longfellow), *Memories* (Whittier)? For a more complete answer to this question, compare the girls in these two poems: *Maidenhood* (Longfellow): —

> "Maiden, with the meek, brown eyes,
> In whose orbs a shadow lies,"

and *In School Days* (Whittier), beginning with the lines where he says of the winter sun long ago: —

> "It touched the tangled golden curls,
> And brown eyes full of grieving."

Matthew Arnold, that severe English critic, called one of these poems perfect of its kind, and Oliver Wendell Holmes cried over one of them. The student who reads these carefully is entitled to rely on his own judgment, without verifying which poem Arnold and Holmes had in mind.

Compare Longfellow's ballads: *The Skeleton in Armor*, *The Birds of Killingworth*, and *The Wreck of the Hesperus*, with Whittier's *Skipper Ireson's Ride*, *Cassandra Southwick*, and *Maud Muller*.

Compare Whittier's *Snow-Bound* with Burns's *Cotter's Saturday Night*. In Whittier's poem, what group of lines descriptive of (*a*) nature, and (*b*) of inmates of the household pleases you most?

What parts of *Hiawatha* do you consider the best? What might be omitted without great damage to the poem?

In *The Courtship of Miles Standish*, which incidents or pictures of the life of the Pilgrims appeal most strongly to you?

What was the underlying purpose in writing *The Biglow Papers* and *One-Hoss Shay*? Do we to-day read them chiefly for this purpose or for other reasons? In what does the humor of each consist?

Prose. — Why is it said that Mrs. Stowe showed a knowledge of psychological values? What were the chief causes of the influence of *Uncle Tom's Cabin*?

What are Webster's chief characteristics? Why does he retain his preëminence among American orators?

What transcendental qualities does Emerson's prose show? From any of his *Essays* select thoughts which justify Tyndall's (p. 192) statement about Emerson's stimulating power. What passages show him to be a great moral teacher?

What was Thoreau's object in going to Walden? Of what is he the interpreter? What was his mission? What passages in *Walden* please you most? What is the reason for such a steady increase in Thoreau's popularity?

Point out the allegory or symbolism in any of Hawthorne's tales. Which of his short stories do you like best? What is Hawthorne's special aim in *The Snow Image* and *The Gentle Boy*? What qualities give special charm to sketches like *The Old Manse* and the *Introduction* to *The Scarlet Letter*? What is the underlying motive to be worked out in *The House of the Seven Gables*? Why is it said that the Ten Commandments reign supreme in Hawthorne's world of fiction? Was he a classicist or a romanticist (p. 219)? What qualities do you notice in his style?

In Lowell's critical essays, what unusual turns of thought do you find to challenge your attention? Does he employ humor in his serious criticism?

What most impresses you in reading selections from *The Autocrat of the Breakfast Table*, the humor, sprightliness, and variety of the thought, or the style? What especially satisfactory pages have you found?

Make a comparison (*a*) of the picturesqueness and color, (*b*) of the energy of presentation, (*c*) of the power to develop interest, and (*d*) of the style, shown in the selections which you have chosen from Prescott, Motley, and Parkman. Compare their style with that of Macaulay in his *History of England*.

CHAPTER V

SOUTHERN LITERATURE

Plantation Life and its Effect upon Literature. — Before the war the South was agricultural. The wealth was in the hands of scattered plantation owners, and less centered in cities than at the North. The result was a rural aristocracy of rich planters, many of them of the highest breeding and culture. A retinue of slaves attended to their work and relieved them from all manual labor. The masters took an active part in public life, traveled and entertained on a lavish scale. Their guests were usually wealthy men of the same rank, who had similar ideals and ambitions. Gracious and attractive as this life made the people, it did not bring in new thought, outside influences, or variety. Men continued to think like their fathers. The transcendental movement which aroused New England was scarcely felt as far south as Virginia. The tide of commercial activity which swept over the East and sent men to explore the West did not affect the character of life at the South. It was separated from every other section of the country by a conservative spirit, an objection to change, and a tendency toward aristocracy.

Such conditions retarded the growth of literature. There were no novel ideas that men felt compelled to utter, as in New England. There was little town life to bring together all classes of men. Such life has always been found essential to literary production. Finally, there was inevitably connected with plantation life a serious question, which occupied men's thoughts.

Slavery. — The question that absorbed the attention of the best southern intellect was slavery. In order to maintain the vast estates of the South, it was necessary to continue the institution of slavery. Many southern men had been anxious to abolish it, but, as time proceeded, they were less able to see how the step could be taken. As a Virginian statesman expressed it, they were holding a wolf by the ears, and it was as dangerous to let him go as to hold on. At the North, slavery was an abstract question of moral right or wrong, which inspired poets and novelists; at the South, slavery was a matter of expediency, even of livelihood. Instead of serving as an incentive to literary activity, the discussion of slavery led men farther away from the channels of literature into the stream of practical politics.

Political versus Literary Ambitions. — The natural ambition of the southern gentleman was political. The South was proud of its famous orators and generals in Revolutionary times and of its long line of statesmen and Presidents, who took such a prominent part in establishing and maintaining the republic. We have seen (p. 68) that Thomas Jefferson of Virginia wrote one of the most memorable political documents in the world, that James Madison, a Virginian President of the United States, aided in producing the *Federalist* papers (p. 71), that George Washington's *Farewell Address* (p. 100) deals with such vital matters as morality almost entirely from a political point of view. Although the South produced before the Civil War a world-famous author in Edgar Allan Poe, her glorious achievements were nevertheless mainly political, and she especially desired to maintain her former reputation in the political world. The law and not literature was therefore the avenue to the southerner's ambition.

Long before the Civil War, slavery became an unusually live subject. There was always some political move to discuss in connection with slavery; such, for instance, as the constitutional interpretation of the whole question, the necessity of balancing the admission of free and slave states to the Union, the war with Mexico, the division of the new territory secured in that conflict, the right of a state to secede from the Union. Consequently, in ante bellum days, the brilliant young men of the South had, like their famous ancestors of Revolutionary times, abundance of material for political and legal exposition, and continued to devote their attention to public questions, to law, and to oratory, instead of to pure literature. They talked while the North wrote.

In the days before the war, literature suffered also because the wealthy classes at the South did not regard it as a dignified profession. Those who could write often published their work anonymously. Richard Henry Wilde (1789–1847), a young lawyer, wrote verses that won Byron's praise, and yet did not acknowledge them until some twenty years later. Sometimes authors tried to suppress the very work by which their names are to-day perpetuated. When a Virginian found that the writer of

> "Thou wast lovelier than the roses
>   In their prime;
> Thy voice excelled the closes
>   Of sweetest rhyme;"

was his neighbor, Philip Pendleton Cooke (1816–1850), he said to the young poet, "I wouldn't waste time on a thing like poetry; you might make yourself, with all your sense and judgment, a useful man in settling neighborhood disputes." A newspaper in Richmond, Virginia, kept a standing offer to publish poetry for one dollar a line.

Educational Handicaps. — Before the war there was no universal free common school system, as at present, to prepare for higher institutions. The children of rich families had private tutors, but the poor frequently went without any schooling. William Gilmore Simms (p. 306) says that he "learned little or nothing" at a public school, and that not one of his instructors could teach him arithmetic. Lack of common educational facilities decreased readers as well as writers.

Until after the war, whatever literature was read by the cultured classes was usually English. The classical school of Dryden and Pope and the eighteenth century English essayists were especially popular. American literature was generally considered trashy or unimportant. So conservative was the South in its opinions, that individuality in literature was often considered an offense against good taste. This was precisely the attitude of the classical school in England during a large part of the eighteenth century. Until after the Civil War, therefore, the South offered few inducements to follow literature as a profession.

The New South. — After the South had passed through the terrible struggle of the Civil War, in which much of her best blood perished, there followed the tragic days of the reconstruction. These were times of readjustment, when a wholly new method of life had to be undertaken by a conservative people; when the uncertain position of the negro led to frequent trouble; when the unscrupulous politician, guided only by desire for personal gain, played on the ignorance of the poor whites and the enfranchised negroes, and almost wrecked the commonwealth. Had Lincoln lived to direct affairs after the war, much suffering might have been avoided, and the wounds of the South might have been more speedily healed.

These days, however, finally passed, and the South began to adapt herself to the changed conditions of modern life. In these years of transition since the Civil War, a new South has been evolved. Cities are growing rapidly. Some parts of the South are developing even faster than any other sections of the country. Men are running mills as well as driving the plow. Small farms have often taken the place of the large plantation. A system of free public schools has been developed, and compulsory education for all has been demanded. Excellent higher institutions of learning have multiplied. Writers and a reading public, both with progressive ideals, have rapidly increased. In short, the South, like the East and the West, has become more democratic and industrial, less completely agricultural, and has paid more attention to the education of the masses.

It would, however, be a mistake to suppose that the southern conservatism, which had been fostered for generations, could at once be effaced. The South still retains much of her innate love of aristocracy, loyalty to tradition, disinclination to be guided by merely practical aims, and aversion to rapid change. This condition is due partly to the fact that the original conservative English stock, which is still dominant, has been more persistent there and less modified by foreign immigration.

Characteristics of Southern Literature. — The one who studies the greatest authors of the South soon finds them worthy of note for certain qualities. Poe was cosmopolitan enough to appeal to foreign lands even more forcibly than to America, and yet we shall find that he has won the admiration of a great part of the world for characteristics, many of which are too essentially southern to be possessed in the same degree by authors in other sections of the country. The poets of the South have placed special emphasis on (1) melody, (2) beauty, (3) artistic workmanship. In creations embodying a combination of such qualities, Poe shows wonderful mastery. More than any other American poet, he has cast on the reader

> " . . . the spell which no slumber
>   Of witchery may test,
> The rhythmical number
>   Which lull'd him to rest."

After reading Poe and Lanier, we feel that we can say to the South what Poe whispered to the fair Ligeia: —

> "No magic shall sever
>   Thy music from thee."

The wealth of sunshine flooding the southern plains, the luxuriance of the foliage and the flowers, and the strong contrasts of light and shade and color are often reflected in the work of southern writers. Such verse as this is characteristic: —

> "Beyond the light that would not die
>   Out of the scarlet-haunted sky,
> Beyond the evening star's white eye
>   Of glittering chalcedony,
> Drained out of dusk the plaintive cry
>   Of 'whippoorwill!' of 'whippoorwill!'" [1]

In the work of her later writers of fiction, the South has presented, often in a realistic setting of natural scenes, a romantic picture of the life distinctive of the various sections, — of the Creoles of Louisiana, of the mountaineers of Tennessee, of the blue grass region of Kentucky, of Virginia in the golden days, and of the Georgia negro, whose folk lore and philosophy are voiced by Uncle Remus.

[1] Cawein, *Red Leaves and Roses*.

EDGAR ALLAN POE, 1809-1849

Early Life. — The most famous of all southern writers and one of the world's greatest literary artists happened to be born in Boston because his parents, who were strolling actors, had come there to fill an engagement. His grandfather, Daniel Poe, a citizen of Baltimore, was a general in the Revolution. His service to his country was sufficiently noteworthy to cause Lafayette to kneel at the old general's grave and say, "Here reposes a noble heart."

An orphan before he was three years old, Poe was reared by Mr. and Mrs. John Allan of Richmond, Virginia. We are given a glimpse of the boy at the age of six, standing on a table, declaiming and drinking wine as a pledge to the health of the guests. If there was ever a child who ought never to have known the taste of wine, that child was Edgar Allan Poe. He could not touch one glass of it without losing moral and physical self-control.

In 1815 his foster parents went to England and placed him for five years in the Manor School House at Stoke Newington, a suburb of London. The headmaster said that Poe was clever, but spoiled by " an extravagant amount of pocket money." This contrast between his school days and adult life should be noted. We shall never hear of his having too much money after he became an author.

In 1820 the boy returned with the Allans to Richmond, where he prepared for college and at the age of seventeen entered the University of Virginia. Here he yielded to the temptation of drinking and gambling, and he lost at the gaming table twenty-five hundred dollars in a few months. Mr. Allan thereupon took him out of college and put him in his own counting room. This act and other causes, which have never been fully ascertained, led Poe to leave Mr. Allan's home. The foster father had perhaps unconsciously sowed the wind in rearing the boy, but objected to reaping the whirlwind.

Poe then went to Boston, where, at the age of eighteen, he published a thin volume entitled *Tamerlane and Other Poems*. Disappointed at not being able to live by his pen, he served two years in the army as a common soldier, giving both an assumed name and age. He finally secured an appointment to West Point after he was actually beyond the legal age of entrance. The cadets said in a joking way that Poe had secured the appointment for his son, but that the father substituted himself after the boy died. Feeling an insatiable ambition to become an author, Poe neglected his duties at West Point, and he was discharged at the age of twenty-two, after less than a year's stay there.

His Great Struggle. — Soon after leaving West Point, Poe went to his kindred in Baltimore. In a garret in that southern city, he first discovered his power in writing prose tales. In 1833 his story, *MS. Found in a Bottle*, won a prize of one hundred dollars offered by a Baltimore paper. In 1834 Mr. Allan died without mentioning Poe in his will; and in spite of his utmost literary efforts, Poe had to borrow money to keep from starving.

After struggling for four years in Baltimore, he went to Richmond and became editor of the *Southern Literary Messenger*. He worked very hard in this position, sometimes contributing to a single number as much as forty pages of matter, mostly editorials and criticisms of books. In Baltimore he had tested his power of writing short stories, but in Richmond his work laid the foundation of his reputation as a literary critic. While here, he married his cousin, Virginia Clemm, but even his affection for her did not enable him to withstand the conviviality of the place. A little drink was poison in his veins, unfitting him for work. Although his genius had increased the circulation of the *Messenger* sevenfold within two years, its proprietor felt obliged to dispense with Poe's services.

The principal part of the rest of his life was passed in Philadelphia and New York, where he served as editor of various periodicals and wrote stories and poems. In the former city, he wrote most of the tales for which he is to-day famous. With the publication of his poem, *The*

Raven, in New York in 1845, he reached the summit of his fame. In that year he wrote to a friend, "*The Raven* has had a great 'run' — but I wrote it for the express purpose of running — just as I did *The Gold Bug,* you know. The bird beat the bug, though, all hollow." And yet, in spite of his fame, he said in the same year, "I have made no money. I am as poor now as ever I was in my life."

POE'S COTTAGE, FORDHAM, NEW YORK

The truth was that it would then have been difficult for the most temperate author to live even in the North without a salaried position, and conditions were worse in the South. Like Hawthorne, Poe tried to get a position in a customhouse, but failed.

He moved to an inexpensive cottage in Fordham, a short

distance from New York City, where he, his wife, and mother-in-law found themselves in 1846 in absolute want of food and warmth. The saddest scene in which any great American author figured was witnessed in that cottage in "the bleak December," when his wife, Virginia, lay dying in the bitter cold. Because there was insufficient bed clothing to keep her warm, Poe gave her his coat and placed the family cat upon her to add its warmth.

Her death made him almost completely irresponsible. The stunning effect of the blow may be seen in the wandering lines of *Ulalume* (1847). The end came to him in Baltimore in 1849, the same year in which he wrote the beautiful dirge of *Annabel Lee* for his dead wife. He was found intoxicated, taken to a hospital, where he conversed "with spectral and imaginary objects," passed into a state of delirium, and died at the age of forty.

VIRGINIA CLEMM

In anticipation of his end, he had written the lines:—

> " And oh, of all tortures,—
> *That* torture the worst
> Has abated — the terrible
> Torture of thirst
> For the napthaline river
> Of Passion accurst:—
> I have drank of a water
> That quenches all thirst."

His Tales. — He wrote more than sixty tales, some of which rank among the world's greatest short stories. The most important of these productions may be classified as tales (1) of the supernatural, like *The Fall of the House of Usher* and *Ligeia*, (2) of conscience, like *William Wilson*, that remarkable forerunner of *Dr. Jekyll and Mr. Hyde*, (3) of pseudo-science, like *A Descent into the Maelstrom*, (4) of analysis or ratiocination, like *The Gold Bug* and that wonderful analytical detective story, the first of its kind, *The Murders in the Rue Morgue*, the predecessor of later detective stories, like *The Adventures of Sherlock Holmes*, and (5) of natural beauty, like *The Domain of Arnheim*.

This classification does not include all of his types, for his powerful story, *The Pit and the Pendulum*, does not belong to any of these classes. He shows remarkable versatility in passing from one type of story to another. He could turn from a tale of the supernatural to write a model for future authors of realistic detective stories. He could solve difficult riddles with masterly analysis, and in his next story place a conscience-stricken wretch on the rack and then turn away calmly to write a tale of natural beauty. He specially liked to invest an impossible story with scientific reality, and he employed Defoe's specific concrete method of mingling fact with fiction. With all the seriousness of a teacher of physics, Poe describes the lunar trip of one Hans Pfaall with his balloon, air-condenser, and cat. He tells how the old cat had difficulty in breathing at a vast altitude, while the kittens, born on the upward journey, and never used to a dense atmosphere, suffered little inconvenience from the rarefaction. He relates in detail the accident which led to the detachment from the balloon of the basket containing the cat and kittens, and we find it impossible not to be interested in their fate. He had the skill of a wizard in presenting in remarkably brief compass suggestion after suggestion to invest his tales with the proper atmosphere and to hypnotize the reader into an unresisting acceptance of the march of events. Even a hostile critic calls him "a conjuror who does not need to have the lights turned down."

In one respect his tales are alike, for they are all romantic (p. 88) and deal with the unusual, the terrible, or the supernatural. Some of these materials suggest Charles Brockden Brown (p. 89), but Poe, working with the genius of a master artist, easily surpassed him.

His Development of the Modern Short Story. — Poe has an almost world-wide reputation for the part which he played in developing the modern short story. The ancient Greeks had short stories, and Irving had written delightful ones while Poe was still a child; but Poe gave this type of literature its modern form. He banished the little essays, the moralizing, and the philosophizing, which his predecessors, and even his great contemporary, Hawthorne, had scattered through their short stories. Poe's aim in writing a short story was to secure by the shortest air-line passage the precise effect which he desired. He was a great literary critic, and his essays, *The Philosophy of Composition* and *The Poetic Principle*, with all their aberrations, have become classic; but his most famous piece of criticism — almost epoch-making, so far as the short story is concerned — is the following: —

"A skillful literary artist has constructed a tale. If wise, he has not fashioned his thoughts to accommodate his incidents; but having conceived, with deliberate care, a certain unique or single *effect* to be wrought out, he then invents such incidents, — he then combines such events as may best aid him in establishing this preconceived effect. If his very initial sentence tend not to the outbringing of this effect, then he has failed in his first step. In the whole composition there should be no word written, of which the tendency, direct or indirect, is not to the one preëstablished design."

Poe's greatest supernatural tale, *The Fall of the House of Usher*, should be read in connection with this criticism. His initial sentence thus indicates the atmosphere of the story: —

"During the whole of a dull, dark, and soundless day in the autumn of the year, when the clouds hung oppressively low in the heavens, I had been passing alone, on horseback, through a singularly dreary tract of country; and at length found myself, as the shades of the evening drew on, within view of the melancholy House of Usher."

Each following stroke of the master's brush adds to the desired effect. The black and lurid tarn, Roderick Usher with his mental disorder, his sister Madeline, subject to trances, buried prematurely in a vault directly underneath the guest's room, the midnight winds blowing from every direction toward the House of Usher, the chance reading of a sentence from an old and musty volume, telling of a mysterious noise, the hearing of a muffled sound and the terrible suggestion of its cause, — all tend to indicate and heighten the gloom of the final catastrophe.

In one of his great stories, which is not supernatural, *The Pit and the Pendulum*, he desires to impress the reader with the horrors of medieval punishment. We may wonder why the underground dungeon is so large, why the ceiling is thirty feet high, why a pendulum appears from an opening in that ceiling. But we know when the dim light, purposely admitted from above, discloses the prisoner strapped immovably on his back, and reveals the giant pendulum, edged with the sharpest steel, slowly descending, its arc of vibration increasing as the terrible edge almost imperceptibly approaches the prisoner. We find ourselves bound with him, suffering from the slow torture. We would escape into the upper air if we could, but Poe's hypnotic power holds us as helpless as a child while that terrible edge descends.

A comparison of these stories and the most successful ones published since Poe's time, on the one hand, with those written by Irving or Hawthorne, on the other, will show the influence of Poe's technique in making almost a new creation of the modern short story.

Poetry. — Poe wrote a comparatively small amount of verse. Of the forty-eight poems which he is known to have written, not more than nine are masterpieces, and all of these are short. It was a favorite article of his poetic creed that there could be no such creation as a long poem, that such a poem would in reality be a series of poems. He thought that each poem should cause only one definite emotional impression, and that a long poem would lack the necessary unity. He says that he determined in advance that *The Raven* should contain about one hundred lines.

HOUSE WHERE POE WROTE "THE RAVEN"
(Near Eighty-fourth Street, New York)

His poetic aim was solely "the creation of beauty." He says: —

"Regarding, then, Beauty as my province, my next question referred to the *tone* of its highest manifestation; and all experience has shown that this tone is one of *sadness*. Beauty of whatever kind, in its supreme development, invariably excites the sensitive soul to tears. Melancholy is thus the most legitimate of all the poetical tones."[1]

[1] *The Philosophy of Composition.*

He then concludes that death is the most melancholy subject available for a poet, and that the death of a beautiful woman "is unquestionably the most poetical topic in the world." From the popularity of *The Raven* at home and abroad, in comparison with other American poems, it would seem as if the many agreed with Poe and felt the fascination of the burden of his song: —

> "Tell this soul with sorrow laden if, within the distant Aidenn,
> It shall clasp a sainted maiden whom the angels name Lenore —
> Clasp a rare and radiant maiden whom the angels name Lenore."

> Annabel Lee
> By Edgar A. Poe.
>
> It was many and many a year ago,
> In a kingdom by the sea,
> That a maiden there lived whom you may know
> By the name of Annabel Lee; —
> And this maiden she lived with no other thought
> Than to love and be loved by me.

FACSIMILE OF FIRST STANZA OF ANNABEL LEE

His most beautiful poem, *Annabel Lee*, is the dirge written for his wife, and it is the one great poem in which he sounds this note of lasting triumph: —

> "And neither the angels in heaven above,
> Nor the demons down under the sea,
> Can ever dissever my soul from the soul
> Of the beautiful ANNABEL LEE."

A few of his great poems, like *Israfel* and *The Bells*, do not sing of death, but most of them make us feel the presence of the great Shadow. The following lines show that it would be wrong to say, as some do, that his thoughts never pass beyond it:—

> "And all my days are trances,
>   And all my nightly dreams
> Are where thy dark eye glances,
>   And where thy footstep gleams—
> In what ethereal dances,
>   By what eternal streams." [1]

It would be difficult to name a poet of any race or age who has surpassed Poe in exquisite melody. His liquid notes soften the harshness of death. No matter what his theme, his verse has something of the quality which he ascribes to the fair Ligeia:—

> "Ligeia! Ligeia!
> My beautiful one!
> Whose harshest idea
> Will to melody run."

The fascination of his verse is not due to the depth of thought, to the spiritual penetration of his imagination, or to the poetic setting of noble ideals, for he lacked these qualities; but he was a master in securing emotional effects with his sad music. He wedded his songs of the death of beautiful women to the most wonderful melodies, which at times almost transcend the limits of language and pass into the realm of pure music. His verses are not all-sufficient for the hunger of the soul; but they supply an element in which Puritan literature was too often lacking, and they justify the transcendental doctrine that beauty is its own excuse for being.

[1] *To One in Paradise.*

General Characteristics. — Poe was a great literary artist, who thought that the creation of beauty was the object of every form of the highest art. His aim in both prose and poetry was to produce a pronounced effect by artistic means. His continued wide circulation shows that he was successful in his aim. An English publisher recently said that he sold in one year 29,000 of Poe's tales, or about three times as many of them as of any other American's work.

The success with which Poe met in producing an effect upon the minds of his readers makes him worthy of careful study by all writers and speakers, who desire to make a vivid impression. Poe selected with great care the point which he wished to emphasize. He then discarded everything which did not serve to draw attention to that point. On his stage the colored lights may come from many different directions, but they all focus on one object.

Hawthorne and Poe, two of the world's great short-story writers, were remarkably unlike in their aims. Hawthorne saw everything in the light of moral consequences. Poe cared nothing for moral issues, except in so far as the immoral was ugly. Hawthorne appreciated beauty only as a true revelation of the inner life. Poe loved beauty and the melody of sound for their own attractiveness. His effects, unlike Hawthorne's, were more physical than moral. Poe exalted the merely technical and formal side of literary excellence more than Hawthorne.

Poe's prose style is direct, energetic, clear, and adequate to the occasion. His mind was too analytic to overload his sentences with ornament, and too definite to be obscure. He had the same aim in his style as in his subject matter, — to secure an effect with the least obstruction.

His poetry is of narrower range than his prose, but his greatest poems hold a unique position for an unusual combination of beauty, melody, and sadness. He retouched and polished them from year to year, until they stand unsurpassed in their restricted field. He received only ten dollars for *The Raven* while he was alive, but the appreciation of his verse has increased to such an extent that the sum of two thousand dollars was recently paid for a copy of the thin little 1827 edition of his poems.

It has been humorously said that the French pray to Poe as a literary saint. They have never ceased to wonder at the unusual combination of his analytic reasoning power with his genius for imaginative presentation of romantic materials, — at the realism of his touch and the romanticism of his thought. It is true that many foreign critics consider Poe America's greatest author. An eminent English critic says that Poe has surpassed all the rest of our writers in playing the part of the Pied Piper of Hamelin to other authors. At home, however, there have been repeated attempts to disbar Poe from the court of great writers. Not until 1910 did the board of electors vote him a tablet in the Hall of Fame for Great Americans.

BUST OF POE IN UNIVERSITY OF VIRGINIA

It may be admitted that Poe was a technical artist, that his main object was effectiveness of impression and beauty of form, that he was not overanxious about the worth of his subject matter to an aspiring soul, and that he would have been vastly greater if he had joined high moral aim to his quest of beauty. He overemphasized the romantic elements of strangeness, sadness, and horror. He was deficient in humor and sentiment, and his guiding standards of criticism often seem too coldly intellectual. Those critics who test him exclusively by the old Puritan standards invariably find him wanting, for the Puritans had no room in their world for the merely beautiful.

Poe's genius, however, was sufficiently remarkable to triumph over these defects, which would have consigned to oblivion other writers of less power. In spite of the most determined hostile criticism that an American author has ever known, the editions of Poe's works continue to increase. The circle of those who fall under his hypnotic charm, in which there is nothing base or unclean, is enlarged with the passing of the years. As a great literary craftsman, he continues to teach others. He is now not likely to be dislodged from that peculiar, narrow field where he holds a unique and original position among the great writers of the world.

WILLIAM GILMORE SIMMS, 1806-1870

William Gilmore Simms, often styled the "Cooper of the South," was born of poor parents in Charleston, South Carolina, in 1806. His mother died when he was very young, and his father moved west into the wilds of Mississippi. The boy was left behind to be reared by his grandmother, a poor but clever woman, who related to him tales of the Revolutionary War, through which she had lived. During a visit to his father, these tales were supplemented by stories of contemporary life on the borders of civilization. In this way Simms acquired a large part of the material for his romances.

He prospered financially, married well, became the owner of a fine estate, and bent every effort to further southern literature and assist southern writers. He became the center of a group of literary men in Charleston, of whom Hayne and Timrod were the most famous. The war, however, ruined Simms. His property and library were destroyed, and, though he continued to write, he never found his place in the new order of life. He failed to catch the public ear of a people satiated with fighting and hair-raising adventures. He survived but six years, and died in Charleston in 1870.

WILLIAM GILMORE SIMMS

Being of humble birth, Simms lacked the advantage of proper schooling. Although he was surrounded by aristocratic and exclusive society, he did not have the association of a literary center, such as the Concord and Cambridge writers enjoyed. He found no publishers nearer than New York, to which city he personally had to carry his manuscripts for publication. Yet with all these handicaps, he achieved fame for himself and his loved Southland. This victory over adverse conditions was won by sheer force of indomitable will, by tremendous activity, and by a great, honest, generous nature.

His writings show an abounding energy and versatility. He wrote poetry, prose fiction, historical essays, and political pamphlets, and amazed his publishers by his speed in composition. His best work is *The Yemassee* (1835), a story of the uprising of the Indians in Carolina. The midnight massacre, the fight at the blockhouse, and the blood-curdling description of the dishonoring of the Indian chief's son are told with infectious vigor and rapidity. *The Partisan* (1835), *Katherine Walton* (1851), and *The Sword and Distaff* (1852), afterwards called *Woodcraft*, also show his ability to tell exciting tales, to understand Indian character, and to commemorate historical events in thrilling narratives.

Simms wrote rapidly and carelessly. He makes mistakes in grammar and construction, and is often stilted and grandiloquent. All of his romances are stories of adventure which are enjoyed by boys, but not much read by others. Nevertheless, his best works fill a large place in southern literature and history. They tell in an interesting way the life of the border states, of southern crossroads towns, of colonial wars, and of Indian customs. What Cooper did for the North, Simms accomplished for the South. He lacked Cooper's skill and variety of invention, and he created no character to compare with Cooper's Leatherstocking; but he excelled Cooper in the more realistic portrayal of Indian character.

HENRY TIMROD, 1829-1867

Henry Timrod was born in Charleston, South Carolina, in 1829. He attended the University of Georgia; but was prevented by delicate health and poverty from taking his degree. He was early thrown upon his own resources to earn a livelihood, and having tried law and found it distasteful, he depended upon teaching and writ ing. His verses were well received, but the times preceding the Civil War were not propitious for a poor poet. As he was not strong enough to bear arms at the outbreak of hostilities, he went to the field as a war correspondent for a newspaper in Charleston and he became later an associate editor in Columbia. His printing office was demolished in Sherman's march to the sea, and at the close of the war Timrod was left in a desperate condition. He was hopelessly ill from consumption; he was in the direst poverty; and he was saddened by the death of his son. There was no relief for Timrod until death released him from his misery in 1867. Yet in spite of all his trials, he desired earnestly to live, and when his sister told him that death would, at least, bring him rest, he replied, "Yes, my sister, but love is sweeter than rest."

Timrod's one small volume of poetry contains some of the most spontaneous nature and love lyrics in the South. In this stanza to *Spring*, the directness and simplicity of his manner may be seen: —

> "In the deep heart of every forest tree
> The blood is all aglee,
> And there's a look about the leafless bowers
> As if they dreamed of flowers."

He says in *A Vision of Poesy* that the poet's mission is to

" . . . turn life's tasteless waters into wine,
And flush them through and through with purple tints."

His best known and most original poem is *The Cotton Boll*. This description of the wide stretches of a white cotton field is one of the best in the poem. He shows the field

" . . . lost afar
Behind the crimson hills and purple lawns
Of sunset, among plains which roll their streams
Against the Evening Star!
And lo!
To the remotest point of sight,
Although I gaze upon no waste of snow,
The endless field is white;
And the whole landscape glows,
For many a shining league away,
With such accumulated light
As Polar lands would flash beneath a tropic day!"

Simplicity and sincerity in language, theme, and feeling are special characteristics of Timrod's verse. His lyrics are short and their volume slight, but a few of them, like *Spring* and *The Lily Confidante*, seem almost to have sung themselves. So vivid is his reproduction of the spirit of the awakening year in his poem *Spring*, that, to quote his own lines: —

" . . . you scarce would start,
If from a beech's heart,
A blue-eyed Dryad, stepping forth, should say,
'Behold me! I am May.'"

Timrod shows the same qualities of simplicity, directness, and genuine feeling in his war poetry. No more ringing lines were written for the southern cause during the Civil War than are to be found in his poems, *Carolina* and *Ethnogenesis*.

PAUL HAMILTON HAYNE, 1830-1886

Paul Hamilton Hayne was born in Charleston, South Carolina, in 1830. His family was rich and influential, and he inherited a fortune in his own right. After graduating at Charleston College, he studied law, but devoted his independent leisure entirely to literature. He became associated with *The Southern Literary Gazette*, and was the first editor of *Russell's Magazine*, an ambitious venture launched by the literary circle at the house of Simms. Hayne married happily, and had every prospect of a prosperous and brilliant career when the war broke out. He enlisted, but his health soon failed, and at the close of the war he found himself an invalid with his fortune destroyed. He went to the Pine Barrens of Georgia, where he built, on land which he named Copse Hill, a hut nearly as rude as Thoreau's at Walden. Handicapped by poverty and disease, Hayne lived here during the remainder of his life, writing his best poems on a desk fashioned out of a workbench. He died in 1886.

Hayne wrote a large amount of poetry, and tried many forms of verse, in almost all of which he maintained a smoothness of meter, a correctness of rhyme, and, in general, a high level of artistic finish. He is a skilled craftsman, his ear is finely attuned to harmonious arrangements of sounds, and he shows an acquaintance with the best melodists in English poetry. The limpid ease and grace in his lines may be judged by this dainty poem: —

> "A tiny rift within the lute
> May sometimes make the music mute!
> By slow degrees, the rift grows wide,
> By slow degrees, the tender tide —
> Harmonious once — of loving thought
> Becomes with harsher measures fraught,
> Until the heart's Arcadian breath
> Lapses thro' discord into death!"

His best poems are nature lyrics. In *The Woodland Phases*, one of the finest of these, he tells how nature is to him a revelation of the divine: —

> "And midway, betwixt heaven and us,
> Stands Nature in her fadeless grace,
> Still pointing to our Father's house,
> His glory on her mystic face."

Hayne found the inspiration for his verse in the scenes about his forest home: in the "fairy South Wind" that "floateth on the subtle wings of balm," in

> ". . . the one small glimmering rill
> That twinkles like a wood-fay's mirthful eye,"

in the solitary lake

> "Shrined in the woodland's secret heart,"

in

> "His blasted pines, smit by the fiery West,
> Uptowering rank on rank, like Titan spears,"

in the storm among the Georgian hills, in the twilight, that

> ". . . on her virginal throat
> Wears for a gem the tremulous vesper star,"

and in the mocking-birds, whose

> ". . . love notes fill the enchanted land;
> Through leaf-wrought bars they storm the stars,
> These love songs of the mocking-birds!"

The chief characteristics of his finest poetry are a tender love of nature, a profusion of figurative language, and a gentle air of meditation.

SIDNEY LANIER, 1842-1881

Life. — Sidney Lanier was the product of a long line of cultured ancestors, among whom appeared, both in England and America, men of striking musical and artistic ability. He was born in Macon, Georgia, in 1842. He served in the Confederate army during the four years of the war, and was taken prisoner and exposed to the hardest conditions, both during his confinement and after his release. The remainder of his life was a losing fight against the ravages of consumption.

He was fairly successful for a short time in his father's law office; but if ever a man believed that it was his duty to devote his every breath to the gift of music and poetry bestowed upon him, that man was Lanier. His wife agreed with him in his ideals and faith, so in 1873 he left his family in Georgia and went to Baltimore, the land of libraries and orchestras. He secured the position of first flute in the Peabody orchestra, and, by sheer force of genius, took up the most difficult scores and faultlessly led all the flutes. He read and studied, wrote and lectured like one who had suffered from mental starvation. In 1879 he received the appointment of lecturer on English literature at the Johns Hopkins University, a position which his friends had long wished to see him fill. He held it only two years, however, before his death. His health had fast been failing. He wrote part of the time while lying on his back, and, because of physical weakness, he delivered some of his lectures in whispers. In search of relief, he was taken to Florida, Texas, and North Carolina, but no permanent benefit came, and he died in his temporary quarters in North Carolina in 1881.

Works.— Lanier wrote both prose and poetry. His prose comprises books for children and critical studies. *The Science of English Verse* (1880) and *The English Novel* (1883) are of interest because of their clear setting forth of his theory of versification and art. In his poetry he strives to embody the ideals proclaimed in his prose work, which are, first, to write nothing that is not moral and elevating in tone, and, second, to express himself in versification which is obedient to the laws of regular musical composition, in rhyme, rhythm, vowel assonance, alliteration, and phrasings.

Lanier's creed, that the poet should be an inspiration for good to his readers, is found in his lines:—

> "The artist's market is the heart of man,
> The artist's price some little good of man."

The great inspiration of his life was love, and he has some fine love poems, such as *My Springs*, *In Absence*, *Evening Song*, and *Laus Mariae*. In *The Symphony*, which voices the social sorrow for the overworked and downtrodden, he says the problem is not one for the head but the heart: —

> "Vainly might Plato's brain revolve it,
> Plainly the heart of a child could solve it."

In ending the poem, he says that even

> "Music is Love in search of a word."

Strong personal love, tender pitying love for humanity, impassioned love of nature, and a reverent love of God are found in Lanier.

The striking musical quality of Lanier's best verse is seen in these stanzas from *Tampa Robins*: —

> "The robin laughed in the orange-tree:
> 'Ho, windy North, a fig for thee:
> While breasts are red and wings are bold
> And green trees wave us globes of gold,
> Time's scythe shall reap but bliss for me
> — Sunlight, song, and the orange-tree.
>
> . . . . . .
>
> "'I'll south with the sun and keep my clime;
> My wing is king of the summer-time;
> My breast to the sun his torch shall hold;
> And I'll call down through the green and gold,
> *Time, take thy scythe, reap bliss for me,*
> *Bestir thee under the orange-tree.*'"

The music of the bird, the sparkle of the sunlight, and the pure joy of living are in this poem, which is one of Lanier's finest lyrical outbursts. *The Song of the Chattahoochee* is another of his great successes in pure melody. The rhymes, the rhythm, the alliteration beautifully express the flowing of the river.

His noblest and most characteristic poem, however, is *The Marshes of Glynn*. It seems to breathe the very spirit of the broad open marshes and to interpret their meaning to the heart of man, while the long, sweeping, melodious lines of the verse convey a rich volume of music, of which he was at times a wonderful master.

> " Oh, what is abroad in the marsh and the terminal sea?
> Somehow my soul seems suddenly free
> From the weighing of fate and the sad discussion of sin,
> By the length and the breadth and the sweep of the marshes of Glynn."

This poem, original and beautiful, both in subject and form, expresses Lanier's strong faith in God. He says: —

> " As the marsh-hen secretly builds on the watery sod,
> Behold, I will build me a nest on the greatness of God:
> I will fly in the greatness of God as the marsh-hen flies
> In the freedom that fills all the space 'twixt the marsh and the skies:
> By so many roots as the marsh-grass sends in the sod
> I will heartily lay me a-hold of the greatness of God."

No Puritan could show a truer faith than Lanier's, nor a faith more poetically and devoutly expressed. In his *Sunrise* he attains at times the beauty of *The Marshes of Glynn*, and voices in some of the lines a veritable rhapsody of faith. Yet for sustained elevation of feeling and for unbroken musical harmonies, *Sunrise* cannot equal *The Marshes of Glynn*, which alone would suffice to keep Lanier's name on the scroll of the greater American poets.

General Characteristics. — Lanier is an ambitious poet. He attempts to voice the unutterable, to feel the intangible, to describe the indescribable, and to clothe this ecstasy in language that will be a harmonious accompaniment to the thought. This striving after practically impossible effects sometimes gives the feeling of artificiality and strain to his verse. It is not always simple, and sometimes one overcharged stanza will mar an otherwise exquisite poem.

On the other hand, Lanier never gives voice to anything that is merely trivial or pretty. He is always in earnest, and the feeling most often aroused by him is a passionate exaltation. He is a nature poet. The color, the sunshine, the cornfields, the hills, and the marshes of the South are found in his work. But more than their outer aspect, he likes to interpret their spirit, — the peace of the marsh, the joy of the bird, the mystery of the forest, and the evidences of love everywhere.

The music of his lines varies with his subjects. It is light and delicate in *Tampa Robins*, rippling and gurgling in *The Song of the Chattahoochee*, and deeply sonorous in *The Marshes of Glynn*. Few surpass him in the long, swinging, grave harmonies of his most highly inspired verse. In individual lines, in selected stanzas, Lanier has few rivals in America. His poetical endowment was rich, his passion for music was a rare gift, his love of beauty was intense, and his soul was on fire with ideals.

FATHER RYAN, 1839-1886

Another poet who will long be remembered for at least one poem is Abram Joseph Ryan (1839–1886), better known as

FATHER RYAN

"Father Ryan." He was a Roman Catholic priest who served as chaplain in the Confederate army, and though longing and waiting only for death in order to go to the land that held joy for him, he wrote and worked for his fellow-man with a gentleness and sympathy that left regret in many hearts when he died in Louisville, Kentucky, in 1886.

He loved the South and pitied her plight, and in his pathetic poem, *The Conquered Banner*, voiced the woe of a heart-broken people: —

> "Furl that Banner, softly, slowly!
> Treat it gently — it is holy —
>   For it droops above the dead.
> Touch it not — unfold it never —
> Let it droop there, furled forever,
>   For its people's hopes are dead."

JOHN BANNISTER TABB, 1845–1909

John Bannister Tabb was born in 1845 on the family estate in Amelia County, Virginia. He was a strong adherent of the southern cause, and during the war he served as clerk on one of the boats carrying military stores. He was taken prisoner, and placed in Point Lookout Prison, where Lanier also was confined. After the war, Tabb devoted some time to music and taught school. His studies led him toward the church, and at the age of thirty-nine he received the priest's orders in the Roman Catholic church. When he died in 1909, he was a teacher in St. Charles College, Ellicott City, Maryland. He had been blind for two years.

Tabb's poems are preëminently "short swallow-flights of song," for most of them are only from four to eight lines long. Some of these verses are comic, while others are grave and full of religious ardor. The most beautiful of all his poems are those of nature. The one called *The Brook* is among the brightest and most fanciful: —

> "It is the mountain to the sea
> That makes a messenger of me:
> And, lest I loiter on the way
> And lose what I am sent to say,
> He sets his reverie to song
> And bids me sing it all day long.
> Farewell! for here the stream is slow,
> And I have many a mile to go."[1]

The Water Lily is another dainty product, full of poetic feeling for nature: —

> "Whence, O fragrant form of light,
> Hast thou drifted through the night,
> Swanlike, to a leafy nest,
> On the restless waves, at rest?
>
> "Art thou from the snowy zone
> Of a mountain-summit blown,
> Or the blossom of a dream,
> Fashioned in the foamy stream?"[2]

In *Quips and Quiddits* he loves to show that type of humor dependent on unexpected changes in the meaning of words. The following lines illustrate this characteristic: —

> "To jewels her taste did incline;
> But she had not a trinket to wear
> Till she slept after taking quinine,
> And awoke with a ring in each ear."

---

[1] *Poems*, 1894.   [2] *The Water Lily*, from *Poems*, 1894.

Tabb's power lay in condensing into a small compass a single thought or feeling and giving it complete artistic expression. The more serious poems, especially the sacred ones, sometimes seem to have too slight a body to carry their full weight of thought, but the idea is always fully expressed, no matter how narrow the compass of the verse. His poetry usually has the qualities of lightness, airiness, and fancifulness.

JOEL CHANDLER HARRIS, 1848-1908

Joel Chandler Harris was born at Eatonton, in the center of Georgia in 1848. He alludes to himself laughingly as "an uncultured Georgia cracker." At the age of twelve, he was setting type for a country newspaper and living upon the plantation of the wealthy owner of this paper, enjoying the freedom of his well-selected library, hunting coons, possums, and rabbits with his dogs, and listening to the stories told by his slaves. The boy thus became well acquainted with many of the animal fables known to the negroes of Georgia. Later in life, he heard a great many more of these tales, while traveling through the cotton states, swapping yarns with the negroes after he had gained their confidence. His knowledge of their hesitancy about telling a story and his sympathy with them made it possible for him to hear

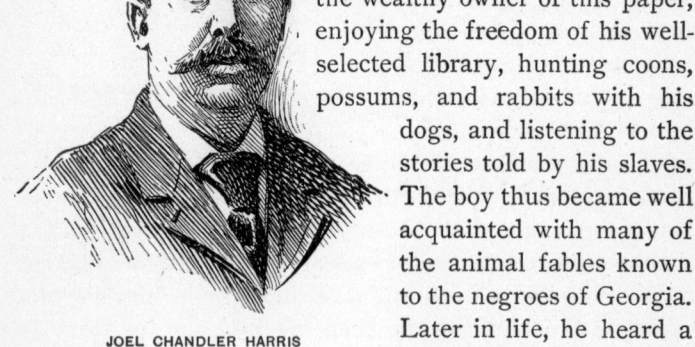

JOEL CHANDLER HARRIS

rare tales when another would probably have found only silence. Sometimes, while waiting for a train, he would saunter up to a group of negroes and start to tell a story himself and soon have them on tiptoe to tell him one that he did not already know. In many ways he became the possessor of a large part of the negro folklore. He loved a story and he early commenced to write down these fables, making of them such delightful works of art that all America is his debtor, not only for thus preserving the folklore of a primitive people in their American environment, but also for the genuine pleasure derived from the stories themselves. They are related with such humor, skill, and poetic spirit that they almost challenge comparison with Kipling's tales of the jungle. The hero is the poor, meek, timid rabbit, but in the tales he becomes the witty, sly, resourceful, bold adventurer, who acts "sassy" and talks big. Harris says that "it needs no scientific investigation to show why he [the negro] selects as his hero the weakest and most harmless of all animals, and brings him out victorious in contests with the bear, the wolf, and the fox. It is not virtue that triumphs, but helplessness; it is not malice, but mischievousness." Sometimes, as is shown in *The Wonderful Tar Baby Story*, a trick of the fox causes serious trouble to the rabbit; but the rabbit usually invents most of the pranks himself. The absurdly incongruous

BRER RABBIT AND THE TAR BABY
(Courtesy of D. Appleton & Co.)

attitude of the rabbit toward the other animals is shown in the following conversation, which occurs in the story of *Brother Rabbit and Brother Tiger*, published in *Uncle Remus and His Friends*: —

"Brer Tiger 'low, ' How come you ain't skeer'd er me, Brer Rabbit? All de yuther creeturs run when dey hear me comin'.'

"Brer Rabbit say, ' How come de fleas on you ain't skeer'd un you? Dey er lots littler dan what I is.'

"Brer Tiger 'low, ' Hit's mighty good fer you dat I done had my dinner, kaze ef I'd a-been hongry I'd a-snapped you up back dar at de creek.'

"Brer Rabbit say, 'Ef you'd done dat, you'd er had mo' sense in yo' hide dan what you got now.'

"Brer Tiger 'low, 'I gwine ter let you off dis time, but nex' time I see you, watch out!'

"Brer Rabbit say, 'Bein's you so monst'us perlite, I'll let you off too, but keep yo' eye open nex' time you see me, kaze I'll git you sho.'"

The glee of the negro in the rabbit's nonchalant bearing is humorously given in this paragraph: —

"Well, I wish ter goodness you could er seed 'im 'bout dat time. He went 'long thoo de woods ez gay ez a colt in a barley-patch. He wunk at de trees, he shuck his fisties at de stumps, he make like he wuz quoilin' wid 'is shadder kaze it foller 'long atter 'im so close; en he went on scan'lous, mon!"

The three books that contain the most remarkable of these tales are: *Uncle Remus, His Songs and His Sayings* (1880), *Nights with Uncle Remus* (1881), *Uncle Remus and His Friends* (1892). In the volume, *Told by Uncle Remus* (1905), the same negro relates more stories to the son of the "little boy," who had many years before listened to the earlier tales. The one thing in these books that is absolutely the creation of Harris is the character of Uncle Remus. He is a patriarchal ex-slave, who seems to be a storehouse of knowledge concerning Brer Rabbit, Brer

Fox, Brer B'ar, and indeed all the animals of those bygone days when animals talked and lived in houses. He understands child nature as well as he knows the animals, and from the corner of his eye he keeps a sharp watch upon his tiny auditor to see how the story affects him. No figure more living, original, and lovable than Uncle Remus appears in southern fiction. In him Harris has created, not a burlesque or a sentimental impossibility, but an imperishable type, the type of the true plantation negro.

Harris also writes entertainingly of the slaves and their masters on the plantation and of the poor free negroes, in such stories as *Mingo and Other Sketches* (1884) and *Free Joe* (1887). He further presents a vivid picture of the Georgia "crackers" and "moonshiners"; but his inimitable animal stories, and Uncle Remus who tells them, have overshadowed all his other work, and remain his most distinctive and original contribution to American literature. These tales bid fair to have something of the immortality of those myths which succeeding generations have for thousands of years enjoyed.

THOMAS NELSON PAGE, 1853—

Thomas Nelson Page was born on Oakland Plantation in Hanover County, Virginia, in 1853. He graduated at Washington and Lee University in 1872, and took a degree in law at the University of Virginia in 1874. He practiced law in Richmond, wrote stories and essays upon the old South, and later moved to Washington to live.

His best stories are the short ones, like *Marse Chan* and *Meh Lady*, in which life on the Virginia plantations during the war is presented. Page is a natural story-teller. He wastes no time in analyzing, describing, and explaining, but sets his simple plots into immediate motion and makes us acquainted with his characters through their actions and speech. The regal mistresses of the plantations, the lordly but kind-hearted masters, the loving, simple-minded slaves, and handsome young men and maidens are far from complex personalities. They have a primitive simplicity and ingenuousness which belong to a bygone civilization. The strongest appeal in the stories is made by the negroes, whose faith in their masters is unquestioning and sometimes pathetic.

THOMAS NELSON PAGE

Some old negro who had been a former slave usually tells the story, and paints his "marster," his "missus," and his "white folks," as the finest in the region. He looks back upon the bygone days as a time when "nuthin' warn too good for niggers," and is sure that if his young "marster" did not get the brush "twuz cause twuz a bob-tailed fox." In *Meh Lady* the negro relating the tale is the true but unconscious hero. This kindly presentation of the finest traits of slave days, the idealizing of the characters, and the sympathetic portrayal of the warm affection existing between master and slave give to Page's books a strong note of romanticism. The humor is mild, quaint, and subtle, and it often lies next to tears. Page is preeminently a short-story writer. He possesses the restraint, the compression, the art, the unity of idea necessary to the production of a good short story.

GEORGE W. CABLE, 1844—

George Washington Cable is of Virginia and New England stock, but he was born in New Orleans in 1844, and called this beautiful city his home until 1884, when he moved to Connecticut. The following year he selected Northampton, Massachusetts, as a permanent residence. He was but fourteen when his father died, leaving the family in straitened circumstances. The boy thereupon left school and went to work. Four years later he entered the Confederate army. So youthful was his appearance, that a planter, catching sight of him, exclaimed, "Great heavens! Abe Lincoln told the truth. We *are* robbing the cradle and the grave!" He served two years in the southern army, and after the war returned penniless to his native city. His efforts to find employment are described in his most realistic novel, *Dr. Sevier*. He was a surveyor, a clerk to cotton merchants, and a reporter on the New Orleans *Picayune;* but his tastes were literary, and after the publication in 1879 of a volume of short stories, *Old Creole Days*, his attention was turned wholly to literature.

Cable's *Old Creole Days* is a collection of picturesque short stories of the romantic Creoles of New Orleans. *Jean-ah-Poquelin*, the story of an old recluse, is most artistically told. There are few incidents; Cable merely describes the former roving life of Jean, tells how suddenly it stopped, how he never again left the old home where he and an African mute lived, and how Jean's younger brother mysteriously disappeared, and the suspicion of his murder rested upon Jean's shoulders. The explanation of these points is unfolded by hints, conjectures, and rare glimpses into the Poquelin grounds at night, and finally by an impressive but simple description of Jean's funeral, at which the terrible secret is completely revealed. The deftest and finest touch of an artist is seen in the working out of this pathetic story.

Madame Delphine, now included in the volume *Old Creole Days*, is equally the product of a refined art. Here is shown the anguish of a quadroon mother who turns frantically from one to another for help to save her beautiful child, the ivory-tinted daughter of the South. When every one fails, the mother heart makes one grand sacrifice by which the end is gained, and she dies at the foot of the altar in an agony of remorse and love. The beautiful land of flowers, the jasmine-scented night of the South, the poetic chivalry of a proud, high-souled race are painted vividly in this idyllic story. Its people are not mortals, its beauty is not of earth, but, like the carved characters on Keats's Grecian urn, they have immortal youth and cannot change. Keats could have said to the lovers in *Madame Delphine*, as to his own upon the vase:—

"Forever wilt thou love, and she be fair!"

Cable's best long works are *The Grandissimes* (1880), *Dr. Sevier* (1884), and *Bonaventure, a Prose Pastoral of Arcadian Louisiana* (1888). Of these three, *The Grandissimes* is easily first in merit. It is a highly romantic work, full of dramatic episodes, and replete with humor. The abundance and variety of interesting characters in this romance evidence the great fertility and power of invention possessed by Cable. First of all, there is the splendid Creole, Honoré Grandissime, the head of the family, — a man who sees far into the future, and places his trust in the young American republic. Combating the narrow prejudices of his family, he leads them in spite of themselves to riches and honor. Opposing him in family counsels is his uncle, Agricola Fusilier, the brave, blustering, fire-eating reactionary. There is also the beautiful quadroon, Palmyre Philosophe. The "united grace and pride of her movement was inspiring, but — what shall we say? — feline? It was a femininity without humanity, — something that made her, with all her superbness, a creature that one would want to find chained." Beside her are the dwarf Congo woman and Clemence, the sharp-tongued negress, who sells her wares in the streets and sends her bright retorts back to the young bloods who taunt her. There is Bras Coupé, the savage slave, who had once been a chief in Africa and who fights like a fiend against enslavement, blights the broad acres with his curse, lives an exile in snake-infested swamps, and finally meets a most tragic fate. These unusual and somewhat sensational characters give high color, warmth, and variety to the romance. The two exquisite Creole women, Aurora and her daughter, Clotilde, are a triumph of delicate characterization, being at one and the same time winning, lovable, illogical, innocent, capable, and noble. The love scene in which Aurora says "no," while she means "yes," and is not taken at her word, is as delicious a bit of humor and sentiment as there is in modern fiction. In neither *Dr. Sevier* nor *Bonaventure* are there the buoyancy, vital interest, and unity of impression of *The Grandissimes*, which is one of the artistic products of American novelists. Cable may not have rendered the Creole character exactly true to life; but he has in a measure done for these high-spirited, emotional, brave people what Irving did for the Knickerbockers of New York and what Hawthorne did for the Puritan.

Cable has also given graphic pictures of New Orleans. His poetic powers of description enabled him to make the picturesque streets, the quaint interiors, the swamps, bayous, forests, and streams very vivid realities to his readers. He has warmth of feeling and a most refined and subtle humor. His scenes are sometimes blood-curdling, his characters unusual, and the deeds described sensational; but in his best work, his manner is so quiet, his English so elegant, and his treatment so poetic, that the effect is never crude or harsh, but always mild and harmonious.

JAMES LANE ALLEN, 1849 —

James Lane Allen was born in 1849 near Lexington, in the rich blue-grass section of Kentucky. He did not leave the state until he was twenty-two, so that his education both at school and college was received in Kentucky, and all his early and most impressionable years were passed amid Kentucky scenes. Many of these years were spent on a farm, where his faculty for observing was used to good advantage. As he grew older, he took his share in the farm work and labored in the fields of hemp, corn, and wheat, which he describes in his works. He graduated from Transylvania College, Lexington, and taught for several years, but after 1884 devoted himself to writing.

In 1891, Allen published *Flute and Violin and Other*

Kentucky Tales and Romances. For artistic completeness, Allen wrote nothing superior to the story in this collection, entitled, *King Solomon of Kentucky*, a tale of an idle vagabond who proved capable of a heroism from which many heroes might have flinched. All of the stories are romantic and pathetic. *The Kentucky Cardinal* (1894) and *Aftermath* (1895) are poetic idyls, whose scenes are practically confined within one small Kentucky garden, where the strawberries grow, the cardinal sings, and the maiden watches across the fence her lover at his weeding. The compass of the garden is not too small to embody the very spirit of out-of-doors, which is continuously present in these two delightful stories.

JAMES LANE ALLEN

From the human point of view, *The Choir Invisible* (1897) is Allen's strongest book. John Gray, Mrs. Falconer, and Amy are convincingly alive. No better proof of the vital interest they arouse is needed than the impatience felt by the reader at John's mistaken act of chivalry, which causes the bitterest sorrow to him and Mrs. Falconer. Allen's later works, *The Reign of Law* (1900), *The Mettle of the Pasture* (1903), *The Bride of the Mistletoe* (1909), lose in charm and grace what they gain as studies of moral problems. The hardness and incompleteness of outline of the character portrayals and the grimness of spirit in the telling of the tales make these novels uninviting after the luxuriance of the earlier books.

The setting is an important part of Allen's stories. He describes with the graphic touch of a true nature lover the witchery of Kentucky's fallow meadows, the beauty of her hempfields, the joys of a June day. A noisy conflict could not occur in the restful garden of *The Kentucky Cardinal*, while in the frontier garden of Mrs. Falconer, in *The Choir Invisible*, the ambitious, fiery John Gray seems not out of harmony because the presence of the adjacent wild forest affects the entire scene. In one way or another, the landscapes, by preparing the reader for the moods of the characters, play a part in all of Allen's novels. He is a master of the art that holds together scenes and actions. His descriptive powers are unusual, and his style is highly wrought. It is more that of the literary essayist than of the simple narrator, and it is full of poetic touches, delicate suggestions, and refined art.

MARY N. MURFREE (CHARLES EGBERT CRADDOCK), 1850 —

Miss Mary Noailles Murfree, better known as Charles Egbert Craddock, was born in Murfreesboro, Tennessee, in 1850. For fifteen years she spent her summers in the Tennessee mountains among the people of whom she writes. Her pen name of Charles Egbert Craddock deceived her publishers into the belief that she was a man. Both Howells and Thomas Bailey Aldrich accepted her stories for the *Atlantic Monthly* without suspecting her sex, and Aldrich was a surprised man the day she entered his office and introduced herself as Charles Egbert Craddock.

The stories that suggested to her editors a masculine hand are lively recitals of family feuds, moonshiners' raids,

MARY N. MURFREE (CHARLES EGBERT CRADDOCK)

circuit court sessions, fights over land grants, discoveries of oil, and many similar incidents, which make up the life of a people separated from the modern world by almost inaccessible mountains. The rifle is used freely by this people, and murder is frequent, but honor and bravery, daring and sacrifice, are not absent, and Craddock finds among the women, as well as the men, examples of magnanimity and heroism that thrill the reader.

The presence of the mountains is always imminent, and seems to impress the lives of the people in some direct way. To Cynthia Ware, for instance, in the story, *Drifting Down Lost Creek*, Pine Mountain seems to stand as a bar to all her ambitions and dreams: —

MARY N. MURFREE
(Charles Egbert Craddock)

"Whether the skies are blue or gray, the dark, austere line of its summit limits the horizon. It stands against the west like a barrier. It seems to Cynthia Ware that nothing which went beyond this barrier ever came back again. One by one the days passed over it, and in splendid apotheosis, in purple and crimson and gold, they were received into the heavens and returned no more. She beheld love go hence, and many a hope. Even Lost Creek itself, meandering for miles between the ranges, suddenly sinks into the earth, tunnels an unknown channel beneath the mountain, and is never seen again."

And, finally, after a tremendous self-sacrifice, when all appears lost and her future looks colorless and hopeless, she fears that the years of her life are "like the floating leaves drifting down Lost Creek, valueless, purposeless, and vaguely vanishing in the mountains." All of the stories are by no means so tragically sad as this one, but all are overshadowed by the mountains. Among the best of the novels, *Down the Ravine* and *The Prophet of the Great Smoky Mountain* may be mentioned. Craddock shows marked ability in delineating this primitive type of level-headed, independent people, and she tells their story with ease and vigor. The individual characters are not strongly differentiated in her many books, and the heroines bear considerable resemblance to each other, but the entire community of mountain folk, their ideals, hopes, and circumscribed lives are clearly and vividly shown.

MADISON J. CAWEIN, 1865-1914

Cawein spent the greater part of his life in Louisville, Kentucky, where he was born in 1865 and died in 1914. He wrote more than twenty volumes of verse, the best of which he collected in five volumes (1907) and later in one volume (1911). The appreciative English critic, Edmund Gosse, in his *Introduction* to the 1907 collection, calls Cawein "the only hermit thrush" singing "through an interval comparatively tuneless." W. D. Howells's (p. 373) *Foreword* in the 1911 volume emphasizes Cawein's unusual power of making common things 'live and glow thereafter with inextinguishable beauty.'

MADISON J. CAWEIN

Cawein actually writes much of his poetry out of doors in the presence of the nature which he is describing. His lyrics of nature are his best verse. He can even diminish the horror of a Kentucky feud by placing it among: —

> "Frail ferns and dewy mosses and dark brush, —
> Impenetrable briers, deep and dense,
> And wiry bushes, — brush, that seemed to crush
> The struggling saplings with its tangle, whence
> Sprawled out the ramble of an old rail-fence."

In his verses the catbird nests in the trumpet vine, the pewee pours forth a woodland welcome, the redbird sings a vesper song, the lilacs are musky of the May, the bluebells and the wind flowers bloom. We hear

> ". . . tinkling in the clover dells,
> The twilight sound of cattle bells."

His verse often shows exactness of observation, characteristic of modern students of nature, as well as a romantic love of the outdoor world. Note the specific references to the shape and color of individual natural objects in these lines from Cawein: —

> "May-apples, ripening yellow, lean
> With oblong fruit, a lemon-green,
> Near Indian-turnips, long of stem,
> That bear an acorn-oval gem."

He loves the nymphs of mythology, the dryads, naiads, and the fairies. One of his poems is called *There Are Fairies*: —

> "There are fairies, I could swear
> I have seen them busy where
> Rose-leaves loose their scented hair,
>
> . . . . .
>
> Leaning from the window sill
> Of a rose or daffodil,
> Listening to their serenade,
> All of cricket music made."

In luxuriance of imagery and profuse appeal to the senses, he is the Keats of the South. Lines like these remind us of the greater poet's *The Eve of St. Agnes:* —

> "Into the sunset's turquoise marge
> The moon dips, like a pearly barge
> Enchantment sails through magic seas
> To fairyland Hesperides."

Keats exclaims : —

> "O for a beaker full of the warm South."

Cawein proceeds to fill the beaker from the summer of a southern land, where

> "The west was hot geranium-red,"

where

> "The dawn is a warp of fever,
> The eve is a woof of fire,"

and where

> "The heliotropes breathe drowsy musk
> Into the jasmine-dreamy air."

Cawein sometimes suffers from profuseness and lack of pruning, but the music, sentiment, imaginative warmth, and profusion of nature's charms in his best lyrics rouse keen delight in any lover of poetry. While he revels in the color, warmth, and joys of nature, it should also be observed that he can occasionally strike that deeper note which characterizes the great nature poets of the English race. In *A Prayer for Old Age*, he asks: —

> "Never to lose my faith in Nature, God:
> But still to find
> Worship in trees; religion in each sod;
> And in the wind
> Sermons that breathe the universal God."

SUMMARY

The lack of towns, the widely separated population, the aristocratic nature of the civilization depending on slave labor, the absorption of the people in political questions, especially the question of slavery, the attitude toward literature as a profession, the poverty of public education, the extreme conservatism and isolation of the South, and, finally, the Civil War, and the period of reconstruction after it, — were all influences that served to retard the development of literature in the South.

The greatest name in southern literature is that of Edgar Allan Poe, the literary artist, the critic, the developer of the modern short story, the writer of superlatively melodious verse. He was followed by Simms, who was among the first in the South to live by his pen. His tales of adventure are still interesting and important for the history that they embody. Timrod's spontaneity and strength appear in lyrics of war, nature, and love. Hayne, a skilled poetic artist, is at his best in lyrics of nature. Lanier's poems of nature embody high ideals in verse of unusual melody, and voice a faith in "the greatness of God," as intense as that of any Puritan poet. Lanier shared with Simms, Hayne, and Timrod the bitter misfortunes of the war. Father Ryan is affectionately remembered for his stirring war lyrics and Father Tabb for his nature poems, sacred verse, and entertaining humor. The nature poetry of Cawein abounds in the color and warmth of the South.

In modern southern fiction there is to be found some of the most imaginative, artistic, and romantic work of the entire country in the latter quarter of the nineteenth century. Rich local color renders much of this fiction attractive. Harris fascinates the ear of the young world with the Georgia negro's tales of Brer Fox and Brer Rabbit. The Virginia negroes live in the stories of Page. Craddock introduces the Tennessee mountaineer, and Allen, the Kentucky farmer, scholar, and gentleman, while Cable paints the refined Creole in the fascinating city of New Orleans.

Notwithstanding the use of dialect and other realistic touches of local color, the fiction is largely romantic. The careful analysis of motives and detailed accounts of the commonplace, such as the eastern realists developed in the last part of the nineteenth century, are for the most part absent from this southern fiction.

A strong distinguishing feature of this body of fiction is the large part played by natural scenes. Allen shows unusual skill in employing nature to heighten his effects. If the poetic and vivid scenes were removed from Cable's stories, they would lose a large part of their charm. When Miss Murfree chooses eastern Tennessee for the scene of her novels, she never permits the mountains to be forgotten. These writers are lovers of nature as well as of human beings. The romantic prose fiction as well as the poetry is invested with color and beauty.

REFERENCES

Page's *The Old South*.
Page's *Social Life in Old Virginia before the War*.
Hart's *Slavery and Abolition*.
Baskerville's *Southern Writers*, 2 vols.
Link's *Pioneers of Southern Literature*, 2 vols.
Moses's *The Literature of the South*.
Holliday's *A History of Southern Literature*.
Manly's *Southern Literature*.
Painter's *Poets of the South*.
Woodberry's *The Life of Edgar Allan Poe, Personal and Literary, with his chief Correspondence with Men of Letters*, 2 vols., 1909. (The best life.)

Woodberry and Stedman's *The Works of Edgar Allan Poe with a Memoir, Critical Introductions, and Notes*, 10 vols.

Harrison's *The Virginia Edition of the Works of Edgar Allan Poe*, 17 vols. (Contains excellent critical essays.)

Harrison's *Life and Letters of Edgar Allan Poe*, 2 vols.

Stedman's *Poets of America*. (Poe.)

Fruit's *The Mind and Art of Poe's Poetry*.

Canby's *The Short Story in English*, Chap. XI. (Poe.)

Baldwin's *American Short Stories*. (Poe.)

Payne's *American Literary Criticism*. (Poe.)

Prescott's *Selections from the Critical Writings of Edgar Allan Poe, edited with an Introduction and Notes*.

Gates's *Studies and Appreciations*. (Poe.)

Trent's *William Gilmore Simms*.

Erskine's *Leading American Novelists*. (Simms.)

Ward's *Memorial of Sidney Lanier*, in *Poems of Sidney Lanier*, edited by his Wife.

Burt's *The Lanier Book*.

Burt and Cable's *The Cable Story Book*.

Page's *The Page Story Book*.

SUGGESTED READINGS

Selections (not always the ones indicated below) from *all* the authors mentioned in this chapter may be found in Trent's *Southern Writers*, 524 pages, and Mims and Payne's *Southern Prose and Poetry for Schools*, 440 pages. Selections from the majority of the poets are given in Painter's *Poets of the South*, 237 pages, and Weber's *Selections from the Southern Poets*, 221 pages. The best poems of Poe and Lanier may be found in Page's *The Chief American Poets*.

POETRY

Poe. — His best poems are short, and may soon be read. They are *Annabel Lee, To One in Paradise, The Raven, The Haunted Palace, The Conqueror Worm, Ulalume, Israfel, Lenore*, and *The Bells*.

Hayne. — *A Dream of the South Winds, Aspects of the Pines, The Woodland Phases*, and *A Storm in the Distance*.

Timrod. — *Spring, The Lily Confidante, An Exotic, The Cotton Boll*, and *Carolina*.

Lanier. — *The Marshes of Glynn, Sunrise, The Song of the Chattahoochee, Tampa Robins, Love and Song, The Stirrup Cup,* and *The Symphony.*

Ryan. — *The Conquered Banner,* and *The Sword of Robert Lee.*

Tabb. — Fourteen of his complete poems may be found on two pages (489 and 490) of Stedman's *An American Anthology.* Much of Tabb's best work is contained in his little volume entitled *Poems* (1894).

Cawein. — *The Whippoorwill, There are Fairies, The Shadow Garden, One Day and Another, In Solitary Places, A Twilight Moth, To a Wind Flower, Beauty and Art, A Prayer for Old Age.*

The best two volumes of general selections from Cawein's verse have been published in England and given the titles, *Kentucky Poems* (1902), 264 pages, edited with an excellent *Introduction* by Edmund Gosse, and *New Poems* (1909), 248 pages. His best nature poetry will be found in his single American volume of selections, entitled *Poems, Selected by the Author* (1911).

PROSE

Poe. — Poe's best short story is *The Fall of the House of Usher,* but it is better to begin with such favorites as either *The Murders in the Rue Morgue, The Gold-Bug,* or *A Descent into the Maelstrom.* There are many poor editions of Poe's *Tales.* Cody's *The Best Tales of Edgar Allan Poe* and Macmillan's *Pocket Classics* edition may be recommended. The best part of his critical remarks on short-story writing is quoted in this text, p. 299. A part of his essay, *The Poetic Principle,* is given in Trent.

Simms. — Mims and Payne give (pp. 50–69) a good selection from *The Yemassee,* describing an Indian episode in the war of 1715, between the Spaniards and the Indians on the one hand, and the English on the other. Trent gives (pp. 186–189) from *The Partisan,* a scene laid at the time of the Revolutionary War.

Harris. — Read anywhere from *Uncle Remus, his Songs, and his Sayings* (1880), *Nights with Uncle Remus* (1881), *Uncle Remus and his Friends* (1892). An excellent selection, *Brother Billy Goat eats his Dinner,* is given in Trent.

Cable. — *Madame Delphine* and *Jean-ah-Poquelin,* two of Cable's best short stories, are published under the title, *Old Creole Days.*

Page, Allen, and Craddock. — From Page, read either *Marse Chan* or *Meh Lady*; from Allen, *King Solomon of Kentucky,* and *Two Gentlemen* of Kentucky, from *Flute and Violin*, or *The Kentucky Cardinal*, or *The Choir Invisible*; from Craddock, selections from *Down the Ravine*, *In the Tennessee Mountains*, or *The Prophet of the Great Smoky Mountain*.

QUESTIONS AND SUGGESTIONS

Poetry. — Which of Poe's nine poems indicated for reading pleases you most and which least? What is the chief source of your pleasure in reading him? Do you feel like reading any of his poems a second time or repeating parts of them? Account for the extraordinary vitality of Poe's verse. What is the subject matter of most of his poems?

What is the subject of Lanier's best verse? Compare his melody and ideals with Poe's. Is Lanier's *Song of the Chattahoochee* as melodious as Tennyson's *The Brook*? Which is the most beautiful stanza in *My Springs*? What are the strongest and most distinguishing qualities of Lanier's verse? Which of these are especially prominent in *The Marshes of Glynn* and *Sunrise*, and which in *Tampa Robins*?

Compare Hayne and Timrod for artistic finish, definiteness, and spontaneity. Does Hayne or Timrod love nature more for herself alone? Select the best stanza from Timrod's *The Lily Confidante* and compare it with your favorite stanza from Lanier's *My Springs*. From each of the poems of Hayne suggested for reading, select some of the most artistic creations of his fancy.

Indicate the patriotism and the pathos in Father Ryan's verse.

Point out some unique qualities in Tabb's poetry. Is the length of his poems in accordance with Poe's dictum? Select some passage showing special delicacy or originality in describing nature.

What in Cawein's verse would indicate that he wrote his poems out of doors? Compare the definiteness of his references to nature with Hayne's. What specific references in Cawein's nature poems please you most? Compare Keats's poems *On the Grasshopper and Cricket*, *Fancy*, and stanzas here and there from *The Eve of St. Agnes* with Cawein's imagery and method of appealing to the senses.

Prose. — Take one of Poe's tales, and point out how it illustrates his theory of the short story given on p. 299. In order to hold the attention of an average audience, should you select for reading one of Irving's, Hawthorne's, or Poe's short stories? Should you use the same principle in selecting one of these stories for a friend to read quietly by himself?

Is Simms dramatic? In what particulars does he remind you of Cooper? In the selection from *The Yemassee* (Mims and Payne) are there any qualities which Poe indicates for a short story?

What is the secret of the attractiveness of the stories of Joel Chandler Harris? Point out some valuable philosophy of human nature which frequently crops out. What special characteristics of Uncle Remus are revealed in these tales? What are the most prominent qualities of Brer Rabbit? Why does the negro select him for his hero? What is the final result of Brer Fox's trick in *The Wonderful Tar Baby Story?* What resemblances and differences can you find between the animal stories of Harris and Kipling?

Why are Cable's stories called romantic? What remarkable feature do you notice about their local color? Give instances of his poetic touch and of his power to draw character. Does he reveal his characters in a plain, matter-of-fact manner, or by means of subtle touches and unexpected revelations?

Compare Page's negroes with Uncle Remus. What characteristics of Virginia life do the stories of Page reveal? What do you find most attractive in him as a story-teller?

What impression does Allen's *King Solomon of Kentucky* make on you? What are some of the strong situations in *The Choir Invisible?* What effect does the natural setting have on his scenes?

In the presentation of what scenes does Craddock excel? What are some of the characteristics of her mountain people? Is the individuality of the characters strongly marked or are they more frequently general types? In what parts of the South are the scenes of the stories of Cable, Page, Allen, and Craddock chiefly laid? How should you define "local color" in terms of the work of each of these writers?

CHAPTER VI

WESTERN LITERATURE

The Newness of the West.—It is difficult for the young of to-day to realize that Wisconsin and Iowa were not states when Hawthorne published his Twice Told Tales (1837), that Lowell's *The Vision of Sir Launfal* (1848) was finished ten years before Minnesota became a state, that Longfellow's *Hiawatha* (1855) appeared six years before the admission of Kansas, and Holmes's *The Autocrat of the Breakfast Table* (1858), nine years before the admission of Nebraska. In 1861 Mark Twain went to the West in a primitive stagecoach. Bret Harte had finished *The Luck of Roaring Camp* (1868) before San Francisco was reached by a transcontinental railroad.

Even after the early pioneers had done their work, the population of the leading states of the West underwent too rapid a change for quick assimilation. Between 1870 and 1880 the population of Minnesota increased 77 per cent; Kansas, 173 per cent; Nebraska, 267 per cent. This population was mostly agricultural, and it was busy subduing the soil and getting creature comforts.

Mark Twain says of the advance guard of the pioneers who went to the far West to conquer this new country:—

"It was the *only* population of the kind that the world has ever seen gathered together, and it is not likely that the world will ever see its like again. For, observe, it was an assemblage of two hundred thousand *young* men — not simpering, dainty, kid-gloved weaklings, but stalwart, muscular, dauntless young braves, brimful of push and energy, and royally endowed with every attribute that goes to make up a peerless and magnificent manhood — the very pick and choice of the world's glorious ones."[1]

In even as recent a period as the twenty years from 1880 to 1900, the population of Minnesota increased 124 per cent; Nebraska, 135 per cent; and Colorado, 177 per cent. This increase indicates something of the strenuous work necessary on the physical side to prepare comfortable permanent homes in the country, town, and city, and to plan and execute the other material adaptations necessary for progressive civilized life and trade. It is manifest that such a period of stress is not favorable to the development of literature. Although the population of California increased 60 per cent and that of the state of Washington 120 per cent between 1900 and 1910, the extreme stress, due to pioneer life and to rapid increase in population, has already abated in the vast majority of places throughout the West, which is rapidly becoming as stable as any other section of the country.

The Democratic Spirit. — In settling the West, everybody worked shoulder to shoulder. There were no privileged classes to be excepted from the common toils and privations. All met on common ground, shared each other's troubles, and assisted each other in difficult work. All were outspoken and championed their own opinions without restraint. At few times in the history of the civilized world has the home been a more independent unit. Never have pioneers been more self-reliant, more able to cope with difficulties, more determined to have their rights.

This democratic spirit is reflected in the works of western authors. It made Mark Twain the champion of the weak, the impartial upholder of justice to the Maid of

[1] *Roughing It.*

Orleans, to a slave, or to a vivisected dog. It made him join the school of Cervantes and puncture the hypocrisy of pretension in classes or individuals. The Clemens family had believed in the aristocracy of slavery, but the great democratic spirit of the West molded Mark Twain as a growing boy. All the characters of worth in the great stories of his young life are democratic. The son of the drunkard, the slave mother, the crowds on the steamboats, the far western pioneers, belong to the great democracy of man.

Abraham Lincoln owes his fame in oratory to this democratic spirit, to the feeling that prompted him to say, "With malice toward none; with charity for all." Bret Harte's world-famous short stories picture the rough mining camps. Eugene Field is a poet of that age of universal democracy, the age of childhood. The poetry of James Whitcomb Riley is popular because it speaks directly to the common human heart.

Although the West has already begun a period of greater repose, she has been fortunate to retain an Elizabethan enthusiasm and interest in many-sided life. This quality, so apparent in much of the work discussed in this chapter, is full of virile promise for the future.

ABRAHAM LINCOLN, 1809-1865

Migrating from his birthplace in Kentucky, first to Indiana and then to Illinois, where he helped to clear the unbroken forest, Abraham Lincoln was one of America's greatest pioneers. Shackled by poverty and lack of education, his indomitable will first broke his own fetters and then those of the slave. History claims him as her own, but some of the plain, sincere, strong English that fell from his lips while he was making history demands attention as literature. Passing by his great debates with Douglas (1858), not because they are unimportant, but because they belong more to the domain of politics and history, we come to his *Gettysburg Address* (1863), which is one of the three greatest American orations. In England, Oxford University displays on its walls this *Address* as a model to show students how much can be said simply and effectively in two hundred and sixty-nine words. Edward Everett, a graduate of Harvard, called the most eloquent man of his time, also spoke at Gettysburg, although few are to-day aware of this fact.

ABRAHAM LINCOLN

The question may well be asked, "How did Lincoln, who had less than one year's schooling, learn the secret of such speech?" The answer will be found in the fixity of purpose and the indomitable will of the pioneer. When he was a boy, he seemed to realize that in order to succeed, he must talk and write plainly. As a lad, he used to practice telling things in such a way that the most ignorant person could understand them. In his youth he had only little scraps of paper or shingles on which to write, and so perforce learned the art of brevity. Only a few books were accessible to him, and he read and reread them until they became a part of him. The volumes that he thus absorbed were the *Bible*, *Æsop's Fables*, *Arabian Nights*, *Robinson Crusoe*, *The Pilgrim's Progress*, *Franklin's Autobiography*, Weems's *Life of Washington*, and two or three textbooks. Without such good reading, which served to guide his practice in writing and speaking, he could never have been President. Later in life he read Shakespeare, especially *Macbeth*.

Parts of his *Second Inaugural Address* (1865) show even better than his *Gettysburg Address* the influence of the *Bible* on his thought and style. One reason why there is so much weak and ineffective prose written to-day is because books like the *Bible* and *The Pilgrim's Progress* are not read and reread as much as formerly. Of the North and the South, he says in his *Second Inaugural:*—

"Both read the same Bible, and pray to the same God; and each invokes his aid against the other. It may seem strange that any men should dare to ask a just God's assistance in wringing their bread from the sweat of other men's faces; but let us judge not, that we be not judged. The prayers of both could not be answered — that of neither has been answered fully. . . .

"With malice toward none; with charity for all; with firmness in the right, as God gives us to see the right, let us strive on to finish the work we are in; to bind up the nation's wounds. . . ."

Absolute sincerity is the most striking quality in his masterpieces. Simplicity and brevity are next in evidence; to these are sometimes added the pathos and intensity of a Hebrew prophet.

BRET HARTE, 1839-1902

Life. — The father of Bret Harte was professor of Greek in the Albany, New York, Female College, where his son, named Francis Bret, was born in 1839. The boy never attended an institution of learning higher than a common school. Fatherless at the age of fifteen, he went with his mother to California in 1854. Here he tried teaching school, mining, going on stages as an express messenger, printing, government service, and editing. Of his experience in California, he writes: —

"Here I was thrown among the strangest social conditions that the latter-day world has perhaps seen. . . . Amid rushing waters and wildwood freedom, an army of strong men, in red shirts and top-boots, were feverishly in search of the buried gold of earth. . . . It was a land of perfect freedom, limited only by the instinct and the habit of law which prevailed in the mass. . . . Strong passions brought quick climaxes, all the better and worse forces of manhood being in unbridled play. To me it was like a strange, ever-varying panorama, so novel that it was difficult to grasp comprehensively."

BRET HARTE
(From a painting by John Pettie, R. A.)

Amid such surroundings he was educated for his life work, and his idealization of these experiences is what entitles him to a sure place in American literature.

After spending sixteen years in California, he returned in 1871 to the East, where he wrote and lectured; but these subsequent years are of comparatively small interest to the student of literature. In 1878 he went as consul to Crefeld in Germany. He was soon transferred from there to Glasgow, Scotland, the consulship of which he held until his removal by President Cleveland in 1885. These two sentences from William Black, the English novelist, may explain the presidential action: "Bret Harte was to have been back from Paris last night, but he is a wandering comet. The only place he is sure not to be found is at the Glasgow consulate." Bret Harte was something of a lion in a congenial English literary set, and he never returned to America. He continued to write until his death at Camberly, Surrey, in 1902. The tourist may find his grave in Frimley churchyard, England.

Works. — Bret Harte was a voluminous writer. His authorized publishers have issued twenty-eight volumes of his prose and one volume of his collected poems. While his *Plain Language from Truthful James*, known as his "Heathen Chinee" poem, was very popular, his short stories in prose are his masterpieces. The best of these were written before 1871, when he left California for the East. Much of his later work was a repetition of what he had done as well or better in his youth.

The Overland Magazine, a San Francisco periodical, which Bret Harte was editing, published in 1868 his own short story, *The Luck of Roaring Camp*. This is our greatest short story of pioneer life. England recognized its greatness as quickly as did America. The first two sentences challenge our curiosity, and remind us of Poe's dictum concerning the writing of a story (p. 299): —

"There was commotion in Roaring Camp. It could not have been a fight, for in 1850 that was not novel enough to have called together the entire settlement."

We at once stand face to face with the characters of that mining camp. "The assemblage numbered about a hundred men. One or two of these were actual fugitives from justice, some were criminal, and all were reckless." We shall remember "Kentuck" and Oakhurst and "Stumpy," christening the baby: —

"'I proclaim you Thomas Luck, according to the laws of the United States and the State of California, so help me God.' It was the first time that the name of the Deity had been otherwise uttered than profanely in the camp."

There are two sentences describing the situation of Roaring Camp:—

"The camp lay in a triangular valley between two hills and a river. The only outlet was a steep trail over the summit of a hill that faced the cabin, now illuminated by the rising moon."

Poe would have approved of the introduction of this bit of description, for it heightens the pathetic effect and focuses attention upon the mother. Even that "steep trail" is so artistically introduced that she

". . . might have seen it from the rude bunk whereon she lay,— seen it winding like a silver thread until it was lost in the stars above. . . . Within an hour she had climbed, as it were, that rugged road that led to the stars, and so passed out of Roaring Camp, its sin and shame, forever."

Bret Harte in a few words relates how these miners reared the child, how they were unconsciously influenced by it, and how one day an expressman rushed into an adjacent village saying:—

"They've a street up there in 'Roaring,' that would lay over any street in Red Dog. They've got vines and flowers round their houses, and they wash themselves twice a day."

He had, as we have seen, something of the remarkable technique of which Poe was a master. The influence of Dickens, especially his sentimentalism, is often apparent in Harte's work. Some have accused him of caricature or exaggeration, but these terms, when applied to his best work, signify little except the use of emphasis and selection, of which Homer and Shakespeare freely availed themselves. The author of *The Luck of Roaring Camp*, *The Outcasts of Poker Flat*, and *Tennessee's Partner* seemed to know almost instinctively what he must emphasize or neglect in order to give his readers a vivid impression of the California argonauts. He mingles humor and pathos, realism and idealism, in a masterly way. No other author has had the necessary dramatic touch to endow those times with such a powerful romantic appeal to our imagination. No one else has rescued them from the oblivion which usually overtakes all transitory stages of human development.

Bret Harte's pages afford us the rare privilege of again communing with genuine primitive feeling, with eternal human qualities, not deflected or warped by convention. He gives us the literature of democracy. In self-forgetfulness, sympathy, love for his kind, Tennessee's partner in his unkempt dress is the peer of any wearer of the broadcloth.

Bret Harte's best work is as bracing, as tonic, as instinct with the spirit of vigorous youth, as the mountain air which has never before been breathed. Woodberry well says: "He created lasting pictures of human life, some of which have the eternal outline and pose of a Theocritean idyl. The supreme nature of his gift is shown by the fact that he had no rival and left no successor. His work is as unique as that of Poe or Hawthorne."[1]

EUGENE FIELD, 1850–1895

The Poet Laureate of Children. — Eugene Field was born in St. Louis in 1850. Of this western group of authors he was the only member who went to college. He completed the junior year at the University of Missouri, but did not graduate. At the age of twenty-three he began newspaper work there, and he continued this work in various places

[1] Woodberry: *America in Literature.*

until his death in Chicago in 1895. For the last twelve years of his life he was connected with the Chicago *Daily News*.

He wrote many poems and prose tales, but the work by which he will probably live in literature is his poetry for children. For his title of poet-laureate of children, he has had few worthy competitors. His *Little Boy Blue* will be read as long as there are parents who have lost a child. "What a world of little people was left unrepresented in the realms of poetry until Eugene Field came!" exclaimed a noted teacher. Children listen almost breathlessly to the story of the duel between "the gingham dog and the calico cat," and to the ballad of "The Rock-a-By Lady from Hushaby Street," and the dreams which she brings: —

> "There is one little dream of a big sugar plum,
> And lo! thick and fast the other dreams come
> Of popguns that bang, and tin tops that hum,
> And a trumpet that bloweth!"

He loved children, and any one else who loves them, whether old or young, will enjoy reading his poems of childhood. Who, for instance, will admit that he does not like the story of *Wynken, Blynken, and Nod?*

EUGENE FIELD

"Wynken, Blynken, and Nod one night
    Sailed off in a wooden shoe —
Sailed on a river of crystal light,
    Into a sea of dew.
'Where are you going, and what do you wish?'
The old moon asked the three.
'We have come to fish for the herring fish
    That live in this beautiful sea;
Nets of silver and gold have we!'
        Said Wynken,
        Blynken,
        And Nod.

"The old moon laughed and sang a song,
    As they rocked in the wooden shoe,
And the wind that sped them all night long
    Ruffled the waves of dew."

Who does not wish to complete this story to find out what became of the children? Who does not like Krinken?

"Krinken was a little child, —
    It was summer when he smiled."

Field could write exquisitely beautiful verse. His tender heart had felt the pathos of life, and he knew how to set this pathos to music. He was naturally a humorist, and his humor often caused him to take a right angle turn in the midst of serious thoughts. Parents have for nearly a quarter of a century used the combination of humor and pathos in his poem, *The Little Peach*, to keep their children from eating green fruit: —

"A little peach in the orchard grew, —
    A little peach of emerald hue;
Warmed by the sun and wet by the dew,
    It grew.

"John took a bite and Sue a chew,
And then the trouble began to brew, —
Trouble the doctor couldn't subdue.
    Too true!

"Under the turf where the daisies grew
They planted John and his sister Sue,
And their little souls to the angels flew, —
    Boo hoo!"

Time is not likely to rob Eugene Field of the fame of having written *The Canterbury Tales of Childhood*.

JAMES WHITCOMB RILEY, 1853-1916

The poet of our time who has most widely voiced the everyday feeling of democracy, of the man on the farm, in the workshop, and in his home circle, is James Whitcomb Riley. His popularity with this generation suggests the part which the ballad makers played in developing a love for verse before Shakespeare came.

He was born in the little country town of Greenfield, twenty miles east of Indianapolis. Like Bret Harte and Mark Twain, Riley had only a common school education. He became a sign painter, and traveled widely, first painting advertisements for patent medicines and then for the leading business firms in the various towns he visited. After this, he did work on newspapers and became a traveling lecturer, and reader of his own poems.

Much of his poetry charms us with its presentation of

rural life. In *The Old Swimmin'-Hole and 'Leven More Poems* (1883), it is a delight to accompany him

> "When the frost is on the punkin and the fodder's in the shock,"

or when

> "The summer winds is sniffin' round the bloomin' locus' trees,
> And the clover in the pastur' is a big day fer the bees,"

or again, in *Neighborly Poems* (1891), as he listens to *The First Bluebird* singing with

> "A breezy, treesy, beesy hum,
> Too sweet fer anything!"

We welcome him as the champion of a new democratic flower. In his poem, *The Clover*, he says: —

> "But what is the lily and all of the rest
> Of the flowers, to a man with a hart in his brest
> That was dipped brimmin' full of the honey and dew
> Of the sweet clover-blossoms his babyhood knew?"

Like Eugene Field, Riley loved children. His *Rhymes of Childhood* (1890) contains such favorites as *The Raggedy Man*, *Our Hired Girl*, *Little Orphant Annie*, with its bewitching warning about the "*Gobble-uns,*" and the pathetic *Little Mahala Ashcraft*.

But no matter whether his verses take us to the farm, to the child, to the inner circle of the home, or to a neighborly gathering, their first characteristic is simplicity. Some of his best verse entered the homes of the common people more easily because it was written in the Hoosier dialect. He is a democratic poet, and the common people listen to him. In *Afterwhiles* (1887), he says: —

> "The tanned face, garlanded with mirth,
> It hath the kingliest smile on earth —
> The swart brow, diamonded with sweat,
> Hath never need of coronet."

In like vein are his lines from *Griggsby's Station:*—

"Le's go a-visitin' back to Griggsby's Station —
Back where the latch string's a-hangin' from the door,
And ever' neighbor 'round the place is dear as a relation —
Back where we ust to be so happy and so pore!"

In lines like the following from *Afterwhiles*, there is a rare mingling of pathos and hope and kindly optimism:—

"I cannot say, and I will not say
That he is dead. — He is just away!

"With a cheery smile and a wave of the hand,
He has wandered into an unknown land,

"And left us dreaming how very fair
It needs must be, since he lingers there."

The charitable optimism of his lines:—

"I would sing of love that lives
On the errors it forgives,"

has touched many human hearts.

Furthermore, he has unusual humor, which is as delightful and as pervasive as the odor of his clover fields. Humor drives home to us the application of the optimistic philosophy in these lines:—

"When a man's jest glad plum through,
God's pleased with him, same as you."

"When God sorts out the weather and sends rain,
W'y, rain's my choice."

In poems like *Griggsby's Station* he shows his power in making a subject pathetic and humorous at the same time.

Albert J. Beveridge says of Riley, "The aristocrat may make verses whose perfect art renders them immortal, like Horace, or state high truths in austere beauty, like Arnold. But only the brother of the common man can tell what the common heart longs for and feels, and only he lives in the understanding and affection of the millions."

SAMUEL L. CLEMENS, 1835-1910

Life in the Mississippi Valley. — The author who is known in every village of the United States by the pen name of Mark Twain, which is the river phrase for two fathoms of water, was born in Florida, Missouri, in 1835. He says of his birthplace: "The village contained a hundred people, and I increased the population by one per cent. It is more than the best man in history ever did for any other town." When he was two and a half years old, the family moved to Hannibal on the Mississippi, thirty miles away.

The most impressionable years of his boyhood were spent in Hannibal, which he calls "a loafing, down-at-the-heels, slave-holding Mississippi town." He attended only a common school, a picture of which is given in *The Adventures of Tom Sawyer*. Even this schooling ceased at the age of twelve, when his father died. Like Benjamin Franklin and W. D. Howells, the boy then became a printer, and followed this trade in various places for nearly eight years, traveling east as far as New York City. He next became a "cub," or under pilot, on the Mississippi River. After an eighteen months' apprenticeship, he was an excellent pilot, and he received two hundred and fifty dollars a month for his services. He says of these days: "Time drifted smoothly and prosperously on, and I supposed — and hoped — that I was going to follow the river the rest of my days, and die at the wheel when my mission was ended. But by and by the war came, commerce was suspended, my occupation was gone." For an inimitable account of these days, the first twenty-one chapters of his *Life on the Mississippi* (1883) should be read.

". . . in that brief, sharp schooling, I got personally and familiarly acquainted with about all the different types of human nature that are to be found in fiction, biography, or history. The fact is daily borne in upon me, that the average shore employment requires as much as forty years to equip a man with this sort of education. . . . When I find a well-drawn character in fiction or biography, I generally take a warm personal interest in him, for the reason that I have known him before — met him on the river."[1]

No other work in American literature or history can take the place of this book and of his three great stories

---

[1] *Life on the Mississippi*, Chapter XVIII.

(pp. 359-361), which bring us face to face with life in the great Mississippi Valley in the middle of the nineteenth century.

Life in the Far West. — In 1861 he went to Nevada as private secretary to his brother, who had been appointed secretary of that territory. Mark Twain intended to stay there but a short time. He says, "I little thought that I would not see the end of that three-month pleasure excursion for six or seven uncommonly long years."

The account of his experiences in our far West is given in the volume called *Roughing It* (1871). This book should be read as a chapter in the early history of that section. The trip from St. Joseph to Nevada by stage, the outlaws, murders, sagebrush, jackass rabbits, coyotes, mining camps, — all the varied life of the time — is thrown distinctly on the screen in the pages of *Roughing It.* While in the West, he caught the mining fever, but he soon became a newspaper reporter and editor, and in this capacity he discovered the gold mine of his genius as a writer. The experience of these years was only second in importance to his remarkable life in the Mississippi Valley. No other American writer has received such a variety of training in the university of human nature.

Later Life. — In 1867, he supplemented his purely American training with a trip to Europe, Egypt, and the Holy Land. The story of his journey is given in *The Innocents Abroad* (1869), the work which first made him known in every part of the United States. *A Tramp Abroad* (1880), and *Following the Equator: A Journey Around the World* (1897), are records of other foreign travels. While they are largely autobiographical, and show in an unusually entertaining way how he became one of the most cosmopolitan of our authors, these works are less important than those which throb with the heart beats of that American life of which he was a part in his younger days.

In 1884 he became a partner in the publishing house of Charles L. Webster and Co. This firm incurred risks against his advice, and failed. The failure not only swallowed up every cent that he had saved, but left him, past sixty, staggering under a load of debt that would have been a despair to most young men. Like Sir Walter Scott in a similar misfortune, Mark Twain made it a point of honor to assume the whole debt. He lectured, he wrote, he traveled, till finally, unlike Scott, he was able to pay off the last penny of the firm's indebtedness. His life thus set a standard of honor to Americans, which is to them a legacy the peer of any left by any author to his nation.

After his early pioneer days, his American homes were chiefly in New England. For many years he lived in Hartford, Connecticut. In 1908 he went to a new home at Redding, Connecticut. His last years were saddened by the death of his daughter and his wife. His death in 1910 made plain the fact that few American authors had won a more secure place in the affections of all classes.

It does not seem possible that the life of any other American author can ever closely resemble his. He had Elizabethan fullness of experience. Even Sir Walter Raleigh's life was no more varied; for Mark Twain was a printer, pilot, soldier, miner, newspaper reporter, editor, special correspondent, traveler around the world, lecturer, biographer, writer of romances, historian, publisher, and philosopher.

Stories of the Mississippi Valley. — The works by which Mark Twain will probably be longest known are those dealing with the scenes of his youth. He is the historian of an epoch that will never return. His works that reveal the bygone life of the Mississippi Valley are not unlikely to increase in fame as the years pass. He resembles Hawthorne in presenting the early history of a section of our country. New England was old when Hawthorne was a boy, and he imaginatively reconstructed the life of its former days. When Mark Twain was young, the West was new; hence his task in literature was to preserve contemporary life. He has accomplished this mission better than any other writer of the middle West.

The Adventures of Tom Sawyer (1876) is a story of life in a Missouri town on the Mississippi River. Tom Sawyer, the hero, is "a combination," says the author, "of the characteristics of three boys whom I knew." Probably Mark Twain himself is the largest part of this combination. The book is the record of a wide-awake boy's impression of the life of that day. The wretched common school, the pranks of the boys, the Sunday school, the preacher and his sermon, the task of whitewashing the fence, the belief in witches and charms, the half-breed Indian, the drunkard, the murder scene, and the camp life of the boys on an island in the Mississippi, — are all described with a vividness and interest due to actual experience. The author distinctly says, "Most of the adventures recorded in this book really occurred; one or two were experiences of my own, the rest those of boys who were schoolmates of mine."

Huckleberry Finn (1885) has been called the *Odyssey* of the Mississippi. This is a story of life on and along the great river, just before the middle of the nineteenth century. Huckleberry Finn, the son of a drunkard, and the friend of Tom Sawyer, is the hero of the book. The reader becomes deeply interested in the fortunes of Jim, a runaway slave, who accompanies Huck on a raft down the river, and who is almost hourly in danger of being caught and returned or again enslaved by some chance white man.

One of the strongest scenes in the story is where Huck debates with himself whether he shall write the owner where to capture Jim, or whether he shall aid the poor creature to secure his freedom. Since Huck was a child of the South, there was no doubt in his mind that punishment in the great hereafter awaited one who deprived another of his property, and Jim was worth eight hundred dollars. Huck did not wish to lose his soul, and so he wrote a letter to the owner. Before sending it, however, he, like Hamlet, argued the case with himself. Should he send the letter or forfeit human respect and his soul? The conclusion that Huck reached is thoroughly characteristic of Mark Twain's attitude toward the weak. The thirty-first chapter of *Huckleberry Finn*, in which this incident occurs, could not have been written by one who did not thoroughly appreciate the way in which the South regarded those who aided in the escape of a slave. Another unique episode of the story is the

HUCKLEBERRY FINN
(From "Huckleberry Finn," Copyright, 1884, by Samuel L. Clemens.)

remarkable dramatic description of the deadly feud between the families of the Shepherdsons and the Grangerfords.

This story is Mark Twain's masterpiece, and it is not improbable that it will continue to be read as long as the Mississippi flows toward the Gulf. Of Mark Twain's achievement in these two tales, Professor William Lyon Phelps of Yale says: "He has done something which many popular novelists have signally failed to accomplish — he has created real characters. His two wonderful boys, Tom Sawyer and Huckleberry Finn, are wonderful in quite different ways. The creator of Tom exhibited remarkable observation; the creator of Huck showed the divine touch of imagination. . . . *Tom Sawyer* and *Huckleberry Finn* are prose epics of American life."

Mark Twain says that he was reared to believe slavery a divine institution. This fact makes his third story of western life, *Pudd'nhead Wilson*, interesting for its pictures of the negro and slavery, from a different point of view from that taken by Mrs. Stowe in *Uncle Tom's Cabin*.

General Characteristics. — During his lifetime, Mark Twain's humor was the chief cause of his well-nigh universal popularity. The public had never before read a book exactly like his *Innocents Abroad*. Speaking of an Italian town, he says, "It is well the alleys are not wider, because they hold as much smell now as a person can stand, and, of course, if they were wider they would hold more, and then the people would die." Incongruity, or the association of dissimilar ideas, is the most frequent cause of laughter to his readers. His famous cablegram from England that the report of his death was much exaggerated is of this order, as is also the following sentence from *Roughing It:* —

"Then he rode over and began to rebuke the stranger with a six-shooter, and the stranger began to explain with another."

Such sentences convey something more than a humorous impression. They surpass the usual historical records in revealing in an incisive way the social characteristics of those pioneer days. His humor is often only a means of more forcibly impressing on readers some phase of the philosophy of history. Even careless readers frequently recognize that this statement is true of much of the humor in *A Connecticut Yankee at King Arthur's Court*, which is one of his most successful exhibitions of humor based on incongruity.

While his humor is sometimes mechanical, coarse, and forced, we must not forget that it also often reveals the thoughtful philosopher. To confirm this statement, one has only to glance at the humorous philosophy that constitutes *Pudd'nhead Wilson's Calendar*.

Mark Twain's future place in literature will probably be due less to humor than to his ability as a philosopher and a historian. Humor will undoubtedly act on his writings as a preservative salt, but salt is valuable only to preserve substantial things. If matter of vital worth is not present in any written work, mere humor will not keep it alive.

One of his most humorous scenes may be found in the chapter where Tom Sawyer succeeds in getting other boys to relieve him of the drudgery of whitewashing a fence. That episode was introduced to enable the author to make more impressive his philosophy of a certain phase of human action: —

"He had discovered a great law of human action without knowing it — namely, that in order to make a man or a boy covet a thing, it is only necessary to make the thing difficult to attain. If he had been a great and wise philosopher, like the writer of this book, he would now have comprehended that Work consists of whatever a body is *obliged* to do, and that Play consists of whatever a body is not obliged to do."

His statement about illusions shows that his philosophy does not always have a humorous setting: —

"The illusions are the only things that are valuable, and God help the man who reaches the time when he meets only the realities."

Hatred of hypocrisy is one of his emphatic characteristics. If Tom Sawyer enjoyed himself more in watching a dog play with a pinch-bug in church than in listening to a doctrinal sermon, if he had a better time playing hookey than in attending the execrably dull school, Mark Twain is eager to expose the hypocrisy of those who would misrepresent Tom's real attitude toward church and school. While Mark Twain is determined to present life faithfully as he sees it, he dislikes as much as any Puritan to see evil triumph. In his stories, wrongdoing usually digs its own grave.

His strong sense of justice led him to write *Personal Recollections of Joan of Arc* (1896), to defend the Maid of Orleans. Because he loved to protect the weak, he wrote *A Dog's Tale* (1904). For the same reason he paid all the expenses of a negro through an eastern college.

Although he was self-taught, he gradually came to use the English language with artistic effect and finish. His style is direct and energetic, and it shows his determination to say a thing as simply and as effectively as possible. One of the rules in *Pudd'nhead Wilson's Calendar* is, "As to the Adjective: when in doubt, strike it out." He followed this rule. Some have complained that the great humorist's mind, like Emerson's, often worked in a disconnected fashion, but this trait has been exaggerated in the case of both. Mark Twain has certainly made a stronger impression than many authors whose "sixthly" follows more inevitably. It is true that his romances do not gather up every loose end, that they do not close with a grand climax which settles everything; but they reflect the spirit of the western life, which also had many loose ends and left much unsettled.

His mingled humor and philosophy, his vivid, interesting, contemporary history, which gives a broad and sympathetic delineation of important phases of western life and development, fill a place that American literature could ill afford to leave vacant.

SUMMARY

Lincoln spoke to the common people in simple virile English, which serves as a model for the students of Oxford University. Bret Harte wrote stories filled with the humor and the pathos of the rough mining camps of the far West. Eugene Field's simple songs appeal to all children. The virtues of humble homes, the smiles and tears of everyday life, are presented in James Whitcomb Riley's poems. Mark Twain, philosopher, reformer of the type of Cervantes, and romantic historian, has, largely by means of his humor, made a vivid impression on millions of Americans. Every member of this group had an unusual development of humor. Each one was imbued with the democratic spirit and eager to present the elemental facts of life. For these reasons, the audiences of this group have been numbered by millions.

REFERENCES

Roosevelt's *The Winning of the West*.
Turner's *Rise of the New West*.
Hart's *National Ideals Historically Traced*.
Johnston's *High School History of the United States* (612 pp.).

Clemens's *Life on the Mississippi*.
Clemens's *Roughing It*.
Schurz's *Abraham Lincoln*. (Excellent.)
Morse's *Abraham Lincoln*.
Chubb's *Selections from the Addresses, Inaugurals, and Letters of Abraham Lincoln*, edited with an Introduction and Notes. (Macmillan's Pocket Classics.)
Boynton's *Bret Harte*.
Pemberton's *The Life of Bret Harte*.
Erskine's *Leading American Novelists*, pp. 325-379. (Harte.)
Canby's *The Short Story in English*, Chap. XIV. (Harte.)
Field's *The Eugene Field Book*, edited by Burt and Cable. (Contains autobiographical matter and Field's best juvenile poems and stories.)
Thompson's *Eugene Field*, 2 vols.
Field's *The Writings in Prose and Verse of Eugene Field*, Sabine Edition, 12 vols.
Garland's *A Dialogue between James Whitcomb Riley and Hamlin Garland*, in *McClure's Magazine*, February, 1894.
In Honor of James Whitcomb Riley, with a Brief Sketch of his Life, by Hughes, Beveridge, and Others, Indianapolis: Bobbs-Merrill Company, 1906.
Clemens's *Autobiography*.
Matthews's *Biographical Criticism of Mark Twain*, in the *Introduction* to *The Innocents Abroad*.
Phelps's *Essays on Modern Novelists*. (Mark Twain; excellent.)
Henderson's *Mark Twain*, in *Harper's Magazine*, May, 1909.
Howells's *My Mark Twain*.

SUGGESTED READINGS

Lincoln. — *The Gettysburg Address*, part of the *Second Inaugural Address*.

Harte. — *Tennessee's Partner*, and *How Santa Claus came to Simpson's Bar*. Harte's two greatest stories, *The Luck of Roaring Camp* and *The Outcasts of Poker Flat*, should be read in mature years. These stories may all be found in the single volume, entitled *The Luck of Roaring Camp and Other Stories*. (Riverside Aldine Press Series.)

Field. — *Little Boy Blue, The Duel, Krinken, Wynken, Blynken*, and

Nod, The Rock-a-By Lady. These poems may all be found in Burt and Cable's *The Eugene Field Book.*

Riley. — *When the Frost is on the Punkin, The Clover, The First Bluebird, Ike Walton's Prayer, A Life Lesson, Away, Griggsby's Station, Little Mahala Ashcraft, Our Hired Girl, Little Orphant Annie.* These poems may be found in the three volumes, entitled *Neighborly Poems, Afterwhiles,* and *Rhymes of Childhood.*

Mark Twain. — *Life on the Mississippi,* Chaps. VIII., IX., XIII. *Roughing It,* Chap. II. If the first two chapters of *The Adventures of Tom Sawyer* and *The Adventures of Huckleberry Finn* are read, the time will probably be found to finish the books. For specimens of his humor at its best, read *Pudd'nhead Wilson's Calendar,* printed at the beginning of the twenty-one chapters of *Pudd'nhead Wilson.* His humor depending on incongruity is well shown in *A Connecticut Yankee in King Arthur's Court.* *The Prince and the Pauper* is a fascinating story of sixteenth-century England.

QUESTIONS AND SUGGESTIONS

Why does Oxford University display on its walls *The Gettysburg Address* of Lincoln? What books helped mold his style?

What period of our development do Bret Harte's stories illustrate? What are some special characteristics of his short stories? Does he belong to the school of Poe or Hawthorne? Which one of our great short story writers has the most humor, — Irving, Hawthorne, Poe, or Harte? Which one of them do you enjoy the most?

Why is Eugene Field called the poet-laureate of children? Which of his poems indicated for reading do you prefer? What are the most striking qualities of his verse?

Point out the chief characteristics of Riley's verse. What lines please you most for their humor, references to rural life, optimism, kindly spirit, and pathos? Why is he so widely popular?

Which of Mark Twain's works are most valuable to the student of American literature and history? In what sense is he a historian? What phases of western development does he describe? Give instances (*a*) of his humor which depends on incongruity, (*b*) of his philosophical humor, (*c*) of his hatred of hypocrisy, and (*d*) of his solicitude for the weak. Why is he said to belong to the school of Cervantes? What specially impresses you about Mark Twain's style?

CHAPTER VII

THE EASTERN REALISTS

From Romanticism toward Realism. — The enormous circulation of magazines in the United States has furnished a wide market for the writers of fiction. Magazines have especially stimulated the production of short stories, which show how much technique their authors have learned from Poe. The increased attention paid to fiction has led to a careful study of its guiding principles and to the formation of new rules for the practice of the art.

When we look back at the best work of earlier writers of American fiction, we shall find that it is nearly all romantic. In the eighteenth century, Charles Brockden Brown wrote in conformity to the principles of early romanticism, and combined the elements of strangeness and terror in his tales. The modified romanticism persisting through the greater part of the nineteenth century demanded that the *unusual* should at least be retained in fiction as a dominating factor. Irving's *Rip Van Winkle* has the older element of the impossible, and *The Legend of Sleepy Hollow* shows fascinating combinations of the unusual. Cooper achieved his greatest success in presenting the Indians and the stalwart figure of the pioneer against the mysterious forest as a background. Hawthorne occasionally availed himself of the older romantic materials, as in *The Snow Image*, *Rappaccini's Daughter*, and *Young Goodman Brown*, but he was more often attracted by the newer elements, the strange and the unusual, as in *The*

Scarlet Letter and *The House of the Seven Gables*. Poe followed with a combination of all the romantic materials, — the supernatural, the terrible, and the unusual. Bret Harte applied his magnifying glass to unusual crises in the strange lives of the western pioneers. By a skillful use of light and shadow, Mark Twain heightened the effect of the strange scenes through which he passed in his young days. Almost all the southern writers, from Simms to Cable and Harris, loved to throw strong lights on unusual characters and romantic situations.

The question which the romanticists, or idealists, as they were often called in later times, had accustomed themselves to ask, was, "Have these characters or incidents the unusual beauty or ugliness or goodness necessary to make an impression and to hold the attention?" The masters of the new eastern school of fiction took a different view, and asked, "Is our matter absolutely true to life?"

Realism in Fiction. — The two greatest representatives of the new school of realism in fiction are William D. Howells and Henry James. Both have set forth in special essays the realist's art of fiction. The growing interest in democracy was the moving force in realism. In that realist's textbook, *Criticism and Fiction* (1891), Howells says of the aristocratic spirit in literature : —

"It is averse to the mass of men; it consents to know them only in some conventionalized and artificial guise. . . . Democracy in literature is the reverse of all this. It wishes to know and to tell the truth, confident that consolation and delight are there; it does not care to paint the marvelous and impossible for the vulgar many, or to sentimentalize and falsify the actual for the vulgar few."

"Realism is nothing more and nothing less than the truthful treatment of material," says Howells. He sometimes insists on considering "honesty" and "realism" as synonymous terms. His primary object is not merely to amuse by a pleasant story or to startle by a horrible one. His object is to reflect life as he finds it, not only unusual or exceptional life. He believes that it is false to real life to overemphasize certain facts, to overlook the trivial, and to make all life dramatic. He says that the realist in fiction "cannot look upon human life and declare this thing or that thing unworthy of notice, any more than the scientist can declare a fact of the material world beneath the dignity of his inquiry."

Howells recognizes the great importance of the spirit of romanticism, and says that it was at the beginning of the nineteenth century

". . . making the same fight against effete classicism which realism is making to-day against effete romanticism. . . . The romantic of that day and the real of this are in certain degree the same. Romanticism then sought, as realism seeks now, to widen the bounds of sympathy, to level every barrier against æsthetic freedom, to escape from the paralysis of tradition. It exhausted itself in this impulse; and it remained for realism to assert that fidelity to experience and probability of motive are essential conditions of a great imaginative literature."

Henry James in his essay, *The Art of Fiction*, denies that the novelist is less concerned than the historian about the quest for truth. He says, "The only reason for the existence of a novel is that it *does* compete with life. When it ceases to compete as the canvas of the painter competes, it will have arrived at a very strange pass." To the intending novelist he says: —

"All life belongs to you, and don't listen either to those who would shut you up into corners of it and tell you that it is only here and there that art inhabits, or to those who would persuade you that this heavenly messenger wings her way outside of life altogether, breathing a superfine air and turning away her head from the truth of things."

It must not be supposed that Howells and James were the original founders of the realistic school, any more than Wordsworth, Coleridge, and their associates were the originators of the romantic school. History has not yet discovered the first realist or the first romanticist. Both schools have from time to time been needed to hold each other in check. Howells makes no claim to being considered the first realist. He distinctly says that Jane Austen (1775–1817) had treated material with entire truthfulness. Henry James might have discovered that Fielding had preceded him in writing, "It is our business to discharge the part of a faithful historian, and to describe human nature as it is, not as we would wish it to be."

An occasional revolt against extreme romanticism is needed to bring literature closer to everyday life. The tendency of the followers of any school is to push its conclusions to such an extreme that reaction necessarily sets in. Some turned to seek for the soul of reality in the uninteresting commonplace. Others learned from Shakespeare the necessity of looking at life from the combined point of view of the realist and the romanticist, and they discovered that the great dramatist's romantic pictures sometimes convey a truer idea of life than the most literal ones of the painstaking realist. Critics have pointed out that the original *History of Dr. Faustus* furnished Marlowe with a realistic account of Helen of Troy's hair, eyes, "pleasant round face," lips, "neck, white like a swan," general figure, and purple velvet gown, but that his two romantic lines : —

> "Was this the face that launch'd a thousand ships,
> And burnt the topless towers of Ilium?"

enable any imaginative person to realize her fascination better than pages of realistic description. But we must not forget that it was an achievement for the writers of this group to insist that truth must be the foundation for all pictures of life, to demonstrate that even the pillars of romanticism must rest on a firm basis in a world of reality, and to teach the philosophy of realism to a school of younger writers.

By no means all of the eastern fiction, however, is realistic. **Thomas Bailey Aldrich** (1836–1907), for instance, wrote in a romantic vein *The Story of a Bad Boy*, which ranks among the best boys' stories produced in the last half of the nineteenth century. There were many other writers of romantic fiction, but the majority of them at least felt the restraining influence of the realistic school.

Realism in Poetry. — One eastern poet, Walt Whitman, took a step beyond any preceding American poet in endeavoring to paint with realistic touches the democracy of life. He defined the poet as the indicator of the path between reality and the soul. He thus proclaims his realistic creed : —

"I will not have in my writing any elegance or effect or originality to hang in the way between me and the rest like curtains. I will have nothing hang in the way, not the richest curtains. What I tell I tell for precisely what it is. Let who may exalt or startle or fascinate or soothe, I will have purposes as health or heat or snow has and be as regardless of observation. You shall stand by my side and look in the mirror with me."

The subject of his verse is the realities of democracy. No other great American poet had indulged in realism as extreme as this : —

"The butcher-boy puts off his killing-clothes, or sharpens his knife at the stall in the market,
I loiter enjoying his repartee and his shuffle and break-down."

Whitman says boldly : —

"And the cow crunching with depress'd head surpasses any statue."

He discarded ordinary poetic meter, because it seemed to lack the rhythm of nature. It is, however, very easy for a poet to cross the line between realism and idealism, and we sometimes find adherents of the two schools disagreeing whether Whitman was more realist or idealist in some of his work, for instance, in a line or verse unit, like this, when he says: —

"That the hands of the sisters Death and Night incessantly softly wash again, and ever again, this soil'd world."

IDENTITY
(Drawing by Elihu Vedder)

The fact that not all the later eastern poets were realistic needs emphasis. Thomas Bailey Aldrich, perhaps the most noted successor of New England's famous group, was frequently an exquisite romantic artist, or painter in miniature, as these eight lines which constitute the whole of his poem, *Identity*, show: —

"Somewhere — in desolate wind-swept space —
In Twilight-land — in No-man's-land —
Two hurrying Shapes met face to face,
  And bade each other stand.

"'And who are you?' cried one, agape,
Shuddering in the gloaming light.
  'I know not,' said the second Shape,
    'I only died last night!'"

WILLIAM DEAN HOWELLS, 1837—

The foremost leader of realism in modern American fiction, the man who has influenced more young writers than any other novelist of the last quarter of the nineteenth century, is William Dean Howells, who was born in Martin's Ferry, Ohio, in 1837. He never went to college, but obtained valuable training as a printer and editor in various newspaper offices in Ohio. He was for many years editor of the *Atlantic Monthly* and an editorial contributor to the *New York Nation* and *Harper's Magazine*. In these capacities, as well as by his fiction, he reached a wide public. Later he turned his attention mainly to the writing of novels. So many of their scenes are laid in New England that he is often claimed as a New England writer.

WILLIAM DEAN HOWELLS

His strongest novels are *A Modern Instance* (1882), *The Rise of Silas Lapham* (1885), *The Minister's Charge* (1886), *Indian Summer* (1886), and *A Hazard of New Fortunes* (1889). These belong to the middle period of his career. Before this, his mastery of character portrayal had not culminated, and later, his power of artistic selection and repression was not so strictly exercised.

The Rise of Silas Lapham is a story of the home life and business career of a self-made merchant, who has the customary braggadocio and lack of culture, but who possesses a substantial integrity at the root of his nature. The little shortcomings in social polish, so keenly felt by his wife and daughters, as they rise to a position due to great wealth, the small questions of decorum, and the details of business take up a large part of the reader's attention; but they are treated with such ease, naturalness, repressed humor, refinement of art, and truth in sketching provincial types of character, that the story is a triumph of realistic creation. *A Modern Instance* is not so pleasant a book, but the attention is firmly held by the strong, realistic presentation of the jealousy, the boredom, the temptations, and the dishonesty exhibited in a household of a commonplace, ill-mated pair. *Indian Summer* begins well, proceeds well, and ends well. It may be a trifle more conventional than the two other novels just mentioned, but it is altogether delightful. The conversations display keen insight into the heart of the young, imaginative girl and of the older woman and man. *The Minister's Charge* is thoroughly individual. The young boy seems so close to his readers that every detail in his life becomes important. The other people are also full of real blood, while the background is skillfully arranged to heighten the effect of the characters. *A Hazard of New Fortunes* would be decidedly improved if many pages were omitted, but it is full of lifelike characters, and it sometimes approaches the dramatic, in a way unusual with Howells.

In his effort to present life without any misleading ideas of heroism, beauty, or idyllic sweetness, Howells sometimes goes so far toward the opposite extreme as to write stories that seem to be filled with commonplace women, humdrum lives, and men like Northwick in *The Quality of Mercy*, of whom one of the characters says: —

"He was a mere creature of circumstances like the rest of us! His environment made him rich, and his environment made him a rogue. Sometimes I think there *was* nothing to Northwick except what happened to him."

But in such work as the five novels enumerated, Howells shows decided ability in portraying attractive characters, in making their faults human and as interesting as their virtues, in causing ordinary life to yield variety of incident and amusing scenes, and, finally, in engaging his characters in homelike, natural, self-revealing conversations, which are often spiced with wit.

Howells does not always have a plot, that is, a beginning, a climax, and a solution of all the questions suggested. He has, of course, a story, but he does not find it necessary to present the entire life of his characters, if he can accurately portray them by one or more incidents. After that purpose is accomplished, the story often ceases before the reader feels that a real ending has been reached.

Howells rarely startles or thrills; he usually both interests and convinces his readers by a straightforward presentation of everyday, well-known scenes and people. The strongest point in his art is the easy, natural way in which he seems to be retailing faithfully the facts exactly as they happened, without any juggling or rearranging on his part. His characters are so clearly presented that they do not remain in dreary outline, but emerge fully in rounded form, as moving, speaking, feeling beings. His keen insight into human frailties, his delicate, pervading humor, his skill in handling conversations, and his delightfully clear, easy, natural, and familiar style make him a realist of high rank and a worthy teacher of young writers.

HENRY JAMES, 1843-1916

The name most closely associated with Howells is that of Henry James, who was born in New York. William James (1842-1910) the noted psychologist, was an older brother. Henry James is called an "international novelist" because he lived mostly abroad and laid the scenes of his novels in both Europe and America. His sympathy with England in the European war caused him to become a British subject in 1915, eight months before his death in 1916.

Like Howells, James was a leader in modern realistic fiction. His work has been called the "quintessence of realism." But instead of selecting, as Howells does, the well-known types of the average people, James prefers to study the ordinary mind in extraordinary situations, surroundings, and combinations. For this reason, his characters, while realistically presented, rarely seem well-known and obvious types.

James was the first American to succeed in the realistic short story, that is, the story stripped of the supernatural and romantic elements used by Hawthorne and Poe. James selects neither a commonplace nor a dramatic situation, but chooses some difficult and out-of-the-way theme, and clears it up with his keen, subtle, impressionistic art. *A Passionate Pilgrim*, *The Madonna of the Future*, and *The Lesson of the Master* are short stories that show his abstruse, unusual subject matter and his analytical methods.

He was a very prolific writer. He published as many as three volumes in twelve months. Year after year, with few exceptions, he brought out either a novel, a book of essays, or a volume of short stories. His most interesting novels are *Roderick Hudson* (1875), *Daisy Miller: A Study* (1878), *The Portrait of a Lady* (1881), and *The Princess Casamassima* (1886).

Daisy Miller is a brilliant study of the Italian experiences of an American girl of the unconventionally independent type. She is beautiful, frank, original, but whimsical, shallow, and headstrong. One minute she attracts, the next moment she repels. One feels baffled and provoked, but is held to the book by the spell of a writer who is clever, intellectual, a master of style, and a skilled scientist in dissecting human character. In *Roderick Hudson* and *The Portrait of a Lady*, the characters are much more interesting, the situations are larger, the human emotion deeper, and the books richer from every point of view. These novels also show Americans in European surroundings. Isabel Archer and Ralph Touchet in *The Portrait of a Lady* have qualities that deeply stir the admiration and emotions. Every scene in which these characters appear adds to the pleasure in being able to know and love them, even though they are merely characters in a book.

Only a few such persons as these, so rich in the qualities of the heart, appear in James's novels. He has portrayed a greater variety of men and women than any other American writer, but they usually interest him for some other quality than their power to love and suffer. He is tempted to regard life from the intellectual viewpoint, as a problem, a game, and a panorama. He does not, like Hawthorne, enter into the sanctuary and become the hero, laying the lash of remorse upon his back. James stands off, a disinterested onlooker, and exhibits his characters critically, accurately, minutely, as they take their parts in the procession or game. Brilliant and faultless as the portraits are, they too frequently appear cold, pitiless renditions of life, often of life too trivial to seem worthy the searching study that he gives it. Ralph Touchet, Roderick Hudson, Isabel Archer, and Miss Light are sufficient to prove the tremendous power possessed by James to present the emotional side of life. Both in theory and practice, however, he usually prefers to remain the disinterested, impartial, detached spectator.

Like Howells, James does not depend upon a plot. There is little action in his works. The interest is psychological, and a chance word, an encounter on the street, even a look, may serve to change an attitude of mind and affect the outcome.

The popular impression that James is impossible to understand and that he uses words to obscure his meaning is, of course, false, although in his later novels his style is extremely involved and often difficult to follow. In such works as *The Wings of a Dove* (1902) and *The Golden Bowl* (1904), for example, there are long and intricate psychological explanations, which are most abstruse and confusing. It is this later work which has given rise to the common saying that William James wrote psychology like a novelist, and Henry James, novels like a psychologist.

Judged by his best work, however, such as *The Portrait of a Lady* and *Roderick Hudson*, Henry James must be acknowledged a master of English style. His keen analytical mind is reflected in a brilliant, highly polished, and impressively incisive style. In a few perfectly selected words the subtlest thoughts are clearly revealed. In these masterpieces, the reader is constantly delighted by the artist's skill, which leads ever deeper into human motives after it would seem that the heart and mind could disclose no further secrets. Such skill shows a mastery of language rarely surpassed in fiction. At his best, James has a fineness and sureness of touch, and a command of perfectly fitting words, as well as elegance and grace in style.

MARY E. WILKINS FREEMAN, 1862—

Mary Eleanor Wilkins (Mrs. Freeman), known for her realistic stories of the provincial New Englander, was born in Randolph, Massachusetts. With humor to see the little eccentricities of the people among whom she lived and a sympathetic understanding of their heroic qualities, she has created real men and women, — farmers, school teachers, prim spinsters, clergymen, stern Roman matrons, — all unmistakable types of New England village life. Her unfailing ability to transplant the reader into rock-ribbed, snow-clad New England, with its many fond associations for most Americans, is proof of her power as

MARY E. WILKINS FREEMAN

an artist. Her art is subtle, and it commands both attention and admiration, as she reveals every slight move in a simple plot and with extraordinary deftness of touch brings out the most delicate shadings that differentiate her characters.

Her style is easy and clear, and is pervaded by a fine sense of humor. Her short stories are her most artistic work, especially those in the two volumes, *A New England Nun*, and *Silence and Other Tales;* but she can also tell a long story well, as is shown in *Pembroke*, which combines at their best all her qualities as a novelist.

She is distinctly a realist of Howells's school, presenting the daily rounds of the life which she knew intimately, and making complete stories of such meager material as the subterfuges which two poor but proud sisters practiced in order to make one black silk dress, owned in partnership, appear as if each really possessed "a gala dress." She takes stolid, practical characters, who have seemingly nothing attractive in their composition, and by her sympathetic treatment causes them to appeal strongly to human hearts. She discovers heroic qualities in apparently commonplace homes and families, and finds humorous or pathetic possibilities in men and women whom most writers would consider very unpromising. Miss Wilkins knows that in rural New England romantic things do happen, tragedies do occur, and heroes and heroines do appear in unexpected quarters to meet emergencies, and she occasionally transfers such events to her pages, thereby enlivening them without sacrificing the reality of her pictures. But the triumph of her art consists in her facile handling of simple incidents and everyday men and women and her power to carry them without a hint of sentimentality to a natural, artistic, effective climax, heightened usually by a touch of either humor or pathos.

WALT WHITMAN, 1819-1892

Life. — Suffolk County, Long Island, in which is situated the village of West Hills, where Walt Whitman was born in 1819, was in some ways the most remarkable eastern county in the United States. Hemmed in on a narrow strip of land by the ocean on one side and Long Island Sound on the other, the inhabitants saw little of the world unless they led a seafaring life. Many of the well-to-do farmers, as late as the middle of the nineteenth century, never took a land journey of more than twenty miles from home. Because of such restricted environment, the people of Suffolk County were rather insular in early days, yet the average grade of intelligence was high, for some of England's most progressive blood had settled there in the first half of the seventeenth century.

Nowhere else in this country, not even at the West, was there a greater feeling of independence and a more complete exercise of individuality. There was a certainty about life and opinions, a feeling of relationship with everybody, a defiance of convention, that made Suffolk County the fit birthplace of a man who was destined to trample poetic conventions under his feet and to sing the song of democracy. In Walt Whitman's young days, all sorts and conditions of men on Long Island met familiarly on equal terms. The farmer, the blacksmith, the carpenter, the mason, the woodchopper, the sailor, the clergyman, the teacher, the young college student home on his vacation, — all mingled as naturally as members of a family. No human being felt himself inferior to any one else, so long as the moral proprieties were observed. Nowhere else did there exist a more perfect democracy of conscious equals. Although Whitman's family moved to Brooklyn before he was five years old, he returned to visit relatives, and later taught school at various places on Long Island and edited a paper at Huntington, near his birthplace. In various ways Suffolk County was responsible for the most vital part of his early training. In his poem, *There Was a Child Went Forth*, he tells how nature educated him in his island home. In his prose work, *Specimen Days and Collect*, which all who are interested in his autobiography should read, he says, "The successive growth stages of my infancy, childhood, youth, and manhood were all pass'd on Long Island, which I sometimes feel as if I had incorporated."

Like Mark Twain, Walt Whitman received from the schools only a common education but from life he had an uncommon training. His chief education came from associating with all sorts and conditions of people. In Brooklyn he worked as a printer, carpenter, and editor. His closest friends were the pilots and deck hands of ferry boats, the drivers of New York City omnibuses, factory hands, and sailors. After he had become well known, he was unconventional enough to sit with a street car driver in front of a grocery store in a crowded city and eat a watermelon. When people smiled, he said, "They can have the laugh — we have the melon."

His Suffolk County life might have left him democratic but insular; but he traveled widely and gained cosmopolitan experience. In 1848 he went leisurely to New Orleans, where he edited a newspaper, but in a short time he journeyed north along the Mississippi, traveled in Canada, and finally returned to New York, having completed a trip of eight thousand miles.

WHITMAN AT THE AGE OF THIRTY-SIX

After his return, he seems to have worked with his father in Brooklyn for about three years, building and selling houses. He was then also engaged on a collection of poems, which, in 1855, he published under the title of *Leaves of Grass*. From this time he was known as an author.

In 1862 he went South to nurse his brother, who was wounded in the Civil War. For nearly three years, the poet served as a volunteer nurse in the army hospitals in Washington and its vicinity. Few good Samaritans have performed better service. He estimated that he attended on the field and in the hospital eighty thousand of the sick and wounded. In after days many a soldier testified that his recovery was aided by Whitman's kindly ministrations. Finally, however, his own iron constitution gave way under this strain.

When the war closed, he was given a government clerkship in Washington, but was dismissed in 1865, because of hostility aroused by his *Leaves of Grass*. He soon received another appointment, however, which he held until 1873, when a stroke of paralysis forced him to relinquish his position. He went to Camden, New Jersey, where he lived the life of a semi-invalid during the rest of his existence, writing as his health would permit. He died in 1892, and was buried in Harleigh Cemetery, near Camden.

Poetry. — Whitman gave to the world in 1855 the first edition of the poems, which he called *Leaves of Grass*. His favorite expression, "words simple as grass," and his line: —

"I believe a leaf of grass is no less than the journey-work of the stars,"

give a clue to the idea which prompted the choice of such an unusual title. He continued to add to these poems during the rest of his life, and he published in 1892 the tenth edition of *Leaves of Grass*, in a volume containing four hundred and twenty-two closely printed octavo pages.

Whitman intended *Leaves of Grass* to be a realistic epic of American democracy. He tried to sing this song as he heard it echoed in the life of man and man's companion,

Nature. While many of Whitman's poems have the most dissimilar titles, and record experiences as unlike as his early life on Long Island, his dressing of wounds during the Civil War, his comradeship with the democratic mass, his almost Homeric communion with the sea, and his memories of Lincoln, yet according to his scheme, all of this verse was necessary to constitute a complete song of democracy. His poem, *I Hear America Singing*, shows the variety that he wished to give to his democratic songs: —

"I hear America singing, the varied carols I hear,
Those of mechanics, each one singing his as it should be blithe and strong,
The carpenter singing his as he measures his plank or beam,
The mason singing his as he makes ready for work, or leaves off work,
The boatman singing what belongs to him in his boat, the deckhand singing on the steamboat deck,
The shoemaker singing as he sits on his bench, the hatter singing as he stands,
The woodcutter's song, the ploughboy's on his way in the morning, or at noon intermission or at sundown,
The delicious singing of the mother, or of the young wife at work, or of the girl sewing or washing,
Each singing what belongs to him or her and to none else."

His ambition was to put human life in America "freely, fully, and truly on record."

His longest and one of his most typical poems in this collection is called *Song of Myself*, in which he paints himself as a representative member of the democratic mass. He says: —

"Agonies are one of my changes of garments,
I do not ask the wounded person how he feels, I myself become the wounded person,
My hurts turn livid upon me as I lean on a cane and observe.

Not a youngster is taken for larceny but I go up too, and am tried and sentenced."

In these four lines, he states simply what must be the moving impulse of a democratic government if it is to survive. Here is the spirit that is to-day growing among us, the spirit that forbids child labor, cares for orphans, enacts model tenement laws, strives to regenerate the slum districts, and is increasing the altruistic activities of clubs and churches throughout the country. But these verses will not submit to iambic or trochaic scansion, and their form is as strange as a democratic government was a century and a half ago to the monarchies of Europe. Place these lines beside the following couplet from Pope: —

> "Self-love and Reason to one end aspire,
> Pain their aversion, Pleasure their desire."

Here the scansion is regular, the verse polished, the thought undemocratic. The world had long been used to such regular poetry. The form of Whitman's verse came as a distinct shock to the majority.

Sometimes what he said was a greater shock, as, for instance, the line: —

> "I sound my barbaric yawp over the roofs of the world."

For a considerable time many people knew Whitman by this one line alone. They concluded that he was a barbarian and that all that he said was "yawp." Although much of his work certainly deserved this characterization, yet those who persisted in reading him soon discovered that their condemnation was too sweeping, as most were willing to admit after they had read, for instance, *When Lilacs Last in the Dooryard Bloom'd*, a poem that Swinburne called "the most sonorous nocturn yet chanted in the church of the world." The three *motifs* of this song are the lilac, the evening star, and the hermit thrush: —

> "Lilac and star and bird twined with the chant of my soul,
> There in the fragrant pines and the cedars dusk and dim."

In the same class we may place such poems as *Out of the Cradle Endlessly Rocking*, where we listen to a song as if from

> "Out of the mocking-bird's throat, the musical shuttle."

Whitman also wrote in almost regular meter his dirge on Lincoln, the greatest dirge of the Civil War: —

> "O Captain! my Captain! our fearful trip is done,
> The ship has weather'd every rack, the prize we sought is won,
> The port is near, the bells I hear, the people all exulting."

In 1888 Whitman wrote that "from a worldly and business point of view, *Leaves of Grass* has been worse than a failure — that public criticism on the book and myself as author of it yet shows mark'd anger and contempt more than anything else." But he says that he had comfort in "a small band of the dearest friends and upholders ever vouchsafed to man or cause." He was also well received in England. He met with cordial appreciation from Tennyson. John Addington Symonds (1840–1893), a graduate of Oxford and an authority on Greek poetry and the Renaissance, wrote, "*Leaves of Grass*, which I first read at the age of twenty-five, influenced me more, perhaps, than any other book has done except the *Bible;* more than Plato, more than Goethe." Had Whitman lived until 1908, he would probably have been satisfied with the following statement from his biographer, Bliss Perry, formerly professor of English at Princeton, "These primal and ultimate things Whitman felt as few men have ever felt them, and he expressed them, at his best, with a nobility and beauty such as only the world's very greatest poets have surpassed."

General Characteristics. — His most pronounced single characteristic is his presentation of democracy: —

> "Stuff'd with the stuff that is coarse and stuff'd with the stuff that is fine."

He said emphatically, "Without yielding an inch, the working man and working woman were to be in my pages from first to last." He is the only American poet of his rank who remained through life the close companion of day laborers. Yet, although he is the poet of democracy, his poetry is too difficult to be read by the masses, who are for the most part ignorant of the fact that he is their greatest representative poet.

He not only preached democracy, but he also showed in practical ways his intense feeling of comradeship and his sympathy with all. One of his favorite verses was

> "And whoever walks a furlong without sympathy walks to his own funeral drest in his shroud."

His Civil War experiences still further intensified this feeling. He looked on the lifeless face of a son of the South, and wrote: —

> ". . . my enemy is dead, a man divine as myself is dead."

Like Thoreau, Whitman welcomed the return to nature. He says: —

> "I am enamour'd of growing out-doors,
> Of men that live among cattle or taste of the ocean or woods."

He is the poet of nature as well as of man. He tells us how nature educated him: —

> "The early lilacs became part of this child,
>   And grass and white and red morning-glories, and white and red clover, and the song of the phœbe-bird,
>   And the Third-month lambs and the sow's pink-faint litter, and the mare's foal and the cow's calf."

He delights us

" . . . with meadows, rippling tides and trees and flowers and grass,
And the low hum of living breeze — and in the midst God's beautiful
    eternal right hand."

No American poet was more fond of the ocean. Its aspect and music, more than any other object of nature, influenced his verse. He addresses the sea in lines like these : —

" With husky-haughty lips, O sea!
Where day and night I wend thy surf-beat shore,
Imaging to my sense thy varied strange suggestions,
(I see and plainly list thy talk and conference here,)
Thy troops of white-maned racers racing to the goal,
Thy ample, smiling face, dash'd with the sparkling dimples of the
    sun."

He especially loves motion in nature. His poetry abounds in the so-called motor images.[1] He takes pleasure in picturing a scene

"Where the heifers browse, where geese nip their food with short
    jerks,"

or in watching

" The white arms out in the breakers tirelessly tossing."

While his verse is fortunately not without idealistic touches, his poetic theory is uncompromisingly realistic, as may be seen in his critical prose essays, some of which deserve to rank only a little below those of Lowell and Poe. Whitman says : —

"For grounds for *Leaves of Grass*, as a poem, I abandon'd the conventional themes, which do not appear in it : none of the stock ornamentation, or choice plots of love or war, or high exceptional personages

---

[1] For a discussion of the various types of images of the different poets, see the author's *Education of the Central Nervous System*, Chaps. VII., VIII., IX., X.

of Old-World song; nothing, as I may say, for beauty's sake — no legend or myth or romance, nor euphemism, nor rhyme."

His unbalanced desire for realism led him into two mistakes. In the first place, his determination to avoid ornamentation often caused him to insert in his poems mere catalogues of names, which are not bound together by a particle of poetic cement. The following from his *Song of Myself* is an instance: —

"Land of coal and iron! land of gold! land of cotton, sugar, rice!
  Land of wheat, beef, pork! land of wool and hemp! land of the apple and the grape!"

In the second place, he thought that genuine realism forbade his being selective and commanded him to put everything in his verse. He accordingly included some offensive material which was outside the pale of poetic treatment. Had he followed the same rule with his cooking, his chickens would have been served to him without removing the feathers. His refusal to eliminate unpoetic material from his verse has cost him very many readers.

He further concluded that it was unfitting for a democratic poet to be hampered by the verse forms of the Old World. He discarded rhyme almost entirely, but he did employ rhythm, which is determined by the tone of the ideas, not by the number of syllables. This rhythm is often not evident in a single line, but usually becomes manifest as the thought is developed. His verse was intended to be read aloud or chanted. He himself says that his verse construction is "apparently lawless at first perusal, although on closer examination a certain regularity appears, like the recurrence of lesser and larger waves on the seashore, rolling in without intermission, and fitfully rising and falling." There is little doubt that he carried in his ear the music of the waves and endeavored to make his verse in some measure conform to that. He says specifically that while he was listening to the call of a seabird

> ". . . on Paumanok's[1] gray beach,
> With the thousand responsive songs at random,
> My own songs awaked from that hour,
> And with them the key, the word up from the waves."

In ideals he is most like Emerson. Critics have called Whitman a concrete translation of Emerson, and have noticed that he practiced the independence which Emerson preached in the famous lecture on *The American Scholar* (p. 185). In 1855 Emerson wrote to Whitman: "I am not blind to the worth of the wonderful gift of *Leaves of Grass*. I find it the most extraordinary piece of wit and wisdom that America has yet contributed."

Whitman is America's strangest compound of unfiltered realism, alloyed with rich veins of noble idealism. No students of American democracy, its ideals and social spirit, can afford to leave him unread. He sings, "unwarped by any influence save democracy,"

> "Of Life, immense in passion, pulse, and power,
> Cheerful, for freest action form'd under the laws divine."

Intelligent sympathy with the humblest, the power to see himself "in prison shaped like another man and feel the dull unintermitted pain," prompts him to exclaim:—

> "I seize the descending man and raise him with resistless will."

An elemental poet of democracy, embodying its faults as well as its virtues, Whitman is noteworthy for voicing the new social spirit on which the twentieth century is relying for the regeneration of the masses.

---

[1] The Indian name for Long Island.

SUMMARY

American fiction had for the most part been romantic from its beginning until the last part of the nineteenth century. Charles Brockden Brown, Irving, Cooper, Hawthorne, Poe, Bret Harte, and Mark Twain were all tinged with romanticism. In the latter part of the last century, there arose a school of realists who insisted that life should be painted as it is, without any addition to or subtraction from reality. This school did not ask, "Is the matter interesting or exciting?" but, "Is it true to life?"

Howells and James were the leaders of the realists. Howells uses everyday incidents and conversations. James not infrequently takes unusual situations, so long as they conform to reality, and subjects them to the most searching psychological analysis. Mary Wilkins Freeman, a pupil of Howells, shows exceptional skill in depicting with realistic interest the humble life of provincial New England. While this school did not turn all writers into extreme realists, its influence was felt on the mass of contemporary fiction.

Walt Whitman brings excessive realism into the form and matter of verse. For fear of using stock poetic ornaments, he sometimes introduces mere catalogues of names, uninvested with a single poetic touch. He is America's greatest poet of democracy. His work is characterized by altruism, by all-embracing sympathy, by emphasis on the social side of democracy, and by love of nature and the sea.

REFERENCES

Stanton's *A Manual of American Literature*.
Alden's *Magazine Writing and the New Literature*.

Perry's *A Study of Prose Fiction*, Chap. IX., *Realism*.

Howells's *Criticism and Fiction*.

Burt and Howells's *The Howells Story Book*. (Contains biographical matter.)

Henry James's *The Art of Fiction*.

Phelps's *William Dean Howells*, in *Essays on Modern Novelists*.

Brownell's *Henry James*, in *American Prose Masters*.

Canby's *The Short Story in English*. (James.)

Whitman's *Leaves of Grass* (1897), 446 pp. (Contains all of his poems, the publication of which was authorized by himself.)

Triggs's *Selections from the Prose and Poetry of Walt Whitman*. (The best for general readers.)

Perry's *Walt Whitman, his Life, and Work*. (Excellent.)

G. R. Carpenter's *Walt Whitman*.

Platt's *Walt Whitman*. (*Beacon Biographies*.)

Noyes's *An Approach to Walt Whitman*. (Excellent.)

Bucke's *Walt Whitman*. (A biography by one of his executors.)

In Re Walt Whitman, edited by his literary executors. (Supplements Bucke.)

Burroughs's *Whitman: A Study*.

Symonds's *Walt Whitman: A Study*.

Dowden's *The Poetry of Democracy*, in *Studies in Literature*.

Stevenson's *Familiar Studies of Men and Books*. (Whitman.)

Whitman's *Works*, edited by Triggs. (Putnam Subscription Edition.) Vol. X. contains a bibliography and reference list of 98 pp.

SUGGESTED READINGS

The Prose Realists. — Sections II., XV., and XXVIII., from Howells's *Criticism and Fiction*. *Silas Lapham* is the best of his novels. Those who desire to read more should consult the list on p. 373 of this book.

In Henry James, read either *The Portrait of a Lady* or *Roderick Hudson*. *A Passionate Pilgrim*, and *The Madonna of the Future* are two of his best short stories.

Read any or all of these short stories by Mary Wilkins Freeman: *A New England Nun*, *A Gala Dress*, in the volume, *A New England Nun and Other Stories*, *Evelina's Garden*, in the volume, *Silence and Other Stories*. Her best long novel is *Pembroke*.

Walt Whitman. — While the majority of his poems should be left for mature years, the following, carefully edited by Triggs in his volume of *Selections*, need not be deferred: —

Song of Myself, Triggs, pp. 105–120. (Begin with the line on p. 105, " A child said, *What is the Grass ?*"), *Out of the Cradle Endlessly Rocking*, pp. 154–160, *I Hear America Singing*, p. 100, *Reconciliation*, p. 175, *O Captain! My Captain*, p. 184, *When Lilacs Last in the Dooryard Bloom'd*, pp. 176–184, *Patrolling Barnegat*, p. 163, *With Husky-Haughty Lips, O Sea!* p. 232.

Selections from his prose, including *Specimen Days, Memoranda of the War*, and his theories of art and poetry, may be found in Triggs, pp. 3–95.

QUESTIONS AND SUGGESTIONS

The Prose Realists. — To what school did the best writers in American fiction belong, prior to the last quarter of the nineteenth century ? What was the subject of each ? What is the realistic theory advanced by Howells ? In what respects does this differ from the practice of the romantic school ?

Take any chapter of *Silas Lapham* and of either *The Portrait of a Lady*, or of *Roderick Hudson*, and show how Howells and James differ from the romanticists. What difference do you notice in the realistic method and in the style of Howells and of James ?

What special qualities characterize the work of Mary Wilkins Freeman ? What is the secret of her success in so employing a little realistic incident as to hold the reader's attention ? Compare the two short stories, *The Madonna of the Future* (James) and *A New England Nun* (Wilkins Freeman) and show how James's interest lies in the subtle psychological problem, while Mrs. Freeman's depends on the unfolding of simple emotions. It will also be found interesting to compare the method of that early English realist Jane Austen, *e.g.* in her novel *Emma*, with the work of the American realists.

In general, do you think that the romantic or the realistic school has the truer conception of the mission and art of fiction ? Why is it desirable that each school should hold the other in check ?

Walt Whitman. — How did his early life prepare him to be the poet of democracy ? To what voices does he specially listen in his poem, *I Hear America Singing?* In his *Song of Myself*, point out some passages that show the modern spirit of altruism. In *Out of the Cradle*

Endlessly Rocking, what lines best show his lyric gift ? What individual objects stand out most strongly and poetically ? Could this poem have been written by one reared in the middle West ? Why does he select the lilacs, evening star, and hermit thrush, as the *motifs* of the poem, *When Lilacs Last in the Dooryard Bloom'd?* In *Patrolling Barnegat,* do you notice any resemblance to Anglo-Saxon poetry of the sea, *e.g.* to *Beowulf* or *The Seafarer ?* In *With Husky-Haughty Lips, O Sea!* what touches are unlike those of Anglo-Saxon poets ? (See the author's *History of English Literature,* pp. 21, 25, 33, 35, 37.) Which of Whitman's references to nature do you consider the most poetic ? How does *O Captain! My Captain!* differ in form from the other poems indicated for reading ? What qualities in his verse impress you most ?

A GLANCE BACKWARD

Lack of originality is a frequent charge against young literatures, but the best foreign critics have testified to the originality of the Knickerbocker Legend, of Leatherstocking, of the great Puritan romances, in which the Ten Commandments are the supreme law, of the work of that southern wizard who has taught a great part of the world the art of the modern short story and who has charmed the ear of death with his melodies, of America's unique humor, so conspicuous in the service of reform and in rendering the New World philosophy doubly impressive.

American literature has not only produced original work, but it has also delivered a worthy message to humanity. Franklin has voiced an unsurpassed philosophy of the practical. Emerson is a great apostle of the ideal, an unexcelled preacher of New World self-reliance. His teachings, which have become almost as widely diffused as the air we breathe, have added a cubit to the stature of unnumbered pupils. We still respond to the half Celtic, half Saxon, song of one of these: —

> "Luck hates the slow and loves the bold,
> Soon come the darkness and the cold."

American poets and prose writers have disclosed the glory of a new companionship with nature and have shown how we,

> " . . . pocketless of a dime may purchase the pick of the earth."

After association with them, we also feel like exclaiming: —

"Earth of the vitreous pour of the full moon just tinged with blue!
 . . . rich apple-blossom'd earth!
Smile, for your lover comes."

No other literature has so forcibly expressed such an inspiring belief in individuality, the aim to have each human being realize that this plastic world expects to find in him an individual hero. Emerson emphasized "the new importance given to the single person." No philosophy of individuality could be more explicit than Walt Whitman's: —

"The whole theory of the universe is directed unerringly to one single individual, — namely to You."

This emphasis on individuality is an added incentive to try "to yield that particular fruit which each was created to bear." We feel that the universe is our property and that we shall not stop until we have a clear title to that part which we desire. As we study this literature, the moral greatness of the race seems to course afresh through our veins, and our individual strength becomes the strength of ten.

No other nation could have sung America's song of democracy: —

"Stuff'd with the stuff that is coarse and stuff'd with the stuff that is fine."

The East and the West have vied in singing the song of a new social democracy, in holding up as an ideal a

". . . love that lives
 On the errors it forgives,"

in teaching each mother to sing to her child: —

"Thou art one with the world — though I love thee the best,
And to save thee from pain, I must save all the rest.

> Thou wilt weep; and thy mother must dry
> The tears of the world, lest her darling should cry."

True poets, like the great physicians, minister to life by awakening faith. The singers of New England have made us feel that the Divine Presence stands behind the darkest shadow, that the feeble hands groping blindly in the darkness will touch God's strengthening right hand. Amid the snows of his Northland, Whittier wrote: —

> "I know not where his islands lift
> Their fronded palms in air;
> I only know I cannot drift
> Beyond his love and care."

Lanier calls from the southern marshes, fringed with the live oaks " and woven shades of the vine ": —

> "I will fly in the greatness of God as the marsh-hen flies
> In the freedom that fills all the space 'twixt the marsh and the skies:
> By so many roots as the marsh-grass sends in the sod
> I will heartily lay me a-hold on the greatness of God."

The impressive moral lesson taught by American literature is a presence not to be put by. Lowell's utterance is typical of our greatest authors: —

> "Not failure, but low aim, is crime."

Hawthorne wrote his great masterpiece to express this central truth: —

> "To the untrue man, the whole universe is false, — it is impalpable, — it shrinks to nothing within his grasp."

Finally, American literature has striven to impress the truth voiced in these lines: —

> "As children of the Infinite Soul
> Our Birthright is the boundless whole. . . .
>
> "High truths which have not yet been dreamed,
> Realities of all that seemed. . . .
>
> "No fate can rob the earnest soul
> Of his great Birthright in the boundless whole!"

SUPPLEMENTARY LIST OF AUTHORS AND THEIR CHIEF WORKS [1]

EASTERN AUTHORS

Abbott, Jacob (1803–1879), b. Hallowell, Me. One of America's most voluminous writers on all classes of popular subjects. He wrote one hundred and eighty volumes and aided in the preparation of thirty-one more. *Illustrated Histories, The Rollo Books.*

Adams, Henry (1838–   ), b. Boston, Mass. Historian. *History of the United States* from 1801 to 1817, that is, under Jefferson's and Madison's administrations. 9 vols. Excellent for this important period.

Alcott, Louisa May (1832–1888), b. Germantown, Pa. Daughter of Amos Bronson Alcott. Writer of wholesome, humorous, and interesting stories for young people. *Little Women, An Old-Fashioned Girl, Eight Cousins, Rose in Bloom.*

Allston, Washington (1779–1843), b. Waccamaw, S. C. Moved to New England and graduated at Harvard in 1800. Artist, early poet of Wordsworthian school. *The Sylphs of the Seasons, and Other Poems.*

Ames, Fisher (1758–1808), b. Dedham, Mass. Orator, statesman. Best speech, *On the British Treaty* (1796).

Austin, Jane G. (1831–1894), b. Worcester, Mass. Novelist of early colonial New England. *Standish of Standish, Betty Alden, Dr. Le Baron and his Daughters, A Nameless Nobleman, David Alden's Daughter, and Other Stories of Colonial Times.*

Bacheller, Irving (1859–   ), b. Pierrepont, N. Y. Novelist. *Eben Holden, D'ri and I, Darrel of the Blessed Isles.*

---

[1] For a complete record of the work of contemporary authors, consult *Who's Who in America.*

Bancroft, George (1800–1891), b. Worcester, Mass. Historian, diplomatist. *History of the United States, from the Discovery of the Continent to the Establishment of the Constitution in 1789*, 6 vols. *History of the Formation of the Constitution of the United States*, 2 vols. Covers the period to the inauguration of Washington. The volumes on the Revolutionary War and the formation of the Constitution are the best part of the work. While Bancroft's improved methods of research among original authorities almost entitle him to be called the founder of the new American school of historical writing, yet the best critics do not to-day consider his work scientific. They regard it more as an apotheosis of democracy, written by a man who loved truth intensely, who shirked no drudgery in original investigations, but who shows the strong bias of the days of Andrew Jackson in the tendency to believe that what democracy does is almost necessarily right.

Bangs, John Kendrick (1862–   ), b. Yonkers, N.Y. Humorist. *House-Boat on the Styx, The Idiot at Home, A Rebellious Heroine*.

Barr, Amelia E. (1831–   ), b. Ulverston, Lancashire, Eng. Anglo-American novelist. *A Bow of Orange Ribbon, Jan Vedder's Wife, A Daughter of Fife*, and *Between Two Loves*.

Bates, Arlo (1850–   ), b. East Machias, Me. Educator, author. *Under the Beech Tree* (poems), *Talks on the Study of Literature*.

Bedott, Widow. *See* **Whitcher, Frances.**

Beecher, Henry Ward (1813–1887), b. Litchfield, Conn. Congregational clergyman, widely popular as a preacher and lecturer. Delivered noted anti-slavery lectures in England. Some of his published works are *Eyes and Ears, Life Thoughts, Star Papers, Yale Lectures on Preaching*.

"Billings, Josh." *See* **Shaw, Henry Wheeler.**

Boker, Geo. H. (1823–1890), b. Philadelphia, Pa. Dramatist, poet, diplomat. *Francesca da Rimini, Dirge for a Soldier*.

"Breitmann, Hans." *See* **Leland, Charles Godfrey.**

Brooks, Phillips (1835–1893), b. Boston, Mass. Bishop of the

Episcopal Diocese of Massachusetts. One of the foremost preachers of his day. Wrote many works on religious subjects, also *Essays and Addresses, Letters of Travel.*

Brown, Alice (1857–   ), b. Hampton Falls, N. H. Novelist, *The Story of Thyrza, John Winterburn's Family, Country Neighbors, Tiverton Tales, The Mannerings.*

Browne, Charles F. ("Artemus Ward") (1834–1867), b. Waterford, Me. Newspaper writer and lecturer. Famous humorist of the middle of the nineteenth century. *Artemus Ward: His Book, Artemus Ward: His Travels, Artemus Ward in London.*

Brownson, Orestes A. (1803–1876), b. Stockbridge, Vt. Clergyman, journalist, Christian socialist. Brownson's *Quarterly Review* (1844–1875), *New Views of Christianity, Society, and the Church.*

Bunner, Henry Cuyler (1855–1896), b. Oswego, N. Y. Editor of *Puck* for many years. A clever and successful short-story writer. *Short Sixes, Love in Old Cloathes, Zadoc Pine and Other Stories.*

Burroughs, John (1837–   ), b. Roxbury, N. Y. An exact observer of life in the woods and one of the most conservative and entertaining writers on nature. He tells only what he sees and does not draw on his fancy to endow animals with man's power to reason. Some of his nature books are: *Wake-Robin, Signs and Seasons, Pepacton, Riverby, Locusts and Wild Honey, Squirrels and Other Fur-Bearers. Indoor Studies* and *Whitman, A Study,* show keen critical powers and genuine literary appreciation. Burroughs reminds the reader of Thoreau in closeness of observation and honesty of expression, but Burroughs is less of a philosopher and poet and more of a scientist.

Cary, Alice (1820–1871) and her sister **Phœbe Cary** (1824–1871), b. Miami Valley, near Cincinnati, O. Moved to New York City. Poets. *Poems* by Alice and Phœbe Cary.

Chambers, Robert W. (1865–   ), b. Brooklyn, N. Y. Author of exciting romances. *The Red Republic, A King and a Few Dukes, The Conspirators.*

Channing, William Ellery (1780-1842), b. Newport, R. I. Great Unitarian preacher and reformer. *Spiritual Freedom, Evidences of Christianity and of Revealed Religion, Self-Culture, Slavery.*

Child, Lydia Maria (1802-1880), b. Medford, Mass. Novelist, editor. *Hobomok,* a story of life in colonial Salem; *The Rebels,* a tale of the Revolution, introduces James Otis, Governor Hutchinson, and the Boston Massacre; *Appeal for that Class of Americans called Africans.*

Churchill, Winston (1871-   ), b. St. Louis, Mo. Home in Cornish, N. H. Novelist. *Richard Carvel, The Crisis,* and *The Crossing* are interesting novels of American historical events. *Mr. Crewe's Career.*

Clarke, James Freeman (1810-1888), b. Hanover, N. H. Noted Unitarian clergyman. *Orthodoxy: Its Truths and Errors, Ten Great Religions, Self-Culture.*

Cone, Helen Gray (1859-   ), b. New York City. Poet. *Oberon and Puck, The Ride to the Lady, Verses Grave and Gay.*

Cooke, Rose Terry (1827-1892), b. West Hartford, Conn. Poet and short-story writer. *The Two Villages* is her best-known poem, and *The Deacon's Week* one of her best stories.

Craigie, Pearl Mary Teresa ("John Oliver Hobbes") (1867-1906), b. Boston, Mass. Novelist. *School for Saints, The Herb Moon, The Flute of Pan, The Tales of John Oliver Hobbes.*

Cranch, Christopher Pearse (1813-1892), b. Alexandria, Va. Educated in Massachusetts. Artist, transcendental poet, and contributor to *The Dial.* Best poems, *Gnosis, I in Thee.*

Crane, Stephen (1870-1900), b. Newark, N. J. Novelist. *The Red Badge of Courage* is a remarkable romance of the American Civil War.

Crawford, Francis Marion (1854-1909), b. Bagni di Lucca, Italy. Voluminous writer of novels and romances. Some are historical, and the scenes of the best of them are laid in Italy. He wrote his *Zoroaster* and *Marzio's Crucifix* in both English and French, and received a reward of one thousand francs from the French Academy. *Saracinesca, Sant' Ilario,* and *Don Orsino,* a trio of novels about one Roman family, and *Katherine Lauderdale* and its sequel, *The Ralstons*, are among his best works.

Curtis, George William (1824–1892), b. Providence, R. I. Literary and political essayist, civil service reformer, and critic. Was a resident in his youth at Brook Farm. Spent four years of his early life in foreign travel. *Nile Notes of a Howadji* and *The Howadji in Syria* are poetic descriptions of his trip. His masterpiece is *Prue and I*, a prose idyl of simple, contented, humble life. The largest part of his work was done as editor. He was editor of *Putnam's Magazine* at the time of its failure in 1857, and undertook to pay up every creditor, a task which consumed sixteen years. He wrote the *Easy Chair* papers in *Harper's Monthly*. A volume of these essays contains some of his easiest, most urbane, and humorous writings. They are light and in the vein of Addison's *Spectator*. In *Orations and Addresses* are to be found some of his strongest and most polished speeches on moral, historical, and political subjects.

Dana, Richard Henry, Sr. (1787–1879), b. Cambridge, Mass. Author, diplomat, judge. Co-editor *North American Review* when it published Bryant's *Thanatopsis*. Champion of the romantic school of Wordsworth and Coleridge. Dana's best known poem, *The Buccaneer*, shows the influence of this school.

Dana, Richard Henry, Jr. (1815–1882), b. Cambridge, Mass. Lawyer, statesman, author. His *Two Years before the Mast* keeps its place among the best books written for boys during the nineteenth century. The British admiralty officially adopted this book for circulation in the navy.

Davis, Richard Harding (1864–1916), b. Philadelphia, Pa. Journalist, playwright, novelist. Best works are short stories of New York life, such as *Van Bibber and Others*, *Gallegher and Other Stories*. *The Bar Sinister*, which holds boys spellbound, is an excellent story of a dog.

Deland, Margaretta Wade (1857–   ), b. Allegheny, Pa. Voluminous writer of stories. *Old Chester Tales*, *Dr. Lavendar's People*, *John Ward, Preacher*.

Dickinson, Emily (1830–1886), b. Amherst, Mass. Author of unique short lyrics. *Poems*.

Dickinson, John (1732–1808), b. Crosia, Md. Statesman. *The Farmer's Letters to the Inhabitants of the British Colonies*.

Dodge, Mary Mapes (1838–1905), b. New York City. Editor of *Saint Nicholas Magazine*. Among her juvenile books may be mentioned *Hans Brinker, Donald and Dorothy, The Land of Pluck*.

Dorr, Julia C. R. (1825–   ), b. Charleston, S. C. Moved to Vermont. Poet, novelist. *Poems, In Kings' Houses, Farmingdale*.

Dwight, John S. (1813–1893), b. Boston, Mass. Musician, transcendentalist. Best poem, *Rest*, appeared in first number of *The Dial*.

Egan, Maurice Francis (1852–   ), b. Philadelphia. Diplomat, poet, essayist, novelist. *Preludes, Songs and Sonnets, Lectures on English Literature, The Ghost of Hamlet*.

Everett, Edward (1794–1865), b. Dorchester, Mass. Orator, statesman. *Orations and Speeches*.

Fields, James T. (1817–1881), b. Portsmouth, N. H. Editor *Atlantic Monthly* and publisher. *Yesterdays with Authors*.

Fiske, John (1842–1901), b. Hartford, Conn. Scientist and historian. His histories are both philosophical and interesting. *The Critical Period of American History, The Beginnings of New England, The American Revolution, The Discovery of America*.

Ford, Paul Leicester (1865–1902), b. Brooklyn, N. Y. Novelist, historian. *The Honorable Peter Stirling, Janice Meredith*.

Foster, Stephen Collins (1826–1864), b. Pittsburg, Pa. Writer of some of the most widely known songs of the nineteenth century. *Old Folks at Home* ("Down on the Suwanee River"), *My Old Kentucky Home, Nellie was a Lady*.

Frederic, Harold (1856–1898), b. Utica, N. Y. Novelist, journalist. *The Damnation of Theron Ware, Gloria Mundi*.

Gilder, Richard Watson (1844–1909), b. Bordentown, N. J. Editor and poet. Editor of *Century Magazine* until his death. Poems: *The New Day, Five Books of Song, For the Country*.

Goodwin, Maud Wilder (1856–   ), b. Ballston Spa, N. Y. Writer of romances, chiefly historical. *The Colonial Cavalier, or Southern Life before the Revolution, Four Roads to Paradise.*

Grant, Robert (1852–   ), b. Boston, Mass. Novelist, essayist, jurist. *Confessions of a Frivolous Girl, An Average Man, The Art of Living.*

Greeley, Horace (1811–1872), b. Amherst, N. H. Founder and editor of *The Tribune*, New York City. Exerted strong influence on the thought of his time. *Recollections of a Busy Life.*

Green, Anna Katharine (Mrs. Charles Rohlfs) (1846–   ), b. Brooklyn, N. Y. Voluminous writer of interesting detective stories, of which *The Leavenworth Case* is the most noted.

Guiney, Louise Imogen (1861–   ), b. Boston, Mass. Poet, essayist. *The White Sail and Other Poems, A Roadside Harp, The Martyr's Idyl and Shorter Poems.*

Hale, Edward Everett (1822–1909), b. Boston, Mass. Unitarian divine, author, philanthropist. Best known story, *The Man without a Country.* Wrote many miscellaneous essays.

Hardy, Arthur S. (1847–   ), b. Andover, Mass. Educator, novelist, diplomat. *But Yet a Woman, Wind of Destiny, Passe Rose.*

Harland, Henry ("Sidney Luska") (1861–1905), b. St. Petersburg, Russia. Novelist. *The Cardinal's Snuff-Box, My Friend Prospero, The Lady Paramount.*

Hawthorne, Julian (1846–   ), b. Boston, Mass., son of Nathaniel Hawthorne. Novelist, essayist. Deserves to be called his father's Boswell for the excellent and sympathetic two volumes, entitled *Nathaniel Hawthorne and his Wife.*

Hedge, Frederick H. (1805–1890), b. Cambridge, Mass. Clergyman, transcendentalist. Best poem, *Questionings*, appeared in *The Dial.*

Higginson, Thomas Wentworth (1823–   ), b. Cambridge, Mass. Unitarian minister, prominent anti-slavery agitator, author. *Life of Margaret Fuller Ossoli, Cheerful Yesterdays, Contemporaries, Old Cambridge.*

"Hobbes, John Oliver," *See* Craigie, Pearl Mary Teresa.

Holland, J. G. (1819-1881), b. Belchertown, Mass. Editor of the first series of *Scribner's Monthly*, wrote several poems, of which *Bitter-Sweet* was the most popular, and several novels, the best of which is *Arthur Bonnicastle*.

Holley, Marietta (1850-   ), b. Ellisburg, N.Y. Humorist, Author of *Josiah Allen's Wife, My Opinions and Betsey Bobbet's, Sweet Cicely, Samantha at Saratoga*, and *Poems*.

Howard, Blanche Willis (1847-1898), b. Bangor, Me. Novelist. *Guenn* is an unusually strong novel. *One Summer, Aunt Serena*, and *The Open Door* are wholesome, pleasing stories.

Howe, Julia Ward (1819-1910), b. New York City. Philanthropist, author of the famous *Battle Hymn of the Republic*.

Hutchinson, Thomas (1711-1780), b. Boston, Mass. America's greatest historical writer before the nineteenth century. His great work is *The History of the Province of Massachusetts Bay*.

Ireland, John (1838-   ), b. Ireland. Roman Catholic archbishop. *The Church and Modern Society*.

Janvier, Thomas Allibone (1849-1913), b. Philadelphia, Pa. Journalist and author. *Color Studies, Stories of Old New Spain, An Embassy to Provence, The Passing of Thomas*.

Jewett, Sarah Orne (1849-1909), b. South Berwick, Me. Artistic novelist of old New England villages. *Deephaven, The Country of the Pointed Firs, The Tory Lover*. She shows a more genial side of New England life than Miss Wilkins gives.

King, Charles (1844-   ), b. Albany, N.Y. Soldier, novelist. *A War-Time Wooing, The Colonel's Daughter, The Deserter, The General's Double*.

Kirk, Ellen Olney (1842-   ), b. Southington, Conn. Novelist. *Through Winding Ways, A Midsummer Madness, The Story of Margaret Kent, Marcia*.

Larcom, Lucy (1826-1893), b. Beverly Farms, Mass. A factory hand in Lowell, encouraged by Whittier to write. *Poems; A New England Girlhood, Outlined from Memory*.

Lathrop, George P. (1851-1898), b. Oahu, Hawaii. Son-in-law

of Nathaniel Hawthorne, editor, author. *A Study of Hawthorne, Spanish Vistas, Newport.*

Lazarus, Emma (1849–1887), b. New York City. Poet, translator, essayist. *Admetus, Songs of a Semite, Poems.*

Leland, Charles Godfrey ("Hans Breitmann") (1824–1903), b. Philadelphia, Pa. Humorist. *Hans Breitmann's Ballads,* written in what is known as Pennsylvania Dutch dialect.

Locke, David Ross ("Petroleum V. Nasby") (1833–1888), b. Vestal, N. Y. Political satirist. *Nasby Letters.*

Lodge, Henry Cabot (1850–   ), b. Boston, Mass. Statesman, historian, essayist. *A Short History of the English Colonies in America, Alexander Hamilton, Daniel Webster, Studies in History, Hero Tales from American History* (with Theodore Roosevelt).

"**Luska, Sidney.**" *See* **Harland, Henry.**

Mabie, Hamilton W. (1846–1916), b. Cold Spring, N. Y. Editor, essayist. *My Study Fire, William Shakespeare: Poet, Dramatist, and Man, Essays on Books and Culture.*

MacKaye, Percy Wallace (1875–   ), b. New York City. Dramatist. *Jeanne d'Arc, Sappho and Phaon, The Canterbury Pilgrims, Ticonderoga and Other Poems.*

McMaster, John Bach (1852–   ), b. Brooklyn, N. Y. Historian and professor of American history. *A History of the People of the United States from the Revolution to the Civil War.* 7 vols. An entertaining history, sometimes suggestive of Macaulay.

Marks, Mrs. Lionel. *See* **Peabody, Josephine Preston.**

"**Marvel, Ik.**" *See* **Mitchell, Donald G.**

Melville, Herman (1819–1891), b. New York City. Novelist. *Typee Omoo, Mardi, White Jacket or the World in a Man of War, Moby Dick or the White Whale* contain interesting accounts of his wide travels.

Mitchell, Donald Grant ("Ik Marvel") (1822–1908), b. Norwich, Conn. Essayist. *Reveries of a Bachelor, Dream Life.*

Mitchell, S. Weir (1829–   ), b. Philadelphia, Pa. Physician, novelist, and poet. *Hugh Wynne, Free Quaker; The Adventures of François; Dr. North and his Friends;* and *Constance Trescot,*

Moore, Clement Clarke (1779-1863), b. New York City. Oriental scholar and poet. Known to children to-day for his poem, *'Twas the Night before Christmas*.

Moulton, Ellen Louise Chandler (1835-1908), b. Pomfret, Conn. Story writer, poet, correspondent. *Some Women's Hearts, Swallow Flights and Other Poems, In Childhood's Country*.

"Nasby, Petroleum V." *See* **Locke, David Ross**.

Odell, Jonathan (1737-1818), b. Newark, N. J. Clergyman, greatest anti-Revolution poetic satirist. Shows influence of Dryden and Pope. *The American Congress, The American Times*.

O'Reilly, John Boyle (1844-1890), b. Ireland. Journalist, poet. *Songs, Legends and Ballads; Moondyne; Songs from the Southern Seas*.

"Partington, Mrs." *See* **Shillaber, Benjamin P.**

Paulding, James Kirke (1779-1860), b. Pleasant Valley, N.Y. Satirical humorist and descriptive writer. *The Dutchman's Fireside*. Assisted Irving in the *Salmagundi* papers.

Payne, John Howard (1792-1852), b. New York City. Dramatist. Author of the song, *Home, Sweet Home*.

Peabody, Josephine Preston (Mrs. Lionel Marks) (1874-   ) b. New York City. Poet, dramatist. *The Singing Leaves, Fortune and Men's Eyes, Marlowe, The Piper* (Stratford-on-Avon prize drama). Author of excellent poems for children.

Perry, Bliss (1860-   ), b. Williamstown, Mass. Educator, editor, author. *Walt Whitman, A Study of Prose Fiction, John Greenleaf Whittier*.

Read, Thomas Buchanan (1822-1872), b. Chester Co., Pa. Poet and painter. *The New Pastoral, Sheridan's Ride*.

Repplier, Agnes (1857-   ), b. Philadelphia, Pa. Witty essayist. *Books and Men, Points of View, Essays in Idleness*.

Riggs, Mrs. *See* **Wiggin, Kate Douglas**.

Roe, Edward Payson (1838-1888), b. New Windsor, N.Y. Clergyman, novelist. *Barriers Burned Away, Opening a Chestnut Burr, Nature's Serial Story*.

Rohlfs, Mrs. Charles. *See* **Green, Anna Katherine**.

Roosevelt, Theodore (1858–   ), b. New York City. Ex-President of the United States. Lived for awhile on a western ranch and amassed material for some of his most popular works. *Ranch Life and the Hunting Trail, The Winning of the West, The Rough Riders.* He has written also on civil, economic, and ethical subjects with great vigor and incisive clearness. His *African Game Trails* is the record of his trip to Africa.

Sangster, Margaret (1838–   ), b. New Rochelle, N. Y. Editor, writer of stories and poems. *Poems of the Household, Home Fairies and Heart Flowers.*

Saxe, John Godfrey (1816–1887), b. Highgate, Vt. Journalist, writer of humorous verse. *Humorous and Satirical Poems, The Money King and Other Poems.*

Schouler, James (1839–   ), b. Arlington, Mass. Lawyer, historian. *A History of the United States under the Constitution.* 6 vols.

Scollard, Clinton (1860–   ), b. Clinton, N. Y. Educator, poet. *With Reed and Lyre, The Hills of Song, Voices and Visions.*

Sedgwick, Catherine M. (1789–1867), b. Stockbridge, Mass. Novelist. Her best stories are those of simple New England country life. *Redwood, Clarence, A New England Tale.*

Shaw, Henry Wheeler (Josh Billings) (1818–1885), b. Lanesborough, Mass. Humorist. *Farmers' Alminax, Every Boddy's Friend, Josh Billings' Spice Box.*

Shea, John Dawson Gilmary (1824–1892), b. New York City. Editor, historian. *Discovery and Exploration of the Mississippi Valley, History of the Catholic Missions among the Indian Tribes of the United States, History of the Catholic Church in the United States,* and many other historical and religious studies.

Sherman, Frank Dempster (1860–1916), b. Peekskill, N. Y. Professor of architecture, poet. *Madrigals and Catches, Lyrics for a Lute, Lyrics of Joy.*

Shillaber, Benjamin P. ("Mrs. Partington") (1814–1890), b. Portsmouth, N. H. Humorist of Mrs. Malaprop's style, mistaking words of similar sounds but dissimilar sense. *Life and Say-*

ings of Mrs. Partington, Partingtonian Patchwork, Ike and his Friend.

Smith, Samuel F. (1808–1895), b. Boston, Mass. Clergyman. Author of our national poem, *America*. Of him, Holmes wrote, " Fate tried to conceal him by naming him Smith."

Sparks, Jared (1789–1866), b. Willington, Conn. Unitarian minister and historian. *Diplomatic Correspondence of the American Revolution, The Writings of George Washington, The Works of Benjamin Franklin.*

Spofford, Harriet Prescott (1835–   ), b. Calais, Me. Novelist, poet. *The Amber Gods and Other Stories, New England Legends, Poems.*

Stedman, Edmund Clarence (1833–1908), b. Hartford, Conn. Poet, critic. One of America's fairest critics. Did valuable work in compiling and criticizing modern English and American literature. *A Victorian Anthology, An American Anthology, Victorian Poets, Poets of America*. Co-editor of *Library of American Literature* in eleven large octavo volumes.

Stockton, Frank R. (1834–1902), b. Philadelphia, Pa. Novelist and humorist. His novels have a farcical humor, due to ridiculous situations and absurdities, treated in a mock-serious vein. *The Lady or the Tiger? The Late Mrs. Null, The Casting away of Mrs. Lecks and Mrs. Aleshine, The Hundredth Man.*

Stoddard, Charles Warren (1843–1909), b. Rochester, N.Y. Author, educator, traveler. *South Sea Idyls, Lepers of Molokai, Poems.*

Stoddard, Richard Henry (1825–1903), b. Hingham, Mass. Journalist, editor, poet. *Songs of Summer, Abraham Lincoln: a Horatian Ode, The Lion's Cub.*

Story, William Wetmore (1819–1895), b. Salem, Mass. Sculptor, author. *Roba di Roma*, or *Walks and Talks about Rome, Poems, Conversations in a Studio, Excursions in Art and Letters.*

Sumner, Chas. (1811–1874), b. Boston, Mass. Noted anti-slavery statesman. His published speeches and orations fill fifteen volumes.

Taylor, Bayard (1825-1878), b. Kennett Square, Chester Co., Pa. Extensive traveler, wrote twelve different volumes of travels, the first being *Views Afoot, or Europe Seen with Knapsack and Staff* (1846). He wrote also much poetry. Among the best of his shorter poems are *The Bedouin Song*, *Nubia*, and *The Song of the Camp*. *Lars: a Pastoral of Norway* is his best long poem. The work by which he will probably remain longest known in literature is his excellent translation of Goethe's *Faust*.

Thaxter, Celia Laighton (1836-1894), b. Portsmouth, N. H. Spent most of life upon Isles of Shoals. Artist, author. *Poems* (Appledore Edition, 1896). Best single poem, *The Sandpiper*.

Thomas, Edith Matilda (1854-   ) b. Chatham, O. Poet. *A New Year's Masque*, *A Winter Swallow, and Other Verse*, *Fair Shadow Land*, *Lyrics and Sonnets*.

Ticknor, George (1791-1871), b. Boston, Mass. *A History of Spanish Literature*.

Torrey, Bradford (1843-1912), b. Weymouth, Mass. Nature writer. *Birds in the Bush*, *The Footpath Way*, *Footing it in Franconia*. Editor of Thoreau's *Journal*.

Tourgee, Albion W. (1838-1905), b. Williamsfield, O. Educated in New York. Soldier, judge, novelist of the reconstruction period. *A Fool's Errand*, *Bricks without Straw*.

Trowbridge, John Townsend (1827-1916), b. Ogden, N. Y. Editor, novelist, poet, juvenile writer. *My Own Story* (biography). Among his stories for young people are *The Drummer Boy*, *The Prize Cup*, *The Tide-Mill Stories*. Best known poem, *The Vagabonds*.

Van Dyke, Henry (1852-   ), b. Germantown, Pa. Clergyman, professor, essayist, poet. *The Builders and Other Poems*, *Fisherman's Luck and Some Other Uncertain Things*, *The Story of the Other Wise Man*. An interesting, optimistic philosopher, and lover of nature, whose works deserve the widest reading.

Ward, Artemus. *See* **Browne, Charles F.**

Ward, Elizabeth Stuart Phelps (1844-1911), b. Boston, Mass. Novelist. *The Gates Ajar*, *The Story of Avis*, *A Singular Life*.

Warner, Charles Dudley (1829–1900), b. Plainfield, Mass. Traveler, journalist, essayist. Wrote the *Editor's Drawer* and *Editor's Study* of *Harper's Magazine*. *My Summer in a Garden* and *Backlog Studies* are delightful for their subtle humor and style. He wrote many entertaining books of travel, such as *Saunterings, In the Levant, My Winter on the Nile, Baddeck and that Sort of Thing*. He wrote *The Gilded Age* in collaboration with Mark Twain.

Webster, Noah (1758–1843), b. Hartford, Conn. Philologist. Published in 1783 his famous *Speller*, which superseded *The New England Primer*, and which almost deserves to be called "literature by reason of its admirable fables." More than sixty million copies of this *Speller* have been sold.

Westcott, Edward Noyes (1847–1898), b. Syracuse, N.Y. Banker, author of one remarkable novel which was published posthumously, *David Harum*, a story of central New York.

Wharton, Edith (1862–   ), b. New York City. Essayist, novelist. Her fiction deals largely with modern society problems. She treats subtle psychological questions with especial skill in the short story. *The Valley of Decision, Crucial Instances, The House of Mirth, The Fruit of the Tree, Italian Backgrounds*.

Whipple, Edwin Percy (1819–1886), b. Gloucester, Mass. Critic, essayist. *Essays and Reviews, American Literature and Other Papers, Recollections of Eminent Men*.

Whitcher, Frances ("Widow Bedott") (1811–1852), b. Whitestown, N.Y. Humorist. *The Widow Bedott Papers*.

Whitney, Adeline Dutton Train (1824–1906), b. Boston, Mass. Poet, novelist, and writer of juvenile stories. *Faith Gartney's Girlhood, We Girls, Boys at Chequasset, Summer in Leslie Goldthwaite's Life, Poems*.

Wiggin, Kate Douglas (Mrs. Riggs) (1857–   ), b. Philadelphia, Pa. Novelist and writer on kindergarten subjects. Author of *The Bird's Christmas Carol, Timothy's Quest, Rebecca of Sunnybrook Farm, Penelope's Progress, A Cathedral Courtship*. Pathos, humor, and sympathy for the poor, the weak, and the helpless are characteristic qualities of her work. There are few better children's stories than the first two mentioned.

Williams, Roger (1604?-1683), b. probably in London. Founder of Rhode Island. The first great preacher of "soul liberty" in America. *The Bloody Tenent of Persecution for Cause of Conscience Discussed, The Bloody Tenent yet More Bloody.*

Willis, N. P. (1806-1867), b. Portland, Me. Traveler, prose writer, poet, editor. While his work has proved ephemeral, he taught many writers of his day the necessity of artistic finish in their prose. His prose *Letters from under a Bridge*, and his poems, *Parrhasius* and *Unseen Spirits*, may be mentioned.

Winsor, Justin (1831-1897), b. Boston, Mass. Librarian at Harvard, historian, editor of *Narrative and Critical History of America*. Author of *The Mississippi Basin: the Struggle in America between England and France, 1697-1763; The Westward Movement, 1763-1798; Reader's Handbook of the American Revolution, Christopher Columbus.*

Winter, William (1836-), b. Gloucester, Mass. Dramatic editor of the New York *Tribune* from 1865 to 1909. Edited numbers of plays. Author of *Shakespeare's England, Gray Days and Gold, Life and Art of Edwin Booth, Wanderers* (poems).

Winthrop, Theodore (1828-1861), b. New Haven, Conn. Novelist. His best story, *John Brent*, contains some of his western experiences.

Wister, Owen (1860-), b. Philadelphia, Pa. Lawyer and novelist. Gives realistic pictures of the middle West. *New Swiss Family Robinson, The Dragon of Wantley, Red Men and White, Lin McLean, Lady Baltimore*, and *The Virginian*.

Woodberry, Geo. E. (1855-), b. Beverly, Mass. Educator, author of excellent biographies of Poe, Hawthorne, and Emerson. *America in Literature, Poems.*

Woolson, Constance Fenimore (1848-1894), b. Claremont, N. H. Novelist. Best novel, *Horace Chase*. Some of her other novels are *Castle Nowhere, Anne, East Angels, Jupiter Lights, The Old Stone House.*

SUPPLEMENTARY LIST OF AUTHORS

SOUTHERN AUTHORS

Alsop, George (1638– ?), b. England. Published in 1666 an entertaining volume, *A Character of the Province of Maryland.*

Audubon, John J. (1780–1851), b. near New Orleans, La. Noted ornithologist and painter of birds. Published *Birds of America* at one thousand dollars a copy and *Ornithological Biography* in 5 vols.

Azarias, Brother. *See* Mullany, P. F.

Burnett, Frances Hodgson (1849–   ), b. Manchester, Eng. Anglo-American novelist. *Little Lord Fauntleroy, That Lass o' Lowrie's, Haworth's, A Fair Barbarian, A Lady of Quality.*

Calhoun, John C. (1782–1850), b. Abbeville District, S.C. Statesman, orator. Best work, *Disquisition on Government and Discourse on the Constitution and Government of the United States.* Best speech, *Nullification and the Force Bill* (1833).

Clay, Henry (1777–1852), b. near Richmond, Va. Orator, statesman. Best speeches: *On the War of 1812* (1813), *The Seminole War* (1819), *The American System* (1832).

Cooke, John Esten (1830–1886), b. Winchester, Va. Colonial and military story writer. Best romance, *The Virginia Comedians.*

Dixon, Thomas (1864–   ), b. Shelby, N.C. Clergyman, novelist. *The Leopard's Spots, The One Woman, The Clansman.*

Evans, Augusta. *See* Wilson, Augusta Evans.

Fox, John Jr. (1863–   ), b. in Bourbon Co., Kentucky. Novelist of life in the Kentucky mountains. *The Kentuckians, A Mountain Europa, A Cumberland Vendetta, The Little Shepherd of Kingdom Come, The Trail of the Lonesome Pine.*

Gayarré, Charles E. A. (1805–1895), b. New Orleans, La. Jurist, historian. *History of Louisiana.*

Gibbons, James (1834–   ), b. Baltimore, Md. Roman Catholic cardinal. *The Faith of Our Fathers, The Ambassador of Christ.*

Glasgow, Ellen Anderson Gholson (1874–   ), b. Richmond, Va. Novelist. *The Descendant, The Voice of the People, The Deliverance.*

Grady, Henry W. (1851–1889), b. Athens, Ga. Editor, orator. Best oration, *The New South.*

Hearn, Lafcadio (1850–1904), b. in Ionian Islands of Irish and Greek parentage. Journalist, author. Lived many years in New Orleans, went thence to New York, and still later to Japan. Author of *Stray Leaves from Strange Literature, Two Years in the French West Indies, Glimpses of Unfamiliar Japan, Out of the East*. Shows marked descriptive ability.

Hegan, Alice. *See* **Rice, Alice Hegan.**

"Henry, O." *See* **Porter, Sidney.**

Johnston, Mary (1870–   ), b. Buchanan, Va. Writer of vigorous, well-handled romances of Virginia history. *Prisoners of Hope, To Have and to Hold, Audrey, Lewis Rand.*

Johnston, Richard Malcolm (1822–1898), b. Hancock Co., Ga. Lawyer, professor of English. Writer of Georgia stories. *Dukesborough Tales.*

Kennedy, J. P. (1795–1870), b. Baltimore, Md. Wrote three works of fiction, *Swallow Barn*, a picture of the manners and customs of Virginia at the end of the eighteenth century, *Horse-Shoe Robinson, a Tale of the Tory Ascendency, Rob of the Bowl*, a story of colonial Maryland.

Key, Francis Scott (1780–1843), b. Frederick Co., Md. *The Star-Spangled Banner.*

King, Grace E. (1852–   ), b. New Orleans, La. Novels of Creole life and historical works on De Soto and New Orleans: *Monsieur Motte, Tales of Time and Place, Balcony Stories.*

Longstreet, Augustus B. (1790–1870), b. Augusta, Ga. Judge, and (later) a Methodist minister. His *Georgia Scenes* is one of the liveliest pictures of provincial Georgia life.

Marshall, John (1755–1835), b. Germantown, Va. Great Chief Justice of U. S. *The Life of George Washington.*

Martin, George Madden (1866–   ), b. Louisville, Ky. Novelist. *Emmy Lou — Her Book and Heart.*

Matthews, James Brander (1852–   ), b. New Orleans, La. Lecturer on literature at Columbia College. Critic and story writer. *French Dramatists of the Nineteenth Century, Margery's*

Lovers, A Secret of the Sea and Other Stories, The Story of a Story, The Historical Novel, Study of the Drama, The Short Story.

Mullany, P. F. (Brother Azarias) (1847–1893), b. Ireland. Educator, essayist. *The Development of Old English Thought, Phases of Thought and Criticism.*

O'Hara, Theodore (1820–1867), b. Danville, Ky. Poet. *The Bivouac of the Dead.*

Peck, Samuel Minturn (1854–   ), b. Tuscaloosa, Ala. Poet and novelist. *Caps and Bells, Rhymes and Roses.*

Pike, Albert (1809–1891), b. Boston, Mass. Moved to Arkansas. Teacher, editor, lawyer. Wrote the popular song, *Dixie*, and *To the Mocking Bird.*

Pinkney, Edward Coate (1802–1828), b. London, Eng. Poet. Best lyrics, *A Serenade, A Health, Songs, The Indian's Bride.*

Porter, Sydney ("O. Henry") (1867–1910), b. Greensboro, N. C. Edited newspapers in Texas. Successful short-story writer. *The Four Million, The Heart of the West, The Gentle Grafter, Roads of Destiny, Options, The Voice of the City.*

Prentice, Geo. D. (1802–1870), b. Preston, Conn. Editor Louisville *Journal*, poet. *Poems.* Best poem, *The Closing Year.*

Preston, Margaret Junkin (1825–1897), b. Philadelphia, Pa. Moved to Lexington, Va. Representative woman poet of the Confederacy. *Cartoons, For Love's Sake, Colonial Ballads, Sonnets, and Other Verse.*

Randall, James Ryder (1839–1908), b. Baltimore, Md. Teacher, poet. *Maryland, My Maryland* (song).

Reid, Christian. *See* **Tiernan, Frances F.**

Rice (Alice Hegan) (1870–   ), b. Shelbyville, Ky. A widely popular story writer of humble folk, a humorist of rare power, a cheery, breezy philosopher, and a sympathetic interpreter of the simple heart of the brave poor. *Mrs. Wiggs of the Cabbage Patch, Lovey Mary, Captain June, Sandy, Mr. Opp.*

Rice, Cale Young (1872–   ), b. Dixon, Ky. Author of exquisite lyrics. One of the greatest of the younger poetic dramatists whose plays have acting qualities. Poems: *From Dusk* *to Dusk, With Omar, Song-Surf, Nirvana Days.* Plays: *Charles di Tocca, David, Yolanda of Cyprus, A Night in Avignon.*

Rives, Amélie (Princess Troubetskoy) (1863–   ), b. Richmond, Va. Novelist. *The Quick or the Dead, Virginia of Virginia.*

Russell, Irwin (1853–1879), b. Port Gibson, Miss. Caricaturist, musician, poet. He was among the first to see the possibilities of the negro dialect in verse. *Poems.*

Seawell, Molly Elliot (1860–1916), b. Gloucester Co., Va. Novelist. *Little Jarvis* (awarded a $500 prize), *Sprightly Romance of Marsac* (awarded a $3000 prize), *Throckmorton.*

Smith, F. Hopkinson (1838–1915), b. Baltimore, Md. Artist, author, engineer. *Colonel Carter of Cartersville* is his most enduring work. The Colonel is a remarkable portrait. *A Gentleman Vagabond and Some Others, Caleb West: Master Diver, A Day at Laguerre's and Other Days, The Fortunes of Oliver Horn.*

Stith, William (1689–1755), b. Virginia. Scholarly historian who was so painstaking and detailed in his accounts that he was almost neglected until the present time. *History of Virginia from the First Discovery to the Dissolution of the London Company.*

Stuart, Ruth McEnery (1856–   ), b. in parish of Avoyelles, La. Specially liked for her humorous negro and plantation stories. *A Golden Wedding and Other Tales, Sonny, Holly and Pizen.*

Thompson, William Tappan (1812–1882), b. Ravenna, O. Georgia journalist and humorist. *Major Jones's Courtship.*

Tiernan, Frances F. ("Christian Reid") (1846–   ), b. Salisbury, N.C. Novelist. *Child of Mary, Heart of Steel.*

Troubetskoy, Princess. See **Rives, Amélie.**

Weems, Mason Locke (1760–1825), b. Dumfries, Va. Clergyman, biographer. *Life of Washington.*

Wilson, Augusta Evans (1835–1909), b. Columbus, Ga. Prolific novelist. Best novel, *Saint Elmo.*

Wilson, Woodrow (1856–   ), b. Staunton, Va. Educator, historian, statesman. *A History of the American People.*

Wirt, William (1772–1834), b. Bladensburg, Md. Lawyer. *Life and Character of Patrick Henry, Letters of the British Spy.*

WESTERN AUTHORS

Atherton, Gertrude Franklin (1859–   ), b. San Francisco, Cal. Novelist. *The Doomswoman, The Aristocrats, The Conqueror.*

Baldwin, James (1841–   ), b. Westfield, Ind. Writer of excellent stories for children. *The Story of Siegfried, Old Greek Stories, Stories of the King, Discovery of the Old Northwest, The Book Lover.*

Bierce, Ambrose (1842–   ), b. Ohio. For many years a San Francisco journalist. *Can Such Things Be? In the Midst of Life* (tales of soldiers and civilians).

Burdette, Robert Jones (1844–1914), b. Greensboro, Pa. Journalist on Burlington (Ia.) *Hawkeye* and other papers, lecturer, humorist, clergyman. *The Rise and Fall of the Moustache, Hawkeyetems, Life of William Penn.*

Burnham, Clara Louise (1854–   ) b. Newton, Mass. Moved to Chicago. Novelist. *Dr. Latimer, The Wise Woman.*

Carleton, Will (1845–1912), b. Hudson, Mich. Poet, editor, lecturer. *Farm Ballads, Farm Legends, Farm Festivals, City Ballads. Over the Hills to the Poor House,* best known single poem.

Catherwood, Mary Hartwell (1847–1902), b. Luray, O. Writer of historical tales of Canada and the Northwest. *A Woman in Armour, The Lady of Fort St. John, The Romance of Dollard, The White Islander, a Story of Mackinac, Lazarre.*

Cheney, John Vance (1848–   ), b. Groveland, N.Y. Moved to the West. Poet and critic. *Thistle-Drift, Wood-Blooms, Queen Helen and Other Poems.* Critical Works: *That Dome in Air* and *The Golden Guess.*

Dunbar, Paul Laurence (1872–1906), b. Dayton, O. African descent. Journalist, poet. Wrote many fine lyrics. *Oak and Ivy, Lyrics of Lowly Life, Lyrics of the Hearthside.*

Dunne, Finley Peter (1867–   ), b. Chicago, Ill. Humorist, journalist. *Mr. Dooley's Philosophy.*

Eggleston, Edward (1837–1902), b. Vevay, Ind. Novelist of the early life of southern Indiana. *The Hoosier Schoolmaster, The Hoosier Schoolboy, Roxy, The Graysons.*

Foote, Mary Hallock (1847–   ), b. Milton, N. Y. Her novels give vivid representations of western life. *The Led Horse Claim, The Chosen Valley, Cœur d'Alène.*

French, Alice ("Octave Thanet") (1850–   ), b. Andover, Mass. Novelist. *Knitters in the Sun, Stories of a Western Town, A Book of True Lovers, The Man of the Hour.*

Garland, Hamlin (1860–   ), b. West Salem, Wis. Presents graphic pictures of the middle West in such stories as *Main-Traveled Roads, Prairie Folks, Rose of Dutcher's Coolly, Boy Life on the Prairie.*

Hay, John (1838–1905), b. Salem, Ind. Private secretary to President Lincoln. Lawyer, journalist, diplomatist, and statesman. *Pike County Ballads.* Joint author with J. G. Nicolay of *Abraham Lincoln: A History*, 9 vols.

Herrick, Robert (1868–   ), b. Cambridge, Mass. Professor (University of Chicago), novelist. *The Web of Life, The Common Lot, The Master of the Inn.*

Hovey, Richard (1864–1900), b. Normal, Ill. Poet, dramatist. *Songs from Vagabondia, The Marriage of Guenevere, Taliesin: A Masque.*

Jackson, Helen Hunt (1831–1885), b. Amherst, Mass. Novelist, poet. Her great western novel, *Ramona*, stands in the same relation to the Indian as *Uncle Tom's Cabin* to the negro. Her *Century of Dishonor* shows the wrongs done to the Indian race. *Poems.*

London, Jack (1876–1916), b. San Francisco, Cal. Novelist of adventure. *The Call of the Wild, The Children of the Frost, The Sea Wolf, The Game.*

Lummis, Charles F. (1859–   ), b. Lynn, Mass. Traveler, librarian, writer. *The Spanish Pioneers, The Man Who Married the Moon, The Enchanted Burro.*

McCutcheon, Geo. Barr (1866–   ), b. Tippecanoe Co., Ind. Novelist. *Castle Craneycrow, Brewster's Millions, Beverly of Graustark.*

Markham, Edwin (1852–   ), b. Oregon City, Ore. Poet. *The Man with the Hoe and Other Poems.*

Miller, Cincinnatus Heine (Joaquin Miller) (1841–1913), b. Wabash District, Ind. Lived in the far West, about which he writes in his poetry. *Songs of the Sierras, Songs of the Sunlands, Songs of the Desert.*

Moody, William Vaughan (1869–1910), b. Spencer, Ind. Poet, dramatist. *The Masque of Judgment, The Fire Bringer, The Great Divide* (play).

Nicholson, Meredith (1866–   ), b. Crawfordsville, Ind. Novelist. *The House of a Thousand Candles, The Port of Missing Men, The Hoosiers* (in *National Studies in American Letters*).

Norris, Frank (1870–1902), b. Chicago, Ill. Realistic novel writer. *McTeague, The Octopus, The Pit.*

Phillips, David Graham (1867–1911), b. Madison, Ind. Novelist. *The Social Secretary, The Second Generation, The Fashionable Adventures of Joshua Craig.*

Piatt, John James (1835–   ), b. James Mills, Ind. Poet. *Western Windows, Idyls and Lyrics of the Ohio Valley, Poems of Two Friends* (with W. D. Howells).

Rhodes, James Ford (1848–   ), b. Cleveland, O. Historian. *History of the United States from the Compromise of 1850*, 7 vols. The seventh volume ends with 1877.

Seton, Ernest Thompson (1860–   ), b. South Shields, Eng. Painter, naturalist. *Wild Animals I Have Known, Lives of the Hunted, Natural History of the Ten Commandments, The Trail of the Sandhill Stag, The Biography of a Grizzly.*

Sill, Edward Rowland (1841–1887), b. Windsor, Conn. Professor in University of California. Transcendental poet. Some fine verse may be found in his volumes, *Hermione and Other Poems* and *The Hermitage and Later Poems.*

Spalding, John L. (1840–   ), b. Lebanon, Ky. Roman Catholic archbishop. *Education and the Higher Life, Things of the Mind, Socialism and Labor.*

Spearman, Frank H. (1859–   ), b. Buffalo, N. Y. Moved to Wisconsin. Novelist, essayist. *Whispering Smith, The Daughter of a Magnate, The Nerve of Foley.*

Tarkington, Newton Booth (1869-   ), b. Indianapolis, Ind. Novelist. *The Gentleman from Indiana, Monsieur Beaucaire, The Two Vanrevels, Cherry, The Conquest of Canaan.*

"**Thanet, Octave.**" *See* **French, Alice.**

Thompson, Maurice (1844-1901), b. Fairfield, Ind. Novelist, naturalist, poet. Best known works, *By-Ways and Bird Notes, My Winter Garden, Alice of Old Vincennes.*

Wallace, Lew (1827-1905), b. Brookville, Ind. Lawyer, diplomat, author. *Ben Hur*, a tale of remarkable power; *The Fair God, The Prince of India.*

White, Stewart Edward (1873-   ), b. Grand Rapids, Mich. Writer of vigorous stories of western mountain life. *The Blazed Trail, The Silent Places, The Claim Jumpers, The Riverman.*

Wilcox, Ella Wheeler (1855-   ), b. Johnstown Center, Wis. Journalist and poet. *Poems of Passion, Poems of Pleasure, Poems of Power, Poems of Sentiment.*

INDEX

Abbott, Jacob, 399.
Adams, Henry, 399.
Adams, John, 73, 75, 101.
Adams, John Quincy, 147.
Adams, Samuel, 74, 75, 102, 105, 106.
Addison, Joseph, 55, 83, 98, 114, 121, 123, 124, 149, 152.
Alcott, Amos Bronson, 159, 160, 164, 209.
Alcott, Louisa May, 160, 399.
Aldrich, Thomas Bailey, 330, 371, 372.
Alhambra, 115, 120.
Allen, James Lane,
  life and works of, 328–330, 336.
  questions and suggestions on, 340.
  references on, 336, 337, 338, 339.
  suggested readings in, 338, 339.
Allston, Washington, 399.
Alsop, George, 414.
American Note Books, 166, 167, 207, 208.
American Scholar, The, 185, 186.
Ames, Fisher, 399.
Amsterdam, New, 117, 118.
Annabel Lee, 297, 302.
Arber, Edwin, 19, 20.
Armada, Spanish, 15.
Arnold, Matthew, 274, 285.
Atherton, Gertrude Franklin, 418.
Atlantic Monthly, 248, 251, 263.
Audubon, John J., 414.
Austen, Jane, 370, 394.
Austin, Jane G., 399.
Autobiography, Franklin's, 76–79.
Autocrat of the Breakfast Table, The, 262, 263, 264, 265.
Azarias, Brother (Mullany, P. F.), 416.

Bacheller, Irving, 399.
Bacon, Nathaniel, 22, 59.
Baldwin, James, 418.
Bancroft, George, 400.
Bangs, John Kendrick, 400.
Barlow, Joel, 93, 94, 103, 105, 106.
Barr, Amelia E., 400.
Bates, Arlo, 400.
Bay Psalm Book, 37, 38.
Bedott, Widow, 412.
Beecher, Henry Ward, 169, 400.
Berkeley, Sir William, 25.
Beveridge, Albert J., 354.
Beverley, Robert, 23, 59.

Bible, The, 136, 235, 345.
Bierce, Ambrose, 418.
Biglow Papers, 247, 249, 250, 251, 252, 264, 275.
"Billings, Josh" (Shaw, Henry Wheeler), 409.
Blithedale Romance, 219.
Boker, George H., 400.
Bradford, William, 26–28, 60, 61, 62, 64.
Bradstreet, Anne, 39–41, 59, 61, 63, 258.
Breitmann, Hans (Leland, C. G.), 409.
Bridge, Horatio, 206, 209.
Brook Farm, 165–167, 169, 207, 219, 278.
Brooks, Phillips, 400.
Brown, Alice, 401.
Brown, Charles Brockden, 86, 88, 89–92, 99, 103, 104, 105, 106, 125, 299, 367, 392.
Browne, Charles F. ("Artemus Ward"), 401.
Browning, Robert, 274.
  Whittier's comment on, 275.
Brownson, Orestes A., 401.
Bryant, William Cullen, 99, 108, 135–145, 149, 150, 151, 152, 231, 253.
  betrothal prayer of, 138.
  compared with Wordsworth, 143, 144, 145.
  general characteristics of, 143–145.
  life of, 135–140.
  Lowell on, 253.
  moral qualities of, 136, 137, 143, 145.
  poetry of, 139, 140–145.
  Puritan training of, 136.
  questions and suggestions on, 152.
  references on, 151.
  suggested readings in, 152.
  translates Homer, 140.
Bunner, Henry Cuyler, 401.
Bunyan, John, 10, 55, 83.
Burdette, Robert Jones, 418.
Burke, Edmund, 98.
Burnett, Frances Hodgson, 414.
Burnham, Clara Louise, 418.
Burns, Robert, 25, 99, 235, 243, 244, 275.
Burroughs, John, 401.
Burwell Papers, 22.
Butler, Samuel, 96.
Byrd, William, 23, 26, 59.
Byron, Lord, 145, 289.

423

INDEX

Cable, George Washington, **336, 368.**
   life and works of, 325–328.
   questions and suggestions on, **340.**
   references on, 336, 337, 338.
   suggested readings in, 338.
Calhoun, John C., 176, 414.
Calvin, John, 34.
Cambridge University, 16.
Carleton, Will, 418.
Carlyle, Thomas, 43, 162, **183, 192,** 274.
Cary, Alice and Phœbe, 401.
Catherwood, Mary Hartwell, **418.**
Cawein, Madison J., 292, **335.**
   life and works of, 332–334.
   questions and suggestions on, **339.**
   references on, 336, 338.
   suggested readings in, 338.
Cervantes, 364, 366.
Chambered Nautilus, The, 261.
Chambers, Robert W., 401.
Channing, William, 163.
Channing, William Ellery, **154, 402.**
Charles I, 12, 14, 15.
Chaucer, Geoffrey, 10, 254.
Cheney, John Vance, 418.
Cherry Valley Massacre, 126.
Child, Lydia Maria, 402.
Churchill, Winston, 402.
Civil War, 11, 251, 290, 291, 335, **384, 388.**
Clarke, James Freeman, 402.
Classic School, 86.
Clay, Henry, 414.
Clemens, Samuel L. ("Mark Twain"), 10, 172, 341, 342, 343, 355–364, **365, 366,** 368.
   general characteristics of, 361–364.
   humor of, 355, 361, 362, 364.
   life of, 355–358.
   moral quality of, 358, 363.
   personal philosophy of, 362, 364.
   questions and suggestions on, 366.
   references on, 365, 366.
   stories of Mississippi Valley, 358–361.
   style of, 363, 364.
   suggested readings in, 366.
Clergy (New England), 35–37, 75, **136.**
Coleridge, Samuel Taylor, 88, 97, 99, 103, 110, 145, 254, 370.
Colonial literature, 9–64.
   questions and suggestions on, **63, 64.**
   references on, 60, 61.
   suggested readings in, 62, 63.
   summary of, 58–60.
Columbus, Christopher, 121, **122.**
Communipaw, 118.
Comus, 51, 52, 55.
Concord Bridge, 179, 246.
Concord, Mass., 181, 182, 194, 196, 211.
Concord group, 278.

Cone, Helen Gray, 402.
Conway, Moncure D., 209.
Cooke, John Esten, 414.
Cooke, Philip Pendleton, 289.
Cooke, Rose Terry, 402.
Cooper, James Fenimore, 10, 88, 91, 125–134, 150, 151, 152, 186, 219, 308, 340, 367.
   general characteristics of, 133, 134.
   life of, 125–130.
   moral quality of, 134.
   pioneer and Indian tales of, 130–133, 149.
   questions and suggestions on, 152.
   references on, 150, 151.
   sea tales of, 133, 151.
   style of, 134.
   suggested readings in, **151.**
Cooperstown, 126, 128, 130.
Copyright law, 96, 278.
Cotton, John, 14, 35, 36, 37, 46.
Courtship of Miles Standish, 231, 232, 284, 286.
Cowper, William, 99.
Craddock, Charles Egbert. *See* Murfree, Mary N.
Craigie, Pearl Mary Teresa ("John Oliver Hobbes"), 402.
Cranch, Christopher Pearse, 402.
Crane, Ichabod, 119, 122.
Crane, Stephen, 402.
Crawford, F. Marion, 402.
"Croakers," The, 108, 109, 148, 151, 152.
Cromwell, Oliver, 15.
Culprit Fay, The, 110.
Curtis, George William, 166, 403.

Dana, Charles A., 166.
Dana, R. H. Sr., 403.
Dana, R. H. Jr., 403.
Dante, 50, 52, 224.
Darwin, Charles, 274.
Davis, Richard Harding, 403.
Defoe, Daniel, 55, 98.
Deland, Margaretta W., 403.
Democratic spirit of American literature, 68–70, 225, 226, 243, 342–364, 382–391, 397.
De Quincey, Thomas, 146.
Dial, The, 162–165, 169, 278, **282.**
Dickens, Charles, 274, 348.
Dickinson, Emily, 404.
Dickinson, John, 404.
Disraeli, Benjamin, 183.
Dixon, Thomas, 414.
Dodge, Mary Mapes, 404.
Dorr, Julia C. R., 404.
Dowden, Edward, 11.
Drake, Joseph Rodman, 108–111, 148, 151, 152.

INDEX 425

Drayton, Michael, 12.
Dryden, John, 22, 24, 55, 87, 290.
Du Bartas, 40.
Dunbar, Paul Lawrence, 418.
Dunne, Finley Peter, 418.
Dutch, The, 112, 117, 121, 135.
Dwight, John S., 404.
Dwight, Timothy, 85, 92, 93, 103, 105, 106.

Edwards, Jonathan, 50–54, 59, 60, 70, 77, 80, 85.
   questions and suggestions on, 64.
   references on, 61, 63.
   sermon on hell fire, 153, 154, 157.
   suggested readings in, 63.
Egan, Maurice Francis, 404.
Eggleston, Edward, 418.
Eliot, George, 274.
Elizabeth, Queen, 15, 16, 17.
Emerson, Ralph Waldo, 158, 159, 161, 162, 163, 169, 178–193, 246, 396, 397.
   essays of, 186–188.
   general characteristics of, 191–193.
   idealistic philosophy of, 185, 190, 192.
   life of, 178–183.
   Lowell on, 253.
   moral quality of, 179, 185, 186, 188, 191, 192.
   personal philosophy of, 190.
   poetry of, 182, 188–191.
   prose of, 183–188.
   questions and suggestions on, 284, 285, 286.
   references on, 281, 282, 283.
   style of, 193.
   suggested readings in, 282, 283.
England, literary dependence on, 127.
English literature, America's debt to, 9, 10.
   classical age of, 87.
   from 1607 to 1754, 54, 55.
   in first part of the nineteenth century, 145, 146.
   in second half of the eighteenth century, 98, 99.
   in Victorian age, 274, 275.
   influence of, on early American fiction, 85–88.
   romantic movement in, 86–88, 110.
Evangeline, 228, 229, 279.
Evans, Augusta, 417.
Evening Post, New York, 116, 139.
Everett, Edward, 173, 175, 344, 404.

Fable for Critics, 247, 250, 253.
Faerie Queene, 206.
Federalist, 71, 288.
Fiction. *See also* Morton, Sarah; Brown, C. B.; Irving; Cooper; Hawthorne; Poe; Simms; Cable; Allen; Harte; Clemens; Howells; James; Wilkins Freeman.
   early American, 85–92.
   Gothic element in, 88, 90, 91.
   influence of Richardson on, 86.
   realistic school of, 367–371, 373–380.
   romantic element in, 88, 90, 91, 119, 120, 123, 124, 125, 130, 131, 211–221, 297–301, 305, 306, 307, 308, 309, 326–328, 329, 347–349, 358–361.
Field, Eugene, 343, 349–352, 353.
   questions and suggestions on, 366.
   references on, 365, 366.
   suggested readings in, 365, 366.
Fielding, Henry, 55, 85, 86, 98, 370.
Fields, James T., 404.
Fiske, John, 404.
Foote, Mary Hallock, 419.
Ford, Paul Leicester, 404.
Foster, Stephen Collins, 404.
Fox, John Jr., 414.
Franklin, Benjamin, 25, 47, 76–83, 84, 89, 102, 103, 130, 396.
   general characteristics of, 80–83, 102.
   humor of, 82.
   most widely read colonial writer, 80.
   philosophy of, 80, 81, 82.
   Poor Richard's maxims, 81, 82.
   questions and suggestions on, 106.
   references on, 104.
   suggested readings in, 105.
Frederic, Harold, 404.
Freeman, Mary E. Wilkins, 379, 380, 392.
   characteristics of, 380.
   questions and suggestions on, 394.
   references on, 392, 393.
   suggested readings in, 393.
French, Alice ("Octave Thanet"), 419.
French and Indian War, 65, 100.
Freneau, Philip, 66, 96–98, 99, 103, 105, 106.
Fugitive Slave Act, 170, 275.
Fuller, Margaret, 158, 159, 162, 166.

Garland, Hamlin, 419.
Garrison, William Lloyd, 169, 235.
Gayarré, Charles E. A., 414.
Gettysburg Address, 177, 344.
Gibbon, Edward, 98.
Gibbons, James, 414.
Gilder, Richard Watson, 404.
Glasgow, Ellen Anderson Gholson, 414.
Godwin, William, 90, 99.
Goethe, 387, 411.
Goldsmith, Oliver, 114, 122, 124.
Goodwin, Maud Wilder, 405.
Gosse, Edmund, 332.
"Gothic," 88, 90.

INDEX

Grady, Henry W., **414**.
Grant, Robert, 405.
Greeley, Horace, 405.
Green, Anna Katherine, 405.
Guiney, Louise Imogen, 405.

Hale, Edward Everett, 405.
Halleck, Fitz-Greene, 108–111, 145, 148, 152, 157.
Hamilton, Alexander, 70, 71, 75, 102–105.
Hardy, Arthur S., 405.
Harland, Henry ("Sidney Luska"), 405.
Harris, Joel Chandler, 368.
  life and works of, 320–323.
  questions and suggestions on, 340.
  references on, 336, 337.
  suggested readings in, 338.
Harte, Bret, 10, 341, 343, 345–349, 352.
  life of, 345–347.
  questions and suggestions on, 366.
  references on, 365.
  suggested readings in, 365.
  works of, 347–349.
Hartford Wits, 92, 96, 103.
Hawkeye, 130.
Hawthorne, Julian, 405.
Hawthorne, Nathaniel, 10, 88, 91, 161, 166, 167, 204–221, 296, 301, 304, 328, 339, 341, 359, 366, 367, 376, 392, 398.
  at Brook Farm, 166, 167.
  general characteristics of, 219–221.
  great romances of, 214–219, 283, 286.
  life of, 204–211.
  moral quality of, 212, 214, 215, 216, 218, 219, 221, 279, 304, 398.
  on Emerson, 183, 189.
  questions and suggestions on, 286.
  references on, 281.
  short stories of, 211–214, 283, 286.
  style of, 221.
  suggested readings in, 283.
Hay, John, 419.
Hayne, Paul Hamilton, 238, 307, 335.
  life and works of, 311, 312.
  questions and suggestions on, 339.
  references on, 336, 337.
  suggested readings in, 337.
Hearn, Lafcadio, 415.
Hedge, Frederic H., 405.
Hegan, Alice (Rice, Alice Hegan), 416.
Henry, O. (Porter, Sydney), 416.
Henry, Patrick, 73, 74, 75, 102, 105, 106, 177.
Herbert, George, 40.
Herrick, Robert, 419.
Hiawatha, 228, 229–231, 279.
Higginson, Thomas Wentworth, 405.
Hobbes, John Oliver (Craigie, Pearl Mary), 402.

Hoffman, Matilda, **115**.
Holland, J. G., 406.
Holley, Marietta, 406.
Holmes, Oliver Wendell, 155, 168, 182, 185, 191, 258–265.
  humor of, 259, 260, 263, 264.
  life of, 258–260.
  moral quality of, 261, 265.
  poetry of, 260–262, 279, 284, 285.
  prose of, 263–265, 279, 286.
  questions and suggestions on, 285, 286.
  references on, 281, 282.
  suggested readings in, 284.
Hooker, Rev. Thomas, 16.
House of the Seven Gables, The, 214, 216 217, 221, 283, 286.
Hovey, Richard, 419.
Howard, Blanche Willis, 406.
Howe, Julia Ward, 406.
Howells, William Dean, 330, 368, 369, 370, 373–376, 378, 392.
  best novels of, 373.
  characteristics of his work, 374, 375.
  questions and suggestions on, 394.
  references on, 392, 393.
  suggested readings in, 393.
Huckleberry Finn, 172, 359–361.
Hudson, Hendrick, 113, 117, 119.
Hudson River, 113, 114, 124, 135.
Hutchinson, Thomas, 402, 406.

Idealism, 185, 368, 372. *See also* Romanticism.
Ideals. *See* Moral Ideals.
Identity, 372.
Independence, Declaration of, 68, 69, 74, 100.
Indian, 18, 28, 91, 92, 117, 125, 132, 308.
Ireland, John, 406.
Irving, Washington, 107, 112–124, 133, 219, 266, 301, 328, 339, 366, 367.
  explores Sleepy Hollow, 113.
  general characteristics of, 123, 124, 149.
  humor of, 117, 118, 123, 152.
  invents the "Knickerbocker Legend," 116, 117.
  life of, 112–116.
  Lowell's recipe for, 253.
  profits from writing, 115, 116.
  questions and suggestions on, 152.
  references on, 150, 151.
  style of, 124.
  suggested readings in, 151.
  works of, 116–124.

Jackson, Andrew, 147, 148, **186**.
Jackson, Helen Hunt, 419.
James I, 14.

INDEX

James, Henry, 368, 369, 370, 376–379, 392, 393, 394.
  best work of, 377.
  characteristics of his work, 376–379.
  compared with Howells, 396.
  questions and suggestions on, 394.
  references on, 392, 393.
  suggested readings in, 393.
James, Henry, Sr., 376.
James, William, 376, 378.
Jamestown, 11, 13.
Janvier, Thomas Allibone, 406.
Jefferson, Thomas, 68–70, 75, 102, 105, 106, 288.
Jewett, Sarah Orne, 406.
Job, 136.
Johnson, Samuel, 87, 98, 99.
Johnston, Mary, 415.
Johnston, Richard Malcolm, 415.

Kant, 156.
Keats, John, 88, 142, 146, 275, 326, 334, 399.
Kennedy, J. P., 415.
Key, Francis Scott, 415.
King, Charles, 406.
King, Grace, 415.
Kipling, Rudyard, 321, 340.
Kirk, Ellen Olney, 406.
Knickerbocker, Diedrich, 116, 122, 123.
Knickerbocker's History of New York, 107, 123, 151, 152, 266.
Knickerbocker Legend, 119, 135, 149, 396.

Lamb, Charles, 83, 146.
Lanier, Sidney, 292, 313–317, 335, 398.
  general characteristics of, 316, 317.
  life of, 313, 314.
  questions and suggestions on, 339.
  references on, 336, 337.
  suggested readings in, 338.
  works of, 314–316.
Larcom, Lucy, 406.
Lathrop, George P., 406.
Laud, Archbishop, 14, 15.
Lazarus, Emma, 407.
Leatherstocking Tales, 130–133, 149.
Leaves of Grass, 383–391.
Leland, Charles Godfrey, 407.
Lincoln, Abraham, 177, 276, 290, 325, 343–345, 364, 365, 366, 387.
Locke, David Ross, 407.
Locke, John, 50, 156.
Lodge, Henry Cabot, 407.
London, Jack, 419.
Longfellow, Henry W., 222–233, 243, 249, 279, 283, 285, 341.
  ballads of, 227, 228, 284.
  compared with Whittier, 243.
  general characteristics of, 232, 233.
  laureate of common heart, 225, 226.
  life of, 222–225.
  longer poems of, 228–232, 283, 284, 285, 286.
  moral quality of, 226, 232, 233.
  questions and suggestions on, 285, 286.
  references on, 281, 282.
  suggested readings in, 283, 284.
Longstreet, Augustus, 415.
Lounsbury, T. R.,
  on Cooper, 130.
Lowell, James Russell, 96, 162, 169, 245–257, 263, 275, 279, 341, 389, 398.
  as a critic, 254, 255, 257.
  as a poet of nature, 252, 255, 256.
  early years of, 245–247.
  genius of, 257.
  humor of, 251, 252, 255, 257.
  influence of marriage on, 247, 248.
  later work of, 248–250.
  moral quality of, 247, 250, 253, 254, 256, 398.
  on Emerson, 183, 192, 193.
  on Thoreau's style, 202.
  poetry of, 250–253, 255–257, 284, 285, 286.
  prose of, 249, 254, 255, 257.
  questions and suggestions on, 285, 286.
  references on, 282.
  suggested readings in, 284.
  versatility of, 257.
Lummis, Charles F., 419.
Luska, Sydney (Henry Harland), 405.

Mabie, Hamilton W., 407.
Macaulay, T. B., 274, 407.
MacKaye, Percy Wallace, 407.
Madison, James, 101, 288.
Magnalia, 59.
Manse, Old, 178.
Marble Faun, 210, 214, 217, 218.
Markham, Edwin, 419.
Marks, Mrs. Lionel (Peabody, Josephine Preston), 408.
Marlowe, Christopher, 370.
Marshall, John, 415.
Martin, George Madden, 415.
Martineau, Harriet, 186.
Marvel, Ik (Mitchell, Donald Grant), 407.
Materialism, 147, 148, 150, 191.
Mather, Cotton, 39, 46–50, 59, 61, 63, 64, 77, 82.
Matthews, James Brander, 415.
McCutcheon, George Barr, 419.
McMaster, John Bach, 407.
Melville, Herman, 407.
Mexican War, 148, 251.

INDEX

Miller, Cincinnatus Heine (Joaquin), Miller, 420.
Milton, John, 10, 39, 40, 51, 54, 55.
Mitchell, Donald Grant (Ik Marvel), 407.
Mitchell, S. Weir, 407.
Moody, William Vaughn, 420.
Moore, Clement Clarke, 408.
Moral Ideals,
  Bryant's, 136, 143, 145.
  Cawein's, 334.
  Cooper's, 134.
  Emerson's, 185, 186, 187, 188, 191, 192, 193.
  Franklin's, 80, 81, 102.
  Hawthorne's, 212, 214, 215, 216, 218, 219, 220, 221, 304, 398.
  Howells's, 369.
  Lanier's, 316, 398.
  Lincoln's, 345.
  Longfellow's, 226, 232.
  Lowell's, 247, 253, 255, 256, 279, 398.
  of democracy, 32, 37, 69, 72, 73, 101, 147, 148, 185, 186, 255, 342, 343, 361, 368, 385, 386, 388, 391, 392, 397.
  of Jonathan Edwards, 52.
  of New England authors, 167, 168, 172, 268, 280, 398.
  of the founder of the Virginia colony, 13.
  of the Puritans, 13, 32, 33, 34–37, 47, 51, 52, 54, 60, 72, 85, 102, 136, 138.
  of the realistic school, 368, 369, 371, 389.
  Thoreau's, 195, 202.
  Twain's, Mark, 343, 363, 364.
  Whitman's, 384, 385, 386, 388, 389, 391, 397.
  Whittier's, 237, 238, 242, 244, 261, 265, 280, 398.
  Woolman's, 83, 84.
Morse, S. F. B., 133.
Morton, Mrs. Sarah, 85, 86.
Mosses from an Old Manse, 211, 213, 283.
Motley, John Lothrop, 267–269, 280.
Moulton, Ellen Louise Chandler, 408.
Mullany, P. F. (Brother Azarias), 416.
Murfree, Mary Noailles (Craddock, Charles Egbert), 330–332, 336.
  life and works, 330–332.
  questions and suggestions on, 340.
  references on, 336, 337.
  suggested readings in, 339.

Nasby, Petroleum V. (Locke, David Ross), 408.
Nature,
  Charles Brockden Brown's use of, 91, 92.
  Emerson on, 184, 185, 188–190, 193.
  in Allen's stories, 330, 336.
  in Bryant's verse, 99, 137, 138, 139, 140, 141, 145, 146.
  in Burroughs's writings, 401.
  in Cawein's verse, 292, 332–334.
  in Craddock's stories, 331, 336.
  in Drake's verse, 110.
  in Freneau's verse, 97, 98.
  in Hayne's verse, 312.
  in Lanier's verse, 315, 316.
  in Longfellow's verse, 229, 230, 231.
  in Lowell's verse, 252, 255, 256, 279.
  in Riley's verse, 353.
  in Tabb's verse, 319.
  in Timrod's verse, 309, 310.
  in Whitman's verse, 387, 388, 389, 396, 397.
  in Whittier's verse, 235, 240, 241, 242.
  new view of, 161, 162.
  Thoreau's companionship with, 194–200, 202, 203.
  transcendental feeling for, 158, 161, 162, 184, 185, 188–190, 202, 203.
  Wordsworth's view of, 99, 144, 146.
New England. *See also* Moral Ideals.
  clergy of, 35–37, 59.
  colonization of, 13, 14, 15.
  Elizabethan traits in early colonists of, 15–17.
  ideals of, 13, 30, 33, 34, 167, 168, 398.
  literature of, 26–55, 59, 60, 153–286, 379, 380.
  renaissance of, 153, 155, 156.
New England Primer, 34, 412.
New York, as a literary center, 107, 148.
New York Evening Post, 116, 139.
Nicholson, Meredith, 420.
Norris, Frank, 420.
North American Review, 140, 142.
Novel. *See* Fiction.

Odell, Jonathan, 408.
O'Hara, Theodore, 416.
Oldstyle, Jonathan, 114.
Oratorical Dictionary, 175.
Orators, 71–75, 102, 105, 106, 173–177, 283, 288, 289, 343–345, 365.
O'Reilly, John Boyle, 408.
Oregon Trail, 270, 271.
Orphic Sayings, 164.
Otis, James, 71–73, 102, 105, 106.
Oxford University, 122, 262.

Page, Thomas Nelson, 323, 324, 336, 337, 338.
  questions and suggestions on, 340.
  references on, 336, 337.
  suggested readings in, 338.
Paine, Thomas, 67, 68, 102, 104.
Parkman, Francis, 270–273, 280.
Partington, Mrs. (Shillaber, Benjamin P.), 408.

INDEX

Paulding, James K., 114.
Payne, John Howard, 408.
Peabody, Josephine Preston (Mrs. Lionel Marks), 408.
Peabody, Sophia, 207, 208.
Peck, Samuel Minturn, 416.
Pennell, Joseph, 120.
Perry, Bliss, 387, 408.
Phelps, William L., 361.
Phillips, David Graham, 420.
Phillips, Wendell, 173.
Piatt, John James, 420.
Pierce, Franklin, 206, 209, 210, 211.
Pierrepont, Sarah, 50, 51, 52, 53.
Pike, Albert, 416.
Pilgrims. *See* Puritans.
Pilgrim's Progress, 55, 77, 206, 344, 345.
Pinkney, Edward Coate, 416.
Plato, 28, 192, 387.
Plymouth, Bradford's history of, 26-28, 60, 64.
Pocahontas, 19, 20.
Poe, Edgar Allan, 10, 88, 91, 288, 292, 293-306, 335, 336, 337, 338, 339, 340, 366, 367, 368, 376, 392, 396.
  critical prose of, 295, 299, 301, 337.
  develops modern short story, 299.
  general characteristics of, 304-306, 335.
  life of, 293-297.
  poetry of, 296, 297, 301-303, 305, 335, 337, 339.
  questions and suggestions on, 339.
  references on, 336, 337.
  style of, 304-306.
  suggested readings in, 337, 338.
  tales of, 297-301, 304, 335, 338.
Poor Richard's Almanac, 81, 82.
Pope, Alexander, 22, 55, 87, 103, 255, 290, 386.
Porter, Sydney ("O. Henry"), 416.
Portrait of a Lady, 377.
Prentice, Geo. D., 416.
Prescott, William H., 266, 267, 280.
Preston, Margaret Junkin, 416.
Printing, early, 25, 38.
Puritans, 13-15, 25, 26-37, 44, 46, 47, 48, 51, 69, 216, 217, 219, 303, 306, 316, 363.
  clergy of, 35-37.
  religion of, 13, 33, 34, 153-155.

Raleigh, Sir Walter, 16, 358.
Randall, James Ryder, 416.
Read, Thomas Buchanan, 408.
Realism, 367-372, 392, 393-395.
Realists, the Eastern, 373-392.
Reformation, 16.
  New England's, 151-155.
Reid, Christian, 417.
Renaissance, New England's, 155-167.

Religion, 33-35, 39, 60, 101, 136, 153-155, 398. *See also* Channing, Wm. Ellery; Clergy; Edwards, Jonathan; Mather, Cotton; Moral Ideals; Puritans; Reformation; Unitarianism.
Repplier, Agnes, 408.
Revival of Learning, 16, 155, 156.
Revolution, literary history of, 65-106.
Revolutionary War, 11, 65, 66, 71, 72, 75, 80, 96, 97, 100, 101, 103, 123, 293, 306.
Rhodes, James Ford, 420.
Rice, Alice Hegan, 416.
Rice, Cale Young, 416.
Richardson, Samuel, 55, 85, 86, 98, 102.
Riggs, Mrs., 412.
Riley, James Whitcomb, 343, 352-354, 364, 365, 366.
  life and works of, 352-354.
  questions and suggestions on, 366.
  references on, 365.
  suggested readings in, 366.
Ripley, George, 165.
Rip Van Winkle, 119, 122, 123, 124, 149, 151, 152, 367.
Rives, Amélie (Princess Troubetskoy), 417.
Roe, Edward Payson, 408.
Rohlfs, Mrs. Charles (Green, Anna Katherine), 405.
Romanticism, 86-88, 110, 123, 367, 368, 369, 370, 371, 392.
Roosevelt, Theodore, 409.
Russell, Irwin, 417.
Ryan, Father, 317, 318, 335, 339.

Salem, 204, 205, 206, 209.
Salmagundi, 114.
Sandys, George, 21, 22, 59.
Sangster, Margaret, 409.
Saxe, John Godfrey, 409.
Scarlet Letter, The, 209, 214, 215, 216, 218, 220, 221, 283, 286, 398.
Schouler, James, 409.
Scollard, Clinton, 409.
Scott, Sir Walter, 128, 134, 146, 227, 358.
Seawell, Molly Elliot, 417.
Sedgwick, Catherine M., 409.
Seton, Ernest Thompson, 420.
Sewall, Samuel, 43-45, 59, 63, 64.
Shakespeare, William, 9, 10, 15, 16, 17, 20, 21, 59, 87, 215, 254, 257, 345, 370.
Shaw, Henry Wheeler ("Josh Billings"), 409.
Shea, John Dawson Gilmary, 409.
Shelley, Percy Bysshe, 54, 90, 142, 145, 146.
Shepard, Thomas, 34, 48.
Sherman, Frank Dempster, 409.
Shillaber, Benjamin P. ("Mrs. Partington"), 409.

INDEX

Short Story, the, 119–121, 211–214, 299–301, 321, 323, 324, 325, 329, 376, 377, 380, 396.
Sidney, Sir Philip, 16, 204.
Sill, Edward Rowland, 420.
Simms, William Gilmore, 290, 306–308, 335, 338, 340.
   life and works of, 306–308.
   questions and suggestions on, 340.
   references on, 336, 337.
   style of, 308.
   suggested readings in, 338.
Simple Cobbler of Agawam, 41, 42, 59, 82.
Sketch Book, 115, 118, 119, 152.
Slavery, 148, 168–173, 237, 238, 239, 250, 251, 260, 275, 276, 278, 283, 288, 289, 335, 360, 361.
Smith, Captain John, 13, 17–20, 61, 62, 63, 64, 91.
Smith, F. Hopkinson, 417.
Smith, Samuel F., 410.
Snow-Bound, 238, 240–243.
South, the New, 290–292.
Southern Literature, 17–26, 59, 68–70, 71, 73, 74, 101, 102, 287–340, 396, 398, 414–417.
Southern Literary Messenger, 295.
Spalding, John L., 420.
Sparks, Jared, 410.
Spearman, Frank H., 420.
Spectator, The, 77, 114.
Spens, Sir Patrick, 245, 246.
Spenser, Edmund, 10, 206.
Spofford, Harriet Prescott, 410.
Standish, Miles, 28, 231, 232.
Stanley, A. P., 217.
Stedman, Edmund Clarence, 410.
Steele, Richard, 98.
Stephen, Leslie, 85.
Stevenson, Robert Louis, 11.
Stith, William, 417.
Stockton, Frank R., 410.
Stoddard, Charles Warren, 410.
Stoddard, Richard Henry, 410.
Story, William Wetmore, 410.
Story. *See* Short Story *and* Fiction.
Stowe, Harriet Beecher, 169–173, 278, 281, 283, 286, 361.
Strachey, William, 20, 21, 62, 64.
Stuart, Ruth McEnery, 417.
Sumner, Charles, 173, 410.
Sunnyside, 115, 116.
Swift, Jonathan, 55, 98.
Symonds, John Addington, 11, 387.

Tabb, John Bannister, 318–320, 335, 337, 339.
   questions and suggestions on, 339.
   references on, 336, 337.
   suggested readings in, 338.

Tanglewood Tales, 213, 214.
Tarkington, Newton Booth, 421.
Taylor, Bayard, 411.
Ten Commandments, 14, 185, 219, 286, 396.
Tennyson, Alfred, 243, 274, 275, 339, 387.
Thackeray, W. M., 274.
Thanatopsis, 138, 140, 141, 150, 151, 152.
Thanet, Octave (French, Alice), 419.
Thaxter, Celia Laighton, 411.
Thomas, Edith, 411.
Thompson, Maurice, 421.
Thompson, William Tappan, 417.
Thoreau, Henry D., 157, 162, 169, 182, 194–203, 213, 246, 279, 283, 286, 311, 388, 401.
   Emerson and, 196.
   general characteristics of, 200–203, 411.
   Journal of, 199, 200, 202, 203, 411.
   life of, 194–197.
   Lowell on, 202.
   moral quality of, 195, 202.
   naturalist, 195, 197, 199, 200, 201–203.
   questions and suggestions on, 286.
   references on, 281.
   style of, 202, 203.
   suggested readings in, 283.
   works of, 197–203.
Threnody, 182.
Ticknor, George, 411.
Tiernan, Frances F., 417.
Timrod, Henry, 238, 308–310, 335, 337, 339.
   life and works of, 308–310.
   questions and suggestions on, 339.
   references on, 336, 337.
   suggested readings in, 337.
Tocqueville, Alexis de, 185.
Torrey, Bradford, 411.
Tourgée, Albion W., 411.
Transcendentalism, 156–161.
Trent, W. P., 173.
Troubetskoy, Princess, 417.
Trowbridge, John Townsend, 411.
Trumbull, John, 92, 94–96, 103, 105, 106.
Tucker, Ellen, 180.
Twain, Mark. *See* Clemens, Samuel L.
Twice Told Tales, 207.
Tyler, M. C., 14, 15.
Tyndall, John, 192, 286.

Uncas, 132, 134.
Uncle Remus, 292, 322, 323.
Uncle Tom's Cabin, 170–173, 275, 278, 283.
   Sand, George, on, 173.
   Trent, W. P., on, 173.
Unitarianism, 154, 155. *See also* Religion.

Van Dyke, Henry, 411.
Van Tassel, Katrina, 119, 120.

INDEX

Van Twiller, Wouter, 118.
Virginia, 11, 12, 18, 20, 21, 24, 61, 62, 287–289, 294, 318, 323. *See also* Southern Literature.
  Elizabethan characteristics of early settlers of, 15–17.
  ideals of founder of, 13.
Vision of Sir Launfal, 247, 250, 252, 253, 275.

Walden, 195, 197, 198, 199.
Wallace, Lew, 421.
Walpole, Horace, 88.
Ward, Artemus (Browne, Charles F.), 401.
Ward, Elizabeth Stuart Phelps, 411.
Ward, Nathaniel, 41–43, 59, 61, 63, 64.
Warner, Charles Dudley, 412.
Washington, George, 25, 67, 83, 100, 122, 123, 147, 249, 256, 288.
Webster, Daniel, 174–177, 239, 240, 278, 283.
  greatest orations of, 176, 177.
  questions and suggestions on, 286.
  references on, 280, 281, 283.
  suggested readings in, 283.
  training for speaking of, 174, **175**.
  Whittier on, 174, 239, 240.
Webster, Noah, 412.
Weed, Thurlow, 129.
Weems, Mason Locke, 417.
West, The,
  democratic spirit of, 342, 343, **361**, 364.
  newness of, 341, 342.
  writers of, 341–366, 418–421.
Westcott, Edward Noyes, 412.
Wharton, Edith, 412.
Whipple, Edwin Percy, 412.
Whitcher, Frances ("Widow Bedott"), 412.
White, Maria, 247, 248.
White, Stewart Edward, 421.
Whitman, Walt, 371, 372, 381–391, 392, 393, 394, 395, 397.
  altruistic qualities of, 384, 385, 386, 388, 391.
  an individualist, 397.
  democratic spirit of, 382, 384, 385, 386, 388, 390, 391.
  fondness for the sea, 389, **390, 391.**
  general characteristics of, 388–**391.**
  ideals of, 384, 385, 386, 388, 391.
  life of, 381–384.
  nature in, 387, 388, 389, 396, 397.
  poetry of, 384–391, 394, 395.
  prose of, 382, 389, 394.
  questions and suggestions on, 394, 395.
  realism of, 371, 372, 385, 389, 390–392.
  references on, 393.
  suggested readings in, 393, 394.
Whitney, Adeline Dutton Train, 412.
Whittier, John Greenleaf, 84, 162, 169, 234–244, 279, 284, 285, 398.
  an opponent of slavery, 237, 238, 239, **240.**
  compared with Longfellow, 243.
  general characteristics of, 243, 244.
  life of, 234–239.
  moral quality of, 238, 242, 244, 279, 398.
  poetry of, 239–244.
  questions and suggestions on, 285.
  references on, 282.
  suggested readings in, 284.
Wiggin, Kate Douglas (Mrs. Riggs), **412.**
Wigglesworth, Michael, 38, 39, 59, 63.
Wilcox, Ella Wheeler, 421.
Wilde, Richard Henry, 289.
Wilkins, Mary E. *See* Freeman, **Mary** E. Wilkins.
Williams, Roger, 36, 155, 413.
Willis, N. P., 413.
Wilson, Augusta Evans, **417.**
Wilson, Woodrow, 417.
Winsor, Justin, 413.
Winter, William, 413.
Winthrop, John, 16, 29–33, **30, 36, 59,** 61, 63, 64.
Winthrop, Theodore, 413.
Wirt, William, 417.
Wister, Owen, 413.
Wonder Book, 213, 214, **283.**
Woodberry, George E., 349, 413.
Woolman, John, 83, 84, 102, 105, **106.**
Woolson, Constance Fenimore, 413.
Wordsworth, William, 10, 88, 99, 103, **137,** 142, 143, 144, 146, 149, 152, 162, **254,** 275, 370.